Health Policy in a Globalising World

Edited by

Kelley Lee, Kent Buse and Suzanne Fustukian

CAMBRIDGE
UNIVERSITY PRESS

PUBLISHED BY THE PRESS SYNDICATE OF THE UNIVERSITY OF CAMBRIDGE
The Pitt Building, Trumpington Street, Cambridge, United Kingdom

CAMBRIDGE UNIVERSITY PRESS
The Edinburgh Building, Cambridge CB2 2RU, UK
40 West 20th Street, New York, NY 10011-4211, USA
477 Williamstown Road, Port Melbourne, VIC 3207, Australia
Ruiz de Alarcón 13, 28014 Madrid, Spain
Dock House, The Waterfront, Cape Town 8001, South Africa

www.cambridge.org
Information on this title: www.cambridge.org/9780521804196

First published 2002
Reprinted 2003

Typeface Plantin 10/12 pt.   *System* LATEX 2$_\varepsilon$ [TB]

A catalogue record for this book is available from the British Library.

Library of Congress Cataloguing in Publication data
Health Policy in a Globalising World / edited by Kelley Lee, Kent Buse
and Suzanne Fustukian.

 p. cm.
ISBN 0 521 80419 1 (hardback) – ISBN 0 521 00943 X (paperback)
1. World health. 2. Globalization – Health aspects. 3. Medical policy.
I. Lee, Kelley, 1962– II. Buse, Kent. III. Fustukian, Suzanne, 1953– .

RA441 .H44 2001
362.1 – dc21   2001035097

ISBN-13 978-0-521-80419-6 hardback
ISBN-10 0-521-80419-1 hardback

ISBN-13 978-0-521-00943-0 paperback
ISBN-10 0-521-00943-X paperback

Transferred to digital printing 2005

Increasing recognition of the impact that globalisation may be having on public health has led to widespread concern about the risks arising from emerging and re-emerging diseases, environmental degradation and demographic change. This book argues that health policy-making is being affected by globalisation and that these effects are, in turn, contributing to the kind of global health issues being faced today. The book explores how the actors, context, processes and content of health policy are changing as a result of globalisation, raising concerns about growing differences in who can influence health policy, what priorities are set, what interventions are deemed appropriate and, ultimately, who enjoys good and bad health. Bringing together a distinguished, international group of contributors, this book covers a comprehensive range of topics and geographic regions and will be invaluable for all those interested in health, social and public policy and globalisation.

KELLEY LEE is Senior Lecturer in Global Health Policy and Co-director of the Centre on Globalisation, Environmental Change and Health at the London School of Hygiene and Tropical Medicine. Her publications include *Global telecommunications regulation: a political economy perspective* (1996), *A historical dictionary of the World Health Organisation* (1999), and *Globalisation and Health: An introduction* (forthcoming).

KENT BUSE is Assistant Professor of International Health in the School of Public Health at the Yale University School of Medicine. He has published in a range of journals including *Social Science and Medicine, Health Policy and Planning, Health Policy, The Lancet, The Bulletin of the World Health Organisation,* the *Journal of Public Health Medicine* and the *Journal of International Development.*

SUZANNE FUSTUKIAN is Senior Lecturer in International Health at the Centre for International Health Studies, Queen Margaret University College, Edinburgh. Her current research areas include pro-poor health policy, poverty reduction and health, the role of civil society in global governance for health, and health and social policy in conflict and post-conflict settings.

To our children – Rowan, Jenny, Salvador, Alexander and Isis – who we hope will enjoy the benefits of globalisation with a humane face.

Contents

Figures

Tables

Boxes

Notes on contributors

ROBERT BEAGLEHOLE trained in medicine in New Zealand and then in epidemiology and public health at the London School of Hygiene and Tropical Medicine and the University of North Carolina at Chapel Hill. He is currently on leave from his position as Professor of Community Health at the University of Auckland, New Zealand and is working in the Department of Health and Sustainable Development at WHO, Geneva on several emerging public health issues.

RUAIRI BRUGHA is Senior Lecturer in public health in the Health Policy Unit of the London School of Hygiene and Tropical Medicine (LSHTM). His main area of research is assessing the role and potential of for-private providers in the delivery of services of public health importance, including malaria, sexually transmitted diseases and tuberculosis. He is joint editor of *Health Policy and Planning*.

KENT BUSE is Assistant Professor of International Health in the School of Public Health at the Yale University School of Medicine. As a political-economist, he undertakes research and publishes on health sector governance and policy at the global, international and national levels. Current research includes the role of the commercial sector in global health governance and the political economy of public–private partnership. He has worked and consulted for a variety of NGOs and intergovernmental organisations.

CARLOS M. CORREA is an Argentine lawyer and economist with a Ph.D. from the University of Buenos Aires. He is Director of the Master Program on Science and Technology Policy and Management and Director of the postgraduate course on Intellectual Property of the University of Buenos Aires. He is also Director of the quarterly journal *Temas de Derecho Industrial y de la Competencia*, which is based in Buenos Aires. Dr Correa is a consultant to UNCTAD, UNIDO, WHO, FAO, Interamerican Development Bank, INTAL, World Bank, SELA, ECLA, and other regional and international organizations. He has authored several books and articles on technology and intellectual property published in national and foreign journals

DR NICK DRAGER is Coordinator: Globlization, Cross Sectoral Policies and Human Rights in the Department of Health and Sustainable Development with the World Health Organisation. He has over 10 years of experience working worldwide with senior government officials of low-income countries and their development partners. Dr Drager's work has focused on the areas of health policy and strategy development, setting priorities for external assistance, building consensus in support of these priorities and in negotiating aid agreements in bilateral and multilateral settings. His current work focuses on enabling countries to analyse and act on broader determinants of health development, as well as placing public health interests higher on the international development agenda to improve health outcomes for the poor. Dr Drager has an MD from McGill University and a Ph.D. in Economics from Hautes Etudes Internationales, University of Geneva.

SUZANNE FUSTUKIAN is Senior Lecturer in International Health at the Centre for International Health Studies, Queen Margaret University College, Edinburgh. She previously held a lectureship in international health at the University of Bristol and was a Research Fellow in the Health Policy Unit at the London School of Hygiene and Tropical Medicine. Her current research interests include post-conflict health and social policy, poverty and health; urban social policy; civil society and its role in governance; and globalisation and social policy. She was Co-Director for eight years of Appropriate Health Resources and Technologies Action Group (now Healthlink Worldwide) and principal editor of *Health Action*, produced by AHRTAG.

HILARY GOODMAN is a lecturer in health policy in the Health Policy Unit. Trained in economics and history she became a health economist, undertaking research in health sector financing and user-fees. Subsequent work has involved the cost-effectiveness of HIV prevention strategies. Most recently she has been course organiser for the M.Sc. in Health Policy, Planning and Financing.

LILANI KUMARANAYAKE is a Lecturer in Health Policy and Economics in the Health Policy Unit at LSHTM. Her areas of specialisation include regulation of health systems, the economics of HIV/AIDS, and globalisation. She has worked in a range of countries in sub-Saharan Africa and been a technical advisor to a number of bilateral and multilateral agencies.

SALLY LAKE was a Research Fellow on the Health Economics and Financing Programme within the Health Policy Unit at the time of writing. She is currently working as a consultant on issues of health sector financing and development in sub-Saharan Africa. Recent publications include: Kumaranayake, L., Lake, S., Mujinja, P. G. M., Hongoro, C. and Mpembeni, R. 'How do countries regulate the health sector: evidence from sub-Saharan Africa', *Health Policy and Planning* 15 (4) (2000), and Mujinja, P. G. M., Mpembeni, R. and Lake, S. 'Awareness and effectiveness of regulations governing private drug outlets in Dar es Salaam: perceptions of key stakeholders', in Soderlund, N. and Mendoza-Arana, P. (eds.) *The new public–private mix in health: exploring changing landscapes*, Geneva: Alliance for Health Policy and Systems Research (forthcoming in 2001).

KELLEY LEE is Senior Lecturer in Global Health Policy and Co-director of the Centre on Globalisation, Environmental Change and Health at LSHTM. She chairs the WHO Scientific Resource Group on Globalisation, Trade and Health, and is a founding member of the UK Partnership for Global Health. She is involved in a number of projects analysing the impacts of globalisation on public health with particular interest in infectious diseases, tobacco control policies and global governance. Her recent publications include: *A historical dictionary of the World Health Organization* (1999); 'Globalisation and cholera: implications for global governance', *Global Governance* (2000) with Richard Dodgson; and *Globalisation and health: an introduction* (Palgrave, forthcoming).

PETER LLOYD-SHERLOCK is a Lecturer in Social Development at the University of East Anglia. He previously held a lectureship in the Health Policy Unit at LSHTM. Published work includes *Old age and urban poverty: the shanty towns of Buenos Aires*, Macmillan Press (1997) and *Healthcare reform and poverty in Latin America*, Institute of Latin American Studies/Brookings Institution (2000).

SUSANNAH H. MAYHEW conducted Ph.D. and subsequent research work at the Health Policy Unit of LSHTM focusing on policy analysis and integrating reproductive health services. She is currently a Research Fellow in the International Division of the Nuffield Institute for Health, University of Leeds, and the London School of Hygiene and Tropical Medicure, working on sexual and reproductive health including policy, management and service delivery issues in Sub-Saharan Africa and South East Asia. Publications include: 'Integrating MCH/FP and STD/HIV services: current debates and future directions', *Health Policy and Planning* 11 (4): 339–53 (1996); Lush, L., Cleland, J., Walt, G. and Mayhew, S., 'Integrating reproductive health: myth and ideology', *Bulletin of World Health Organisation* 77 (9): 771–7 (1999); and Mayhew, S. H., 'Integration of STI services in rural Ghana: the health service and social contexts of implementation', *Reproductive Health Matters* (2000).

BARBARA MCPAKE is Senior Lecturer in Health Economics in the Health Policy Unit with interests in the economics of health systems in Africa and Latin America. She is currently carrying out research on hospital policy in Zambia, Uganda and Colombia. She has been a member of the Health Policy Unit and the Health Economics and Financing Programme since 1991.

DR ZAFAR MIRZA is a public health specialist. He heads a national consumer protection organisation in Pakistan and combines research pursuits with activism at national and international level. More recently he has been involved in discourses in consumer protection, trade as a determinant of public health, TRIPS and its implications, treatment access campaigns, anti-tobacco work, drug policy issues etc. He is a member of the WHO Scientific Resource Group on Globalisation, Trade and Health.

JESSICA OGDEN is Senior Lecturer in Social Anthropology in the Health Policy Unit. She has a Ph.D. in Social Anthropology from the University of Hull (1996). Her doctoral research focused on the relationship between gender, reproductive identity and HIV/AIDS in Kampala, Uganda. She joined the School in 1995 to work on the DFID Tuberculosis Programme, and has been involved in operations research on the Revised National Tuberculosis Programme in India, in a collaborative research project on improving TB control in West Africa, and on a study exploring the transfer of international TB and STI policy from international to national level in South Africa and Mozambique. Current interests include improving the relationship between social science and biomedicine for the development of effective and sustainable community-based interventions for infectious disease.

JOHN PORTER is Reader in International Public Health in the Health Policy Unit. He coordinates a Tuberculosis Research Programme and, through his work on TB and HIV, has become increasingly interested in how health policy is created and dispersed. He teaches a course on ethics, public health and human rights and is also involved in work with displaced populations in areas of conflict.

M. KENT RANSON, MD (McMaster), MPH (Harvard) is a Ph.D. candidate in the Health Policy Unit of LSHTM. His Ph.D. work focuses on the impact of two community-based health insurance schemes in rural India.

DINESH SETHI is a Lecturer in International Public Health in the Health Policy Unit. He studied medicine in Liverpool and trained in public health in North Thames and the London School of Hygiene and Tropical Medicine. His interests in international public health include injury prevention and control, globalisation and workers' safety, the evaluation of emergency medical services and exploration of the most appropriate means of organising such services in low- and middle-income countries. He is currently collaborating with colleagues to investigate the cost-effectiveness of trauma services in Malaysia and is conducting studies to examine the causes and consequences of injuries and violence in refugees in northern Uganda. In the United Kingdom he is involved in the Study of Infectious Intestinal Disease in England and the response of health professionals to domestic violence in north London. Publications include: Sethi, D. and Zwi, A. B., 'Traffic accidents: another disaster?', *European Journal of Public Health* 9: 65–67 (1999); and Sethi, D., Saperi, S., Aljunid, S. and Zwi, A. 'Injury care in low and middle income countries: identifying potential for change', *Injury Control and Safety Promotion* (in press).

DAMIAN WALKER obtained his B.Sc. (Hons) in Economics and M.Sc. in Health Economics from the University of York. A Research Fellow in the Health Policy Unit at LSHTM, his main area of research is the economic evaluation of health care programmes in developing countries, with particular interest in HIV/AIDS and TB prevention strategies, the introduction of new vaccines to routine immunisation programmes and safe motherhood initiatives.

GILL WALT is Professor in International Health Policy and has worked in a number of low-income countries, especially in Southern Africa. Her best-known book is *Health policy: an introduction to process and power.* Current research focuses on policy transfer between and within international and national jurisdictions, with a special interest in global public–private partnerships in international health.

CHARLOTTE WATTS is Senior Lecturer in Epidemiology and Health Policy in the Health Policy Unit of the London School of Hygiene and Tropical Medicine. She is conducting research on the international public health burden of violence against women; and is Senior Technical Advisor to the WHO multicountry study on Women's Health and Domestic Violence Against Women. Her research interests include trafficking in women, and the planning and evaluation of HIV/AIDs prevention activities. She teaches a course on Science, Politics and Policy.

ANTHONY ZWI was born in South Africa where he undertook his medical degree and postgraduate diplomas in occupational health and tropical medicine. He subsequently trained in epidemiology, public health and international health at the London School of Hygiene and Tropical Medicine, and the National Health Service. He headed the Health Policy Unit at the London School of Hygiene and Tropical Medicine from 1997 to 2000 and has actively promoted the study of public health and health systems in humanitarian crises. He has long-standing interest in how conflict impacts upon health and health systems and has promoted the establishment of a network to adapt and transfer analytic tools and response strategies between countries emerging from major periods of conflict.

Foreword

Dr Gro Harlem Brundtland
Director General, World Health Organisation

Globalisation is one of the key challenges that public health faces in the twenty-first century. It is a major theme that is confronting many fields of public policy, but it is the health field that particularly illustrates the shared consequences of a globalising world, both its potential rewards and hazards. Infectious diseases, global trade, collective violence, ageing, health sector reform – all of these issues have determinants and consequences beyond individual countries. We are thus pressed to understand better the globalising processes that are confronting public health and somehow engage with them in order to make globalisation work better for health. We are pointedly aware that we are only beginning to do this. Globalisation in its present form could well be contributing to worsening health as long as a substantial number of people are being marginalised and disadvantaged by the process. Making globalisation work to the advantage of all – rich or poor – is a hard challenge.

This book is a timely contribution. It is important reading for those who want to understand some of the major health consequences of globalisation better. More specifically, the book's concern with how health policy is made – who is involved, which processes are taking place, what changes are happening to the broader context of policy-making – has not yet been addressed elsewhere. The case studies provided illustrate that domestic and foreign policy is being increasingly blurred, and that globalisation is far from creating a globally inclusive policy environment. We must appreciate not only that there are broad determinants of health emerging from globalisation, but that we must go beyond our familiar intellectual, technical and operational borders within the health sector to address them effectively. Only in this way can we begin to put health much higher on the agendas of those who are driving globalisation. This book contributes importantly to this vital task before us.

Preface

Anthony Zwi

The origins of this book lay in a decision taken in 1998 by members of the Health Policy Unit at the London School of Hygiene and Tropical Medicine to collaborate on a joint academic project. Members of the Unit, as in other academic institutions, focus their attention on advancing their own and collective research agendas, pursuing those for which research funding is available while seeking funding to move forward their other research interests. In such focused and competitive environments, the potential for broader collective academic activity and debate, and for more creative and searching exploration of important issues, tends to suffer.

The Health Policy Unit at the London School of Hygiene and Tropical Medicine hosts around thirty members of staff and a similar number of doctoral students. The Unit seeks to inform and strengthen the development and implementation of appropriate health policy and to increase understanding of the process of policy development at global, national and local levels. Areas of expertise include comparative health policy and health systems analysis, health economics and international public health. While many Unit members have a particular interest in the challenges facing low- and middle-income countries, the Unit is increasingly cognisant of the interconnectedness between developments in different parts of the world. Staff come from disciplines ranging from sociology, social policy and political science, to anthropology, health economics, public health and epidemiology. The Unit houses a number of substantive areas of activity including health systems, health economics and financing, economic evaluation, infectious disease policy, modelling of HIV infection and preventive efforts, violence against women, globalisation, political economy of tobacco control, policy transfer, humanitarian aid and public health, and post-conflict health sector development.

Our objectives for developing a joint Health Policy Unit project were to explore an area which cut across all our respective research agendas, to collaborate with one another in different teams and more combinations than usual, and to examine and contribute to building understanding around an important current challenge in international public health and policy. Three possible themes were considered – equity, poverty and social exclusion; North–South research collaboration and its attendant challenges; and globalisation, global health and their linkages with health policy and its transfer. Our concerns with equity, poverty and social exclusion reflected a commitment to recognising inequalities in the distribution of global, national and local resources, and the negative impact of this for development, health and well-being. The topic would challenge us to think through how we could conceptualise the current inequities and contribute to the debate regarding the appropriate balance between efficiency and equity concerns. Focusing on North–South research collaboration, and asking questions about whose agendas we research and why, and how we could more appropriately balance northern and southern perspectives, objectives and power over research content and processes, reflected our everyday concerns and activities. Staff within the Health Policy Unit recognise the privileged position in which we find ourselves, and the particular challenge of working effectively and equitably with partners in under-resourced settings. The third possibility, to explore issues of globalisation and global health policy, posed the challenge of engaging with ongoing debates taking place in international relations, politics and development studies, exploring their interfaces with those in international health. Underlying all three possibilities was the recognition that the world is changing rapidly and, in many ways, fundamentally, and that we need to reflect on the implications of this for international health work.

This book represents the product of the third option: globalisation and health policy. Many of us believed that we are witnessing profound changes worldwide and that neglecting to understand and relate to these changes will hamper our work, and its value, in relation to international health policy. In working on this project together, we had to get to grips with a number of issues, including the imprecision with which the term globalisation is often applied, the importance of understanding the benefits, opportunities and negative effects of aspects of current forms of globalisation, and the challenge of identifying a way forward in analysing and influencing policy debate in international health. 'Globalisation' as a term and concept is at risk of being rendered meaningless by over-use and excessive claims regarding its ability to explain too many different aspects of international relations, politics and economics. None the less, most agree that there is something qualitatively different happening in the contemporary world and that understanding these changes and assessing their implications for our own areas of work is crucial.

As researchers and practitioners seeking to promote health and improve the quality of life for all, we must examine both the negative and positive dimensions of globalisation. Through our work in many parts of the world, we have seen some of the negative human consequences of globalisation driven solely by the so-called logic of the market. Globalisation brings a complex set of costs and benefits to individuals, communities and societies around the world; it is simultaneously integrating and fragmenting, leaving both winners and losers in its wake.

We argue for a more humane globalisation, one that builds connections without disrupting others, creating many more winners than losers, and keeping basic human values of dignity and equity at its core. The new technologies of global communication will assist in making visible what is often invisible, making heard what is often unheard, making explicit what is often implicit, and promoting accountability and transparency among those who exercise power over the lives of others; we need to learn to tame and use these technologies to ensure that all aspects of the debate are heard and considered.

The process of producing the book followed from our objectives: we sought to work with, write and debate with one another, and in so doing, to sharpen understanding of our own areas of work and to link our concepts and concerns with others being critiqued in the development community. A number of chapters provided the basis for intense exchange within the Unit; while intellectual sparring usually takes up a small proportion of our time, it is always particularly invigorating, challenging and affirming when it occurs. Many chapters were carefully reviewed by outside peer reviewers as well as by the editors, Kelley Lee, Kent Buse and Suzanne Fustukian, who have worked to ensure that we clarify our thoughts and concepts, sharpen our arguments and seek linkages with literature we normally neglect. They, with the support of the Unit but with a great deal of personal commitment and energy, have ensured that this project has been tackled as effectively as it has, and that we have a product to show for it.

We owe a note of thanks to the Department of Health and Development (formerly the Department of Health in Sustainable Development) of the World Health Organisation that had the foresight and commitment to back our initiative. WHO provided arm's-length support to the production of this book, collaborating on two chapters, providing an important contribution from Dr Brundtland, the Director General, and assisting in the distribution of the book to resource-poor settings.

Through the process of producing this book, we have each examined our work in a different way from usual. We have come to believe that

Acknowledgements

This volume began as a project to involve as many members of the Health Policy Unit (HPU), London School of Hygiene and Tropical Medicine (LSHTM), as possible in a collective effort to cross our disciplinary boundaries. The resulting book bears the names of the chapter contributors, but many others were involved at various times in the initial conceptualisation of the project and refining of its ideas. Each chapter was reviewed in an HPU research workshop where many useful comments were forthcoming. We would thus like to thank all of our colleagues for the generosity of their time and intellectual energies during the writing of this book. A special thanks goes to Patrick Vaughan who lent his experience to the editorial team in the early stages of this project. Most particularly, we would like to express our gratitude to Anthony Zwi, Head of Unit, who originally conceived of the idea of a Unit project, and doggedly gave his consistent support for it through the ups and downs of the past two years.

In addition to being a joint project of LSHTM colleagues, the book represents the fruits of a collaboration with the Department of Health and Development, World Health Organisation. Nick Drager provided his support for the project from its beginnings. As well as generous financial support, he and colleagues contributed substantially to the chapter on multilateral trade agreements.

As well as navigating through workshops, many of the chapters were additionally reviewed by named experts who provided thoughtful and conscientious insights. We gratefully thank Sara Bennett, Karen Bissell, Lucy Gilson, Anne-Marie Foltz (Yale University), Anne Mills and John Martin (WHO).

Finally, our gratitude to Sarah Caro at Cambridge University Press for shepherding this book through its various stages of production. The production of this book was facilitated enormously by the sharp eyes and editorial skills of Tamsin Kelk who graciously agreed to tackle this project in spite of other heavy responsibilities. We thank her for agreeing to add this manuscript to the large piles of papers already on her desk.

Our appreciation also to Lucy Paul, Linda Amarfio, Nicola Lord and Jane Cook who provided ongoing logistical and administrative support for this project, as well as putting up with us disorganised academics for the rest of the time.

Abbreviations

AB	Appellate Body
ACTUP	AIDS Coalition to Unleash Power
AGP	Agreement on Government Procurement
AIDS	acquired immune deficiency syndrome
ARV	antiretroviral
BCG	Bacille Calmette–Guérin
BI	Bamako Initiative
CBA	cost–benefit analyses
CEA	cost-effectiveness analysis
CEO	Corporate Europe Observatory
CL	compulsory licensing
CPEs	complex political emergencies
CPT	Consumer Project on Technology
CSW	Commission on the Status of Women
CUA	cost-utility analysis
DALE	disability-adjusted life expectancy
DALY	disability-adjusted life-year
ddI	didanosine
DFID	Department for International Development
DOTS	directly observed therapy, short course
DSB	Dispute Settlement Body
DSU	dispute settlement understanding
ECOSOC	UN Economic and Social Council
EPA	Environmental Protection Agency
EPI	Expanded Programme on Immunisation
EPZs	export processing zones
EQC	Choosing Interventions: Costs, Effectiveness, Quality and Ethics
FAO	Food and Agriculture Organisation
GATS	General Agreement on Trade in Services
GATT	General Agreement on Tariffs and Trade
GAVI	Global Alliance for Vaccines and Immunization

GDP	gross domestic product
GNP	gross national product
GOBI-FFF	Growth monitoring, Oral rehydration, Breast-feeding, Immunisation, Food supplements, Family spacing and Female literacy
GP	General Practitioner
GPPPs	global public–private partnerships
GSDF	Global sustainable development facility
HAI	Health Action International
HCF	health care financing
HEFP	Health Economics and Financing Programme
HFS	Health Financing and Sustainability Program
HIV	human immunodeficiency virus
HMOs	health care maintenance organisations
HPU	Health Policy Unit
HUMCs	health unit management committees
IAVI	International AIDS Vaccine Initiative
ICC	International Chamber of Commerce
ICFTU	International Confederation of Free Trade Unions
ICPD	International Conference on Population and Development
ICRC	International Committee of the Red Cross
IDB	InterAmerican Development Bank
IFBWW	International Federation of Building and Wood Workers
IFPMA	International Federation of Pharmaceutical Manufacturers Associations
IFRC	International Federation of Red Cross and Red Crescent Societies
ILO	International Labour Organisation
IMF	International Monetary Fund
IMO	International Maritime Organisation
INGO	international nongovernmental organisation
IPPC	International Plant Protection Convention
IPPF	International Planned Parenthood Federation
IPRP	intellectual property rights protection
ISO	International Standards Organisation
ITS	International Trade Secretariats
ITTO	International Timber Treaty Organisation
ITU	International Telecommunications Union
IUATLD	International Union against Tuberculosis and Lung Disease
LATAG	Latin American Trade Advisory Group

LDC	least-developed country
LICs	low-income countries
LMICs	low- and middle-income countries
LSE	London School of Economics
LSHTM	London School of Hygiene and Tropical Medicine
MDRTB	multi-drug resistant tuberculosis
MEC	Mectizan® Expert Committee
MFN	most-favoured-nation
MSF	Médecins sans Frontières
MTAs	multilateral trade agreements
NATO	North Atlantic Treaty Organisation
NGO	non-governmental organisation
NHS	UK National Health Service
NRC	National Resistance Council
NTB	non-tariff barrier
ODA	UK Overseas Development Administration
OECD	Organisation for Economic Co-operation and Development
OSHA	American Occupational Safety and Health Administration
PAHO	Pan-American Health Organisation
PAMI	Integrated Programme of Medical Attention (Argentina)
PATH	Program for Appropriate Technology
PHC	primary health care
PHN	Population, Health and Nutrition Division
PhRMA	American Pharmaceutical Manufacturers Association
PI	parallel importing
PPMs	production and processing methods
PSPs	private sector providers
PYLL	potential years of life lost
QALY	quality-adjusted life-year
R & D	research and development
RDFs	revolving drug funds
SAC	Strategic Advisory Council
SADC	Southern African Development Council
SAPs	structural adjustment policies
SHS	Strengthening Health Systems
SMP	Safety Monitoring Programme
SPS	Sanitary and Phytosanitary Measures
STDs	sexually transmitted diseases
STIs	sexually transmitted infections

TB	tuberculosis
TBT	Technical Barriers to Trade
TFCSD	Task Force on Child Survival and Development
TNCs	transnational corporations
TRIPS	Trade-Related Aspects of Intellectual Property Rights
TUAC	Trade Union Advisory Committee
UK	United Kingdom
UN	United Nations
UNAIDS	Joint United Nations Programme on HIV/AIDS
UNCTAD	United Nations Conference on Trade and Development
UNDP	United Nations Development Programme
UNFPA	United Nations Population Fund
UNHCR	United Nations High Commissioner for Refugees
UNICEF	United Nations Children's Fund
UNRISD	United Nations Research Institute for Social Development
US	United States
USAID	United States Agency for International Development
USTR	United States trade representative
VAW	violence against women
WBCSD	World Business Council on Sustainable Development
WDR	*World Development Report*
WHO	World Health Organisation
WTO	World Trade Organisation

1   An introduction to global health policy

Kelley Lee, Suzanne Fustukian and Kent Buse

Globalisation is among the most discussed, and is undoubtedly one of the most disputed, terms to have come into common parlance in recent years. Scholarly and popular writing about globalisation has grown exponentially over the past decade or so, spurred by often heated debates over whether or not the process is actually occurring, to what extent, for what reasons, in what forms and with what consequences. Economic globalisation has initially received the lion's share of attention, but recognition of the political, social, cultural, technological, environmental and other aspects of globalisation has rapidly grown in more recent years.

It is in the latter context that this book, which explores how health policy-making is being affected by forces broadly defined as globalisation, was conceived. Health is an important sector of most economies and a core area of social policy. For example, total expenditure on health as a proportion of Gross Domestic Product (GDP) is as high as 14 per cent in the US and is over 10 per cent in a number of additional OECD (Organization for Economic Co-operation and Development) member countries. Public expenditure on health as a proportion of total public expenditure varies widely between countries, with India and Indonesia spending 3.9 and 3.0 per cent respectively, and Andorra and Argentina spending 38.5 and 21.6 per cent respectively (WHO 2000a). As such, the health sector has been the focus of much policy reform effort over the past two decades, to coincide with shifting ideas worldwide about the welfare state and the role of the public and private sectors in health care financing and provision. Ultimately the subject of health policy is a universally relevant one. Global health has featured prominently on the agendas of the major international political conferences of the 1990s, and has recently been framed as a security issue in the US and at the UN Security Council. Moreover, we are all concerned with our own and others health status, and the factors that optimise it. The health status of individuals and populations is a significant barometer of social progress, broadly reflecting the sustainability of current, and prospective, forms of how we order our lives both locally and globally.

Attention to the links between globalisation and health has increased rapidly since the mid 1990s, initially spurred by concerns over perceived changing threats to national and human security. These concerns have widened, as understanding of the diverse and uneven impacts of globalisation on human health has grown, to include international trade agreements, global financial and trade flows, and global environmental change. Accompanying this attention have been efforts to explore the implications of these challenges to existing institutions and practices of health governance – how should collective action be taken to mediate the positive and negative impacts of globalisation on human health?

The purpose of this book sits between seeking to better understand the impacts of globalisation and finding ways forward to strengthen health governance. We are especially interested in the changing actors, processes and contexts of policy-making, along with the actual policies adopted. In many ways, these four components are intertwined with each other. Yet it is useful to analytically tease them out in relation to how globalisation is impacting on each of them. Selected areas of health policy have been focused on, with a particular emphasis on low- and middle-income countries (LMICs), to illustrate the impact of globalisation on health policy-making. The areas covered are by no means exhaustive, however, and the issues they raise in relation to health policy-making are not exclusive to these countries and regions. Indeed, one of the key messages of this volume is that no population group is immune from the health-related causes and consequences of globalisation.

The impacts of globalisation on health

An appreciation of the diversity of impacts that globalisation is having on health is rapidly growing, resulting in a variety of initiatives seeking more detailed understanding of these impacts and designing effective policy responses to them. These initiatives, in turn, have led to the term 'global health' which is being increasingly recognised among scholars, policy-makers and practitioners as distinct from 'international health', although the difference is not always made sufficiently clear. Indeed, both terms are variably defined and frequently used interchangeably, and there is consequently confusion between them.

International health is a familiar and longstanding term that broadly refers to health matters that concern two or more countries. Alternatively, within the development community, international health usually refers to health matters relevant to the developing world. While all sorts of public and private sector actors (both individuals and groups) may be involved in international health, it is the primacy of the state and state-defined actors that distinguishes international health. For example, the regular transport of infectious diseases such as plague by trade ships from Asia to western Europe from the twelfth century onwards led to the adoption of maritime quarantine systems by Italian city states and later other European countries, as the foundations of the modern surveillance and control systems. The practice essentially excluded a suspect ship and its passengers from landing at a port of call for a given time until it was granted plague-free status by local authorities. The important feature of this system, which Carmichael (1997) describes as 'an undeniable stimulus to the growth of the modern bureaucratic state', is its efforts to shore up the territorial boundaries of the state against a health threat. If somehow the threat could be kept at bay outside of the given state's borders, the population within would remain safe.

Many of the health issues that policy-makers face today remain, strictly speaking, international health issues. The threat of food-borne diseases from increased international trade, for example, in principle could be addressed by improved national, regional and multilateral regulation of food production and trade. Increased risk from infectious diseases as a result of highly mobile populations, at least those affecting individuals who enter and leave countries legally, could (theoretically) be regulated by customs authorities and public health officials at points of entry into a given country. In practice, as a number of chapters to this volume demonstrate, this is difficult to achieve given the limited capacity of many LMIC governments.

However, international health becomes global health when the causes or consequences of a health issue circumvent, undermine or are oblivious to the territorial boundaries of states and, thus, beyond the capacity of states to address effectively through state institutions alone. The illicit drug trade is conducted in a highly covert way, using global transportation, communications, banking and financial infrastructures to directly challenge law-enforcement authorities worldwide. As Stares (1996) argues, the illicit drug industry has its own geographical rationalism of closely linked producing and consuming populations. The health effects of environmental degradation, such as global climate change or the Chernobyl nuclear accident, can also transcend state boundaries and directly challenge the capacity of the state alone to address its causes and consequences.

Global health is also concerned with factors that contribute to changes in the capacity of states to deal with the determinants of health. The global economic crisis of the late 1990s is recognised as having had profound impacts on public sector expenditure on health programmes such as family planning and basic health services (UNFPA/Australian National

University 1998). Cheaper and more widely available transportation technologies, for example, have led to a significant increase in the number of people crossing national borders each week. While the sheer volume of international population movements challenges the logistical capacity of public health officials to cope with screening of travellers for health risks, the global movement of more vulnerable groups, such as economic migrants, refugees or trafficked individuals, places the inadequacy of international health (both conceptually and operationally) in starker relief.

One of the first premises of this book is that the scope of global health is expanding as a consequence of the processes of globalisation. Globalisation can be defined as 'processes that are changing the nature of human interaction across a wide range of spheres including the socio-cultural, political, economic, technological and ecological' (Lee 2001). These processes are global, in the sense that at least three types of boundaries hitherto separating human interaction – spatial, temporal and cognitive – are being redefined. These are discussed in greater depth in Lee (2001) but can be summarised briefly as follows.

Spatial or geographical boundaries, in particular the territorial borders of states, are becoming relatively less important as a consequence of globalisation. Perhaps more accurately, a reterritorialisation of geographical boundaries is occurring by which globalising processes are redefining geographical space in alternative and innovative ways. For example, global civil society, virtual communities and cyberspace increasingly defy the logic of territorially defined geography, giving rise to the importance of, on the one hand, aterritorial social arrangements and, on the other, competing loyalties and identities (Scholte 2000). Transnational activities such as foreign-exchange trading and the Internet have become deterritorialised in the sense that geographical location matters little. Other transnational activities, although not deterritorialised as such, have intensified to such an extent that they are transforming societies around the world. Most fundamental of these is the 'global shift' of the world economy, which, through the interrelated actions of transnational corporations (TNCs) and states, is affecting local communities around the globe (Dicken 1998).

In the health field, this reterritorialisation of human interactions is impacting on both cause (health determinants) and effect (health status). As discussed above, globalisation in the economic, political, social, cultural, ecological and technological spheres of human activity needs to be taken into account as part of the broader determinants of health. The impacts of these processes of change, in turn, are leading to new patterns of human health and disease that do not necessarily conform to, or are revealed by, national boundaries alone.

This reconfiguration of the geography of health determinants and status, along with other geographies (e.g. financial resources, production and trade, cultural identity), has called into question traditional ways in which we categorise health needs. The familiar dichotomy between developed and developing countries has long been recognised as overly crude but broadly useful in distinguishing the needs and realistic options of countries of different levels of wealth. Global health issues are thus those that are not confined to a specific country or groups of countries, but are transborder in cause or effect; this suggests that the ways in which we conceptualise the geographical boundaries of the world, and the health issues related to them, need to adapt to processes that are transborder in nature.

Importantly, this does not mean that we should ignore the often stark inequities in impact that are being experienced within and across population groups. While global health, by definition, makes all individuals and groups potentially vulnerable given their transborder nature, those who have the necessary resources, skills and mobility to reduce or avoid the costs of globalisation are at a clear advantage over those who do not. Most agree that there are winners and losers arising from the processes of globalisation. The proportion of winners to losers, and the long-term distribution of costs and benefits among them, remain highly disputed. Supporters of neo-liberalism maintain that benefits will eventually 'trickle down' to more and more people, raising the overall standard of living for all (World Bank 2000). Others, however, disagree that these trickle-down benefits are occurring sufficiently or fast enough. Bauman (1998), for example, argues that a minority of extraterritorial elites are enjoying a disproportionate share of the benefits of globalisation, while the bulk of the world's population, a 'localised majority', bears the brunt of its risks and problems. Similarly, Coburn (2000) writes that 'the links between globalisation and health initially stemmed from concerns within the health sector that economic globalisation in its present form is having adverse impacts on human health, in particular worsening equity and health status within certain vulnerable populations'. Measures to redistribute costs and benefits more directly are thus advocated, such as the Jubilee 2000 initiative on debt relief or the Tobin Tax, to generate resources for addressing global health inequalities.

Temporal boundaries, the way in which we perceive and experience time, are also changing as a result of globalisation. For the most part, globalisation has been characterised by an acceleration of the pace of our lives, a feeling of time compression created by what has become possible technologically and aspirationally. As Gleick (1999: 9–10) writes:

We are in a rush. We are making haste. A compression of time characterizes the life of the century now closing ... We believe that we possess too little of it [time]: that is a myth we now live by. What is true is that we are awash in things, in information, in news, in the old rubble and shiny new toys of our complex civilization, and – strange, perhaps – stuff means speed. The wave patterns of all these facts and choices flow and crash about us at a heightened frequency. We live in the buzz. We wish to live intensely, and we wonder about the consequences.

The effects of this temporal change on health are again relevant to both the determinants of health and health status. Changes in certain health determinants can manifest more rapidly or operate within an altered timescale. Our destruction of the natural environment, for example, is happening at an unprecedented and accelerating rate with direct consequences for the survival of the human species (McMichael 1993). Lee and Dodgson (2000) observe that the seventh cholera pandemic began in 1963 and spread worldwide more quickly than the previous six. Furthermore, its duration of about 40 years is by far the longest cholera pandemic in history, eluding public health efforts to definitively contain it because of its capacity to re-emerge in different parts of the world as a result of such features of globalisation as human hypermobility, political instability and the food trade.

Third, globalisation has a cognitive dimension that concerns the thought processes that shape our perceptions of ourselves and the world around us. Wallerstein (1991) refers to a globalising cognitive framework that he calls 'geoculture', in which 'particular patterns of thought and behaviour – even language – inscribed in geoculture, are not only essential to ensure that the modern world-system functions effectively, but also provide much of its underlying legitimation' (Murden 1997). Globalisation is changing how thought processes are produced and reproduced, particularly through the spread of communication technologies in the mass media, research community and interpersonal communications (e.g. email), as well as what thoughts are being produced (e.g. values, beliefs, ideologies, ethics, cultural identity). There is disagreement as to whether these changes are integrating societies for good or bad. Liberal advocates of the 'global village' vision observe that: 'The world is becoming a single place, in which different institutions function as parts of one system and distant peoples share a common understanding of living together on one planet. This world society has a culture; it instils in many people a budding consciousness of living in a world society' (Lechner and Boli 2000: xiii). Others are worried that dominant western-derived values, characterised by rampant consumerism, materialism and individualism, are being replicated around the world:

onrushing economic, technological, and ecological forces that demand integration and uniformity and that mesmerize peoples everywhere with fast music, fast computers, and fast food – MTV, Macintosh, and McDonald's – pressing nations into one homogenous global theme park, one McWorld tied together by communications, information, entertainment and commerce. (Barber 2000: 21)

Most overtly, the impact of the cognitive dimension of globalisation on health is its direct consequences for diet and life style. Since the end of the Second World War, populations in high-income countries have become less physically active while at the same time consuming increased fat and sugar levels. Smoking rates have declined in many high-income countries, although the health consequences after many decades of high rates of smoking are now being experienced. The result is a steadily rising incidence of obesity, coronary heart disease, certain cancers and diabetes. Importantly, these changes can be linked to the multi-billion pound marketing of particular life styles via the mass media and other channels of advertising, promotion and sponsorship. According to Wallack and Montgomery (1992: 205), processed foods, soft drinks, cigarettes, alcohol, drugs and toiletries account for 80–90 per cent of all international advertising expenditures. The aspirational messages that advertisers have conveyed for decades in high-income countries are becoming globalised, exported to the increasingly affluent in other parts of the world through global trade and production relations, information technologies (notably the mass media), and the liberalisation and privatisation of economies worldwide.

Along with the replication of life style choices on a global scale, the cognitive dimension of globalisation is shaping policy responses that facilitate or hinder their health effects. Individual life style choices are being made within a broader context of global capitalism. Many of the issues raised by this book stem from concerns that cognitive exchanges within current forms of globalisation are undertaken within highly inequitable circumstances. Rather than a 'meeting of minds', health policy is being shaped foremost by a broader context of certain value systems, beliefs, aspirations and so on that seek to maintain a particular world order. This process is aptly captured in the French expression *pensée unique*, explained by Halimi (2000: 18) as follows:

It is the ideological translation of the interests of global capital, of the priorities of financial markets and of those who invest in them. It is the dissemination through leading newspapers of the policies advocated by the international economic institutions which use and abuse the credit, data and expertise they are entrusted with: such institutions as the World Bank, the IMF, the OECD, the World Trade Organization.

This shifting cognitive landscape is clearly discernible in the health field where many of the policies discussed in this book derive. For example, Bettcher and Yach (1998) explore the ways in which public health ethics may be changing as a consequence of globalisation. Similarly, debates over how health should be defined are being reframed, from a concern with how to ensure health as a basic human right available to all and collectively provided, to health as a product whose attainment and consumption by individuals should be regulated by a marketplace. This shift is further reflected in the normative criteria, and resultant analytical tools (e.g. burden of disease, cost-effectiveness analysis), which are applied to translate certain values into decisions over, among other things, the allocation of limited health resources. The cognitive dimension relates to both how societies structure and deliver health care, from the underlying principles that guide health care to the specific technical interventions provided, and the deeper structural level which concerns how we act to mediate and direct globalisation towards agreed goals.

Collectively, changes to spatial, temporal and cognitive boundaries can be described as the dimensions of global change. Efforts to understand and respond effectively to these dimensions of change comprise the broad and growing fields of global health policy and governance (Lee 2001).

What is global health policy?

The focus of this book is on health policy and the ways in which globalisation is affecting how policy-making is being carried out in the health sector (and in other sectors and issue areas that impact on health). Health policy is broadly defined as 'goals and means, policy environments and instruments, processes and styles of decision-making, implementation and assessment. It deals with institutions, political power and influence, people and professionals, at different levels from local to global' (Leppo 1997). Global health policy can thus be understood as the ways in which globalisation may be impacting on health policy and, alternatively, what health policies are needed to respond to the challenges raised by globalising processes.

Interest in global health policy can be seen as an extension of a desire, in more recent literature on globalisation, to understand the knock-on effects of current neo-liberal and market-driven forms of globalisation, on public policy especially in relation to social policy. While much of the globalisation literature remains heavily focused on the economic and financial sectors (World Bank 2000), many of the policy areas neglected until recently are now being addressed. Initially, these efforts have come from scholars in social policy who observe the often adverse effects that globalisation is having on the social sectors such as education, housing and health. Deacon (1997) argues, for example, that national social policy is increasingly determined by global economic competition and certain international organisations. Social policy must thus be understood in terms of global social redistribution, social regulation, social provision and empowerment (Deacon 1997). Alternatively, Kaul *et al.* (1999: 452) conceptualise the shortfalls of globalisation in terms of the undersupply of global public goods defined as exhibiting characteristics which are 'nonexcludable, [and produce] nonrival benefits that cut across borders, generations and populations'.

More recently, attention to the social sectors has come from economic analyses, prompted by externalities of the global financial crisis of the late 1990s, revealing the interconnectedness and mutual vulnerability of national economies and societies. As well as eliciting extensive reflection of the need to strengthen global economic governance (e.g. banking regulation) (Stiglitz 1999), the links between economic and social policy were brought more sharply into focus. As Reinicke (1998: 1) writes:

without a greater effort to understand the origin and nature of the current global transformation and its implications for public policy, we will continue to react to events rather than act to shape the future course of world politics. Such passivity will leave our societies vulnerable to the risks that change will undoubtedly bring, while forgoing the gains that a more active policymaking could realize.

In relation to the health sector, concerns for nascent global public policy has initially centred on threats to national security or at least the security of high-income countries. In the context of reframing post-cold war foreign and defence policy, this perspective has focused on selected health threats such as infectious diseases, biological and chemical weapons, human migration, and illicit drug trafficking. The global health policy agenda in the US, in particular, has sought to channel the so-called 'peace dividend' to health risks arising from globalisation (Institutes of Medicine 1997; Raymond 1997).

Internationally, global health policy has been cast to emphasise the links between health and economic development led by the World Health Organisation (WHO). Recognising economic integration as a key driver of current forms of globalisation, WHO has strengthened its efforts to understand issues such as multilateral trade agreements, capital flows and macroeconomic policy and their implications for public health. In this respect, Director-General Gro Harlem Brundtland has frequently sought to argue that the protection and promotion of public health is a core requirement of sustainable globalisation (Brundtland 1999a).

The intention of this book is to bring these concerns together. A number of questions occur in relation to health policy: is globalisation changing the way health policies are being made? How effectively are societies able to address the risks and benefits of globalisation to human health? Is globalisation broadening or narrowing involvement in priority-setting in health? Is our collective ability to address global health issues strengthened or undermined by the globalisation process? These questions, which are framed by what Held *et al.* (1999: 18) describe as the decisional and institutional impacts of globalisation, are addressed. Decisional impacts are 'the degree to which the relative costs and benefits of the policy choices confronting governments, corporations, collectivities and households are influenced by global forces and conditions'. Institutional impact refers to 'the ways in which organizational and collective agendas reflect the effective choices or range of choices available as a result of globalization'. In short, the volume seeks to advance understanding of the interplay between the dynamics of globalisation and the health policy.

The adverse impacts of globalisation on health, and the seeming incapacity of existing institutions and systems to address them, illustrate the need for, and current weaknesses of, global health governance. Kaul *et al.* (1999), for example, attribute the undersupply of global public goods to three existing weaknesses or 'gaps' in the current institutions of international policy-making:

(a) *jurisdictional gap* – 'the discrepancy between a globalized world and national, separate units of policy-making';

(b) *participation gap* – the continued focus of international co-operation on intergovernmental actors and marginalisation of new global actors, civil society and private sector; and

(c) *incentive gap* – the over reliance of the operationalisation of international agreements on aid mechanisms while ignoring 'many other practical policy options that could make co-operation a preferred strategy for both developing and industrial countries'.

Similarly, Kickbusch (1999) explores the possible characteristics of global health governance and the necessary changes in how policy-making is carried out.

In summary, global health policy is concerned with the ways in which globalisation is affecting the 'goals and means, policy environments and instruments, processes and styles of decision making, implementation and assessment' (Leppo 1997) in the health field. This may eventually lead to the development of global-level policy-making, but global health policy may embrace those aspects of local, national, regional and international policy-making needed to address the impacts of globalisation on health. As described above, the global health policy agenda has thus far been narrowly circumscribed, with selected costs and benefits of globalisation focused upon. It is argued here that global health policy is a broad area encompassing the different spheres of human activity (i.e. economic, political, ecological, technological, cultural) being changed by the processes of globalisation at any level – from the individual to the global.

Conceptual framework of the book

There are admittedly many different models for conceptualising how policy-making takes place, what the most important influences are, and how we should study them. The field is multidisciplinary, offering a diverse and at times incompatible array of theories and approaches. Rather than seek to reconcile differences in disciplinary, epistemological and normative starting points, this book begins with the broad approach taken by Walt and Gilson (1994) that describes health policy in terms of policy actors, processes, context and content. This framework is used, not as a methodological tool, but as a conceptual list to prompt and organise possible analytical questions.

First, how are policy actors in health changing as a consequence of globalisation? This question concerns both who is making policy and their changing power in relation to other actors to influence decision-making. Policy actors may be individuals or groups of individuals with the capacity to influence, either formally or informally, the policy-making process. As well as understanding who participates, it is important to recognise those under-represented by decision-making. Globalisation, as described above, suggests that different actors have gained power over others, notably actors with transnational links and resources. Globalisation is often described as an era of big business and big government. Above all, the book will argue that conventional analyses of health policy, as for other areas of public policy, that narrowly focus on the national level and on state actors alone are becoming increasingly obsolete. This is not to imply that national/local contexts are not important, but that these need to be integrated into a much wider framework of analysis.

Second, how is globalisation affecting the processes by which policy-making is carried out? Much of the criticism of globalisation, from both the political left and right, is that it is an alienating phenomenon that takes power away from individuals and their local communities, and locates it somewhere referred to as the 'global'. Political responsibility and political power are seen to be becoming more separated with the result that an exclusive global elite is able to exert unrivalled power without, to some extent, accountability to those they affect. Decisions taken in the boardrooms of large TNCs can have implications for people around the world. Governments, in turn, theoretically remain responsible to their citizenry but have diminished power to provide for their needs. Large groups of individuals and communities worldwide feel even more disempowered by the globalising forces that seem to be changing modern societies in so many ways. Many writers argue that foremost is the need to democratise globalisation (Amin 2000; Sen 2000).

An alternative vision of policy-making amidst globalisation is what Castells (1996: 469–71) dubs 'the rise of the network society'. He writes that 'dominant functions and processes in the information age are increasingly organized around networks ... A network-based social structure is a highly dynamic, open system, susceptible to innovating without threatening its balance ... Yet the network morphology is also a source of dramatic reorganization of power relationships.' In this sense, the processes of globalisation are potentially democratising, opening up political spaces for a wider range of actors and new interconnections among them. This book explores the extent to which processes of policy-making in the health sector are changing as a consequence of globalisation, and in what ways. Our examples seem to suggest that networks are indeed forming, bringing new configurations of power relations, but that these networks are still relatively exclusive.

Third, how is globalisation changing the context in which policy-making takes place? Policy context concerns the surrounding social, institutional and natural environment that shapes policy-making at a given time. One of the most significant changes to the health policy context in a globalising world is the realisation that the determinants of health are more complex and wide-ranging as a consequence of globalisation. Globalisation brings home the message that the health sector is directly and indirectly affected by other sectors such as trade and finance, environment, labour, communications and transportation. Of course, these connections have long been recognised, but what has become more evident is the increased interrelatedness of these policy areas to an extent unprecedented. Furthermore, there has been what Kaul *et al.* (1999) describe as the blurring of the dividing line between the spheres of domestic and foreign policy, leading to the need 'to review the fundamental principles of policy-making'. National policy-makers have experienced a relative decline in their capacity to control health determinants of domestic populations because globalisation, by its very nature, concerns processes that transcend state boundaries. For example, the global financial crisis of the late 1990s had significant impacts on resources available to health policy-makers in the hardest hit countries (UNFPA/Australian National University 1998). Economic instability from volatile financial markets has been accompanied by political instability in many parts of the world, in turn adversely affecting the capacity to make effective health policies. The worldwide spread of affordable information and communication technologies is changing the evidence base upon which health policies can be made. All of these developments are creating policy contexts influenced by diverse and complex forces, that are rapidly and steadily in flux, and that do not conform to familiar national boundaries.

Finally, is globalisation influencing the content of policies being made? Many of the chapters in this book examine particular policies and locate them within the context of globalisation. Underlying these chapters is the question of why certain policies become globalised, in the sense that policies originating in particular countries, organisations or even individuals are eventually adopted by others as legitimate and useful. Of particular note is what Leppo (1997: 3) describes as 'an epidemic of reforms based on various forms of market principles'. It may be argued that such policies are simply 'good' policies in that they successfully achieve agreed and desired goals. The variable success of policies such as private health insurance, user fees, contracting out and competitive tendering suggests that other factors have influenced their acceptance worldwide.

Structure of the book

We have organised the chapters of this book into three parts. Part I deals with how health policy-making takes place in a globalising world. In so doing, the authors address, among other things, the transfer of values, technologies, practices and policies across a variety of boundaries (e.g. local, national, regional, global). They also explore how policy actors and their interactions are changing as a result of globalising forces. Ranson and colleagues, in their analysis of the public health implications of multilateral trade agreements, explore the shifting patterns of influence among states, multilateral organisations (particularly the WTO) and commercial interests over health policy. The chapter sheds light on the powerful effect that formalised intergovernmental rules enshrined in treaty obligations in one sector (in this case liberalised and harmonised trading rules) can have on public health. Buse and Walt discuss the hybrid institutional form for health policy-making that is embodied in global public–private partnerships. They draw attention to the increasing emphasis placed on such collaboration for health policy and to the need for improved ways of governing these institutions. The chapter by Brugha and Zwi, which reviews the evidence base of policies relating to the regulation of private providers in LMICs, reveals a number of disturbing features. In particular, the authors argue that advice provided by leading donor agencies to privatise health care provision preceded the systematic gathering and analysis of empirical evidence and was instead predicated upon the ideological preferences of powerful external actors. Their case illustrates the hegemony of certain ideas associated with dominant ideologies in a globalising world. A review of the regulation of emerging global health markets by Kumaranayake and Lake highlights the need for more effective regulation and the important role that might be played by non-state actors. Lee and Goodman challenge the orthodox assumption that globalisation opens up political spaces for greater participation in policy development by demonstrating how a small global elite, linked through an epistemic community, came to frame both the terms and the content of health care financing (HCF) reform worldwide. McPake takes up the challenge of understanding policy learning across countries, also in the area of HCF, as well as the promotion of autonomous hospitals, and argues for more sophisticated approaches to policy adaptation. Finally, Kumaranayake and Walker describe the globalisation of specific technical methodology for priority-setting and question its utility in many settings. Collectively, these chapters take a critical look at policy-making within the context of current forms of globalisation.

The chapters in Part II examine selected impacts of globalisation on the content of health policy. These chapters are concerned with how globalising forces are changing the agenda faced by policy-makers, because the determinants of relatively familiar challenges are more complex and multifaceted, or new linkages are emerging between health issues and other areas, or new constellations of interest groups have captured the policy process. Mayhew and Watts demonstrate the critical role that the global women's movement has played in framing the debates on violence against women and reproductive health; using modern communications technology, this movement has formed powerful coalitions to influence global agendas on these issues, despite the often tepid support of state actors. They go on to argue that translating the global rhetoric into national programmes will require pragmatic links to be developed between the services and for them to be context-appropriate. The chapter by Porter *et al.* explores the globalisation of tuberculosis and the role of DOTS (directly observed therapy short course) as a 'global strategy'. Lloyd-Sherlock examines the dynamics behind the ageing agenda; he reveals the global dominance of particular ideological models with grave consequences on equity of health care access. Fustukian *et al.* tackle the neglected area of occupational health and safety as an area of health policy directly affected by the emerging global economy. Finally, Zwi *et al.* consider the implications of collective violence on health policy agendas. They argue that the new forms of collective violence which have emerged since the end of the cold war, notably complex political emergencies (CPEs), are linked to structural features of globalisation. Humanitarian responses to such conflicts, in an appropriate and timely manner, require us to address the root causes of conflict – widening socio-economic inequalities, competition for control of natural resources in a global economy, global arms trade, and privatisation of armed conflict. While these chapters are by no means intended to be a comprehensive discussion of health issues related to globalisation, they seek to demonstrate the need to better integrate consideration of globalising forces into health policy agendas.

In Part III, Buse *et al.* draw conclusions regarding the impact of globalisation on health policy-making. We return to the topic of globalisation and questions of actors, processes, context and content to explore further how globalisation is changing all of these features. However, the editors of this volume are keenly aware that this book only begins to open a corridor to better understanding global health policy. The issues dealt with here to explore global health are necessarily selective and omit, for example, such key areas as global environmental change and non-communicable disease. None the less, in keeping with the multidisciplinary nature of the subject matter, the contributors to this volume approach globalisation from a variety of disciplinary perspectives, including anthropology, development studies, economics, organisation studies, epidemiology, politics and social policy. The chapters illustrate the multiple boundaries being crossed as a result of globalisation – spatial, temporal and cognitive – as well as the need to cross boundaries analytically and operationally to address the health consequences arising from global change.

KEY READINGS

Deacon, B. 1997, *Global social policy, international organizations and the future of welfare*, London: Sage Publications.

Held, D., McGrew, A., Goldblatt, D. and Perraton, J. 1999, *Global transformations: politics, economics and culture*, Stanford University Press.

Kaul, I., Grunberg, I. and Stern, M. (eds.) 1999, *Global public goods: international cooperation in the 21ˢᵗ Century*, Oxford University Press.

Lee, K. 2001, 'Globalisation – a new agenda for health?', in McKee, M., Garner, P. and Stott, R. (eds.) *International co-operation and health*, Oxford University Press.

UNDP 1999, *Human development report 1999*, New York: United Nations Development Programme.

2 The public health implications of multilateral trade agreements

M. Kent Ranson, Robert Beaglehole, Carlos M. Correa,
Zafar Mirza, Kent Buse and Nick Drager

Introduction

An important feature of the modern global trading environment has been the establishment of a comprehensive legal and institutional foundation to regulate international trade in the context of a general desire to enhance political and economic stability. Since 1947, the General Agreement on Tariffs and Trade (GATT) has provided a rules-based regime to govern world trade, but has had limited powers of enforcement. In recognition of the expanding network and volume of world trade, the GATT evolved in 1995 into the World Trade Organization (WTO), an international organisation with the mandate to reduce trade barriers to goods and services and to mediate trade disputes between countries. Under the WTO, the rules and regulations that guide world trade are entrenched in multilateral trade agreements (MTAs) that are enforceable through a binding dispute resolution mechanism. The underlying assumption of the WTO system is that human welfare will increase through economic growth based on trade liberalisation in the context of non-discriminatory rules and transparency. From a public health perspective, this desirable goal requires linking the benefits of the global trading system to sound social policies (Drager 1999).

This chapter explores from a public health perspective the impact, actual and potential, of selected WTO MTAs on health policy, especially in low- and middle-income countries (LMICs). The purpose of this analysis is to suggest policy options for ensuring that existing, and any future, MTAs are more sensitive to public health issues. In the next section, the WTO and some of its Agreements are described, with a brief description of some trade disputes that have been adjudicated since the WTO's inception. The following section discusses the public health implications of MTAs, and describes a range of potential policy options, at national and global levels, aimed at maximising the positive (and minimising the negative) impact of the WTO and its MTAs on public health.

The World Trade Organization: towards binding behind-the-border policy convergence

The WTO is an intergovernmental body that, as of July 2000, had 139 Member States; a further 29 countries, including China, the Russian Federation and Saudi Arabia, are currently negotiating their entry into the WTO. Membership binds parties to adhere to all of the MTAs under the purview of the WTO. The WTO is headquartered in Geneva and governed by a biennial Ministerial Conference composed of representatives of all Member States. Day-to-day operations are overseen by a General Council, which also directs a dispute settlement system and a Trade Policy Review mechanism. Membership on the Council is open to all signatories of the Agreement (WTO 1999a). The WTO has three stated purposes:

1 to assist the free flow of trade by facilitating the removal of trade tariffs or other border restrictions on the import and export of goods and services;
2 to serve as a forum for trade negotiations; and
3 to settle trade disputes based upon an agreed legal foundation.

There are several aspects of the WTO multilateral trading system that are worth recalling here. First, the multilateral trade system's fundamental purpose is to foster the flow of trade between WTO countries by providing a set of rules to regulate trade. An important aim of the WTO is to reduce barriers preventing the free flow of trade, including customs duties (or tariffs), import bans or quotas that selectively restrict trade, and non-tariff barriers. Secondly, the most-favoured-nation clause (MFN) means that each Member Country is obliged to treat all other Members as its 'most favoured' trading partner, i.e. every Member trading-partner country is as favoured as any other for both imports and exports. The third aspect is national treatment, which means non-discrimination between national and foreign goods and services, as well as in relation to trade-related aspects of intellectual property. Important exceptions to the obligations of national treatment are provided in the MTAs. Fourth is transparency, which aims to guarantee openness in the trade policies of WTO Members in goods, services and the protection of intellectual property rights. Fifth is a dispute settlement procedure based on a legal foundation, although the priority is to settle disputes through consultations. This latter procedure is a major change from the GATT, and underscores the rule of law, thus making the trading system more secure and predictable.[1] The final aspect of the WTO system is the recognition of special and differential treatment for developing countries (in particular the least-developed countries, or LDCs) and countries in transition to market economies, including transitional periods for them to implement their WTO obligations. Over three-quarters of WTO Members are developing countries and countries in transition.

Trade and public health under GATT: limits to the sovereign right to protect health?

The GATT, originally adopted in 1947 and incorporated into the WTO Agreements in 1994, does not restrict a Member's freedom to adopt measures based on public health considerations. Article XX (b) of the GATT specifically provides for an exception to GATT rules, including national treatment, when 'necessary to protect human, animal or plant life or health'. Article XX imposes the burden of proving the necessity of the trade-restrictive national measures on the Member invoking an exception (Trebilcock and Howse 1999). With the establishment of the WTO, more specific rules are now found in the Agreements on the Application of Sanitary and Phytosanitary Measures (SPS) and Technical Barriers to Trade (TBT). If there is a conflict between provisions of GATT 1994 and agreements forged in any other MTA contained in Annex A to the WTO Agreement, the provision of the other MTA prevails.

The Thai cigarette case of 1990 illustrates how Article XX(b) has been applied in a dispute. In this case, the panel examined the application of the Article to an import ban on cigarettes imposed by the government of Thailand for public health reasons. The panel concluded that alternatives less restrictive than banning imported cigarettes were available to achieve the health objectives of the Thai government. (Trebilcock and Howse 1999). The panel dismissed the Thai government's argument (which was based on Article XX(b)) that the ban was 'necessary to protect human ... life or health'. While acknowledging 'that this provision clearly allowed contracting parties to give priority to human health over trade liberalization', the panel concluded that Thailand had failed to show that 'there were no alternative measures consistent with the General Agreement, or less inconsistent with it, which Thailand could reasonably be expected to employ to achieve its health policy objectives'. Following this ruling, the domestic market was opened to foreign tobacco companies; however, with the implementation of strong domestic tobacco control policies by the Thai government, the prevalence of cigarette smoking by Thai adults actually declined slightly (Vateesatokit *et al.* 2000).

An example of the application of Article XX(b) following the implementation of the WTO in 1995 is provided by the 'Gasoline case' involving the USA, Venezuela and Brazil in a dispute over gasoline quality (see Box 2.1).

Box 2.1 United States – Standards for Reformulated and Conventional Gasoline (WTO 1996).

At issue in this case (the first ever trade dispute handled by the WTO) was the United State's Environmental Protection Agency (EPA) regulation in relation to the Clean Air Act of 1990. The EPA' s 'Gasoline Rule' aims at preventing worse air pollution in the United States by preventing oil refineries from producing dirtier gasoline. Under the EPA's rule, each domestic US refiner was assigned a baseline, and each refiner was required to produce gasoline no dirtier than the baseline. This baseline was calculated based on the volume and quality of gasoline produced by that refiner in 1990. Foreign refineries (as well as domestic refineries without documentation because they were new or had filing violations), on the other hand, were assigned an average (or 'statutory') baseline that their gasoline had to meet.

Venezuela and Brazil lodged a complaint with the WTO because, they argued, they were placed at a disadvantage in that the ruling created the possibility that imported gasoline that failed to meet the average could be rejected while equally dirty gasoline from the US refiner whose baseline was at the bottom end could be permitted: 'All imported gasoline had to meet the 1990 average expressed in the statutory baseline whereas half of the domestic refineries could sell gasoline which did not meet the statutory baseline.' The US rejected these claims and argued that the Gasoline Rule could be justified under the exceptions contained in Article XX(b). For example, it was argued that:

> air pollution, and in particular ground-level ozone, presented health risks to humans, animals and plants. Toxic air pollution was a cause of cancer, birth defects, damage to the brain or other parts of the nervous system, reproductive disorders and genetic mutation. It could affect not only people with impaired respiratory systems, but healthy adults and children as well ... Thus, its (the Gasoline Rule's) aim was to protect public health and welfare by reducing emissions of toxic pollutants ... Therefore, the Gasoline Rule fell within the range of policies specified in Article XX(b).

Ultimately, the WTO panel ruled that the EPA's Gasoline Rule was not consistent with the GATT, and could not be justified under any of the Article XX exceptions. The US appealed this case in 1996, but the rulings of the panel were upheld by the Appellate Body. Based on the WTO ruling, and facing the prospect of US $150 million in trade sanctions per year, the EPA implemented the WTO's recommendations as of August 1997. Now, a foreign refiner can petition the EPA for an individual baseline. If the EPA approves, then the foreign refiner must supply the same kind of evidence and test data as domestic producers. Gasoline from foreign refiners without an individual baseline will continue to be treated under the average baseline.

The Multilateral Trade Agreements (MTAs): the relevance of the trade regime to health

The legal ground-rules that guide the WTO are covered in multilateral Agreements (along with annexes and schedules). The four Agreements considered particularly relevant to public health are the Agreement on Trade-Related Aspects of Intellectual Property Rights (TRIPS), the Agreement on Technical Barriers to Trade (TBT), the Agreement on the Application of Sanitary and Phytosanitary Measures (SPS), and the General Agreement on Trade in Services (GATS). In terms of controlling trade-restrictive health measures, the SPS Agreement (primarily) and the TBT Agreement (secondarily) are now of more importance from a disputes perspective than GATT Article XX (Fidler 2000).

Agreement on Trade-Related Aspects of Intellectual Property Rights (TRIPS)

This Agreement sets minimum standards of protection for intellectual property rights including patents, copyrights, trademarks and industrial designs. The aim of the TRIPS Agreement is to establish minimum standards of intellectual property rights protection that Member Countries must enforce through national laws. The broad objectives of the TRIPS Agreement are: promotion of technological innovation; transfer and dissemination of technology; and contribution to the mutual advantage of producers and users of technological knowledge in a manner conducive to social and economic welfare. Intellectual property areas covered by TRIPS of particular relevance to health are patents, trademarks and undisclosed information. The TRIPS Agreement set the term of protection for patents at a minimum of 20 years from the filing date (Article 33). For trademarks the term of protection is seven years after the initial registration but this term is renewable indefinitely (Article 18). There is no specified term of protection for undisclosed information, which is protectable under non-exclusive rights in the framework of the disciplines on unfair competition.

Ultimately, all WTO Member Countries are required to provide a minimum level of intellectual property protection. However, transitional arrangements were provided for LMICs in view of the problems they face in upgrading their legal and regulatory systems (patent laws, copyright laws, etc.) to be compliant with TRIPS. From 1 January 1995, the transitional periods agreed were one year for industrialised countries, five years for developing countries and countries in transition, and at least eleven years for LDCs. LMICs that did not provide product patent protection for these

---

Box 2.2   The 'Bolar exception' (WTO WT/DS114/R).

During the term of a patent, the 'Bolar exception' in patent law permits research, development and submission of information and samples required of generic drug manufacturers by regulatory authorities for registration. The purpose of the Bolar exception is to facilitate the approval of a generic product for marketing before patent expiration, thereby permitting a prompt introduction of generic versions after that date, at a lower price than the patented pharmaceuticals. Bolar type provisions are explicitly provided for in the patent laws of many developed and a few developing countries. Bolar provisions do not allow for commercialisation before the expiry of the patent; however, in the Bolar provisions in the Canadian Patent Act, manufacturers were allowed to stockpile for up to six months, so that generic drugs were ready to ship as soon as the patent expires.

In November 1998, the European Commission and their Member States requested the WTO Dispute Settlement Body to establish a panel to examine the application of the Bolar provisions in the Canadian Patent Act in relation to Canada's obligations under the TRIPS Agreement. In March 2000, the Panel concluded that Canada was not in violation of TRIPS in allowing the development and submission of information required to obtain marketing approval for pharmaceutical products carried out without the consent of the patent holder. However, Canada was found to be inconsistent with TRIPS in allowing the manufacturing and stockpiling of pharmaceutical products during the six months immediately prior to the expiry of the twenty-year patent term.

---

products at the date of entry into force of the TRIPS Agreement following these periods were granted an extra five years to amend their patent laws.

Of particular interest to health policy is a case relating to the 'Bolar exception' that has recently come to a decision under the TRIPS Agreement, with important implications for the expeditious availability of generic drugs once the original patents have expired (see Box 2.2).

Agreement on Technical Barriers to Trade (TBT)

The TBT Agreement concerns non-tariff barriers (NTBs) in international trade and has implications for the production, labelling, packaging and quality standards of pharmaceuticals, biological agents and foodstuffs. Although countries introduce product standards and technical regulations for safety and quality reasons, these regulations can also be used, either intentionally or unintentionally, as hidden barriers to trade in goods, especially for imports. According to the US Department of Commerce, almost two-thirds of the US merchandise exports in 1993 were affected by technical standards and requirements in importing countries (Trebilcock and Howse 1999). The TBT Agreement was negotiated to remove these NTBs to international trade. There are three important aspects to the TBT Agreement:

- the basic aim of the Agreement is to ensure that domestic technical standards and regulations do not create unnecessary obstacles to trade;
- the Agreement encourages countries to use international standards where these are appropriate; and
- it does not remove the right of the countries to have higher standards than the international standards, provided they can be justified.

All goods, including industrial and agricultural products, are subject to the provisions of this Agreement. However, purchasing specifications prepared by governmental bodies for their production or consumption requirements are not subject to the provisions of this Agreement.

A panoply of standards for products and services is important to safeguard human health. Governments take measures to protect health through health policies, laws, regulations, codes, standards, guidelines and criteria. A great deal of international trade takes place in goods which are either directly used in health systems (drugs, vaccines, medical equipment, diagnostic instruments and machines) or are important for human health (food items and beverages). Some traded goods are known to have harmful effects on health (tobacco products, pesticides, illicit drugs, etc.). For all these goods, except illegal drugs, a variety of standards and regulations exist both at national and international levels with the aim of protecting human health.

The TBT Agreement acknowledges the importance of standards and regulations for protecting public health. The preamble to the Agreement states that 'no country should be prevented from taking measures necessary to ensure the quality of its exports or for the protection of human, animal, and plant life or health, of the environment, or for the prevention of deceptive practices, at the levels it considers appropriate'. However, Members' regulatory flexibility is limited by the requirement that technical regulations 'are not prepared, adopted or applied with a view to, or with the effect of, creating unnecessary obstacles to trade'. The TBT Agreement requires transparency in the development, adoption and application of standards so that the standards and technical regulations cannot be used as a covert way of discouraging imports.

The Canadian asbestos case has recently come to a decision and may turn out to be a landmark case from a public health perspective, although the details of the judgement have not yet been published officially by the WTO (see Box 2.3).

Box 2.3   Canadian asbestos case.

Asbestos is the leading known cause of occupational cancer whose risks have been extensively documented. In France alone asbestos claims the lives of about 2,000 people each year and a ban on chrysotile (white) asbestos is already in place in nine of the fifteen EU Member States. This case stems from a 1998 challenge by Canada to a complete ban by France in 1996 on the import and use of chrysotile asbestos. Canada was concerned that this ban would be taken up by other countries, particularly its Latin American and Asian trading partners.

Canada challenged the ban on the basis that it was a barrier to trade and that it 'severely damages Canada's economic interests and in particular, its profits for international trade in chrysotile asbestos' (*International Herald Tribune*, 16 June 2000). Canada argued that banning asbestos is an unnecessarily extreme measure because the 'controlled' use of asbestos can reduce the health risks to acceptable levels. Many governments, however, have already rejected the notion that the controlled use of asbestos is safe, even in the context of developed countries. In LMICs, the controlled use of asbestos is not usual. Canada also argued that France was trying to protect its domestic producers of substitute products. The USA and the European Union, which represented France at the WTO panel, sided with France in asking the WTO panel to reject the Canadian complaint.

The outcome of this case was announced in June 2000. The adjudicating panel rejected Canada's claim that the ban constituted an unnecessary obstacle to trade under Article 2 of the TBT agreement, arguing that the ban is not a technical regulation and therefore does not fall under the scope of the Agreement. The panel stated that although the French ban was incompatible with the national treatment provisions outlined in Article III of GATT, France nevertheless had a right to apply the ban under GATT Article XX(b) (General Exceptions). A first ruling was issued in September 2000, following review by both parties. This ruling is the first time in the history of the WTO – and in more than 500 filed trade disputes – that trade-restrictive measures have been upheld as necessary to protect human health (*International Herald Tribune*, 16 June 2000).

Another important consideration is the process of international standards development and the participation of developing countries in the work of international standard-setting organisations. Primarily due to lack of resources, the participation of developing countries in international standard-setting organisations has been quite limited. This may reduce the chances of their compliance with the provisions of the Agreement. Special and differential treatment of developing countries is authorised under the Agreement with the aim of encouraging its implementation.

In addition, the Agreement calls upon developed countries to provide LMICs with appropriate technical assistance.

Agreement on the Application of Sanitary and Phytosanitary Measures (SPS)

The SPS Agreement deals with specific measures taken by countries to protect the health of humans, animals and plants, and is especially concerned with food safety. The SPS Agreement, while recognising the right of countries to take measures to protect health and life, aims to minimise the chances of these measures being used as trade barriers. For countries to restrict trade in food products they have to show scientific evidence of risks to health, although the Agreement does allow countries to implement provisional measures in the absence of such evidence. A multilateral framework of rules and disciplines has been established by the SPS to guide the development, adoption and enforcement of national sanitary and phytosanitary measures that are consistent with international standards, guidelines and recommendations in order to minimise their negative effects on international trade. According to the Agreement, sanitary and phytosanitary measures are defined as any measures applied to:

- protect human or animal life or health from risks arising from additives, contaminants, toxins or disease-causing organisms in foods, beverages or feed stuffs;
- protect human life or health from plant or animal carried diseases;
- protect animal or plant life or health from pests, diseases or disease-causing organisms; and
- prevent or limit other damage to a country from the entry, establishment or spread of pests.

With a view to ensuring compliance with the provisions of this Agreement by LMIC Members, the WTO SPS Committee is able to grant time-limited exceptions in whole or in part from the obligations under this Agreement, taking into account financial, trade and development needs. Provision of technical assistance to LMIC Members has also been agreed, either bilaterally or through appropriate international organisations.

The SPS Agreement explicitly refers to three standard-setting international organisations whose activities are particularly relevant to its objectives: the FAO/WHO Codex Alimentarius Commission, the Office International des Epizooties (also called World Animal Health Organisation), and the international and regional organisations operating within

---

Box 2.4   European community – measures affecting meat and meat products (hormones) (WTO 1998a).

Since 1988, the EU has enforced a ban on the sale of beef from cattle treated with artificial hormones. Although the association between human consumption of artificial hormone residues and health problems has not been empirically established, anecdotal evidence suggests that consumption may be associated with cancer, nerve disorders and other health problems. Rather than exposing its population to possible risk, the EU implemented the ban.

In January 1996, the US challenged the decision of the EU as inconsistent with the SPS Agreement. In 1998, the WTO ruled that the ban was illegal, in part because the EU had not based its ban on a scientific risk assessment that conformed to procedures laid out in the WTO Agreement. The WTO Appellate Body affirmed the decision of the panel and the EU was ordered to allow imports of US beef treated with artificial hormones by 13 May 1999. Subsequent to the EU's refusal to lift the ban, on 12 July 1999 the WTO authorised a US request to impose retaliatory sanctions. The health effects of the WTO ruling may never be precisely known.

---

the framework of the FAO International Plant Protection Convention (IPPC). By 1998, Member Countries of the Codex numbered 161. Despite the importance conferred on the work of the Codex Alimentarius Commission by the SPS Agreement, only half of the Member Countries of the Codex participate in the Commission sessions. Furthermore, only 50 per cent of these delegations had representation from ministries of health (CI 1994; WHO 1998a).

From 1 January 1995 to 16 November 1999, violations of the SPS Agreement have been alleged in sixteen invocations of the formal dispute settlement provisions of the WTO. One important case decided under this Agreement is summarised in Box 2.4.

General Agreement on Trade in Services (GATS)

The concept of international trade in services is relatively new. The GATS Agreement is a response to the growing trade in services and, from a health perspective, covers: the movement of consumers and providers across borders to receive and supply health care, foreign direct investment in health, and the emerging area of electronic commerce and telemedicine.[2] The volume, scope and value of trade in health services is increasing, irrespective of whether or not formal commitments (i.e. Members' undertakings to comply with GATS Agreements in specific and named sectors) under GATS have been made.

Table 2.1 *Modes of health services trade under GATS*

Modes of trade	Health services
1. Cross-border supply	• Telemedicine.
2. Consumption abroad	• Patients seeking health care in foreign countries. • Medical/health educational services provided to foreign students.
3. Commercial presence	• Foreign commercial presence: a. in the hospital operation/management sector; b. in the health insurance sector; c. in the educational sector.
4. Presence of natural persons	• Temporary movement of medical/health professionals to provide services abroad.

GATS aims to establish a multilateral framework of principles and rules for trade in services with a view to the expansion of this trade under conditions of transparency and progressive liberalisation.[3] The GATS Agreement defines trade in services in four modes. The application of these modes to trade in health services are summarised in Table 2.1.

The pattern of commitments in health services under the GATS Agreement is diverse and generally at a low level. Seventy-six Member Countries have undertaken GATS commitments on health insurance, 49 on medical and dental services and 39 on hospital services (WTO 1998b).

There are no exact figures available about the volume of trade in health services, but it appears that the volume of international trade in medical and health services is still relatively modest. In the US, for example, it is estimated that 'exports' of health care services (covering the activities of the US majority-owned suppliers abroad and the services provided to foreigners in the US) is less than 0.2 per cent of total domestic health care spending.

Health implications and policy options

Health implications of the WTO MTAs

Below, an attempt has been made to identify some of the potential public health consequences of the WTO MTAs. Given the recent implementation of the WTO, much of the evidence presented is speculative.

GATT 1994

The exception under Article XX(b) provided in the GATT, as described above, has been interpreted narrowly in a number of cases so as to limit the extent of trade-restrictive environmental, health and safety regulations. In addition, if there is a conflict between the provisions of GATT 1994 and Agreements forged in any other WTO MTA on trade in goods, the provision of the other MTA prevails and has the potential to limit the applicability of the Article XX(b) exception.

Trade-Related aspects of Intellectual Property Rights Agreement: little room for optimism

The TRIPS Agreement has implications for public health in developing countries because of its impact on the production and trade in pharmaceuticals and vaccines (Velasquez and Boulet 1999). Will, for example, more effective patent protection lead to new drugs for diseases affecting the poor in developing countries, or will TRIPS exacerbate the lack of access to new drugs by increasing prices? At this stage, there is little evidence to suggest any major benefits for developing countries in terms of the availability of new and cheaper drugs as a result of TRIPS, although it must be recognised that the development and marketing of new products has a long lead-time. However, the imbalance is clear when we consider that the 75 per cent of the world's population who live in developing countries consume only 14 per cent of the world's drug supply, and more than 80 per cent of drug production takes place in industrialised countries (UNDP 1999). An overview of new drug development between 1975 and 1997, for example, found that of the 1,223 new chemical entities marketed during this period, 379 (31 per cent) were therapeutic innovations but only 13 (1 per cent) were useful for tropical diseases (Pecoul et al. 1999). Furthermore, a multicountry study (India, Indonesia, Pakistan, the Philippines and Thailand) in 1995 found the possible welfare and price effects of introducing product patents for pharmaceuticals to be negative. Inflation-adjusted price increases, estimated as a result of TRIPS for patented drugs, ranged from 5 per cent to 67 per cent (Subramaniam 1995). Similarly for Argentina, a likely drug price increase of 71 per cent has been estimated (Chambouleyron 1995).

Developed countries currently hold 97 per cent of all patents worldwide; more than 80 per cent of the patents that have been granted in developing countries also belong to residents of developed countries (UNDP 1999). Research and development (R & D) of new drugs is mainly undertaken by pharmaceutical transnational corporations (TNCs). The main argument used by the TNCs in support of patents is that without assured profit returns (through strong and prolonged intellectual property rights protection), they could not continue to invest in R & D. However, it is debatable whether the extension of patent protection to developing countries will lead TNCs to invest in R & D for drugs needed in developing countries, as there is limited effective demand for drugs that treat many highly prevalent diseases. At present only 0.2 per cent of the annual global health expenditure related to R & D is for pneumonia, diarrhoeal diseases and tuberculosis, despite their accounting for 18 per cent of the global disease burden (UNDP 1999).

Pharmaceutical companies in developing countries conduct very little research on the development of new drugs. Most of the research by these companies focuses on developing process technologies, formulations or combinations of existing drugs, but they lack the resources and state support (largely available in industrialised countries) to undertake more basic research on new products. In Argentina, for instance, Julio Nogués (cited in Pecoul *et al.* 1999) found no reason to expect an increase in domestic R & D in pharmaceuticals due to the recognition of product patents, because the development of new chemical entities would be outside the R & D capacity of local companies.

Technical Barriers to Trade Agreement: scope for health gains through higher standards

The TBT Agreement may be a useful step towards enhancing public health in a globalised world. It promotes universal standards for protecting certain aspects of human life and health and does not stop Member Countries from maintaining higher standards for protection of public health, as long as they do not represent a disguised barrier to trade. For consumers, the TBT Agreement can be positive for two reasons:

- through universal standards it promises acceptable quality of some of the products which directly or indirectly affect human health; and
- by setting up a system of standard-setting, it minimises the chances of standards being used as a protective shield for domestic products and, hence, promotes trade and more choice and lower prices for consumers.

However, international standards may be perceived as too high and too costly by developing countries, at least in the short term, and may negatively affect the exports of goods from the developing countries (Evans 1994). Many developing countries – China, India, Brazil, South Korea and Pakistan – have considerable export markets in products used directly in the health care system, for example pharmaceutical products, surgical instruments and diagnostic equipment. With the imposition of higher international standards, these countries may see their export markets diminish (see chapter by Fustukian *et al.* this volume).

Agreement on Sanitary and Phytosanitary Measures: the devil is in the detail

Public health may benefit from this Agreement in many ways. By adhering to internationally acceptable standards of food safety and animal health, national authorities can safeguard the health of their citizens. According to the WHO/FAO (Food and Agriculture Organisation) Expert Committee on Food Safety, illnesses due to contaminated food are a leading health problem (WHO 1998a). Since most developing country economies are predominantly agricultural, food processing is one of the basic value-added activities they undertake. Food-safety control programmes in these countries are important from health and export points of views. With unreliable food-safety programmes, the exports of food products from developing countries would not be acceptable. Harmonised food standards across Member Countries can provide a level playing field to trading partners as long as these standards themselves are not used as covert protection from import competition.

The SPS Agreement has conferred a new status on the Codex Alimentarius Commission, an international body charged with developing food codes to protect the health of consumers and to ensure fair practices in food trade. The benefits that the SPS Agreement offers in the area of food safety and trade are: transparency in standard setting; international harmonisation of standards; acceptance of the importance of risk assessment; and equivalence of the relevant measures of other member countries (WTO 1999b).

Public interest groups in the United States have feared that by promoting harmonisation of standards for food safety, the SPS is compelling countries to compromise on national public health safeguards. For example, in July 1999, the Codex Alimentarius approved pesticides residues that do not take into account their impacts on children, as is required under US law (Center of Science in the Public Interest 1999).[4] The same meeting also approved a safety standard for dairy products that does not require pasteurisation, whereas the US Food and Drug Administration has this requirement.

Many concerns have been expressed about the SPS Agreement's acceptance of the Codex standards for food safety. The Codex is not just a scientific body set up for developing global food-safety standards; rather, one of the goals of the Codex is to facilitate international trade in food (FAO/WHO 1999). It has been suggested that the Codex mandate to protect public health is often secondary to its competing mandate to promote international trade (Wallach and Sforza 1999).

General Agreement on Trade in Services: both pros and cons

Increased trade in health services could open the sector to increased competition, bringing with it needed technology and management expertise, and, for some countries, increased export earnings. It could also deepen current inequalities in access and promote the migration of skilled health professionals from already under-serviced areas (Drager 1999).

Some developing countries regard the emigration of their health personnel (Table 2.1: mode 4) as their principal health services export, and seek to have the barriers to the movement of personnel from LMICs to developed countries removed. While benefiting developing countries, mode 4 commitments could also alleviate personnel shortages in developed countries. Countries having a comparative advantage in health services would benefit from trade liberalisation under GATS. Although much of this advantage lies with industrialised countries, some developing countries also enjoy market niches in certain areas of health services. In the following section, we review the evidence on the health impact of the trade in health services under GATS.

Cross-border supply   Telemedicine is the main form of cross-border supply of health services. Many types of health-related data and information can be communicated through telecommunication, for example health management information, clinical information, surveillance and epidemiological information, literature and knowledge. There is a significant potential for cross-border trade, although presently telemedicine appears to have been used mainly to overcome geographical barriers within individual countries and to improve health care in remote regions (WTO 1998b). Telemedicine may contribute to improving the quality of health care services in a cost-effective manner. It can, for example, assist health professionals in remote areas to communicate with specialists in big cities and enable physicians to guide paramedical staff and patients located in remote areas. Although the telecommunication infrastructure, especially broadband real-time video, is expensive, some projects report a 65 to 70 per cent reduction in unnecessary referrals (Mandil 1998). In developing countries, telemedicine has so far been used in a limited way (Mandil 1998; Singkaew and Chaichana 1998). Despite the potential for improving health service quality, most developing countries do not have the resources and infrastructure to invest in telemedicine to enhance the quality of, and geographical access to, health services.

Consumption abroad   'Consumption abroad' means movement of consumers/patients and students to foreign countries for treatment and education. For example, this could facilitate easier access to high-quality services in developed countries by those in LMICs who can afford to do so. Traffic the other way, from developed countries to LMICs by, for example, patients seeking 'exotic' therapies or less expensive treatment in cases not covered by health insurers (e.g. cosmetic surgery), could also be facilitated.

Attracting foreign patients can be a source of increased foreign exchange for developing countries. India has considerable potential for attracting foreign patients, both from neighbouring countries and from the wider Asia–Pacific region. Indian clinics can offer sophisticated treatment, including cardiovascular surgery, as well as standard and specialised therapies at prices estimated at about one-fifth to one-tenth of those charged in industrialised countries for similar interventions (Prassad 1997). Cuba has also been developing a supply of services designed specifically for foreign patients (Diaz and Hurtado 1994). An important consideration, however, for all countries is that the provision of health services to paying foreign patients should not be at the expense of health services provision to the local population.

Medical (and allied) students also move between countries for educational and training purposes. The direction of this movement is predominantly from developing to developed countries. Of concern to many 'sending' countries is that many such students do not return to their countries of origin after completion of their studies.

Commercial presence Commercial presence or establishment trade involves the commercial provision of health services via foreign-invested facilities. Typically such trade takes place as a joint venture with local health service providers. In most Member Countries the foreign commercial presence is restricted to foreign investment in domestic health sectors, especially hospital management and health insurance. Quantitative information about establishment trade in health services is limited. According to the information available from the United States in 1995 the sales by foreign-based affiliates of US majority-owned health care providers amounted to US $469 million. This contrasts, in the same year, with services sales worth US $1.8 billion by foreign-owned health care suppliers in the US (Diaz and Hurtado 1994).

Foreign commercial presence in the health sector has been encouraged by increased privatisation in health care provision in developing countries promoted by the World Bank. The liberalisation of trade in health services under GATS may accentuate this. Most WTO Members have made specific commitments to trade liberalisation in the area of health insurance. In LMICs, the establishment of foreign health insurance companies would benefit only the relatively affluent. The other area of attraction to foreign investors in health services in developing countries is hospital management. This could lead to improved quality standards through sophisticated technology and techniques, but at a considerable cost. The presence of foreign health service providers, alone or in joint venture with local business, may bring variety and higher 'quality' care and would increase the size of the private health care sector.

Presence of natural persons   Presence of 'natural persons' refers to the movement of individuals supplying services as opposed to organisational entities involved in 'commercial presence'. In the case of health services this most commonly involves movement of health professionals between countries who engage in supplying health services. The main direction of this movement is generally from LMICs to industrialised countries, although migration between LMICs and between developed countries is also prevalent. Health professionals move to industrialised countries attracted by higher salaries, better living conditions and brighter career opportunities. In the late 1970s it was estimated that 56 per cent of all migrating physicians came from developing countries (Mejia *et al.* 1979). This represents a huge resource loss both in terms of public spending and health service capacity in developing countries. The GATS might offer an opportunity to conduct this exchange in natural persons within a transparent and predictable framework of legally enforceable disciplines.

Policy options for constructing a health-friendly trade regime

Before turning to the question of how to sensitise and re-orient the present MTA system towards public health, it is useful to consider some of the linkages of the trade regime to the unfolding processes of globalisation (see chapter 1). *First,* the significance of a near universal mechanism with binding legal authority to condition and reshape national policy cannot be too strongly stressed. The fact that this authority has been largely directed towards the free-flow of trade at the expense of other national objectives cannot detract from the hitherto unprecedented opportunity which the regime itself affords for global behind-the-border policy convergence that promotes and protects health. *Secondly,* it should be noted that the MTA process itself represents the 'globalising' of intergovernmental policy-making in that it has begun to close what Kaul *et al.* (1999) refer to as the participation gap. To date, it would appear that the system has largely opened itself to the involvement of for-profit interests in framing the rules of the game (see, e.g. Sell 1999 for a detailed discussion of the drafting of the TRIPS Agreement by a network of twelve CEOs of multinational corporations) and in interpreting the Agreements (Dunoff 1998, p. 433). Although civil society has remained largely at the margins of the debate, directing attention to the perceived pitfalls of trade harmonisation, its increasing prominence may result in a more influential and participative role. In this regard, the need for greater inclusion of developing country interests (both governmental and non-governmental) has also been highlighted. Moreover, the trade arena reinforces the need to move beyond national interests and boundaries in both analysis and practice. Representing all these legitimate interests reinforces the need for increased transparency in WTO procedures and more inclusiveness to ensure that the interests of all parties are adequately heard. *Thirdly*, although trade liberalisation has forcefully reminded the public health community of the breadth of the determinants of health, the increasing volume of global trade (facilitated by the MTAs) results in numerous positive and negative externalities (McMichael and Beaglehole 2000) with which the present intergovernmental MTAs appear ill-equipped to deal. Collectively, these considerations provide a strong case for close analysis and monitoring of the MTA agreements to ensure consistency with development objectives.

A crucial issue from a public health perspective is how to ensure that health-related issues are fully taken into account in the trading system. Tension can exist between the trade interests reflected in the WTO Agreements and public health. The WTO system recognises the need to protect health, but via exceptions which have often been construed rather narrowly. The nature of the exceptions under Article XX of the GATT and under other WTO Agreements puts the onus on the Member State arguing public health interests to provide scientific justification for deviations from its general obligations. This burden will make it very difficult for poor countries to ensure that the MTAs do not adversely impact on the health status of their populations. A related concern is the need to develop the capacity of the public health workforce, especially in developing countries, such that the public health perspective persuasively informs the negotiating stance of national trade officials. An informed and influential public health voice at the national level is a prerequisite for influencing future trade negotiations and for ensuring that existing opportunities within the MTAs can be exploited to the fullest extent. WHO has an important role in providing appropriate training courses and materials to support public health professionals as they begin to engage with the complex issues raised by MTAs.

The development of a more 'health-sensitive' trading system will require the progressive application and interpretation of WTO rules through the evolution of the WTO jurisprudence, on a case-by-case basis. The resolution of possible conflicts between public health and trade interests could be left to decisions taken by existing bodies and procedures under the existing rules. However, negotiations have so far lacked the transparency required for a balanced incorporation of civil society views, and have been strongly influenced by specific industries and commercial interests. The dispute resolution process, for example, relies on closed-doors reviews by panels of trade experts (generally lawyers or diplomats) with no expertise on technical aspects such as those involved in public health issues. The shortcomings of a secretive process of decision-making have been recognised by many WTO Members, especially developing countries. It is encouraging that the US government, for instance, has offered to open up every panel it is party to.[5] It will be important to ensure strong representation from the scientific public health perspective in these processes and to strengthen appropriate country-level capacity and expertise. The need to improve transparency in the WTO operation is recognised by developing and developed countries alike.

A basic question is, therefore, how to achieve a balanced consideration of possible competing trade and public health interests, in a manner that prevents trade perspectives from dominating the interpretation of the WTO Agreements while ensuring public health and other exceptions are not used to unfairly restrict trade.

The need to reconcile trade commitments with national policies, including those on public health, has been recognised as one of the tasks of the WTO. The methods and criteria applied to solve the tensions between the satisfaction of national public interests, and compliance with the general WTO obligations, will determine the scope that sovereign nations retain to pursue legitimate national objectives. Solving such tensions is not, however, an easy task since it may be difficult to distinguish between legitimate measures, least trade-restrictive measures, and those adopted with a purely protectionist intent. Different approaches have been suggested to address conflicts that arise.

One approach is to reaffirm the sovereign rights of states to deal with public health related and other public policy issues. Under this view, national health policies and rules should prevail over multilateral disciplines when a conflict arises. In particular, a 'sovereignty school' has developed in the area of environmental policies, according to which environmental policy-making should be left entirely to national politicians and the WTO stripped of all authority to challenge nationally determined policies. While some supporters of the sovereignty school would accept the review of environmental policies by the WTO to determine if they are really disguised protectionism, others would permit no international oversight whatsoever (Esty 1994).

A second approach suggests reinforcing and expanding the role of the WTO to deal more systematically with trade-related issues of global interest. This new role would be necessary in order to address the restrictions to market access, which derive from diverging attitudes towards new technologies and risks, as well as to address the protection of global goods and of interests of common concern. Under this 'constitutional role' the WTO should no longer be based on a negative integration scheme (i.e. prohibiting restrictions) as its sole task in construing trade-related rules. Under such an expanded role, the WTO should develop new international norms for the protection of global commons and of interests of common concern, such as health or the environment, rather than allowing these matters to be approached under traditional doctrines of exclusive national sovereignty and jurisdiction (Cottier 1998).

Possible approaches

A possible general approach for the integration of trade and public health interests may be to develop agreed interpretations of the MTAs through the WTO General Council decisions on critical issues, in terms of both substance and procedures. This is not, however, a simple task, since the approval of an agreed interpretation requires three-quarters of Members' votes.

Another, more modest, approach would be to try to ensure, on a *case-by-case* basis, that the panels and the Appellate Body (AB) become more sensitive to broader public policy conceptions, such as of public health, through the increasing and effective participation of Members that are not parties to a dispute, and international organisations, such as WHO, in the decision-making process. In fact, firms and other private interest groups have been very active and influential in policy-making and dispute settlement procedures (Dunoff 1998). To counterbalance this influence it will be necessary to strengthen the public health voice at these deliberations by ensuring the participation of relevant public health and non-governmental players.

It should be noted that, according to Article 13 of the dispute settlement understanding (DSU), panels are authorised to obtain opinion and information from any source. Article 13 is broad and appears to give full discretion to panels to decide whether and what type of information or technical advice they need from any source. This provision, however, is addressed only to panels and not to the Appellate Body. Consequently, some legal experts argue that the faculty to obtain outside information is limited to evidence, as opposed to legal arguments. Unlike the procedures before other courts (such as the European Court of Justice), the DSU procedures do not explicitly envisage the possibility for the panels or Appellate Body to invite *'amicus briefs'* from NGOs and other organisations (Marceau and Pedersen 1999: 34). Panels and the Appellate Body may benefit from opinion and advice from WHO whenever the application of health-related exceptions under Article XX(b) of the GATT, the SPS and other WTO Agreements are at stake. WHO may become more active in this respect, although WHO will need to strengthen its capacity to act effectively on these issues on behalf of its members. This would require that the WHO Secretariat be given a broader mandate to act in these matters.

A further alternative would be to propose changes in existing rules, including substantive and procedural norms, such as those relating to the burden of proof. One possible approach would be to adopt a 'patently unreasonable' standard which would require the country, whose domestic policies are under challenge, to produce evidence sufficient to suggest that the policy choice is not 'patently unreasonable', i.e. it is a plausible means of attempting to achieve the policy objectives, even if the reviewing body could itself imagine superior instruments. This approach would be respectful of domestic political sovereignty and policy autonomy (Trebilcock and Howse 1999).

Finally, substantive reforms may be required. In the case of the TRIPS Agreement, for instance, if a 'public health' approach were adopted, some articles may require revision. Clarification of article 31 in relation to the granting and scope of compulsory licences for public health reasons may also be considered.

Conclusions: bringing health proponents into the trade debate

The primary aim of the GATT/WTO system is to reduce tariffs and other barriers to international trade. The GATT, as adopted in 1947, recognised that conflicts may arise between specific trade objectives and those emerging from other public concerns, such as health, safety and the environment. Given the basic objective of the system, however, these concerns have been dealt with as limited exceptions allowable under narrowly defined conditions. Though health and other public concerns have been taken into account in several of the Agreements adopted in 1994, these Agreements have not substantially altered the dominance of trade interests in cases of public health interest.

The tensions between trade and health interests may increase as the globalisation of the economy proceeds and health is increasingly recognised as a global public good. The importance of health regulations has substantially increased since the inception of the GATT system, while in many countries trade liberalisation has increased income distribution inequalities and worsened the opportunities for access to medicines, particularly by the poor.

A crucial issue is, therefore, how such tensions may be resolved within the WTO system in a manner that fully recognises public health concerns and includes full consideration of the norms and standards established by competent intergovernmental organisations. A possible approach, as described above, may be to reinforce the sovereign rights of Member States to deal with such issues of public concern, through a deeper involvement of specialised organisations, such as WHO, and the reform of certain substantive or procedural aspects of the WTO Agreements.

Increased transparency in WTO procedures for dispute settlement, and the systematic recourse to expert advice by panels, may enhance the sensitivity of the WTO system to public health concerns. However, procedural and substantive reforms may also be required.

Given the diversity of groups concerned by the WTO Agreements, the push for a reform of the GATT/WTO system in a health-sensitive direction is not likely to emerge from industry groups. It will be up to national governments to demand and define a health-agenda in possible future negotiations in the WTO in order to ensure that health interests, as determined by national authorities, are not unduly subordinated to trade perceptions. In turn, there is a strong need for health workers to become involved in national and global discussions on the issues addressed in this chapter to ensure and support a strong Member-initiated effort to introduce changes at the WTO General Council.

NOTES

1 The dispute settlement process is outlined in the Understanding on Rules and Procedures Governing the Settlement of Disputes, abbreviated as DSU (dispute settlement understanding). It is administered by the Dispute Settlement Body (DSB) made up of WTO Members. A report is made by a panel and endorsed (or rejected) by the WTO's full membership. Appeals based on points of law can be made to an Appellate Body (AB) at the request of any of the parties to a dispute.
2 Telemedicine is the process of medical care using audio, visual and data communications; this includes medical care delivery, consultation, diagnosis, treatment, education and the transfer of medical data.
3 From preamble of GATS.
4 See also US Law at 405 of the Food Quality Protection Act of 1996, amending section 408(b) of the Federal Food, Drug and Cosmetic Act, 21 USC. Section 34a(B) as quoted in Wallach and Sforza (1999: 73).
5 See the submission of the US president at the 2nd WTO Ministerial Conference.

KEY READINGS

Bettcher, D., Yach, D. and Guindon, G. E. 2000, 'Global trade and health: key linkages and future challenges', *Bulletin of the World Health Organization* 78 (4): 521–34.

Correa, C. 2000, 'Implementing national public health policies in the framework of WTO agreements', *Journal of World Trade* 34 (5): 89–121.

Kinnon, C. 1998, 'World trade: bringing health into the picture', *World Health Forum* 19: 397–406.

Koivusalo, M. 1999, 'World Trade Organization and trade-creep in health and social policies', *GASPP Occasional Papers no. 4*, Helsinki.

Pollock, A. M. and Price D. 2000, 'Rewriting the regulations: how the World Trade Organisation could accelerate privatisation in health-care systems', *The Lancet* 356, 9 December: 1995–2000.

3 Globalisation and multilateral public–private health partnerships: issues for health policy

Kent Buse and Gill Walt

Introduction

Other chapters in this book demonstrate the profound changes accompanying globalisation, which are altering the manner and the ability of nation-states (particularly in low-income countries) to formulate and implement health policy. More specifically, later chapters expose how a variety of challenges cannot be met efficiently at the national level, but require additional collective international, if not global, approaches. Moreover, the ascendancy of organised capital over the power of the nation-state adds impetus to intergovernmental co-operation. Indeed, it has been argued that: 'short of a backlash against globalisation, states will have little choice but to pool their sovereignty to exercise public power in a global environment now mostly shaped by private actors' (Reinicke and Witte 1999). Consequently, new multilateral institutions and instruments are being established, others reformed and some given hitherto unprecedented powers (e.g. the binding nature of the World Trade Organization Agreements), and a number of new forms of global governance are emerging. As globalisation forces a shift from state-centric politics to more complex forms of multicentred governance, and makes the desirability of global level mechanisms for the governance of global problems more apparent, a new set of challenges to the existing multilateral system comes into play.

In relation to the United Nations (UN), two trends in the nature of the emerging global governance architecture are observable, although the notion of the emergence of any system of global governance remains contested (Dodgson *et al.* 2000). The first is that some emerging structures and instruments of global governance side-step the UN and its organisations (ODI 1999). The second involves the establishment of new forms of governance in which the UN enters into horizontal networks, alliances and partnerships with other multilateral institutions, international non-governmental organisations, commercial enterprises and governments. This chapter will address some of the implications of this second trend.

We argue that the burgeoning increase in the number of global public–private partnerships (GPPPs), which, in part, is driven by globalisation, is changing key attributes of the UN system.

During the 1990s there was an explosion in the number of health sector partnerships between UN agencies and the private sector (Buse and Walt 2000b). GPPPs are created so as to achieve the objectives of both private and public partners, and thereby to meet mutually identified needs (resulting from a mixture of public and market failure). However, although GPPPs are heralded as being able to address problems that proved intractable in the absence of partnership, they will transform the relationship between public and private actors as values, roles and responsibilities are mediated through the partnering process. We argue that this transformation is likely to have significant implications for the exercise of governance of health through the multilateral UN regime, and may lead to the further weakening of the UN system. The specialised agencies of the UN, such as the World Health Organisation (WHO), have enjoyed relative global authority and legitimacy, accorded in part by their near universal member state representation, but this may be changing as a result of GPPPs. Although the UN is beset by many problems and weaknesses, we are concerned that, without adequate safeguards, GPPPs may undermine the ability of WHO to effectively contribute to health governance at the global level.

This chapter begins with a short discussion of the concepts under consideration, including globalisation, governance and partnership. The subsequent section demonstrates how four trends associated with globalisation have induced greater co-operation between the UN and the private-for-profit sector, which accounts for the rise in GPPPs. The final section explores some of the likely implications of GPPPs on the nature of health governance at the multilateral level.

Globalisation and the emerging challenges and innovations in governance

Globalisation is a highly contested phenomenon in terms of its conceptualisation, causal dynamics, socio-economic consequences and the implications for state and interstate governance (Held *et al.* 1999). The range of definitions proposed over the past decades is large, tending to reflect select aspects of the process. For our purposes, globalisation may be defined as 'the process of increasing economic, political and social interdependence and global integration that takes place as capital, traded goods, persons, concepts, images, ideas, and values diffuse across state boundaries' (Hurrell and Woods 1995). Reinicke and Witte (1999) make a useful distinction between the processes of growing interdependence and globalisation. The first, a phenomenon largely of the post-Second World War era, was structured and managed mainly by functionally equivalent nation-states and resulted in a variety of international institutions and regimes to provide a rule-based framework to manage their relations. The second process, namely globalisation, is mainly structured by private actors and is notable in that it has brought about a qualitative shift in power relations. In particular, as approximately 70 per cent of trade is now accounted for by intra-industry and intra-firm trade (OECD 1996), global corporate networks are increasingly powerful in relation to nation-states. Here we are suggesting that GPPPs represent a qualitatively new hybrid form of governance in which the two processes of interdependence and globalisation interact. Institutions such as the World Trade Organization (WTO) provide another form of governance at this interface (see Ranson *et al.* this volume). However, we argue that, in contrast to the WTO, the rules governing GPPPs remain inadequately developed.

As globalisation diminishes the influence and power of some nation-states, it subjects the intergovernmental regime to new disciplines and challenges (Knight 1995). One consequence of this changed environment is that multilateral governance increasingly occurs alongside other forms of global governance exercised by transnational networks, issue-networks, organised corporate interests, and other political forces which transcend state boundaries. Globalisation thus provides the context and a force driving the emergence of GPPPs as multilateral organisations and the commercial sector attempt to adjust to a new world order. Yet what sort of governance do GPPPs provide?

Governance, broadly defined, is concerned with the manner in which an organisation or society steers itself (Rosenau 1995). In more operational terms, we are concerned with legitimacy and representation, accountability and competency, appropriateness and respect for due process (World Bank 1994a). Our discussion focuses on the issue of governance at two levels. First, we consider it in relation to international (*ipso facto* 'global' once the private sector is involved) health policy-making and the manner in which GPPPs alter agenda setting, resource allocation, decision-making mechanisms, representation and participation in the governance of global health. As noted above, GPPPs are emerging as one form of global governance, yet there has been very little analysis of these arrangements nor the operational questions they raise. Second, we examine the issues arising in relation to the institutional arrangements that are established to govern and manage the partnerships themselves. But what are such partnerships?

Partnerships and health GPPPs: our units of analyses

Lending specificity to the notion of partnership remains problematic (see Box 3.1). This reflects, in part, the fact that partnering has extended to describe a wide range of activities involving an ever-expanding web of relationships between donors and low-income country governments, between donors and non-governmental organisations (NGOs), between NGOs (including not-for-profit foundations) and communities, among NGOs and, increasingly, between these actors and the private-for-profit sector, including its representatives. In this discussion, however, we employ a narrow and specific definition of a global public–private partnership for health. Health GPPPs are those collaborative relationships which transcend national boundaries and bring together at least three parties, among them a corporation (and/or industry association) and an intergovernmental organisation, so as to achieve a shared health-creating goal on the basis of a mutually agreed and explicitly defined division of labour (adapted from Buse and Walt 2000a). The modus operandi, whereby a governance structure is established, objectives are set, a division of labour agreed and the partnership is monitored, is of central importance as regards implications of GPPPs for global health governance.

Although in this chapter we focus on the interface between multilateral organisations and the private-for-profit sector, health GPPPs often include other partners, such as civil society groups or national governmental agencies or donor agencies, who are often critical for effective

---

Box 3.1   The partnership–network continuum.

The terms partnership, alliance, network, coalition and consortium are often used interchangeably, and there appears to be little agreement on which most accurately describes these different institutional arrangements. None the less, it is possible that these arrangements be considered along a continuum. Partnership can be placed at one end of a continuum, with networks at the other end, and alliances somewhere in between. The partnership end involves more formalised agreements and consequently fewer parties, while the network involves a looser grouping of a greater number of parties who share common interests. It might be that, over time, networks and alliances might evolve into more tightly integrated partnerships.

implementation of partnership activities. For example, public and private actors often partner through an intermediary NGO or charitable foundation: Merck & Co.'s 'Mectizan® Donation Program' operates through the Task Force on Child Survival and Development, while Pfizer's donation of Zithromax® is governed by the 'International Trachoma Initiative', an NGO established under Helen Keller International (Frost and Reich 1998; Cook 1999). The 'International AIDS Vaccine Initiative' is a partnership between the World Bank, the joint UN Programme on HIV/AIDS (UNAIDS), private sector sponsors (e.g. Levi Strauss), private laboratories, the development agencies of the Swiss and UK governments, numerous foundations and academia (Berkley and Lenton 1999).

Elsewhere we have proposed a goal-oriented, three-category classification of health GPPPs: product-based, product development-based, and issues/systems-based (Buse and Walt 2000b). *Product-based partnerships* (see Box 3.2) consist primarily of drug donation programmes. Drug donation programmes are generally established after the discovery that an existing drug (for animals or humans) is found to be effective in the treatment of some condition for which there is limited *effective demand* (i.e. lack of willingness and ability to pay; e.g. Zithromax® for the treatment of trachoma). Pharmaceutical companies generally initiate such partnerships so as to lower the cost and increase the chance of ensuring the drug reaches those who need, but cannot afford, it. While the private sector companies may seek short-term objectives through such GPPPs (e.g. establishing political contacts at global and country levels), it would appear that establishing their reputations as ethically oriented is what is ultimately sought.

Although drug donation programmes would at first instance appear relatively non-controversial, a number of critiques of specific programmes have recently appeared in the literature. Shretta *et al.* (2000), for example, raise a number of concerns regarding the implementation of the Malarone® Donation Program in Kenya. In particular, they calculate that despite the donation by Glaxo Wellcome of Malarone®, a relatively expensive anti-malarial for the treatment of malaria, the drug will not be affordable, thus limiting the likelihood that pilot projects could be scaled-up and prove sustainable at the national level. Moreover, their research suggests that the programme will encourage the inappropriate use of the drug as a first-line therapy (heightening drug-resistant malaria) and, as Malarone® has been registered for use in the private sector, will encourage health workers to sell the drug to enhance their meagre wages and thereby likely exacerbate an already inequitable access to drugs. In so doing the authors provide additional evidence of the

---

Box 3.2   The Mectizan® Donation Program –
a product-based health GPPP.

The Mectizan® Donation Program, launched in 1987, has established itself as the pioneer of product-based public–private health partnerships. It aims to eliminate river blindness by treating everyone with Mectizan® who needs it, for as long as necessary, at no charge. The partnership represents an open-ended commitment by its corporate sponsor, Merck & Co. Drugs worth a reported US $500 million have been provided through the programme to all thirty-four endemic countries. The Mectizan® Donation Program consists of the Mectizan® Expert Committee (MEC) and its Secretariat which is based in the Task Force on Child Survival and Development (TFCSD). The MEC consists of seven independent experts and three liaison (non-voting) members representing WHO, Centers for Disease Control, USA (CDC) and Merck. The MEC chairperson and members are appointed by Merck. The MEC reports biannually and the Secretariat monthly to Merck. Because Merck meets the Program's expenses and appoints MEC members, the independence of the Program has been questioned.

---

potential and actual problems associated with pharmaceutical donation programmes in developing countries (Kale 1999) which are not yet adequately addressed by WHO guidelines on the subject (WHO 1999a).

Product development partnerships (Box 3.3) differ from product donation partnerships in a number of respects. First, they are not targeted at specific countries. Secondly, these partnerships are generally initiated by the public sector. Thirdly, the product development partnerships are not premised so much on ineffective demand as on *market failure*. Most of these products are perceived by the public sector as worthy of societal investment, but the market fails to allocate resources to their discovery and development because industry perceives that the potential returns do not justify the opportunity cost of investment. For example, although research on an AIDS vaccine is considered an important public good, industry is not certain that expenditure on research will be rewarded with a large enough market to justify development and commercialisation, nor what the potential cost of liability and regulation will amount to (IAVI 1996). Product development GPPPs usually entail the public sector assuming a number of risks associated with product discovery, development and/or commercialisation (i.e. providing a public subsidy), thereby offsetting the opportunity cost of industry's involvement. One feature of some product development GPPPs is retention of the intellectual property rights by

---

Box 3.3   The International AIDS Vaccine Initiative – a product development-based health GPPP.

The International AIDS Vaccine Initiative (IAVI) was established in 1996. It aims to ensure the development of safe, effective, accessible, preventive HIV vaccines for use throughout the world. IAVI is an international, non-profit NGO governed by a board of 12 members representing scientists, public sector member organisations, policy-makers and industry leaders. It has a scientific advisory committee drawn from public and private sectors. By 1999, IAVI had supported the establishment of two vaccine development partnerships between biotech companies and academia with US $9 million in grant funding. IAVI negotiates intellectual property agreements leveraging its 'social venture capital' so as to ensure that the public sector retains the rights to eventual vaccines. The Bill and Melinda Gates Foundation contributed US $25 million to IAVI in 1999. Other partners include: World Bank, UNAIDS, Rockefeller Foundation, AP Sloan Foundation, Foundation Marcel Merieux, DFID, Glaxo Wellcome, Levi Strauss International, as well as a number of academic institutions and other charitable foundations.

---

the partnership organisation so as to keep a lever over eventual product pricing (e.g. International AIDS Vaccine Initiative and the Medicines for Malaria Venture). Corporations may engage in product development partnerships so as to mobilise a subsidy for research, obtain assistance in the conduct of clinical trials, or they may be pursuing longer-term interests (financial returns and proximity to regulatory processes). Finally, companies may be seeking to portray themselves in a favourable light, which may help them secure entry into emerging drug markets.

The *systems/issues-based partnerships* (Box 3.4) are a more eclectic group. Some systems GPPPs have been established to complement the efforts of governments, such as the 'Secure the Future' partnership (BMS 1999) and others to tap non-medical private resources for disease control, such as the 'World Alliance for Research and Control of Communicable Diseases' (TDR/WHO 1999). A number of high-profile issue-based GPPPs have been launched which seek to harmonise or bring strategic consistency among the approaches of various actors and to raise the profiles of single diseases on the health policy agenda (e.g. 'Roll Back Malaria' and the 'Stop TB' initiative). By exploring the interests which motivate public and private actors to partner, the following section provides the basis for speculating on the potential implications of partnerships for the different sectors and for public health more generally.

Box 3.4   The Bill and Melinda Gates Children's Vaccine Program – a systems/issues-based health GPPP.

The Bill and Melinda Gates Children's Vaccine Program was established in 1998 with a US $100 million grant from the Bill and Melinda Gates Foundation. The programme aims to reduce or eliminate the time lag in the introduction of new vaccines for children that exists between the developing and developed world. The principal partners are the Bill and Melinda Gates Foundation and the Program for Appropriate Technology (PATH) with a number of other parties involved mainly in activity implementation (these include vaccine manufacturers, UNICEF, WHO, World Bank, International Vaccine Institute, Ministries of Health, NGOs and academia). The Children's Vaccine Program is implemented through: a Secretariat (PATH) which reports to it's principal funding source, the Bill & Melinda Gates Foundation; a Strategic Advisory Council (SAC); a Vaccine Producers Liaison Group, and collaborating partners. The SAC is composed of 6–10 individuals chosen to serve in an independent capacity (one with industry background). The SAC members select their chair and meet once or twice a year. The SAC and Secretariat also draw on three Technical Experts. The Vaccines Producers Liaison Group is linked to the SAC by a liaison member. Industry contributes to the Program through donation of vaccines for model programmes, provision of data for regulatory submissions, and by undertaking financial and market surveys. The programme is set to last 10 years with the initial focus on 3 new vaccines in 18 countries.

Globalising forces and the rise of public–private partnerships

Industry–UN partnership: incorporating industry interests in global governance

During the 1990s, industry began to recognise the potential benefits of alliances with the UN and other intergovernmental groupings. For example, according to Maria Cattaui, Secretary-General of International Chamber of Commerce (ICC):[1] 'Business believes that the rules of the game for the market economy, previously laid down almost exclusively by national governments, must be applied globally if they are to be effective. For that global framework of rules, business looks to the United Nations and its agencies' (Cattaui 1998a). Maucher (1998) the ICC president, supported this position, arguing that: 'In this process of modernisation and globalization of rules, ICC is making a positive contribution, both as an advisor and through its own standard setting ... Broader efforts should now follow in order to foster rules-based freedom for business, with the WTO assuming a key role.' While the ICC conceded the need for additional authority for intergovernmental organisations, this was 'with the proviso that they must pay closer attention to the contribution of business'. For example, as Maucher (1997) had noted earlier: 'We want neither to be the secret girlfriend of the WTO nor should the ICC have to enter the World Trade Organisation through the servants entrance.' The ICC was, however, concerned that the 'power of world business' has been 'poorly ... organised on the international level to make its voice heard' (quoted in CEO 1998). Consequently, the ICC established, in its words, a 'systematic dialogue with the United Nations' in an effort to redress this perceived threat to its interests (Cattaui 1998b).

Industry has embarked upon a multi-pronged strategy to gain access to and influence multilateral and UN decision-making. For example, with respect to the Trade Related Aspects of Intellectual Property Rights Agreement, Sell (1999: 171) provides a comprehensive account of the machinations of the Intellectual Property Committee, whose membership of twelve chief executive officers of US-based multinational corporations 'succeeded in getting most of what they wanted from an intellectual property agreement, which now has the status of public international law'. On a separate front, in June 1997 the Executive Director of the World Business Council on Sustainable Development (WBCSD)[2] co-hosted a meeting with the president of the UN General Assembly to 'examine steps toward establishing terms of reference for business sector participation in the policy-setting process of the UN and partnering in the uses of UN development assistance funds' (Korten 1997). The meeting, which was attended by fifteen high-level government officials (including three heads of state), the UN (including the Secretary-General), and the ICC (including ten CEOs), concluded that 'a framework' for corporate involvement in UN decision-making be worked out under the auspices of the Commission on Sustainable Development (Korten 1997). On yet another front, the ICC conceived the Geneva Business Partnership. Established in September 1998, the Partnership enabled 450 business leaders to meet with representatives of international organisations so as to determine 'how to establish global rules for an ordered liberalism' (CEO 1998).

One outcome of the industry effort is a joint UN–ICC statement on common interests (United Nations 1998). The statement proposed that: 'broad political and economic changes have opened up new opportunities for dialogue and co-operation between the United Nations and the private sector'. Two main areas were proposed: (1) establishing an effective regulatory framework for globalisation; and (2) raising the productive potential of poor countries by promoting the private sector. Within this context, there was a call to 'intensify the search for partnerships'. The articulation of common interests was followed in 1999 by the two organisations entering into a 'Compact'. A press release indicated that the compact 'of shared values and principles, will give a human face to the global market' and would focus on human rights, labour standards and environmental practice (Cattaui 1999). The Compact has proven controversial and a coalition of civil society groups have proposed an alternative 'Citizen's Compact on the United Nations and Corporations' which demands that the UN develop rules which would bind corporate behaviour globally to UN endorsed norms within a legally binding framework (CEO 2000). In response, in his inaugural address, ICC president Adnan Kassar added what he called an important proviso to ICC's support of the nine core values enshrined in Annan's Global Compact: 'There must be no suggestion of hedging the Global Compact with formal prescriptive rules. We would resist any tendency for this to happen' (ICC 2000).

In the health sector there have been calls for global standards and, reflecting trends in other sectors, it has been argued that the private sector should have a voice in the articulation of these standards. For example, a meeting on public–private partnerships in Biotech/Pharma hosted by the Rockefeller Foundation in 1999 proposed the need for a global orphan drugs[3] policy. The meeting concluded that a policy be negotiated between the WTO, WHO and heads of industry (among others) which would guide the standardised development and efficient implementation of intellectual property rights, clinical trials standards, harmonisation of the regulatory process, good manufacturing practices, tax incentives and tiered pricing (Rockefeller 1999). This initiative is taking place against a background of different interests which seek regulatory action in the health sector, but for whom the implications and focus of concern may be different. For example, for the public sector, including multilateral organisations, the concentration may be on rule setting, and the normative standards functions, focusing on health, safety and affordability. For the private-for-profit sector, the central issues are likely to be related to market access, protection of intellectual property rights, licensing and setting single global launch prices for new products (Reich and Govindaraj 1998). As advances in genetics and biotechnology occur, issues related to privacy, patents, therapies and reproductive technologies are creating new ethical dilemmas (Koivusalo and Ollila 1997) that demand regulation.

Exploration to establish common ground between the pharmaceutical industry and multilateral (and other) organisations has been taking place since the beginning of the 1990s (Mitchell *et al.* 1993). Just one expression of this exploration has involved a series of round-table discussions between WHO and the International Federation of Pharmaceutical

Manufacturers Associations (IFPMA), which began in October 1998 (Brundtland 1999b). Among the outcomes of such dialogue are the establishment of new GPPPs. For example, at the annual high-profile World Economic Forum (popularly known as the Davos Summit) in January 2000, the Global Alliance for Vaccines and Immunization (GAVI) – a major GPPP – was launched by Bill Gates together with the executive heads of WHO, UNICEF, the World Bank and Merck & Co.

The formation of GPPPs may also reflect the impact of globalisation on the structure of the global economy (and within various industries) and on ways of doing business. In particular, three, possibly interrelated, elements stand out. First, as noted above, within the context of an increasingly polycentric political–economic system, transnational corporations, the lynch-pins of the world economy, are, generally speaking, gaining some powers formerly monopolised by the state (Held *et al.* 1999: 281). As a consequence of this redefinition of the scope and position of the influence of these institutions, corporations are seeking and engaging in more prominent roles in intergovernmental decision-making (Cutler *et al.* 1999b: 16). Thus, for example, Gorden Cloney of the International Insurance Council describes the WTO Financial Services Agreement in the following terms: 'This agreement is like taking back the neighbourhood. We need a policeman on the block. We can't have governments behaving in thuggish ways' (quoted in Freudman and Maggs 1997). Such influence may also be exercised through GPPPs.

Secondly, numerous industries have become more highly concentrated (Garten 1999). Increasing concentration has affected the pharmaceutical industry (Tarabusi and Vickery 1998). Indeed, horizontal acquisitions and mergers within the industry, and vertical concentration resulting from the take over of biotechnology companies by all of the major research-based pharmaceutical companies during the 1990s, has, according to Mytelka and Delapierre (1999), resulted in a global 'networked, knowledge-based biopharmaceutical oligopoly'. Oligopolies and increasing concentration empower individual mega-companies in relation to both state and intergovernmental organisations, but also increase the possibilities for industry-wide association and organisation (e.g. IFPMA in the case of pharmaceuticals). Consequently, we have seen a rise in self-organisation and market-driven regulation (e.g. ISO standards, Codex Alimentarius) as well as small groups of company executives directly influencing the articulation of intergovernmental agreements (e.g. the TRIPS Agreement – see Sell 1999).

Thirdly, there have been changes in the form of business organisation. It has been argued that globalisation is fuelling corporate alliances (and may indeed be replacing mergers). It is, for example, speculated that 'the average large company, which had no alliances a decade ago, now has in excess of 30' (*Business Week*, 25 October 1999: 106). Strategic alliances, often short-term in nature, allow competing companies in one market to collaborate in other markets (Kanter 1994). The commercial world is increasingly organising itself in alliances and partnerships, and it is natural that it extends this form of organisation (often short term and mercenary) to its relations with governmental entities.

In summary, it is evident that the private sector seeks to articulate its interests and wield power in intergovernmental forums. GPPPs provide an avenue through which to pursue this objective. Consequently, elsewhere, we have concluded that public–private partnerships constitute a form of neo-global corporatism (Buse and Walt 2000a).

GPPPs as a vehicle for penetrating emerging markets

As noted in the introductory chapter to this volume, globalisation has increasingly concentrated wealth in fewer countries, and within countries in fewer hands (UNDP 1999: 3). In more than eighty countries, per capita incomes were lower at the end of the 1990s than a decade earlier. The UN portrays poverty as a 'down side of globalisation' but also suggests that poverty is both a threat and an opportunity to industry interests; a threat in the sense that mass poverty could lead to destabilisation (and thereby jeopardise the smooth functioning of the market) and an opportunity in terms of a potential market-in-waiting. The United Nations Development Programme (UNDP) (1998) goes as far as to assert that: 'Corporate success will be increasingly dependent on harnessing these new markets and production opportunities'. Apparently industry is beginning to appreciate this potential market. According to Waddell (1999), Unilever has recently concluded that most companies should be considering the poor as a target market.

Two GPPPs illustrate how the UN is using poverty as the focus of partnership with the private sector. First, over the course of 1998 and 1999, UNDP attempted to establish the Global Sustainable Development Facility (GSDF). It aimed to bring together leading corporations and UNDP in an effort to ensure the inclusion of two billion new people in the global market economy by the year 2020 (UNDP 1998). The GSDF was to be established as a separate legal entity outside the UN system that would be 'primarily governed by participating corporations and [would] benefit from the advice and support of the UNDP through a special relationship' (UNDP 1998). It was envisioned that the Facility would mainly be funded through contributions from the participating corporations. Activities of the Facility included 'developing products and services adapted to the emerging markets of the poor' (UNDP 1998). As of March 1999, sixteen corporations had joined project discussions. Each of the firms provided UNDP with US $50,000 for the project's design and a number had agreed to be represented on a steering committee and to act as special advisors. Due to the controversial nature of the partnership, it was discontinued in June 2000 (New 2000). Second, the United Nations Conference on Trade and Development (UNCTAD) launched a GPPP in 1999, which it hoped would stimulate foreign direct investment into the forty-eight least developed countries. Through the initiative, UNCTAD and the International Chamber of Commerce work jointly to produce investment guides. In each country a large transnational corporation sponsors the exercise (CEO 1998).

Thus, public–private partnerships are proposed as priming-the-pump of economic globalisation in those areas where the market is not well enmeshed in the global economy, but also as an opportunity to expand markets. As the president of the medical systems unit of Becton Dickinson & Co has said of one GPPP: 'Of course we want to help eradicate neonatal tetanus, but we also want to stimulate the use of non-reusable injection devices, and to build relationships with ministries of health that might buy other products from us as their economies develop' (Deutsch 1999).

GPPPs and economic and technological globalisation

Changing markets and technology associated with globalisation have heightened the appreciation of interdependence between the public and private sectors leading to the development of GPPPs. In particular, new developments in biotechnology are making drug and vaccine development increasingly expensive (Mahoney and Maynard 1999), as are changes in the patenting regime (IAVI 1996). Concomitantly, extensive consolidation of the pharmaceutical industry has led to greater competition within companies, thus increasing the opportunity costs associated with investment in tropical diseases (Tarabusi and Vickery 1998). These changes have led some health advocates to begin to explore ways in which public and private decision-makers can work together to overcome both market and public failures, so as to develop and make available public and merit goods at a cost developing countries could afford while minimising the risk and guaranteeing a return to the private sector (Buse and Walt 2000a). The Medicine for Malaria Venture, for example, represents a partnership to find new anti-malarial drugs, where funds will be provided primarily by the public sector, while industry will provide the sort of support that money cannot buy – in-kind resources such as access to chemical libraries and to their technologies in the areas of genomics and pathogenomics, combinatorial chemistry and bioinformatics (Bruyere 1999).

GPPPs as a strategy to enhance corporate citizenship

Where once one might have characterised the relationship between the UN and corporate sector as often confrontational or distant, over the past decade there has been significant movement from polar positions to a search for common ground. On the one hand, the Secretary-General of the United Nations has recognised the need for international organisations to work with business: 'in today's interdependent world, the United Nations and the private sector need each other' (ICC 1998). On the other hand, Annan has suggested that because 'globalisation is under intense pressure, and business is in the line of fire', business must be 'seen to be committed to global corporate citizenship' (Annan 1999). The World Bank is similarly putting 'its shoulder behind corporate citizenship', a concept it equates with tripartite partnerships between public, private and civil society organisations (Chaparro and Gevers, undated). The Bank's Corporate Citizen Program hopes 'to make partners of captains of industry in transforming education, health care, and other vital building blocks in developing countries'. Corporate citizenship is:

the practice of match-making companies with the rest of society . . . Pure philanthropy it is not. Rather, in a world obsessed by maximising returns and expanding market share, traditional philanthropy is outdated. Companies realise that investing in the well-being of their host communities is more and more of a strategic interest: it helps them build a stable reputation and a brand; and it critically reduces the risk inherent to any foreign investment. (Chaparro and Gevers undated)

Debate surrounding the WTO Agreement on Trade-Related Aspects of Intellectual Property Rights (TRIPS) is illustrative of the manner in which GPPPs provide industry an opportunity to demonstrate its caring face through corporate citizenship. Concerns have been raised that the Agreement will limit access to essential drugs in developing countries (Velasquez and Boulet 1999). Industry acknowledges that access to medicines in poorer countries is an issue but suggests that the 'long-term donation programs instituted by pharmaceutical companies for such debilitating diseases as trachoma, filariasis and river blindness' (i.e. high-profile GPPPs) provide a means to redress the access problem (Bale 1999). Similarly, UN–industry partnerships are also seen as a solution to another contentious issue arising out of the implementation of TRIPS, namely compulsory licensing (see Ranson *et al.* this volume). The case against the use of compulsory licences has been bolstered by reference to alternative strategies to protect the poor, specifically public–private partnerships. Thus the Bristol–Myers Squib's partnership with UNAIDS and a variety of actors in southern Africa, 'Bridging the Gap,' has been cited as the way forward in lieu of compulsory licensing (*Chicago Tribune*, 1999).

Public–private partnerships and the United Nations

The preceding discussion suggests that public–private partnerships between the UN and the business sector will influence the work of the UN. This section explores some of the potential changes – both positive and negative. We organise the section around a framework which proposes that an ideal-type multilateral organisation should play five critical functions with respect to global health. Such an organisation would be enabled to fulfil these unique functions, to varying degrees, by a number of facilitating attributes. The manner in which partnership impinges upon these attributes constitutes the substance of this section. In arguing that such an ideal organisation should undertake these functions, we are not suggesting that the UN has been able to do so in an effective or consistent manner in the past. We acknowledge the many weaknesses that beset the UN and WHO in particular (Godlee 1994). While these shortcomings have circumscribed WHO's ability to meet its ideal mandate, here we draw attention to the manner in which partnership with the private-for-profit sector might compound WHO's limitations. In this short discussion we generalise about the nature and interests of commercial entities – clearly these differ tremendously across a number of criteria (e.g. their propensity to observe rules of law or engage in strategic philanthropy, etc.).

The impact of GPPPs on ethical frameworks: human rights and equity vs. shareholder value

The UN aims to organise world affairs according to the principle, among others, that nation-states are bound to a series of 'universal' norms and values (Cassese 1986). The UN plays a vital role providing a platform for the discussion, negotiation and promotion of these norms and values. Public and private partners bring different values to each partnership. At one end of the continuum are the interests of the UN: 'our main stock in trade . . . is to promote values: the universal values of equality, tolerance, freedom and justice that are found in the UN Charter' (Annan 1999).

At this end of the continuum one finds WHO's concern for the health of the marginalised and dispossessed and its avowal to be the world's health conscience. WHO's values derive from its constitution while its claims to universality are legitimated by its wide membership.

At the opposite end of the spectrum one encounters the bottom-line values that drive the corporate world. Its aim is to maximise profits so as to increase shareholder value. Increasingly, such aims are couched within company mission statements that acknowledge the desirability of good corporate citizenry – with terms such as 'responsible share-holder-value optimisation'. However, as Milton Friedman once observed 'there is one and only one social responsibility of business – to use its resources and engage in activities designed to increase its profits' (quoted in *The Economist* 2000).

At the centre of this continuum are the GPPPs that provide some middle ground where, it is hoped, the differing values of each partner can be submerged as their common interests are pursued. There is, however, debate over whether or not private and public goals are mutually compatible. Several mechanisms have been identified through which profit maximisation may undermine the goal of better health (Hancock 1998). Within partnerships, the question arises as to whether or not private sector goals will ultimately predominate as the UN and industry move closer towards jointly defining their goals through GPPPs, as the values of the weaker partner are captured by the more powerful. Alternatively, is it possible to ensure that core public and private identities and values are preserved as partnerships limit themselves to specific win–win situations?

Because of the potential clash between partners over principles and values, multilateral agencies have recognised the need to exercise caution in selection of their private sector partners (Dukes 1997; Kickbusch and Quick 1998; Bellamy 1999). In practice, given the financial incentives which sometimes motivate UN organisations to enter into partnerships with the private sector, it may be difficult to refuse corporate offers which do not comply with internal guidelines. For example, UNDP is alleged to have disregarded its fund-raising guidelines in pursuance of its controversial 'Global Sustainable Development Facility' partnership (Klein 1999). In relation to health partnerships, Hancock urges 'sober second thoughts' regarding the suitability of the pharmaceutical industry as a partner for WHO, at least in terms of health promotion, because of 'perceived or actual conflict of interests' (Hancock 1998).

While public–private partnerships raise difficult questions concerning the maintenance of publicly oriented values within the public realm, there is also room for optimism. Involving the private-for-profit sector in UN debates may encourage more socially responsible entities and practices in both sectors. In addition, privately generated funds may be utilised to implement and enforce the universal norms and values espoused by the UN.

The impact of partnerships on technical norms and standards: the erosion of public competence?

The UN plays an important role in the area of facilitating and developing technical standards that are used by others to govern activities in all spheres of life (from shipping lanes to postal services). A series of attributes enables it to play this role including legitimacy and authority, and, relative to directly vested parties, impartiality and neutrality. These attributes, which are in some ways interlinked, derive from, and rest upon, the governing arrangements of the UN. Partnerships with the commercial sector may entail reform of these arrangements and therefore raise questions of how to preserve these crucial attributes upon which technical norms and standards are developed which support the ethical framework described above.

For example, the question of legitimate representation in public–private partnerships raises the question of whose interests should be represented in a partnership and whose should not. Most UN organisations derive some of their legitimacy from near universal membership in their governing bodies. For example, the World Health Assembly is currently attended by 191 member states (although its state-centric and narrow biomedical biases raise their own problems of legitimacy), all of whom have equal voting rights irrespective of size of financial contribution (in practice, strong states and interest groups do affect priority-setting in the Organisation). In contrast, representation in global public–private partnerships is both narrower and more eclectic. For example, no health GPPP can claim near universal membership of nation-states (which would make them unwieldy in any event), but, more importantly, few partnerships include low-income country representation, not all of them include WHO on their governing boards and technical committees, and in some cases it would appear that the private sector representation is ad hoc and based on personal contacts.

The legitimacy of GPPPs will depend largely on the expert committees that are established to advise them. Whereas the specialised agencies of the UN, such as WHO, rely on extensive networks of technical experts and have established means for selecting and operating expert groups, there are concerns that GPPP expert groups may be chosen from exclusive epistemic communities (see Lee and Goodman, this volume, for a discussion of epistemic community), may (due to funding) suffer from a lack of independence and may have circumscribed powers (Buse and Walt 2000b).[4] Although many analysts have drawn attention to the extent to which international agenda setting and formulation of policy is controlled by transnational policy elites (Haas 1989), the implications of the increasing prominence of the private sector in policy networks on global standard setting has yet to receive much attention (see Lee *et al.* 1997 and Cutler *et al.* 1999b for some exceptions).

Partnerships also raise difficult questions in relation to competence and appropriateness. As global responsibility for specific health issues is transferred from WHO programmes to GPPPs, there is the potential that WHO will fail to continue to establish expert groups on these issues so as not to duplicate the technical committees established under the aegis of the partnerships (whose membership is vetted by the corporate sponsors). Does this raise the spectre of the erosion of WHO's normative function in relation to global health? Where the private sector assumes a greater voice through partnership in WHO technical discussions, will global standards and norms not begin more closely to reflect private interests, thereby jeopardising their credibility? One must also question the technical credentials of some of the non-state actors involved in GPPPs. In relation to competence and appropriateness, the need for best-practice guidelines and codes of conduct governing partnership are called for. Looking at partnership from a more optimistic perspective, it might prove the case that through interaction with the for-profit sector, publicly endorsed standards may enjoy a more global reach and private interests may be more amenable to respecting them as a function of their involvement in establishing them.

Partnering and the global health commons: externalities, global public goods and country level co-operation

As noted in the introductory chapter, the determinants of health, as well as the means to address them, are influenced increasingly by global processes. It was, therefore, argued that the imperative for nation-state collaboration to address problems of the global health commons is more compelling than ever. The promotion of global public goods, such as research and development, knowledge, harmonised norms, regulation, etc., and the control of international externalities such as transborder spill over of environmental risks, drug resistance, etc. are therefore gaining increased attention and a central role for the UN has been proposed (Kaul *et al.* 1999). A number of GPPPs have been established so as to address problems of the global health commons (such as the 'Stop TB' initiative). Consequently, it can be argued that the addition of private resources through GPPPs further enables collective global action in critical areas. The challenge, however, remains to establish systems for priority-setting that are fair and just (i.e. which public goods to produce and which externalities to control and how to prioritise among them). Moreover, is it possible that the private sector may not support the regulation of externalities when it runs contrary to its interests (e.g. rules to contain the spread of antibiotic resistance may run counter to pharmaceutical interests)?

In a world marked by increasing inequalities, the UN plays a role, within the health and other sectors of low-income countries, of protecting the health of vulnerable populations and providing development support (e.g. capacity development). While the UN shares this role with a host of other agencies, its aid need not be conditional upon political and economic objectives (as is often the case with bilateral aid) and can, therefore, theoretically be allocated according to measures of need (although this is patently not always the case). Partnerships can enable the UN to further its work in underserved areas, as illustrated by the UNAIDS and Bristol–Myers Squibb partnership in support of AIDS activities in Southern Africa. The introduction of partnerships, however, might exacerbate favouritism. Countries and population groups that do not benefit from particular partnerships might feel abandoned. And partnerships may increase inequities within societies: for example, the World Alliance for Community Health, which includes Rio Tinto, Placer Dome and other multinational corporations, aided by the World Health Organisation, is helping companies develop a 'business plan' for health, 'to improve health of firms as well as ordinary people' (*The Economist* 1999). While potentially bringing better-quality primary health services to workers and their families, such efforts may undermine universal health systems. Worse yet, if activities which are in vogue are hived off to special partnerships, there is the potential that bilateral funds which might have been allocated to the UN may be redirected to those special activities, thereby further imperilling the financial situation of the organisations, as well as undermining (or devaluing) government efforts. Hence, as GPPPs 'privatise' some areas of health development, there is concern that public resources will follow private ones, leaving some public priorities untended to.

In summary, there are potential pros and cons of partnerships depending on the selection of partners, balance of power among private and public parties, and the nature of the structures and processes established to oversee the partnerships. The extent, therefore, to which a partnership will be beneficial will depend on its governance as well as how the health co-operation, including GPPPs, are governed at the global level.

*Good governance? Representation, accountability and
competency in partnerships*

A number of challenges to good governance confront the UN as it enters
into commercial partnerships. For example, in relation to representative
legitimacy, it would appear that GPPPs provide the commercial sector
with improved access to decision-making within the UN, which is not balanced by special access to recipient countries and marginalised groups.
As noted above, this carries significant risks and will have to be handled
with caution. Accountability, which is broadly concerned with being held
responsible for one's actions, poses similar challenges. Public and private
sectors have well-established mechanisms of accountability. In the private
sector, management is accountable to the company's shareholders. In the
public sector, administrative structures report to political structures that
are accountable to the ruled through the contestability of political power.
However, accountability within public–private partnerships may be less
straightforward, partly because of the distance between the global partners and the beneficiaries, and the length of time for any impact to be felt.
Moreover, actually holding a partner accountable presents difficult challenges, as they are autonomous entities. Presently, systems of sanctions do
not appear to have developed to apply to negligent partners. In a number
of GPPPs, accountability appears to be predominantly oriented towards
the commercial sponsors, for example 'Mectizan® Donation Program'
(Frost and Reich 1998), whereas in others the management group reports to a governing body, whose members report back to their respective organisations, for example the 'International Trachoma Initiative'
(Cook 1999). In relation to competence and appropriateness, we have
described how partnerships may shift the locust of technical groups outside of the remit of the UN organisations, and through this process global
norms and standards may tend more closely to reflect private interests.
Finally, due process in relation to the good governance of GPPPs has
yet to receive much attention. While transparency of decision-making to
the public will be essential, one can envision conflicts of interest in this
regard.

Conclusions: a call for best-practice guidelines and a global system of accreditation

As global health problems increasingly demand global solutions, public–
private partnerships are increasingly utilised to provide such solutions.
Partnerships are often uniquely suited to address problems of market
and public failure, particularly with respect to hitherto intractable health

challenges confronting the poor in many countries. For the UN, access to private resources through partnership has the potential to enable it more effectively and efficiently to pursue its critical mandate in relation to global health. Nevertheless, partnerships bring their own problems. UN organisations are well aware of the potential problems inherent in these partnerships. UNICEF's present Executive Director has warned 'it is dangerous to assume that the goals of the private sector are somehow synonymous with those of the United Nations, because they most emphatically are not' (Bellamy 1999). WHO's recent guidelines on involvement with the commercial sector reflect this concern, for example in its treatment of conflicts of interest (WHO 1999b).

While the internal scrutiny by WHO of proposed and existing partnerships is warranted, the widespread adoption of this institutional approach to global health development raises additional challenges. There is, for example, the need for more empirical research on the institutional features that make such partnership effective. Such empirical work should also aim to identify more generally applicable, good practice guidelines, including principles for 'good partnership governance' (transparency, accountability, etc.). Such analysis is a necessary prerequisite for the establishment of an independent global regulatory and accreditation system for GPPPs. An empirically grounded and publicly debated regulatory framework which can differentiate between acceptable and unacceptable GPPPs, by ensuring that the former meet specific minimum conditions (and thereby allay concerns of public bodies and critics), would appear to be a desirable feature of a future component of global health governance. As Falk (1999) reminds us 'there is little, or no, normative agency associated with this emergent world order: it is virtually designer-free, a partial dystopia that is being formed spontaneously, and in the process endangering some of the achievements of early phases of statist world order'. In relation to public–private partnerships between the UN and the commercial sector, there is a compelling and urgent case for establishing governance arrangements that ensure and strengthen the unique and critical role of these global public institutions as a component of global governance.

Main summary points

- We have limited understanding of how and why partnerships work (not least, agreement on how success would be measured). There is thus urgent need for more systematic comparative research on such partnerships.

- Partnerships that bring together private- and public-interest organisations also raise theoretical and normative questions in relation to governance, authority and accountability. There is a need for a wider debate on these issues.
- The debate on GPPPs needs to address how to arrive at institutional arrangements that might best govern future health partnership initiatives so as to protect the public's interest in them. These should be formalised in best-practice guidelines and enforced through accreditation.

NOTES

Our initial thoughts were clarified with the assistance of our colleagues in the Health Policy Unit. John Martin, Nick Drager, Robert Beaglehole, Kelley Lee and Anthony Zwi provided useful comments on the text.

1 ICC consists of over 7,000 member companies and business associations in more than 130 countries.
2 The WBCSD is a council of transnational corporations established to represent the interests of global corporations at the UN Conference on Environment and Development in Rio in 1992.
3 Orphan drugs are medicines for rare diseases or conditions. In the United States, the Orphan Drug Act of 1983 aimed to encourage the development of drugs then known to be effective against rare diseases, affecting fewer than 200,000 people, in order to encourage industry to continue development and marketing of what might otherwise have been seen to be market risks (Harrison and Lederberg 1997).
4 For example, the advice of the Technical Advisory Group of the International Trachoma Initiative regarding the choice of recipient countries was not heeded.

KEY READINGS

Buse, K. and Walt, G. 2000a, 'Global public–private partnerships: Part 1 – a new development in health?', *International Bulletin of the World Health Organisation* 78 (5): 549–61.

Buse, K. and Walt, G. 2000b, 'Global public–private partnerships: Part II – what are the issues for global governance?', *International Bulletin of the World Health Organisation* 78 (4): 699–709.

Karliner, J., Cavanagh, J., Bennis, P. and Morehouse, W. 1999, *A perilous partnership: the United Nations development programme's flirtation with corporate collaboration*, The Transnational Resource and Action Centre, www.corpwatch.org, 12 March 1999.

Reich, M. R. 2000, 'Public–private health partnership for public health', *Nature Medicine* 6 (6): 617–20.

Widdus, R., Chacko, S., Holm, K. and Currat, L. (forthcoming), 'Towards better defining "public–private partnership" for health'. *Global Forum for Health Research*, Geneva: GFHR.

4   Global approaches to private sector provision: where is the evidence?

Ruairí Brugha and Anthony Zwi

Introduction

The influence of transnational players on the policies promoted in developing countries is receiving critical attention as analysts explore the impact of globalisation on the role of the state, systems of governance and the quality of global policy prescriptions. Health and social policies, developed in the capital cities of North America and Western Europe and promoted worldwide, may have profound impacts on populations and health systems. This policy-making role, alongside the values and powers which are brought to bear to ensure such policies are adopted, carries with it responsibilities. These include the need to ensure that the policies are focused on tackling the most important problems, that they will benefit the population, especially the poor, and that they stand a good chance of succeeding in the range of settings where they are promoted. Success will partly depend on facilitating local commitment and ownership. Global policy advice, if appropriate at all given the wide variation in contexts, must be under-pinned by adequate evidence. We consider the extent to which evidence has supported policy in relation to one strand of international health policy that has evolved over the last decade – the promotion of private health care provision as part of health sector reforms – and the relevance of global policy prescriptions to national health policies and practice in developing countries.

This chapter reviews the evolution of policy advice to developing countries, from international agencies and powerful donors, regarding how the public sector should relate to for-profit private sector providers (PSPs). The focus is primarily on service provision, while recognising that reforms in private financing deserve equal attention. Among PSPs we include both formally trained allopaths (physicians, nurses, pharmacists) who may be in full- or part-time private practice, and the informal, often illegally operating PSPs (e.g. drug retailers) who are important sources of allopathic drugs. We present the rationales for working with PSPs, and critically evaluate proposed mechanisms to ensure that they provide good quality services. We use an exploration of this policy 'strand' to highlight an issue of more general concern: the extent to which the policy advice from international agencies acting at global level has been derived from a strong evidence and experience base. While 'evidence-based policy' may not always be achievable, it is surely possible and desirable to have policy that is cognisant of the best available evidence – or in its absence seeks to fill the evidence-gaps – around criteria such as cost-effectiveness, equity, feasibility and sustainability.

A small number of international agencies, notably the World Bank and the World Health Organisation (WHO), and the more powerful donor agencies such as the United States Agency for International Development (USAID) and the United Kingdom Department for International Development (DFID), are increasingly dominant in setting global health policy agendas, especially for low-income developing countries. These external agencies are powerful because of their knowledge, experience, networks and resources, and are therefore able to promote their prescriptions without challenge, at least not overtly, from national and subnational policy-makers. Under-resourced ministries of health, partly as a consequence of previous policy advice to downsize the state, are typically weak in negotiating key policy directions with these international players. Grindle and Thomas (1991) identified international leverage as one of four key influences on policy decisions in developing countries; the other three being technical information, bureaucratic implications and political stability, all of which are influenced by resource-rich countries and international agencies.

We argue that donor agencies and influential policy setters have a responsibility to ensure that the policies they promote are well founded and based on careful theoretical and empirical analysis, pilot projects and experimentation, and on rigorous monitoring and evaluation, especially where aid is conditional on policy adoption. We question the extent to which some of the leading agencies have fulfilled this responsibility. Enhancing accountability for policy prescriptions is as important for international as for national and local policy-makers, perhaps even more so given the lack of higher authoritative bodies and procedures for ensuring accountability and transparency. The chapter suggests that policy advice on how to relate with PSPs has usually preceded systematically gathered evidence on: the circumstances in which policy formulation and implementation is most feasible; the conditions in which different policy approaches are most likely to be successful; and the mechanisms available for ensuring that the policies promote population access to good-quality public health services, notably for the most poor.

Background

Health care reforms

The mid 1980s saw a shift in the focus of health policy for low-income developing countries, from the primary health care principles enunciated in the Alma-Ata declaration towards a narrower focus on financing and organisational reforms (Cassels 1995; Zwi and Mills 1995). Decentralisation was seen by some as a way of implementing primary health care (Ebrahim and Ranken 1988). The shift in policy emphasis towards financing reforms (see Lee and Goodman this volume, chapter 6) was seen as reflecting both the emergence of neo-liberal approaches to social policy within the context of global recession in the early 1980s, and the widespread promotion of structural adjustment policies that imposed restrictions on public sector health spending in many countries (Abel-Smith 1986). At the same time, WHO failed to provide international health policy leadership (Kickbusch, 2000) and the World Bank became increasingly influential in shaping international health policy (Zwi and Mills 1995). In 1987, the Bank recommended that governments: 'Encourage the management sector (including non-profit groups, private physicians, pharmacists and other health practitioners) to provide health services for which consumers are willing to pay' (World Bank 1987). In its influential 1993 *World development report* (WDR), it recommended that governments shift elements of service provision from the public to the private for-profit health sector (World Bank 1993). Justification for this shift was partly based on a belief in the greater technical efficiency of the private sector and the desirability of promoting competition. The Bank advised national governments to limit government action to formulating policies, providing a limited package of public health interventions with positive externalities, developing and enforcing regulations, and financing essential clinical services for target groups, notably those who are unable to pay for private care.

USAID has been particularly active in funding and supporting private sector provision initiatives since the mid 1980s; for example, through the use of social marketing to create demand for private sector commodities and services, and by assisting governments to work with the private sector to expand service delivery coverage, especially of family planning services and products (Skaar 1998). USAID's policy was to explicitly support collaboration with the private sector, both to mobilise private sector resources and to increase private sector capacity to design, implement and evaluate reproductive health services (Skaar 1998). The aim was to work with both for-profit and not-for-profit partners ostensibly as a way of promoting sustainable programmes; an additional rationale being 'the *presumed* greater cost-effectiveness of the private sector as compared to the public sector' (Skaar 1998; our italics). Skaar cites USAID's first two major projects (1985 to 1990) that were aimed specifically at collaborating with the private sector, the aim of one of which was to 'identify, develop, and test private-sector models which would demonstrate the ability of the private-sector to provide family planning services on a sustainable basis, largely or entirely at their own cost' (The Enterprise Program, in Skaar 1998). The aim of 'demonstrating' rather than 'testing' suggests the ideological predisposition of US policy towards promoting the for-profit private sector in developing countries, a policy which the financial power of the donor agency could strongly promote.

The position of WHO with regard to private sector provision was more cautious. The report of a 1991 WHO meeting (WHO 1991a) recognised the lack of evidence to support a generalisable policy of promoting the contracting of clinical service provision to the private sector in developing countries (see 'Contracting health care provision', later in this chapter). A proposed policy position for WHO towards the private sector indicated the need to take into account major differences in the private provider market between different low-income countries; and between them and middle-income countries (WHO 1996a). The report acknowledged inequities in access to PSPs, possible private sector inefficiencies relative to the public sector, and the complexities of developing and implementing national private health sector policies. It highlighted the frequency of dual public–private practice in which the same providers operate in both sectors, and called for the recognition of contextual differences, relating to the economic and political histories of countries, in the provision of global policy advice.

Privatisation of health care provision

The WDR strongly advocated the utility of competition in the delivery of health services, arguing that 'because competition can improve quality and drive down costs, governments should foster competition and diversity in the supply of health services and inputs, particularly drugs, supplies and equipment' (World Bank 1993). Scepticism from independent commentators about the application of 'neo-classical' economic theory to the health sector has been widespread: the prerequisites to achieving efficiency improvements through privatisation – a competitive market, government capacity to regulate and manage the market to prevent market failure, and purchasers of services to have reliable information – are often absent (Adam *et al.* 1992; Bennett *et al.* 1997b). An analysis of how competition worked among private hospitals in Thailand suggested that the cost of care rose, increasing the profit to hospitals without evidence of concomitant improvements in quality (Bennett 1997). There is a wide degree of consensus that market imperfections mean that market principles cannot simply be applied in relation to health service utilisation (LeGrand and Bartlett 1993; Rosenthal and Newbrander 1996; Bennett *et al.* 1997b). Ugalde and Jackson (1995), warning that the public and private sectors have different motives and objectives, argued that historical inefficiencies of the public sector in many countries were being used to justify the policy advice to national governments to sideline – and in effect undermine – public sector health care provision, thereby facilitating growth in private health care provision (Ugalde and Jackson 1995: 530).

The Bank has provided little guidance to national policy-makers on the specific challenges and constraints to working with the private health sector or on tested methods for doing so in developing countries. Elsewhere in this book, Lee and Goodman (see chapter 6) and McPake (see chapter 7) consider the evidence underpinning the policy of introducing user fees, a policy which indirectly promoted the privatisation of health care provision, often with negative consequences. For example, the introduction of user charges at a referral centre for sexually transmitted infections (STIs) in Kenya was associated with a reduction in attendance to 40 per cent of pre-user charge levels; after their abolition, attendance by men rose to only 64 per cent of pre-user charge levels (Moses *et al.* 1992).

While there have been a few examples of explicit deregulation so as to permit private practice, such as in Tanzania, Malawi and Mozambique (Bennett *et al.* 1997b), growth of the private health care sector in developing countries has been mainly due to the state withdrawing from or failing to provide health services, creating demand and opening up market opportunities for private providers (Ogunbekun *et al.* 1999). In 1990 private sector expenditure, as a percentage of gross national product (GNP), exceeded public sector expenditure on health in 10 of 14 Asian countries (World Bank 1993). Over the subsequent five years, public expenditure, as a percentage of GNP, fell in eight of these countries (World Bank 1997a). Between 1990 and 1995, the share of private expenditure rose in 15 of the 22 countries of Latin America (Govindaraj *et al.* 1995). In India, private health expenditure has grown at a rate of 12.5 per cent per annum, far higher than increases in per capita income, and now makes up 75 per cent of all health expenditure; about 80 per cent of registered medical practitioners are in the private sector (Bhat 1996). The relative decrease in public expenditure on health, which partly reflects the growing importance of user fees, provides indirect evidence of the privatisation of

Table 4.1 *Percentage of private physicians, private beds and visits made to private facilities by the poorest and richest 20 per cent of the population in selected countries*

Country	Private doctors as percentage of total number of doctors[a]	Private beds as percentage of total number of beds[a]	Visits made by poorest 20 per cent to private facilities as percentage of all visits made by this group[b]	Visits made by richest 20 per cent to private facilities as percentage of all visits made by this group[b]
Ecuador			42	58
Guinea			65	75
India	73	31	85	100
Madagascar			27	40
Mongolia			0	17
Pakistan	32	17	78	84
Tanzania		49	21	61
Trinidad & Tobago			43	61
Average for 28 LMICs weighted by population	55			
Average for 33 LMICs weighted by population		28		
Unweighted average for 9 LICs			47	59

Source: [a] Hanson and Berman (1998); [b] Gwatkin (1999).

Notes: A limitation of the available data is that 'private' includes for-profit and non-profit beds, facilities, and doctors (i.e. doctors working for non-profit organisations). These national level data are also limited by provider type (only physicians) and facility type (hospital beds). The data from Hanson and Berman (1998) come from national ministry of health reports, WHO and World Bank reports, and academic and grey literature. The data from Gwatkin (1999) come from a range of World Bank, international and national reports. Comparability between the two main sources, in particular, may not be valid. However, they appear to support the picture of large numbers of small-scale PSPs and generally high utilisation of the private sector, but with large cross-country variations.

LMICs = low and middle income countries; LICs = low income countries.

provision, and has also contributed to driving the process (WHO 1996a). Recent reviews of the limited data demonstrate the scale of the private health care market in low-income developing countries (Table 4.1). An average of 47 per cent of visits to PSPs are by the poorest quintile of the population, not much less than the 59 per cent of visits to PSPs by the richest quintile (Gwatkin 1999).

Influencing private sector providers

Rationale and challenges

PSPs are the principal primary care providers in many developing countries. The remainder of this chapter focuses particularly on the lack of evidence to underpin policies governing private primary care provision, primarily as provided through individual practitioners (PSPs). In many developing countries, priority public health conditions such as tuberculosis (TB), malaria, and STIs, for which effective interventions are available and which benefit the population generally, are usually managed in the ambulatory, private primary care sector (Uplekar and Rangan 1993; Swan and Zwi 1997; Brugha and Zwi 1998; Brugha and Zwi 1999), often through self-treatment using direct over-the-counter purchases of drugs (McCombie 1996). There is growing evidence pointing to poor-quality care in different settings (Dartnall *et al.* 1997; Uplekar *et al.* 1998): standard diagnosis and treatment guidelines are usually not followed, practitioners are unaware of such guidelines, appropriate investigations are not made prior to treatment, and inadequate follow-up and public health responses are typical. A solution to the over-supply of diagnostic and therapeutic interventions by PSPs, as recommended in the 1993 WDR, is by 'encouraging the for-profit sector to move away from fee-for-service to prepaid coverage (through, for example, encouraging health maintenance organizations)' (World Bank 1993). While this may be desirable in the longer term, it is unlikely to be feasible in many countries in the short term. In any case, in contexts where most providers are single-handed and operating out of small-scale facilities with low patient turnover, opportunities to influence their practice through third-party payment mechanisms will be limited. Large numbers of small-scale private clinics and other facilities represent a challenge to a weak public sector that is often unable to assure the quality of its own service delivery.

The characteristics of PSPs are under-researched and poorly understood. As a result, the approaches recommended by policy-makers, and the tools currently available to managers for controlling and influencing their practices, remain immature. Furthermore, the unregulated informal private sector, which predominates in rural areas and urban slums in many developing countries, remains hidden and ignored, thriving in the absence of alternative accessible and affordable sources of care. Although global policy-makers are increasingly recognising the importance of individual PSPs (WHO 1999c), the ambitious policy direction proposed rests on a number of untested hypotheses. WHO (1999c) has argued that:

A strong purchaser, setting standard rates of remuneration and enforcing a common set of quality and utilisation regulations, will enable the most efficient providers of services to flourish. Such arrangements will allow the very large number of private providers, who are essentially the first points of contact with the health system in many low-income countries, to be brought within a structured but pluralistic health care system, benefiting from its resources and subject to sanction and regulation by professional and public bodies.

Bearing in mind that individual consumers, rather than the state or third-party payers, are the main purchasers of services in most low-income developing countries, we challenge this optimistic viewpoint.

The 'strong purchaser'

International policies for the private sector have been predicated on the untested assumption that the informed 'consumer' can drive quality and efficiency improvements: 'governments, by making information about cost-effectiveness available, can often help improve the decisions of private consumers, providers and insurers', and 'simply by defining an essential clinical package, the public sector provides valuable guidance on what is and is not cost-effective. This distinction may then influence the design of private or social insurance packages and the behaviour of individual providers and patients' (World Bank 1993). The concept of the 'strong purchaser' has also been propagated by WHO (1999c), along with the implication that individual patients can play this role. Although social marketing campaigns have successfully created demand for quality-assured family planning services such as the 'Green Star' project in Pakistan (Agha *et al.* 1997), successful branding campaigns are hugely resource-intensive, and non-approved PSPs may advertise with fake brands to attract service users (Bruce McKay, personal communication). The evidence that these models can be extended to more complex clinical services, which would require service users to be trained to play a role in monitoring technical quality, is as yet limited.

Rosenthal and Newbrander (1996) state that 'it is fundamental to the nature of medical practice that patients assign to providers the responsibility for determining what should be provided, thereby giving up a role of importance in achieving market efficiency in quality as well as cost minimization'. The nature of the principal (patient) – agent (provider) relationship, recognising the inherent asymmetry of information, means that patients look to whatever providers are accessible and affordable to act in their best interest. PSPs, in areas where they are numerous such as in urban India, operate in a highly competitive environment with low profit margins from patients' fees. They rely on client loyalty and seek to maximise patient numbers to maintain or increase their income (Bhat 1999). Service users appear to place a high value on having a family doctor. They typically perceive PSPs as offering a range of benefits: continuity of care, privacy, more time and attention, and responsiveness to their identified needs (Aljunid 1995). Where they have located a 'good doctor', service users assume that the PSP operates in their best interests. An analysis of the supply-side, however, reveals a depressing picture (Bhat 1999). Over half of the 108 private doctors surveyed in Ahmadabad, India, believed that fee-splitting (unnecessary referrals to other doctors or laboratories with the referring doctor receiving part of the fee), over-prescribing of drugs and over-use of diagnostics were high or moderately prevalent practices, primarily as a means of increasing doctors' incomes.

Contracting health care provision

There has been considerable interest among international health policy-makers in contracting as a tool for increasing efficiency in the private health care market, assigning the role of purchaser to the state or some other authoritative body (World Bank 1993, 1997a). However, from an early stage, critics pointed out some of the inherent limitations of this approach, such as asymmetry of information between the purchasers and providers of services and difficulties in specifying and monitoring contracts (Williamson 1987). WHO again adopted a more cautious position: a 1991 WHO meeting that reviewed examples of contracting from seven countries concluded that the necessary conditions for contracting clinical services (effective competition between providers) did not exist in most developing countries (WHO 1991a). The paucity of evidence as to the advantages and pitfalls was noted (WHO 1996a; Walsh, cited in Mills 1997a), as was the lack of evaluations of pilot contract schemes in developing countries, especially where clinical services were being contracted (Mills 1997a). Where contracting has worked in relation to health care (as opposed to non-clinical services such as catering and laundry services), it has usually been through contracting services, including preventive care, to not-for-profit organisations (Marek et al. 1999). Mills (1997a) suggested there was insufficient evidence to show that efficiency improvements could not be better achieved through public sector reforms.

The policy of promoting contracting gained considerable hold in the early 1990s in some high-income countries, such as the UK and New Zealand, where many of the preconditions for successful implementation existed. In many developing countries, especially in the Indian subcontinent, the private sector is mainly composed of single-handed PSPs who lack the capacity, time and resources to manage comparatively sophisticated financing schemes or to enter into contractual relationships with major purchasers. Identification of the necessary prerequisites is essential, before extrapolating lessons and promoting them in different contexts.

Regulation

The development of national regulatory frameworks and the enforcement of regulatory controls has been one of the main planks of global policy for controlling PSPs, through licensing to restrict practice entry, facility registration and inspection (World Bank 1993). The limited success of legal interventions, recognised a decade ago in international agency reports (WHO 1991a) as well as by independent commentators (Cassels 1995; Rosenthal and Newbrander 1996; Kumaranayake 1997), can be attributed to a lack of resources and capacity in the public sector for monitoring and enforcement (WHO 1991a; World Bank 1997a). Enforcement has been a problem in relatively better off middle-income countries such as Thailand, and – in regulating the insurance market – imposes high administrative costs on both the regulator and regulatee (Kumaranayake 1997). It is probably least effective in countries where the state has made a minimal commitment to health, as reflected in health spending as a proportion of GNP, and where single-handed PSPs predominate. In such contexts, those charged with responsibility for enforcing regulations are vulnerable to 'regulatory capture'.

The failure of regulation as an effective tool in many developing countries contradicts the assumption that governments have at their disposal – but are not selecting – effective financial, informational and regulatory instruments for improving performance in the private market (World Bank 1993). Where alternative legal avenues have been used, such as the use of the 1986 Consumer Protection Act in India to protect patients' rights (Bhat 1996), the unwillingness of medical councils and professionals to participate has constrained the ability of the judicial system to make sound judgements around technical quality of care. The availability of routine data is an essential element in monitoring quality of care, but record-keeping and auditing is often poor. Most single-handed PSPs keep rudimentary or no patient records and would be unable to provide useful data on care provided, were they willing to do so. Beyond instituting a simple regulatory framework of professional and facility registration, regulation – unsupported by other strategies – appears to be a weak tool for influencing private sector activity, especially quality of care, in many developing countries. Elsewhere, Kumaranayake and Lake (see chapter 5) consider how the development of global markets could predispose to the development of regulations in the area of price, quantity and competitive practices.

Other approaches

Professional associations have recently been proposed as potential key players for influencing PSP practices (World Bank 1997a; WHO 1999c, 2000a). However, national policy-makers have received little guidance on how to mobilise and work with such bodies, or on the limitations of such approaches. Professional self-regulation has been proposed (DFID 1999a; WHO 1999c, 2000a). The medical profession, like other professions, is typically focused on protecting the interests of its members, and there is little evidence of willingness to give greater weight to promoting standards and protecting societal interests (Roemer 1991; Bennett and Ngalande-Banda 1994; Asian Development Bank 1999).

Small-scale hospital owners, professional bodies and government officials in Mumbai, India, all expressed interest in accreditation, as an alternative mechanism for assuring quality (Nandraj et al. forthcoming). The major concern raised by the authors was the resource implications for a country which invests relatively little in health and where most PSPs, including small hospitals, struggle to survive in a highly competitive environment. Again, the evidence to underpin policy directions is lacking and the authors recommended the need for small-scale pilot projects. In South Africa, full-time PSPs have little contact with public sector control programmes and receive no guidance or up-to-date information and guidance on diagnosis and treatment (Dartnall et al. 1997), which we have also found to be the case in ongoing research in India and Cambodia. The failure of national ministries of health to forge links with professional organisations representing PSPs, and to implement simple interventions such as the dissemination of national guidelines and other evidence, poses an interesting question that we have not attempted to answer: do the policies promoted by international policy-making agencies, in fact, often have limited impact on national policies?

Conclusion

Much of the focus of international health policy debates and prescriptions on private sector provision has been on the development of contractual and other pre-payment mechanisms for working with large-scale private provider facilities. Some agencies, such as the World Bank and USAID, have been enthusiastic in promoting such policy prescriptions; others, such as WHO, have been more cautious, recognising the weakness of the evidence. Little advice or guidance has been forthcoming on how to work with the formal and informal private for-profit health workers who provide services to high proportions of populations in the poorest developing countries. Despite recognition of the need to balance controls on PSPs with supports and incentives, such as subsidised or free provision of drugs to control diseases of public health importance (Bennett and Ngalande-Banda 1994), the lack of small-scale pilot projects and evaluations to map out approaches and identify pitfalls is striking.

Country-level policy-makers have been faced with the options of collaborating with, suppressing or simply ignoring such PSPs. The failure of global policy-makers to conduct or fund empirical analyses and develop frameworks for understanding the influences on their professional practice has resulted in a lack of policy guidance on how to collaborate with PSPs. In its absence, some states have opted for suppression, without the capacity to implement such a policy. The usual result is that the private sector becomes less visible, due to a growth in illegal private practice and 'moonlighting', thereby becoming more refractory to interventions. Or the better-qualified professionals simply emigrate, as did 170 doctors from Tanzania following the introduction of legislation to suppress private practice in 1967 (WHO 1991a). Many governments, recognising the unworkability of suppression of private health care provision, and unsure of how to proceed, have opted to ignore the private sector (WHO 1996a). The Asian Development Bank (1999) has recently expressed concern about the widespread promotion of private sector provision, arguing that relying on it to provide health care services should only take place when two criteria are shown to have been met: efficiency is enhanced and other policy objectives, such as promoting equity, are advanced. In the same document a strong plea is made, as we do, for cautious implementation of policies to enhance the private sector's role in delivering health care, and careful study of both anticipated and unanticipated effects.

Put simply, while there is now a clearer picture of population needs and of *what* interventions are cost-effective, there is insufficient knowledge of *how* to ensure that these interventions are available and utilised effectively by those who need them. 'Far too little attention has been paid to effective

means for securing better health outcomes from the private sector, or
to achieving greater complementarity between private and public sectors' (DFID 1999a; our italics). The evidence-base for achieving the objectives of 'effective legislative and regulatory frameworks...improving
consumer information and rights, and...encouraging quality assurance
mechanisms' (DFID 1999a) has yet to be established. The frequently
cited use of consumer protection legislation in India as an alternative
channel to protect patients' rights (Bhat 1996) is an inadequate basis
for proposing that the users of formal and informal PSPs in developing
countries can be transformed into informed and strong purchasers. In
addition, a major gap in the evidence base exists around how to scale-
up lessons learned in successful projects to national programmes. This
raises questions about how these projects have been conceived and developed, and whether the support or opposition of powerful stakeholders
at the project design phase has been established, with implications for
longer-term sustainability (Brugha and Zwi 1999).

The enthusiastic endorsement by some powerful international policy-
makers of the need to involve private providers in co-ordinated service
provision has been combined with a puzzling neglect of the need for better
evidence on how to do so. Such globally propagated policy prescriptions
appear to have been based more on a neo-liberal conception of the state
and the private sector than on empirical analysis of how the latter actually
works, and reflect a primary concern with financing mechanisms as the
principal tools for influencing practice, as suggested by Lee and Goodman
(see chapter 6). A draft policy position for WHO, which contrasted the
concerns of European donors about improving governance and redefining
the roles of governments with the positions adopted by the World Bank
and USAID, stated:

A combination of domestic concerns with health reform and strong leverage on
health policy in developing countries has made donors important players in the
re-thinking of policy towards the private sector in many developing countries.
Often, the advice has focused on particular mechanisms, such as insurance, user
fees or community financing, rather than on how particular mechanisms fit with
(or distort) progress towards each country's overall policy goals. Countries are
vulnerable to particular donor enthusiasms when they lack a clear policy framework for health development generally, or for the private sector in particular, and
as the above examples show, donors' interests and advice often differ. (WHO
1996a)

The *Lancet* some years ago highlighted concerns regarding the powerful prescriptions contained in the *World development report* of 1993:
'there is a risk that a report from such an influential and well funded
organization will be used uncritically as the basis for decisions on policy

and resource allocation' (*Lancet*, cited by Ugalde and Jackson 1995). A recent evaluation of World Bank activities in the health sector generally stated that: 'the Bank is often better at specifying *what* practices need to change than *how* to change them or *why* change is difficult' (Johnston and Stout 1999, italics in original). Recent reports and statements from global health policy-making and financing bodies have similarly reflected caution in recommending solutions to developing countries and have called for strategies to be based on better evidence (DFID 1999a; Asian Development Bank 1999).

The WHO's *World health report 2000* is less prescriptive than the policy blueprints espoused by international agencies in the late 1980s and 1990s. It recognises the existence of different health service organisational forms in different contexts, with their attendant strengths and weaknesses; and the need to better align provider incentives, whether provision is through the public or private sector. It also highlights the potential danger of fragmentation in current trends towards greater autonomy in service provision, a situation existing already in many countries where the private sector predominates. It therefore concludes that what is needed is better integration of health systems. This recent trend in global health policy recommendations, based on more critical analyses of the emerging evidence and recognising the need to share lessons learned in different contexts, is to be encouraged: 'Better stewardship requires an emphasis on coordination, consultation and evidence-based communication processes. For the ministry of health to understand the principal challenges to better performance it must have a full picture of what is happening...Overall, governments have too little of the necessary information to draw up effective strategies' (WHO 2000a). The Report recognises that 'local – not textbook – solutions must be found... [and that] ... Experimentation and adaptation will be necessary in most settings'.

These laudable sentiments are being propagated at a time when the hegemony of a small number of international agencies in setting global health policy agendas is reducing, and the involvement of large-scale commercial entities in the policy-making process, through global public–private partnerships with international agencies, is increasing (Buse and Walt 2000a). Concerns have been raised about the implications of these partnerships, whose aim is often to promote the availability of new and expensive drugs that could undermine developing country health policies, especially the management of an uncontrolled private provider sector (Shretta *et al.* 2000). Killick (1998) has suggested that the conditionalities attached to aid have often been ineffective in imposing policy prescriptions and translating them into national-level policies, where national policy-makers have not perceived them to be in their interest. In the case of private sector provision in developing countries, uncontrolled growth has resulted from a lack of informed policy guidance to the state on how to manage the private sector, combined with downsizing of public sector provision. The rapidly growing involvement of major private players in setting the direction and conditions for global health policy-making is a potentially much more dangerous situation. It took a decade for those promoting a policy of working with PSPs to realise that they needed more information, experimentation and evaluation, and that global prescriptions would not work. It is imperative that all actors take heed of this experience and that they press the new public–private partnerships, which are beginning to dominate the international health policy field in the twenty-first century, to demonstrate the evidence for the policies they are promoting, and to ensure that policy promotion is context-sensitive and developed in conjunction with important local players, including the state.

KEY READINGS

Brugha, R. and Zwi, A. B. 1998, 'Improving the delivery of public health services by private practitioners in low and middle income countries', *Health Policy and Planning* 13 (2): 107–20.

Smith, E., Brugha, R. and Zwi, A. 2001, *Working with private sector providers for better health care: an introductory guide.* London: Options and LSHTM.

Swan, M. and Zwi, A. 1997, *Private practitioners and public health: close the gap or increase the distance*, PHP Publication no. 24, Department of Public Health and Policy, London School of Hygiene and Tropical Medicine.

WHO 1991, *The public/private mix in national health systems and the roles of Ministries of Health: report of an interregional meeting. 22–26 July, Morelos State, Mexico*, Geneva.

WHO 2000, *The world health report 2000. Health systems: improving performance*, Geneva.

World Bank 1993, *World development report 1993: investing in health*, Washington DC.

5   Regulation in the context of global health markets

Lilani Kumaranayake and Sally Lake

Introduction

Marketisation and globalisation are phenomena that have recently characterised health sectors around the world. Marketisation refers to the use of market mechanisms to finance and provide health services (Hsiao 1994). Globalisation can be described as the 'process of increasing economic, political, and social interdependence and global integration that takes place as capital, traded goods, persons, concepts, images, ideas, and values diffuse across state boundaries' (Hurrell and Woods 1995). Marketisation and globalisation have been contributing to the emergence of a range of global markets for health-related goods and services. This has led to widespread interest in the role regulation can play in structuring positive benefits and minimising negative consequences from this private sector activity.

This chapter explores the nature and development of marketisation in global health. It reviews the changing role of regulation needed in the health sector, and then considers the potential role of regulation within a globalising context. A case study of the World Trade Organisation and its relationship to the pharmaceutical sector is used to highlight the global–national linkages and difficulties of formal regulation. We conclude by considering the scope for regulatory action in the context of global markets and the nature of alternative mechanisms that can be used.

Marketisation and the emergence of global markets within the health sector

For many low- and middle-income countries (LMICs), the main change in the health sector post-independence has been movement from public sector dominance of health care provision and financing to one where there are substantial levels of private sector activity. For example, in Indonesia more than 60 per cent of health expenditure is spent in the

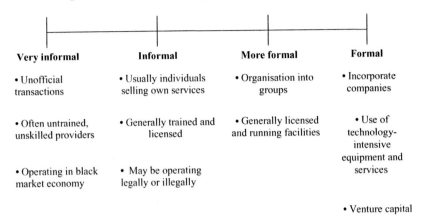

Figure 5.1 Range of private sector activity (adapted from Kumaranayake 1998).

private sector. In India, more than half of the hospitals and 49 per cent of the dispensaries are privately owned (Aljunid 1995; Zwi and Mills 1995). There is a great deal of heterogeneity in the nature of the actors and activities that come under the rubric of private sector activity, including for-profit and non-profit entities. The focus of this chapter will be on the former. Visually we can characterise the range of private sector activity in a simple continuum as shown in Figure 5.1.

There is an important distinction between informal and formal types of private sector activity. At the very informal end, the actors are generally operating on an individual basis and may or may not be operating legally. There is also a wide variation in the range of skills and products being sold: people may be untrained and unlicensed, and products of poor or sub-standard quality. More formal private sector activity is organised into group structures such as companies or health facilities and is much more visible.

In simple terms, a market occurs when there is an exchange between buyers and sellers for a good or service. The health system is not just one market, but rather consists of a series of interconnected sub-markets involving provider services, hospital care and supplies used in health care (e.g. health professionals, pharmaceuticals and medical equipment). The outcomes of the market system reflect the relative power of various stakeholders, particularly trading-off the power of sellers to maximise profits and the ability of consumers to constrain them (Hsiao 1994).

Marketisation is inextricably linked with current forms of globalisation. A key reason for the emphasis on markets within the health sector has been the policy environment, which has promoted markets as means for improved efficiency, choice and quality of health services (World Bank 1993). Marketisation and increasing globalisation in individual sub-markets within the health sector are beginning to generate a range of global markets for health-related goods and services. The pace of globalisation, although not new to the health sector, has rapidly accelerated over the past fifteen years and has manifested itself in the health sector through two mechanisms. First, there has been the increasing exportation of particular models of provision and financing, largely drawing on the private health system of the US. Examples include the expansion of Health Maintenance Organisations into predominantly middle-income markets in Latin America and more recently South Africa (Price *et al.* 1999).

Secondly, we now see the emergence of global markets, where buyers and sellers are exchanging to such a degree as to circumvent national boundaries. With the expansion of communications technology, notably the Internet, major barriers to transferring health-related goods and services between countries are decreasing (Donald 1999). A person living anywhere in the world with access to the Internet can now look up the drugs available for treatment and their current market prices, and, in many cases, purchase them over the web. Much of this activity remains unregulated by national authorities. In relation to health services, there has long been an international labour market for some health sector professionals. While the movement of physicians, for example, is constrained by national licensing laws and language barriers, there has been greater mobility among nurses and other health professionals. This mobility of health professionals worldwide, either actually or virtually, is expected to increase with the growth of global health markets. Developments in the international legal environment are facilitating this process. The aim of the 1995 General Agreement on Trade in Services (GATS) is to facilitate the expansion of the services market, including health-related services. The World Trade Organisation (WTO) argues that, where there is a mixture of private and public funding within the health sector (e.g. user fees, public–private partnerships) in a given country, the service sector should be open to foreign companies. This has facilitated the emergence of capital markets within the health sector with foreign financing being invested in national health sectors (Price *et al.* 1999).

Worldwide, emerging health markets are becoming polarised into very informal and very formal types of private sector activity. For some goods and services, very informal private sector activity is occurring, where there is a vast number of buyers and sellers largely acting across national boundaries by operating largely outside the scope of legal instruments (UNDP 1999). Buyers and sellers are relatively 'invisible' given the informal nature of the transactions. On the other hand, other global markets have actors that are very formal, and highly organised in nature, and these markets are often dominated by a relatively small number of sellers. One important element is that these firms are highly visible, with operations that are transnational. Much of their activity occurs across national boundaries but does so within the sphere of the firm itself (including both the production of goods using various inputs as well as the marketing and distribution of these goods). These transnational companies are now operating in a context where buyers of their products are able to communicate across national boundaries. However, the relative market power of the various actors is still critical in determining the market outcomes. This can be seen clearly in the pharmaceutical industry, where the dominance of large transnational pharmaceutical companies has long had an impact on drug cost and availability in countries throughout the world.

Marketisation and the growth of the private sector have been associated with problems related to the quality, price and distribution of private health services (Bennett 1991; Bennett and Ngalande-Banda 1994; Yesudian 1994; Kumaranayake 1997; Stenson *et al.* 1997; Bhat 1999). These include: poor physical infrastructure and a shortage of qualified staff; low standards of care; poor equipment or inappropriate technology; misuse of public resources within the private sector (e.g. public supplies and time of professional staff diverted to the private sector); and medical malpractice and negligence (Bennett 1991). Globally, concerns have been the concentration of market power among a relatively small number of sellers in particular markets and the growing polarisation between developing and high-income countries in terms of the ability to access and purchase new technologies and new health products.

The growing globalisation of health sector markets also means that there may now be increasing tension between national health objectives and transglobal activities and actors. This highlights the need for effective regulation to ensure that broader governmental objectives for the health sector are not sacrificed for the profit motive, either of private providers within countries or of multinational players who dominate particular markets.

Regulation and regulatory structures and processes

The response to many of the problems found in private markets is a call for the imposition of regulation. Regulation can be thought of as occurring when a state or international body exerts control over the activities of individuals and firms (Roemer 1993). More specifically, regulation has been defined as government 'action to manipulate prices, quantities [and distribution], and quality of products' (Maynard 1982). There are several actors involved in the regulatory process within the health sector: health care professionals, managers, the Ministry of Health, commercial interests, non-governmental organisations, and community and consumer groups.

The World Bank's 1993 *World development report* on health posits a significant role for regulation in achieving positive benefits from privatisation:

Strong government regulation is also crucial, including regulation of privately delivered health insurance to encourage universal access to coverage and to discourage [perverse] practices that lead to overuse of services and escalation of costs . . . As less developed countries take steps to encourage a diversified system of health service delivery, they need to strengthen government's capacity to regulate the private sector. Regulations are required to ensure that quality standards are met, that financial fraud and other abuses do not take place, that those entitled to care are not denied services, and the confidentiality of medical information is respected. (World Bank 1993)

The traditional focus of regulation within the health sector has been on standard-setting, for example ensuring minimum levels of quality and safety. This approach, often called 'social', can be distinguished from the more 'economic' approach, which looks at the role of regulation in the context of markets (Ogus 1994; Kumaranayake *et al.* 2000a). Marketisation requires that a broader set of variables be regulated within the health sector. In addition to its role in setting standards, there is an increased need to consider issues such as the structure of the market (e.g. who is buying), the terms under which health goods or commodities are traded (e.g. licensing) and the nature of competition seen within the market (e.g. concentration of power and anti-competitive practices that lead to perverse outcomes). There is now an economic element to the analysis of the role of regulation within the health sector, as the choice of what to regulate, who to regulate and how to regulate becomes more contingent on the nature of the particular market being considered.

Figure 5.2 presents an analytical framework by which to consider the changing nature of regulation. It reflects the additional market or economic roles that regulation may now need to play, given private sector activity (Kumaranayake and Lake 1998). Regulation occurs when government or the state controls or influences the activities of individuals or organisations through manipulation of target variables (Maynard 1982; Kumaranayake 1997). There is now a broader range of possible variables (labelled as target variables) that may be potentially regulated, including the price and quantity of a good to be sold in the market.

Within a market it is possible to intervene at different levels within its structure (i.e. what to regulate). For example, the broadest interventions

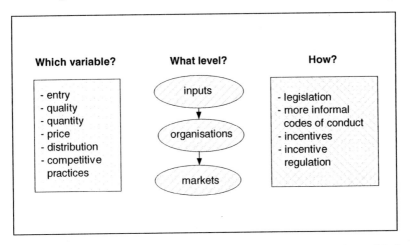

Figure 5.2 The process of regulating (from Kumaranayake and Lake 1998).

could try to regulate the overall market price or the overall number of sellers or output in a market. Other interventions may try to affect market activity by regulating the individual firms or organisations that are operating in the market. A third level at which regulation can operate is the sub-organisational level, focusing on regulating the inputs (e.g. labour, capital) which the organisations use to produce goods and services to sell on the market.

Due to marketisation, regulation now must apply to increasingly sophisticated levels of complexity in the organisation of services, moving from individual inputs such as solo physician practices to hospitals, nursing homes, pharmacies, and then to the broader question of the market structure in general, both in a national and global context. Thus the range of variables that can be targeted applies at all these levels. For example, there are issues regarding entry at the individual input level (e.g. entry of personnel, drugs, medical equipment, and foreign ownership), to the organisation of services (e.g. entry of facilities and clinics) and to markets (e.g. considering issues of entry relative to promoting competition).

The third dimension of the regulatory process is the manner in which regulation is undertaken to affect variables such as entry and price (i.e. the how to regulate). The range of instruments goes from legal controls, where there are sanctions if the regulations are not followed, to incentives and incentive regulation. Incentives are used as a way of changing behaviour and can be either financial (tax or subsidy) or non-financial (e.g. greater recognition, status). A more formalised approach to incentives is seen in the use of incentive regulation, which can be thought of as rules which use verifiable outcomes such as market prices to affect individual participant's behaviour (e.g. prices can only rise by some proportion of market price). Such incentive regulation is often seen in the regulation of former public sector utilities (energy, telecommunications) in industrialised countries.

Another distinction made is between formal and informal regulations. The types of interventions described above can be considered as formal, whereby there is a mixture of formal rule setting and explicit contractual agreements. Informal regulation is described as a system using cooperation between parties (e.g. health professionals, the Ministry of Health, and other interested parties) to achieve desired outcomes (MacKintosh 1997). There may be more informal codes of practice or policy guidelines. Interventions in this case may be the development of good practice norms, for example, where regulation largely works due to the social norms where people behave in accordance with social rewards such as approval or disapproval of others (Lindbeck 1997). These interventions may be structured so that benefits are shared for the different possible outcomes of intervention. These types of informal approaches have also been described as 'institution-light options' rather than 'institution-intensive options' for regulation (World Bank 1997b). They can also include bottom-up regulatory approaches such as public information, local initiatives to strengthen citizens' voices and initiatives by decentralised bodies.

Depending on the mode of regulatory intervention, the nature of the 'regulatory body' will vary. A formal and legal approach will require the existence of a formal regulatory body that oversees, implements and enforces the regulation. Nationally, the nature of regulatory bodies varies between countries, and according to the level under consideration. For example, the regulation of quantity and quality of individual service providers, such as doctors or pharmacists, is often undertaken by a national body such as a Medical Council or Pharmacy Board. This may be a body within a ministry of health or, more frequently, semi-autonomous bodies with a formal linkage to the government health sector through representation on the Council or Board (Kumaranayake *et al.* 2000a). More informal approaches such as regulation codes of conduct may be instituted by peer groups and associations.

Regulation of health markets and global governance

The scope for more formal and legislative regulation within global health markets is clearly contingent on the feasibility of establishing regulatory authority in the broader context of global governance. There is a clear feeling that in order to promote and protect people's health in the emerging global economy, effective rules and regulatory frameworks are needed (Turmen 1999). However, the implementation of regulatory interventions is also highly dependent on the need for strengthening global governance structures: 'the framework of rules, institutions and practices that set limits on the behaviour of individuals, organisations and companies in today's integrating world' (UNDP 1999). There remains considerable debate about what structures are needed, ranging from informal regimes of industry self-regulation and voluntary compliance, to supranational and binding regulations to create 'socially regulated global capitalism' (Deacon 1997).

The creation of the WTO in 1995 is one of the most significant developments towards establishing supranational regulation (see Ranson *et al.* this volume). The Uruguay Round of negotiations led to the creation of a rule-based system of regulation, with the creation of the WTO to enforce a series of multilateral trade agreements. The WTO provides the institutional and legal framework for the multilateral trading system (Drager 1999), and holds substantial power to enforce the trade agreements, including the authority to review a country's national policies, settle disputes and impose substantial sanctions on countries found to be violating the agreement. The enforcement powers of the WTO are substantially larger than those of other international organisations. The Uruguay Round also broadened the scope of the type of commodity covered under the WTO, with agreements extending to services such as insurance and intellectual property rights as well as health care (UNDP 1999). One of the key issues is whether this type of supranational structure can meet the regulatory needs found in global health markets. A closer look at the functioning of the WTO and its implications for health sector regulation are considered below as a case study of the regulation of private health markets in a global economy.

Global regulation of the pharmaceutical industry: a case study

One of the trade agreements emerging from the Uruguay Round was the negotiation of a global agreement on intellectual property rights: the agreement on Trade-Related Aspects of Intellectual Property Rights (TRIPS). A key component of TRIPS in relation to pharmaceuticals, from the perspective of LMICs, is the protection of pharmaceutical patents for a period of 20 years. The TRIPS agreement imposes a patent on both the pharmaceutical process and the final product. Previous to this, only the pharmaceutical process had been patented, allowing domestic companies to use different pharmaceutical processes to produce generic (and much cheaper) versions of brand-name drugs. The TRIPS agreement confers a twenty-year global monopoly[1] to pharmaceutical companies through its patent protection, and so enhances a company's ability to charge premiums for new technologies as well as to ensure that they are not copied (Donald 1999). By 2000, countries, with the exception of least-developing countries, will have had to grant legal protection by patent to pharmaceutical products. The least-developing countries have until 2005/2006 to implement these regulations. Products in the pipeline before 1 January 1995 are exempt from TRIPS (Velasquez and Boulet 1999). These intellectual property rights were largely enshrined following initiatives by industrialised countries (WHO 1998b). The standards imposed by the TRIPS agreement were similar to those held by industrialised countries and were far higher than existing patent protection found in most LMICs.

There are 'out'-clauses within TRIPS to limit patent protection. These include:

1 Compulsory licence (CL): issuance of a CL allows for the legal manufacture and use of generic drugs without the agreement of the patent holder. A judicial or administrative authority (e.g. national body) is allowed by law to grant a licence, without permission from the patent holder, on various grounds of public interest; for example, if a new drug is thought critical to public health such as an AIDS vaccine, or on the grounds of anti-competitive practices (e.g. insufficient quantity or quality or abnormally high prices). The impact of compulsory licensing is really to grant licence to produce essential medicines and is similar to the generic production of drugs in countries such as India. In order to grant CLs, there are rules regarding compensation of the patent holder.

2 Parallel importing (PI): this occurs when branded drugs are purchased from a third party in another country, rather than directly from the manufacturer. This takes advantage of the fact that pharmaceutical companies charge significantly lower prices in one country than another. For example, Retrovir is sold at £125 in the UK, but consumers can purchase this for as little as £54 in other European countries. In the EU, parallel importing of patented products is widely used and is seen as an effective way of equalising prices (Duckett 1999).

There has been tremendous controversy regarding TRIPS and adverse impacts on access to essential drugs (t'Hoen 1999; Mirza 1999).

Events surrounding compulsory licensing of drugs and TRIPS

The recent debate with respect to drugs to treat HIV/AIDS-related illnesses and the role that TRIPS is seen to be playing provides a good example of the role of regulation at the international level and the global and national linkages. In industrialised countries, the use of antiretroviral (ARV) treatment regimens means that AIDS is becoming a chronic illness, as long as these drugs are taken. The major barrier for use of these drugs is their high price (estimated at between $10,000 and $17,000 per person per year). The prices for ARV and other HIV-related drugs mean that they are largely unavailable to people with HIV/AIDS in developing countries. Thus for them, AIDS continues to be a terminal illness with a life expectancy of 7–9 years after infection with HIV. Countries such as Thailand and India have strong domestic drug manufacturers who have been able to produce generic drugs for a fraction of the price of patented versions. However, these countries are now coming under pressure to change their trade practices so as to comply with TRIPS agreement. The massive disparity in prices between patent and generic drugs in these circumstances has led to calls for compulsory licensing, which will allow the generic production of these drugs within countries.

Several less-developed countries have been under pressure from western governments to make changes to their health policy and legislation that would restrict their ability to issue CLs and engage in PI, despite these clauses being consistent with TRIPS (Wilson *et al.* 1999), as they attempt to conform to the WTO deadlines of 2000 and 2005 to be TRIPS compliant. This so-called 'TRIPS-Plus' policy has been highlighted in both Thailand and South Africa (Bond 1999; Wilson *et al.* 1999). Box 5.1 charts the events related to TRIPS and patent protection among a number of countries, particularly South Africa and Thailand, both before and following the creation of the WTO.

Even before the TRIPS agreement was in place, Thailand upheld product patent protection. It is apparent that the 'ratcheting-up' of international regulatory standards on pharmaceutical drugs seen in TRIPS was closely linked to the interests of western countries with strong pharmaceutical manufacturers (Braithwaite and Drahos 1999), and consistent with actions trying to achieve these ends prior to TRIPS. Since 1992, only three generic drugs have been produced and released from the SMP (Safety Monitoring Programme) in Thailand (Wibulpoiprasert 1999), despite the country's exemption from TRIPS.

As the deadline approaches for the TRIPS agreement to be enshrined in law, there is tremendous pressure, particularly from the US

Box 5.1 Activities related to patent protection and the implementation of TRIPS.

- 1979   Thai patent act accepted only process patent for pharmaceuticals. Local generic drug production led to substantially lower prices than patented drugs produced by multinational drug companies (Wibulpolprasert 1999).

- 1986   The US trade representative (USTR) started to investigate the Thai tobacco market, and pressured the Thai government to allow participation of foreign companies. The Thai were threatened with being sanctioned under the US 301 Trade Act. This led to opening of Thai tobacco market to foreign companies.

- 1991   American Pharmaceutical Manufacturers Association (PhRMA) files petition under the US Trade Act alleging that the Government of Thailand does not provide adequate and effective patent protection for pharmaceutical products. USTR initiates investigation.

- 1992   USTR determines that Thai government's acts, policies and practices related to the protection of patents are unreasonable and burden or restrict US commerce. Under the threat from the US to limit textile imports produced in Thailand, the Thai government passed a law to introduce patent product protection. The law covered pharmaceuticals already in the pipeline to be covered under a technical SMP which was negotiated with the USTR. The SMP required all new drugs to be monitored for *at least* two years, thus delaying the registration of generic drugs. Pressure from Thai civic groups led to animals and plants being exempted from product patent as well as allowing CL, parallel importing and the creation of a Pharmaceutical Patent Review Board to collect economic data such as the production cost of pharmaceuticals (Wilson *et al.* 1999).

- 1994   Conclusion of Uruguay Round of negotiations related to multilateral trade, including formulation of TRIPS.

- 1995   Creation of WTO.

- 1997   South African government amends 'Medicines and Related Substances Control Amendment Act, no. 90 of 1997', allowing the Minister of Health to determine prescribed conditions for the supply of more affordable medicines, including fast-track CL and PI (described in clause 15c).

- 1997   On behalf of PhRMA, 40 members of US congress write to President Clinton warning that the Medicines Act threatens the US drug industry and demanding tougher action (Bond 1999).

- 1998   Forty-two pharmaceutical companies (mainly multinational) launched a law-suit against the Government of South Africa, related to its 'Medicines and Related Substances Control Amendment Act, no. 90 of 1997'. This attempts to stop South Africa from adopting compulsory licensing of life-saving drugs (Consumer Project on Technology, undated).

- 1998   Attempt to give WHO a role in monitoring international trade agreements was strongly opposed by US in World Health Assembly, with the US threatening to withdraw its WHO funding.
- 1998   The USTR designates South Africa a special 301 'Watch list' country. The US decided to withhold preferential tariff treatment from certain South African exports, pending adequate progress in intellectual property rights protection in South Africa (Bond 1999).
- 1998   South Africa passes a new *Medicines Act,* which despite US lobbying contains provision about CL and parallel importing which were identical to previous Act in 1997. South Africa takes over three-year leadership of the Non-Aligned Movement.
- 1998   Ongoing discussions between South African government and pharmaceutical companies. USTR sends letter to South African government offering to withhold preferential tariff treatment if a settlement could be reached.
- 1998   In response to the threat of increased trade tariffs on Thai exports to US, the Thai Pharmaceutical Patent Review Board was disbanded and measures taken limiting the right to issue CLs and parallel importing for pharmaceuticals (an example of the US TRIPS-Plus policy) (Wilson *et al.* 1999).
- February 1999   The US PhRMA submission for USTR promotes designation of Thailand and The Dominican Republic as priority watch countries, which may require further punitive action in relation to its pharmaceutical patent protection (Consumer Project on Technology, undated).
- March 1999   Geneva meeting on CL sponsored by three international NGOs – MSF, HAI and CPT – promoting use of CL for essential drugs (McGregor 1999). Representative from US patent and trademarks office quoted saying that US position is more restrictive than the TRIPS agreement, and that the US saw TRIPS as 'a minimum standard of protection' (Bond 1999). Double standards set by US related to CL were highlighted at the meeting.
- April 1999   US pressure intensified on South Africa, with the institution of a formal out-of-cycle review of South Africa and its Medicines Act, which allowed both CL and PI. South Africa seen as one of the first test cases determining the scope of TRIPS.
- May 1999   WHO was given mandate to monitor public-health consequences of international trade agreements at the World Health Assembly.
- June 1999   South African access to drugs and TRIPS becomes major issue in US presidential election. Vice-President Gore targeted by AIDS Coalition to Unleash Power (ACTUP) – a treatment access NGO, and the US media accuses Vice-President Gore of defending the pharmaceutical industry profits at the expense of South African AIDS patients. Gore receiving campaign contributions from the pharmaceutical industry.

- November 1999   Thailand's Government Pharmaceutical Organisation announces that it will negotiate with Bristol–Myers Squibb to manufacture locally a generic version of the antiretroviral drug didanosine (ddI). Generic production would reduce the price of the drug by at least 50 per cent. With this move, Thailand becomes the first developing country to seek a compulsory licence under TRIPS (Nagarajan, 1999).

- November 1999   MSF, HAI and CPT sponsor conference on 'increasing access to essential drugs in a globalised economy'. There was high-profile coverage internationally (Wilson *et al.* 1999; Yamey 1999; Banta 2000).

- December 1999   WTO Ministerial Conference in Seattle, US disrupted by anti-globalisation demonstrators.

- December 1999   Limitation of US TRIPS-Plus policy. US President Clinton ordered a permanent review of the 301 cases on health-related intellectual property matters to 'ensure that application of US trade law related to intellectual property remains sufficiently flexible to respond to legitimate public health crises' by public health authorities (United States Trade Representative 1999). The policy change is important because the US has prevented poor countries from adopting legal measures to produce their own generic versions of patented drugs (Yamey 1999).

- December 1999   The USTR has officially dropped South Africa from 301 'watch lists' (United States Trade Representative 1999). South African newspapers report that Cipla has applied for compulsory licence for Zidouvdine in South Africa.

- January 2000   Discussions held regarding scope of scheduled review of WTO looked at whether to review TRIPS. Draft Common Working Paper of the EC, Hungary, Japan, Korea, Switzerland and Turkey to the Seattle Ministerial Declaration, as it relates to the TRIPS agreement and access to drugs. Working paper suggested use of TRIPS agreement should permit developing countries to grant compulsory licences for drugs appearing on the WHO's essential drugs. Inputs from other countries such as Venezuela which promote idea of WHO essential drug list being exempt from patent compliance of TRIPS. International coalitions are working to promote WTO working groups into reviewing how patent protection may limit affordability of essential medicines to developing world access to essential medicines (Yamey 1999).

- January 2000   Thai government announces it has rejected the ddI compulsory licence, telling protesters that the rejection is based upon US trade pressures (Consumer Project on Technology, undated).

- April 2000   Negotiations within US Congress regarding Africa Trade Bill and sanctions related to TRIPS. Proposed presidential review of African country policies to determine if US government should pressure countries to adopt intellectual property rights that exceed WTO requirements.

- April 2000   The Dominican Republic passes patent bill allowing for CL. US pressure to modify the act before presidential signature, using trade benefits from existing initiatives as leverage.

- May 2000   Reversal of US 'TRIPS-Plus' policy in sub-Saharan Africa with the issuance of a Presidential Executive order related to access to HIV/AIDS pharmaceuticals and medical technologies. The order prohibits the US government from 'taking action pursuant to section 301(b) of the Trade Act of 1974 with respect to any law or policy in beneficiary sub-Saharan African countries that promotes access to HIV/AIDs pharmaceuticals or medical technologies that provide adequate and effective intellectual property protection with the TRIPS agreement' (White House 2000).

- May 2000   Five major pharmaceutical companies offer to negotiate deep cuts in prices for HIV/AIDS related drugs. Negotiations are being held with WHO, the World Bank and UNAIDS, UNICEF and UNFPA. Cuts of more than 80 per cent in drug prices were being mentioned and were seen as an attempt to avoid CL and PI (McNeil 2000).

- June 2000   Health ministers from SADC (Southern African Development Council) countries meet and issue statement saying that they consider CL and PI are critical instruments in improving access to drugs, and would continue to follow actions consistent with TRIPS, circumventing pharmaceutical company drug pricing policies and acquiring essential HIV/AIDs drugs at the cheapest prices (Taitz 2000).

government, to have countries adopt legislation that is even more restrictive than TRIPS and goes so far as banning CL and PI. Debate on these issues is being taken up by consumer and advocacy groups, and there seems to have been some reversals in policy positions in light of these activities. The US president's executive order in May 2000 now prohibits the office of US Trade Representative from interfering with sub-Saharan African countries who operate in a manner consistent with TRIPS. This action was in response to substantial lobbying and advocacy efforts – and implicitly allows both CL and PI to take place without the threat of trade sanctions for countries in sub-Saharan Africa. Within a week of this order, five of the main pharmaceutical companies announced that they would commence negotiations on price cuts for HIV-related drugs with international agencies.

What has also been striking about the recent activity surrounding the TRIPS agreement is the important role that coalitions of consumer and civil society groups have had in highlighting the case of the WTO and access to essential medicines. Key NGOs which have been involved are Médecins sans Frontières (MSF), an international medical aid organisation that won the 1999 Nobel Peace Prize; Health Action International (HAI), an international network of consumer groups concerned with health and development; and the Consumer Project on Technology (CPT), a Washington-based consumer group, part of the Ralph Nader's Public Citizen organisation.

Regulation in perspective

There are some interesting differences between national and global markets, which actually make the possibility of effective international regulation less remote. One key thing is that global markets can equally be seen as involving a formal level of private sector activity (e.g. the pharmaceutical markets) or a very informal level (e.g. spread of information on drug prices by the Internet). While it is very difficult to influence the informal markets directly, the formal markets may be much more amenable to influence.

The case study has shown that, while TRIPS was a good example of regulation at the global level, incorporating rules agreed at the international level, an enforcement structure and regulatory body, in practice its development and impact reflect the relative power of different stakeholders within the market. Regulation is inherently political. While there has been an emergence of supranational global structures such as the WTO, as well as strengthening of international civil society, powerful economic and political interests may not only oppose effective controls but also skew the design of regulation towards their own best interests.

The case study illustrates that even in the presence of supranational or international bodies and legislation which co-ordinates action, actual implementation is very reliant on the interactions and relative power of various stakeholders. This is clearly seen in the formulation and implementation of the TRIPS agreement and the TRIPS-Plus interpretation. The role of the US has been particularly prominent in terms of its international activities in attempting to achieve tighter regulatory standards (favouring pharmaceutical companies) than the TRIPS agreement specifies. This must be clearly interpreted as a response to the powerful lobbying by powerful pharmaceutical companies with a large export market. Domestically however, the US has used CL more than 100 times when it felt that patents were not favourable to the public good. In fact the US federal trade commission has sought compulsory licences on a number of pharmaceutical products as recently as 1997 (Banta 2000). The case study also illustrates the impact that an alliance of strong and vocal consumer and public interest groups (both domestically and globally) can have on the regulatory process.

The differences between events in Thailand and South Africa, and the ability of South Africa to resist and publicise events surrounding TRIPS and threatened trade sanctions, also highlight the differential capacities of countries to both establish and maintain their own domestic policies in the face of global pressure to change. The issue of capacity is even more critical to low-income countries with very few resources available to implement even national regulations. Evidence at the national level shows that, despite the existence of a basic level of regulations in LMICs, the degree to which such regulations are enforced and effective is low (WHO 1991a; Yesudian 1994; Hongoro and Kumaranayake 2000; Mujinja *et al.* 2001). Key reasons for this ineffectiveness relate to lack of information and capacity of the regulatory authority, susceptibility to political influence and weak institutional structures (Kumaranayake 1998). The ability of LMICs to cope with formal regulation in a global context, including their interaction with regulatory structures such as the WTO, is extremely limited, given that most of them cannot even afford permanent missions to the WTO – in contrast to the industrialised countries.

Alternative approaches to regulation

We have discussed that growing marketisation and globalisation now calls for conceptualising action both in using market analysis to understand what is happening within a market, and in using non-legislative mechanisms to influence behaviour. Formal legal regulatory mechanisms highlight the relationship between the regulator (WTO) and regulatee (country). However, the example of the case study amply illustrates that there is a range of other actors who can influence activity and regulatory outcomes. Figure 5.3 highlights the potential, and in some cases actual, role that different institutional structures and actors can play in achieving regulatory goals through both formal and non-formal means. The solid lines indicate the traditional regulator–regulatee relationship; the dashed lines indicate the web of broader relationships that will affect the achievement of regulatory goals.

It is thus important to consider how these relationships can be used to achieve regulatory goals in the context of global markets. Figure 5.3 mentions some of the specific mechanisms that may be used. Traditionally, international actors have played a role in ensuring standard setting. The World Health Organisation has been predominant in this. However, there is now a growing realisation that through functions such as procurement, tendering and negotiation, such agencies can also influence variables such as price (Buse and Walt 2000a). The recent negotiations between WHO/UNAIDS and multinational pharmaceutical companies regarding drugs for the prevention of mother-to-child transmission of HIV are quite illustrative of this. Following the success of clinical trials, which showed that there could be up to a 50 per cent reduction in transmission with the use of Zidovudine, WHO/UNAIDS entered into negotiations with Glaxo Wellcome regarding the price at which it would sell the drug for use in further pilot studies. Further, the impact of lobbying by both international agencies and lobby groups led to Glaxo–Wellcome

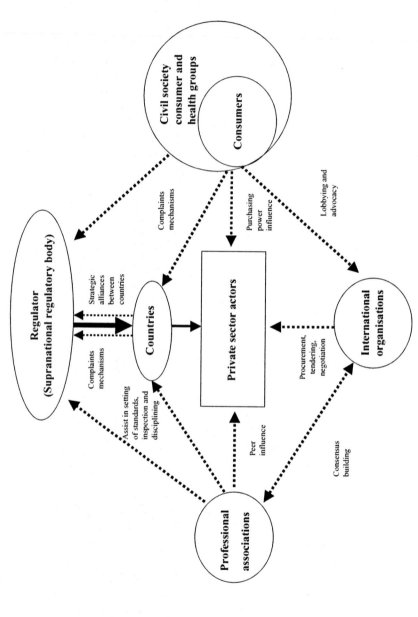

Figure 5.3 Institutional actors and actions to achieve regulatory goals.

halving the drug cost for Zidovudine (UNAIDS 1998). The result of this activity has been a substantial reduction of the drug price in selected countries. While bulk-buying by agencies such as UNICEF has always led to reductions in price, the example of Zidovudine is a clear illustration of how lobbying at a global level has led to changes in prices in a number of countries, which Glaxo Wellcome considered as one global sub-market.

The action around the International Code on the Marketing of Breast Milk Substitutes demonstrates how international codes of conduct which are not legally binding may also achieve regulatory goals by influencing national regulation. The Code was passed by the World Health Assembly in 1981. Monitoring has been taken up by a variety of non- governmental and consumer groups, and, due to problems related to inaction when violations were found, a number of countries were spurred into producing their own legislation. Work in Ghana has found that while international organisations were important in setting up regimes, sustained change required international civil society collaboration with local groups (Chapman 1999).

Conclusion

Despite the existence of basic national legislation on private health financing and provision in most countries, the degree to which these regulations are effectively enforced is low. The experience of LMICs with respect to regulation is in marked contrast to that of Canada and Europe, which have significant private sector activity within their health systems (Muschell 1995). In these countries, a strong regulatory framework is reinforced by public responsibility and resources.

It is increasingly recognised that the role of the state in LMICs as health regulator rather than provider can be problematic given the weaknesses in capacity. Hence, their capacity to contribute to the development and administration of the regulation of emerging global health markets is expected to be even more limited. Their ability to influence the transnational corporations currently dominating emerging global health markets should be questioned. The experience with TRIPS, described in this chapter, suggests that LMICs are considerably disadvantaged in their capacity to influence the regulatory agenda internationally and their implementation nationally.

Our analysis suggests that it is now important not to rely solely on legislative mechanisms (e.g. by multinational or supranational entities), but also to consider non-legal and more informal approaches to achieving desired outcomes. None the less, there are several reasons why regulation might be effectively developed at present. First, the existence of a very formal level of private sector activity, while transnational, means that the key players are visible and potentially amenable to external influence and opinion. Secondly, a national model of regulation transferred to the supranational level may not be the model to follow, but rather more informal and incentive-type mechanisms that have had previous success in influencing the global market. In particular, there is substantial 'buying' power that could be more closely co-ordinated and used to influence large companies. Regional co-operation on regulation might also be effective, as seen by a recent consensus statement by SADC countries (Box 5.1). Third, the emergence of a strengthened international civil society with networks and alliances of non-governmental organisations could be critical for mobilising coalitions of like-minded actors, including donor organisations, national governments and elements of the private sector, to support more effective regulation. The spread of communication and information technologies means that an emerging global civil society, including consumer and advocacy groups, could evolve to play a critical role in mobilising public opinion and exerting pressure on national governments and private companies.

NOTES

We would like to thank our colleagues in the Health Policy Unit (HPU) for their comments and suggestions during the drafting of this chapter, particularly Anthony Zwi, Gill Walt, Anne Mills, Kent Buse and Suzanne Fustukian. Sally Lake is a member of the Health Economics and Financing Programme (HEFP) that is funded by the Department for International Development of the United Kingdom and based at the London School of Hygiene and Tropical Medicine. Lilani Kumaranayake is a member of HEFP and the HPU Globalisation Programme.
1 The monopoly affects all countries who are signatories of the TRIPS.

KEY READINGS

Hsiao, W. C. 1994, 'Marketisation – the illusory magic pill', *Health Economics* 3 (6): 351–8.
Kumaranayake, L. 1997, 'The role of regulation: influencing private sector activity within health sector reform', *Journal of International Development* 9 (4): 641.
Price, D., Pollock, A. M. and Shaoul, J. 1999, 'How the World Trade Organisation is shaping domestic policies in health care', *The Lancet* 354 (9193): 1889–92.
Velasquez, G. and Boulet, P. 1999, 'Essential drugs in the new international economic environment', *Bulletin of the World Health Organisation* 77 (3): 288–92.
Wilson, D., Cawthorne, P., Ford, N. and Aongsonwang, S. 1999, 'Global trade and access to medicines: AIDS treatment in Thailand', *The Lancet* 354: 9193–5.

6   Global policy networks: the propagation of health care financing reform since the 1980s

Kelley Lee and Hilary Goodman

Introduction

Over the last two or three decades, close scrutiny has been given to the issue of health care financing (HCF) in countries at different levels of economic development. The desire for alternative or complementary ways to generate financial resources for health care has in part been driven by need, namely resource shortages and rapidly rising costs. At the same time, however, policy choices have been influenced by particular ideas and values concerning the role of the state, and its perceived responsibilities to finance and provide health care.

Traditional approaches to the study of public policy have focused on the national level and, in particular, the role of the state and government actors as the holders of formal authority to take decisions on behalf of the public interest (Anderson 1975; Rose 1975; Frederickson and Wise 1977). This has been particularly evident in health policy analysis. While certain non-state actors (e.g. private companies, professional associations) have long been recognised as important to public policy-making, they have largely been described as interest groups seeking to influence (e.g. lobbying) a formal process that is essentially focused on the state and its government. Given that the state is taken as the primary unit of analysis, international health is largely equated with comparative analyses of national health policy-making (Leichter 1979).

Since the mid 1980s, analysis of health policy has changed in two main ways. First, there has been recognition of the greater significance, both quantitatively and qualitatively, of non-state actors. These non-state actors include the more familiar private companies and non-governmental organisations (NGOs), as well as consultancy firms, research institutions, charitable foundations, religious and other social movements (e.g. International Women's Health Coalition) and organised crime. Non-state actors appear to have become more numerous within the health field and more visible in their efforts to influence policy-making. Furthermore, their influence of health policy goes beyond efforts directed at the formal processes of government decision-making, in some cases becoming part of the decision-making structure formerly reserved for state actors.

The increased importance of non-state actors in health has led to the development of analytical approaches that seek to understand health policy within a more pluralist environment. Reich (1996), for example, develops the approach of political mapping to try to better capture the diverse range of actors and interests concerned with specific policy issues. The 'comprehensive policy analysis' approach of Frenk (1995) and recent popularity of stakeholder analysis among health researchers (Brugha and Varvasovszky 2000) are similarly motivated. Importantly, these approaches also support a recognition of the porous nature of national-level policy-making, and the importance of actors and forces that cross over state boundaries. This has resulted in a growth in writings about the politics of international health. Walt (1994), for example, extends pluralist theory to the international level in her description of 'international policy networks'. Gordenker *et al.* (1995) explore the role of inter-organisational relations and social networks in facilitating or hindering co-operation on HIV/AIDS.

This chapter seeks to build on these approaches, through an empirical analysis of HCF reform since the early 1980s, to show how globalising forces are changing how health policy is being made and, in turn, how we need to conceptualise it. The chapter begins with a brief review of the changing content of HCF policies since the 1980s and an identification of the key actors involved. This is followed by an introduction to the concept of global policy networks and how it is distinct from analysis of international health policy. A description of the global policy network that has emerged over time around HCF reform is then provided, focusing on key individuals and institutions at the global level. Given the scope of this chapter, detailed discussion of linkages to the national and sub-national level is not given although they are recognised as a critical aspect of the power and influence of these networks. However, implications of the relatively small and tightly structured nature of the HCF network is explored in relation to health governance, and what this may mean for achieving representative and participatory forms of policy-making.

Background: an overview of health care financing in the 1980s and 1990s

HCF is a broad term referring to the mobilisation and use of financial resources in the health sector. It encompasses both resource generation (i.e. the source and mechanisms employed to raise finances), and resource allocation and financial flows. In the context of this chapter, HCF is used to refer largely to resource generation.

While the development of appropriate and effective policies for HCF is no doubt an ongoing task for policy-makers, concerted and widespread efforts internationally to reform HCF policies began in the late 1970s and early 1980s. Following the Alma-Ata Conference and the adoption of the primary health care (PHC) approach in 1978, national governments turned their efforts to its implementation. PHC was not only seen to be desirable ideologically, supported by a political commitment to extend coverage of health services to rural and other underserved populations, but necessary as a cost-effective strategy in resource constrained economies. However, the notion among some that PHC was 'cheap' (Kasongo Project Team 1984) belied the fact that it still demanded large resource commitments (e.g. recurrent costs). The necessary additional resources proved not to be forthcoming, and widespread reallocation from urban hospitals to rural health facilities did not happen on any appreciable scale. Instead, a debate began over the relative merits of comprehensive versus selective primary health care. The latter approach was based on the view that the continued shortage of available resources should temper the ambition of PHC to achieve everything at the same time (Walsh and Warren 1980). UNICEF, a supporter of this view, strongly promoted its GOBI-FFF[1] package as selected priority areas. Others, however, saw this as a contradiction of the basic premise of PHC that would further encourage vertical health programmes.

As financing issues in the health sector became better understood, not least by the development of health economics as a discipline, a clearer picture emerged of the resource gap. De Ferranti (1985) estimated that the worldwide resource gap for implementing comprehensive PHC was US $50 billion per year. At the same time, the macroeconomic context for lower-income countries was one of increasing hardship. World recession, oil crises, falling prices for primary commodities (e.g. copper, cocoa) and a weak tax base engendered severe fiscal deficits for many governments which, in turn, required them to increase foreign debt and pursue structural adjustment policies (SAPs) (Abel-Smith 1986). Importantly, a key feature of SAPs was the policy condition to reduce public expenditure on the social sectors including health. The rationale was that the state was seen to be too large in many countries, resulting in inefficiencies in the administration and allocation of resources. By freeing up countries from a bloated state apparatus, it was believed that private sector, and ultimately resource generating, activity would be encouraged.

As the debate over comprehensive versus selective PHC continued, the search for solutions to fill the resource gap widened. In WHO, the focus was on improving the planning of HCF through fuller and more detailed analysis of national health expenditure (Mach and Abel-Smith 1983).

Better information on income and expenditure patterns in the health sector would form an integral part of the national planning process.

During the same period, working papers by economists in the World Bank began to be circulated that called for more efficient use of available resources, as well as a search for alternative sources. A seminal paper during this period was *Paying for health services in developing countries: an overview* (de Ferranti 1985) which defined categories of health services for which user fees could be levied. This discussion of user fees was followed in 1987 by another influential paper, *Financing health services in developing countries: an agenda for reform* (World Bank 1987), which developed this economic reasoning further. The paper advocated cost-sharing and cost-recovery in the form of user fees at government health facilities, as well as the establishment of pre-payment insurance schemes where appropriate. In addition, it promoted the idea of opening the market to private health care providers, and generally increasing the use of market mechanisms in the health sectors of lower-income countries. The key arguments put forth for user fees were: (a) to raise revenue; (b) to increase efficiency of resource use (i.e. introducing the price signal would promote efficiency through positive influences on provider and user behaviour); and (c) most controversially, to improve equity by using additionally generated revenues to target improved access by the most vulnerable (Birdsall 1986).

For its part, interest in HCF at UNICEF led to the launch of the so-called Bamako Initiative (BI) in 1987. The aim of BI, among other things, was to increase resource availability, primarily through charging for drugs, and to use those resources to improve access for the least well served (UNICEF 1990). It provided start-up funds for community financing schemes such as revolving drug funds (RDFs) or community pre-payment schemes. In the case of RDFs, an initially provided drug-stock would be sold to patients at a mark-up price that, in theory, would provide a self-sustaining means of generating income for supplying drugs to rural communities. This scheme was widely adopted from the late 1980s, although the exact nature of implementation varied from country to country. In some cases, the BI was translated into a national programme involving local retention of revenues raised, usually through user fees (McPake 1993).

Based on these policy approaches, a number of countries around the world, particularly in Africa, were encouraged to introduce or extend user fees in government health facilities. These policies were strongly supported by major donors of health sector aid, notably the World Bank, USAID and UNICEF, which supported financing and technical support for pilot schemes. From the outset, however, there were also strong words of caution against the promotion of user fees for all health care users on the grounds that it would compromise equity and access by the most vulnerable (Cross *et al.* 1986; Gilson 1988; Foster 1989; Waddington and Enyimayew 1989). As evaluative research documenting various country experiences became available, these concerns were shown to be supported by empirical evidence. It became clear that, while general similarities of experience could be drawn across countries, the specific context of each country's health system significantly determined the impact of user fees. As McPake (this volume) describes for Uganda, while the impact of user fees on the demand for health services differed depending on the ways in which they were implemented and how revenues were subsequently allocated, in general user fees did not match expectations that they would raise substantial additional revenues for health care. Proponents of user fees responded by arguing that exemption mechanisms to protect the poor would resolve the equity issue, and that revenues raised needed to be used directly to improve the quality of health care (Litvack and Bodart 1993). Others, however, cautioned that in practice exemption policies were difficult and costly to implement effectively, especially in lower-income countries with weak institutional structures (Dahlgren 1991; Abel-Smith and Rawall 1992). They also pointed to technical difficulties with user fee collection, retention and expenditure (Huff-Rouselle *et al.* 1993; Gilson *et al.* 1995).

Policy debate on user fees, and in particular how to optimise their potential while mitigating their adverse effects, continued throughout the 1990s. Yet by the early to mid 1990s this focus on user fees was already being reframed within the broader context of health sector reform as a whole. It was recognised that HCF, as a fundamentally important component of a health system, could not be reformed in isolation. The thrust of the *World development report 1993: investing in health* (World Bank 1993), for example, was sector wide in perspective, focusing on improving allocative efficiency through, for instance, public sector expenditure on a limited and basic package of health care. In other words, the issue was not only where the financing was to come from, but increasingly what it would be spent on. The dual challenges of raising finances and allocating them more efficiently increasingly defined the policy agenda. Over the decade, a more sophisticated understanding of different insurance schemes, incentive systems and regulatory structures developed, with discussions of HCF embedded within these discussions (Van de Ven 1996). By the late 1990s, widespread acceptance of the need for multiple sources of HCF had replaced debates over public versus private financing, with research and policy discussions shifting to such issues as contracting out, purchaser-provider splits and the public–private mix (Hammer 1996).

Overall, the policy debate on HCF over the past 25 years or so has changed considerably, from a once strong reluctance to consider private financing of selected aspects of health care to a broader acceptance of the need for a public–private mix of financial sources. Importantly, this has been a debate that began in a small number of higher-income countries (i.e. the US, UK) and has gradually spread to many countries at very different levels of economic development. Furthermore, a mixture of state and non-state actors have been involved in this debate, influencing how the 'problem' of HCF reform has been defined, the universe of possible solutions, and the legitimation of certain policy strategies to be taken forward. Understanding how policy-making on HCF has taken place over time, who the key actors were, and how they influenced HCF reform globally and nationally, begins with the concept of global policy networks.

The concept of global policy networks

To analyse the nature of policy-making on HCF reform, this chapter draws on concepts developed in other areas of public and social policy. First, network analysis is useful for understanding interconnections among policy-makers within and across countries. A network can be defined as 'an interconnected group or system', with members of such a group or system being either individuals or collections of individuals. Network analysis is the study of social networks – how and why they form, who their members are, how they work, and what outcomes they produce. Network analysts see networks as crucial to organisational performance, and argue that the effectiveness of a network is inversely proportional to its formality. 'It needs a spider, not a chairman; a list of members, not a set of by-laws; groups, not committees, and a phone number rather than a building' (Handy 1993: 261). The extent to which a network structure has characterised HCF reform, and been important to the effective dissemination of policy reforms, is explored in the next section.

Second, Haas' (1992) concept of an epistemic community is useful to explore who the actors have been and how they have been influential in HCF reform. An epistemic community is 'a network of professionals with recognised expertise and competence in a particular domain and an authoritative claim to policy-relevant knowledge within that domain or issue-area'. While members of an epistemic community may come from different disciplines and backgrounds, they have (a) a shared set of normative and principled beliefs; (b) shared causal beliefs; (c) shared notions of validity; and (d) a common policy enterprise. Importantly, 'control over knowledge and information . . . and . . . the diffusion of new ideas and information' is an important dimension of the power of epistemic communities, as these can lead to 'new patterns of behaviour and . . . international policy co-ordination'. As described below, policy-making on HCF reform has been characterised by the strong presence of an epistemic community. Furthermore, this epistemic community can be described as 'global', in the sense that, it has encompassed a broad range of state and non-state actors across higher, middle and lower-income countries.

The importance given to particular expertise and thus experts, and the transnational nature of their influence over policy-making, also lies behind the concept of a transnational managerial class (Cox 1987). In contrast to descriptions of international health policy as essentially pluralist as a result of the increased participation of non-state actors (Frenk 1995), Cox argues that a new policy elite is emerging that: 'encompasses public officials in the national and international agencies involved with economic management and a whole range of experts and specialists who in some way are connected with the maintenance of the world economy, in which the multinationals thrive – from management consultants, to business educators, to organisational psychologists, to the electronics operators who assemble the information base for business decisions, and the lawyers who put together international business deals.' Together, they serve as the: 'foci for generating the policy consensus for the maintenance and defence of the system. "Interdependence" is the key symbol in an ideology linking economic rationality, social welfare, and political freedom or "modernisation" . . . with a world economy open to corporate movements of goods, capital, and technology.' In other words, the emergence of global policy networks should not necessarily be equated with wider participation and representation in decision-making. Indeed, in the area of HCF, a global elite has come to dominate policy discussions through their control of financial resources and, perhaps more importantly, control of the terms of debate through expert knowledge, support of research, and occupation of key nodes in the global policy network.

In summary, the concept of a global policy network begins with the centrality of social networks that encompass both formal and informal linkages and interactions. Traditional health policy analysis has focused on the former, depicting policy-making in hierarchical (e.g. top-down, bottom-up) and linear terms. Network analysis acknowledges, but also looks beyond, formally defined roles and responsibilities to other ways that link individuals and institutions together (e.g. socio-economic background, education, disciplinary expertise, gender). The type of linkages that bind a network together, in turn, can create exclusivity. In policy areas that require specialist technical knowledge, such as health, elitism can be derived from control over the generation and legitimation of such knowledge. The concept of an epistemic community describes how this elite network can exert influence over policy-making. Similarly, the concept of a transnational managerial class captures the global nature of such an elite network, and challenges the notion that they are value-neutral.

Mapping the global policy network on health care financing reform

In seeking to determine whether HCF reform has been shaped by a global policy network, as described above, this analysis began with a systematic literature search of published and unpublished materials on HCF produced from the late 1970s. MEDLINE and other available databases were used to search more recent literature. Literature not listed on these databases was searched manually. In addition, data on citation of this material was obtained from citation indices as an indicator of level of readership among the scholarly and policy communities. The search produced a list of individuals who had published frequently in prominent scholarly journals[2] on the subject of HCF, or who contributed substantively to policy reports and other documents of the World Bank, WHO, UNICEF, USAID and other relevant organisations. As well as key ideas put forth, where possible their institutional base, source of research funding and nationality were noted.

Having identified key authors, three sets of semi-structured interviews were conducted between 1995 and 1997 with many of the authors, as well as individuals identified as active in the HCF policy area. The interviews were focused on understanding the 'story' behind the HCF reform debates since the late 1970s – what the main issues of debate were, what key policy documents/scholarly works were seen to be most influential, who the key individuals and institutions were seen to be, and what meetings or groupings of these key actors were perceived to be most important. Through these interviews, names of other key informants were identified and followed up.

The task of identifying and ranking network linkages among key actors was informed by a number of sources. Funding for research and other activities was an important link but it was difficult to collect sufficiently comprehensive data beyond information on major initiatives. Key informants were asked about what they believed were the most important international meetings to attend related to HCF and why. Given the invariably crowded diaries of the key informants, it was assumed that this yielded useful information about which groups, of which there was a proliferation over time, were considered worth meeting with. From this information, an 'A' list of international meetings was drawn up. In addition, curriculum vitae were collected from a large number of the key informants as a means of identifying their educational backgrounds and career movements over time. Finally, lists of participants of international meetings related to HCF were examined to identify individuals and their institutional affiliations. A summary of this data in terms of key events and periods identified is provided in Table 6.1.

From this data, network maps were developed that illustrate key institutional actors over time in HCF reform (Figures 6.1–6.3). Key policy initiatives, such as REACH, Partnerships for Health Reform and publication of the *World development report 1993* marked three key periods of policy debate: 1978–86, 1987–93 and 1994–2000. Such initiatives also pointed to collaborative linkages among the main institutional players in the form of funding, personnel or projects. The movement of individuals among these institutions was difficult to capture pictorially given their number and high degree of professional mobility. None the less, data on the career movements of individuals gathered from curriculum vitaes helped to identify and measure in crude terms institutional linkages.

Taken together, these various sources of data suggest that HCF reform has been strongly characterised by a relatively small and tightly integrated network of policy-makers, technical advisers and scholars who have defined and shaped the content and process of policy reform. From the late 1970s to the mid 1980s (Figure 6.1), the network was relatively small and focused on improving information on health financing and expenditure. This led major donor agencies to pay greater attention to financing, not only in the health sector but other social sectors (e.g. education). WHO, in the context of discussions about the affordability of PHC, was actively involved in improving planning of health finances in collaboration with Brian Abel-Smith at the London School of Economics (LSE), Peter Mach and, later, Anne Mills at the London School of Hygiene and Tropical Medicine (LSHTM). Some funding for this work came from the then UK Overseas Development Administration (now Department for International Development).[3]

Across the Atlantic, community financing for PHC began to be discussed. It was the US Agency for International Development (USAID), however, which took the lead by funding projects in a number of American universities (e.g. Harvard, Johns Hopkins) at this point to support improved analysis of expenditure flows and national health accounts in lower-income countries where data remained poor. These projects included influential work on community financing in Senegal (1978) and prepayment schemes in Bolivia (1984–5).[4] The US $8 million REACH project followed in 1985–9, of which one of two components was health financing (US $2 million) led by the consultancy firm John Snow Inc.

Table 6.1 *Summary of key events and periods of policy development*

Date	Event	Individual/Organisation involved
1978–86		
1978	Alma-Ata Conference on Primary Health Care	WHO/UNICEF
1980	GOBI–FFF package promoted	UNICEF
1983	*Planning the finances of the health sector: a manual for developing countries*	Mach and Abel-Smith (WHO)
1985	*Paying for health services in developing countries: an overview*	de Ferranti (World Bank)
1985–89	REACH Project	USAID/John Snow/Abt Associates
1987–93		
1987	Launch of Bamako Initiative	UNICEF
1987	Creation of Division of Strengthening Health Systems	WHO
1987	*Financing health services in developing countries: an agenda for reform*	Akin, Birdsall and de Ferranti (World Bank)
1988	*Problems and priorities regarding recurrent costs*	UNICEF
1988	'Recurrent costs in the health sector – problems and policy options in three countries'	Abel-Smith and Creese, eds. (WHO)
1988	*Government health care charges: is equity being abandoned?*	Gilson (LSHTM)
1989	Health Economics and Financing Programme	UK ODA/LSHTM
1989–95	Health Financing and Sustainability Programme	USAID/Abt Associates
1991	*Cost analysis in primary health care. A training manual for programme managers*	Creese and Parker (WHO/UNICEF)
1991–9	Data for Decision Making Project	Harvard University
1993	*World development report: investing in health*	Jamison *et al.* (World Bank)
1994– 2000		
1995	*A strategic framework for setting priorities for research, analysis, and information dissemination on health sector financing in sub-Saharan Africa*	Health and Human Resources Analysis in Africa Project/ Support for Analysis and Research in Africa (USAID)
1995– 2000	Partnerships for Health Reform Project	USAID/Abt Associates
1995	Forum on Health Sector Reform	WHO
1997	Innovations in Health Care Financing Conference	World Bank
1999	Alliance for Health Policy and Systems Research	WHO/Global Forum for Health Research
2000	Commission on Macroeconomics and Health	WHO

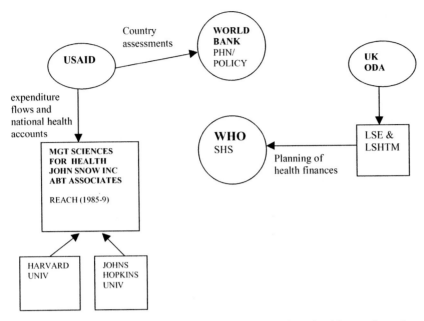

Figure 6.1 Institutional map of global network on health care financing reform (1978–1986).

Importantly, Abt Associates was a subcontractor to this project, which allowed individuals within the consultancy firm to develop specialist health financing expertise and research in French Africa.[5]

By the mid 1980s, important work by David de Ferranti in the Population, Health and Nutrition Division (PHN) of the World Bank began to be disseminated. In 1984 the Bank published *Toward sustained development in subSaharan Africa*, which, while containing only one page on health and not mentioning financing, raised fundamental questions about how lower-income countries did things. As well as contributing to this report, de Ferranti published *Paying for health services in developing countries: an overview* in 1985, which, for the first time, paid attention to recurrent costs, sustainability in developing countries and paying for health care.

The period 1987–93 (Figure 6.2) saw a significant increase in policy work on HCF, with the World Bank substantially developing its technical expertise in health financing and taking a lead role in influencing policy debates. A number of now prominent economic analysts joined the Bank from American universities during this period including John Akin, Mead Over and David Dunlop. The publication of *Financing health services in developing countries: an agenda for reform* (World Bank 1987) threw

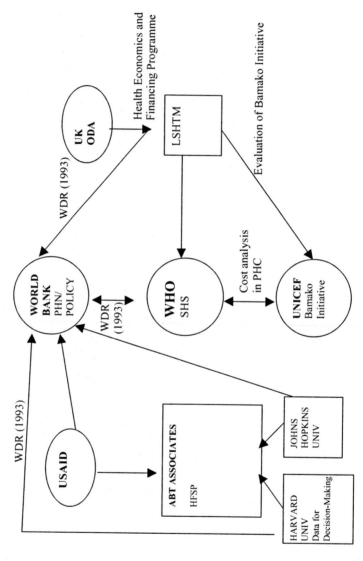

Figure 6.2 Institutional map of global network on health care financing reform (1987–1993).

down a conceptual gauntlet in that it delved directly into the issues of priority-setting and public versus private financing of health care. As well as signalling that the World Bank was surging forward in its work on health financing, the report opened an active intellectual debate both within and outside the World Bank on the role of economics in health development. Many public health professionals were alarmed at the apparent undermining of the fundamental principle of universal access to basic health care. Some economists also did not like the report because there 'wasn't much economics in it'.[6]

Significantly, the report laid the groundwork for the *World development report 1993: investing in health* (World Bank 1993), which remains a seminal, if controversial, policy document on HCF reform. The fact that an annual *World development report* (WDR), a flagship publication of World Bank policy, was dedicated to health financing indicated the importance that the Bank was giving to the issue. The official World Bank position was that preparation of the report was carried out with WHO as a 'full partner', with additional technical inputs from a plethora of scholars in prominent public health institutions. However, the degree of collaboration and consensus is widely disputed, not least because of continued disagreement over the basic tenets of the report. While substantive debate on the content of the report can be found elsewhere (Ugalde and Jackson 1995), what is relevant here is the clear leadership role played by the World Bank in subsequent debates on HCF reform in establishing new concepts and ideas (e.g. disability adjusted life-years, global burden of disease).

Despite its named role as a full partner, WHO and its regional organisations remained a relatively low-key player during this period. The organisation still had limited expertise in health economics, with the exception of Andrew Creese who began to build such expertise in the mid 1980s. This situation continued to be the case into the 1990s, in large part a reflection of WHO's lack of financial resources for health development comparable to the World Bank. As a former Director of the Office of Health in USAID commented, WHO had good technical people but did not worry about the cost of PHC. It remained focused on administration and management at a time when the World Bank, UNICEF and others were exploring user fees and other sources of finance. These subjects remained anathema to traditional attitudes within WHO that PHC should be funded by public financing.[7]

The launch of the Bamako Initiative in 1987 was also amidst disagreement as to whether WHO was an actual collaborator with UNICEF. While announced by UNICEF Executive Director James Grant at a WHO/AFRO meeting of ministers of health, the initiative took WHO by surprise, not least for its focus on user fees. Piloting of BI-inspired projects did lead to a 'thickening' of the HCF reform network with academic institutions such as LSHTM, which undertook a major evaluation in the early 1990s. USAID was also prominent during this period but its contribution was closely tied to the political climate in the United States. The ideological climate under the Reagan Administration favoured greater privatisation, cost containment and efficiency savings, and USAID thus encountered resistance to funding stand-alone projects on health financing. The REACH project was required to combine this work with child survival and immunisation. Funding of US $19 million was finally forthcoming for a major health financing project in 1989, Health Financing and Sustainability (HFS), but its successor (HFS II) was nearly not funded because the government was unconvinced of its relevance. The increase in attention to HCF reform from 1987 to 1993 also led to the creation of major initiatives within key academic institutions. Among these were the Data for Decision Making project at Harvard University (1991–9) and Health Economics and Financing Programme (1989–present) at LSHTM, both of which have played central roles in research and policy advice at both the global and national levels, as discussed below.

The third period (1994–present) suggests a globalisation of the policy network around HCF reform, in the sense that the linkages among key institutions and individuals have become more solidified through a relative convergence of policy positions (Figure 6.3). The World Bank has remained the leading influence in reform debates, largely as a result of its unrivalled financial resources, yet recognition of the adverse social consequences of its policy initiatives, especially on the poor, has led to reflection. De Ferranti, for example, believes now that the Bank was somewhat naïve in basing its policies on a prototype of an African country rather than recognising the diversity among countries. The Bank also focused overly on encouraging ministries of health to introduce user fees when there may have been 'better ways to get to better places'.[8]

The apparent softening of the World Bank's position towards HCF, accompanied by a change in leadership and pursuit of more socially sensitive policy initiatives, has also coincided with a shift within WHO. With the election of Gro Harlem Bruntland as Director-General of WHO in 1998 has come an influx of new staff and advisers who had formerly contributed to the WDR (1993), including Christopher Murray and Alan Lopez (who carried out global burden of disease work at Harvard University) and Dean Jamison (who led the preparation team for the WDR at the World Bank). In addition, new initiatives have been introduced, such as the Forum on Health Sector Reform, Alliance for Health Policy and Systems Research and, more recently, the WHO Commission

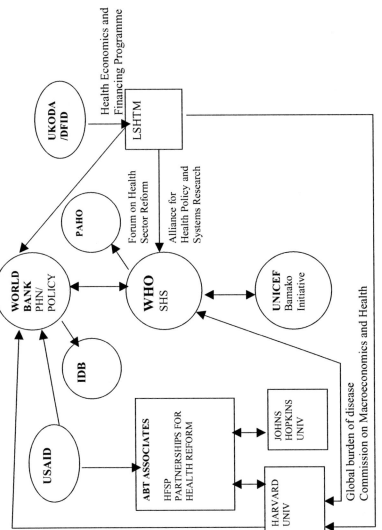

Figure 6.3 Institutional map of global network on health care financing reform (1994–2000).

on Macroeconomics and Health, that are weaving a web of meetings and collaborative work among the major institutional actors. The extension of this tighter network from the US and UK, to the 'traditional' developing world of Africa, Asia and Latin America, to the 'emerging economies' of eastern and central Europe, is explored in greater detail in the next section.

A transnational policy elite: power and influence in global health policy

The brief discussion above suggests that a global policy network on HCF reform has emerged from an initially disparate collection of institutions with a shared concern about the inadequacy of resources for health development. Their early contributions to defining the 'problem' of HCF, and potential solutions, reflected their particular expertise and ideological standpoint. As initiatives proliferated, linkages among these institutions increased in the form of projects, individuals and policy ideas. This process of an evolving policy network can be observed to have three major features.

First, one prominent feature of this global policy network has been a 'revolving door' of career progression that has facilitated the movement of individuals among these institutions. A common pattern, for example, has been how individuals have moved among the key institutions described. A typical career pattern would be Ph.D. training (usually in economics) and then faculty position in a prominent academic institution; project funding from a donor agency such as USAID or World Bank; move to the donor agency as a staff member or technical adviser; and/or recruitment by one of a small number of consultancy firms that have worked closely with donor agencies on HCF issues (i.e. Abt Associates Inc., John Snow Inc.).

Secondly, there is evidence of a strong epistemic community involved with HCF reform centred on economic and public health expertise. Both are areas of specialist technical knowledge and expertise, and the emergent discipline of health economics has developed rapidly since the 1980s into a prominent field of research and policy advice led by a relatively small number of individuals. Typically, these individuals have played multiple roles, engaging in empirical research and academic publishing, while simultaneously contributing to key policy debates through meetings, consultancies and other advisory activities. For example, Brian Abel-Smith engaged in academic research at LSE, advised the UK Overseas Development Administration (ODA), USAID and other governments worldwide on health and social sector financing, and undertook numerous consultancies for donor agencies (Mach and Abel-Smith 1983;

Abel-Smith 1986). In the 1990s, Anne Mills established the ODA-funded Health Economics and Financing Programme at LSHTM that has worked closely with prominent donor agencies and national governments on a range of financing issues. As well as publishing extensively on health sector reform, Mills chairs a number of prominent bodies such as the Alliance for Health Policy and Systems Research and is a member of the WHO Commission on Macroeconomics and Health.

A third feature of the global policy network has been the intellectual debate between public health and economics. As described above, prior to the 1980s public health issues overshadowed discussions of HCF, with emphasis given to improving coverage and strengthening comprehensive PHC. Health for All and the Alma-Ata Declaration were public health initiatives concerned foremost with providing basic health care for all. In contrast, the mid 1980s onwards saw increasing emphasis given to economic criteria for prioritising health needs and recipients. Individuals propounding these views were more often trained in economics than public health (e.g. Nancy Birdsall, Mead Over). Interviews of key informants who were actively involved in shaping the policy debate during this period cited disagreement in fundamental principles and approaches between public health and economic technical experts. In the World Bank, this was played out during the late 1980s between the public health dominated PHN, on the one hand, and the regional bureaux and Policy Research Department, on the other hand. Publication of *Financing health services in developing countries* in 1987 was seen as a largely economist-defined agenda for HCF reform. The WDR (1993) was a retreat from this agenda, with efforts made to bring together the two groups under Dean Jamison, a professor from the University of California at Berkeley with expertise in both economics and public health. Whether this was achieved successfully remains a point of debate, but the stronger emphasis in the Bank since the mid 1990s on human capital and social sector lending suggests continued efforts at reconciliation.

A fourth feature has been an intellectual and policy divide over the past twenty years between two hubs based around Washington DC and London. In Washington, the World Bank and USAID have been most prominent, supporting academic institutions and consultancy firms (John Snow Inc., Abt Associates Inc., Management Sciences for Health) through funding of major projects (e.g. Health Financing and Sustainability I & II; Partnerships for Health Reform). In more recent years, the InterAmerican Development Bank (IDB) has become more active in the field, not least because of Nancy Birdsall's move from the World Bank to serve as director of health in 1993. Similarly, in London the UK ODA established the Health Economics and Financing Programme at

LSHTM, with staff members playing prominent roles in HCF research and policy debates. Individuals at LSE (notably Brian Abel-Smith) and the Liverpool School of Tropical Medicine (e.g. Catriona Waddington) can also be seen as part of this extended hub, who linked at the international level to WHO and UNICEF.

This early transatlantic divide in institutional terms was also manifested in policy debates concerning user fees for lower-income countries. The strongest (and earliest) proponents of user fees came from the US (e.g. Nancy Birdsall, David de Ferranti, John Akin), while the critics raising equity concerns were largely European (e.g. Lucy Gilson, Catriona Waddington). This is most likely explained by differences in the underlying values and principles that shape the US and European health care systems. The creation in 1948 of the National Health Service in the UK, and similar systems throughout Europe after the Second World War, was based on the principle that health care is a social good and should be shared by all who need it regardless of ability to pay. In the US, health care is more commonly viewed in terms of private consumption, with procurement and financing an individual responsibility (Reinhardt 1996). This admittedly crude characterisation none the less forms part of the socio-political context of HCF debates around the two hubs.

Outside of these two *loci* for policy discussion, there was a notable absence of certain institutions and nationals from key debates. For example, as described above, WHO (including PAHO) was not an active player until the mid 1990s and, even to date, continues to have limited health economics expertise on staff. In the case of the Pan-American Health Organisation (PAHO), which boasted two or three health economists at its headquarters in Washington DC and the same at country level throughout the region, there has been a reliance on its links to collaborating centres to provide needed expertise.[9] This may also be explained by the fact that many Latin American countries have social insurance systems, so the issue of user fees is less relevant. Also surprisingly notable by their absence were NGOs, which generally did not engage in the HCF debate. The notable exception is the work by Health Action International on the Bamako Initiative, and Save the Children Fund on sustainability during the mid 1990s (Save the Children Fund 1996).

Finally, and perhaps most importantly in terms of the global propagation of HCF policies, have been linkages between the above described policy network and national level implementation, particularly in lower-income countries. It is beyond the scope of this chapter to analyse in detail the numerous connections that have evolved among key institutions and individuals concerned with HCF reform globally and nationally. However, this analysis identifies types of linkages that could usefully be followed up in future research to more fully understand the way in which policy ideas and practice are becoming globalised. One important type of link has been through research training and projects. Research on HCF at the country level was initially undertaken from the two hubs identified. The Washington hub of institutions focused, for example, on Latin America, the Philippines, Egypt and Francophone Africa (e.g. Niger, Cameroon), while the London hub was especially active in Southern and East Africa, and Thailand. This does not reflect a conscious 'division of labour' but rather historical similarities in health systems (e.g. ex-colonies and the British health care system), as well as an extension of general aid relations. Early links largely consisted of country case studies or pilot schemes to test different financing mechanisms. By the late 1980s, these project links began to be reinforced by the training of research students from lower-income countries by key individuals within core academic institutions. Support for research training has come from a number of initiatives such as the International Clearinghouse for Health Sector Reform Initiatives and International Health Policy Program. These links have been further strengthened by the promotion of former students to policy-making positions in lower-income countries or international health organisations from which they have built collaborative links with the institutions where they trained.

Global health governance and the transnational managerial class

Governance can be broadly defined as the means by which a society steers itself towards achieving agreed goals. Global health governance concerns the collective forms of governance, from the sub-national to the global level, which address health issues with global dimensions. It is increasingly recognised that 'good' governance, by which governance is carried out in an effective and appropriate way, adheres to certain principles such as accountability, transparency and representativeness. The extent to which a discernible global policy network on HCF reform has emerged over the past twenty years, characterised by a small number of individuals and institutions tightly linked through research and policy activity, raises issues concerned with the nature of global health governance.

The extent to which HCF reform has been the shaped by a more or less participatory and inclusive process is a key issue. That there have been clear individual and institutional leaders in policy debates is not necessarily in itself a point of concern. How representative that leadership is of relevant interests affected by policy changes, however, is important to the legitimacy and appropriateness of reforms. In the case of HCF reform, it is argued in this chapter that the global policy network has been narrowly based in a small number of institutions, led by the World Bank and USAID, and in the nationality and disciplinary backgrounds of the key individuals involved. While key institutions and individuals have supported or undertaken research and policy activities in a wide range of lower-income countries, analysis of policy changes over time suggests that the process of policy initiation and formulation has been largely top-down, developed and supported through the Washington and London hubs. This is not to say that there has not been a diversity of viewpoints; indeed, there has been considerable debate as to the merits and demerits of certain financing mechanisms (e.g. user fees). None the less, the network is tightly focused at the global and national levels on a relatively small number of individuals with similar backgrounds.

This suggests that HCF reform worldwide has been fostered by the emergence of a policy elite, rather than a rational convergence of health needs and solutions. This, in itself, is not a new revelation to long-time critics of development aid and its domination by powerful Western governments (Amin 1996). However, what is different about this policy network that makes it a 'global' elite is its inclusion of public and private interests, and sometimes a mixture of the two within the same institutional structure (e.g. Health Financing and Sustainability Project), across countries (i.e. transnational). The exertion of influence over policy reform has been through a combination of coercive and consensual means. The former, which is well described in development studies literature, has stemmed from the vulnerability of lower-income countries to donor-led policies as a consequence of severe resource constraints including the capacity to engage in full policy dialogue with the aid community. Inequalities in economic and intellectual power have given donors the ability to set implicit or explicit conditionalities on aid.

Effective as coercive means can be, the propagation of HCF reform has also been shaped by the building of consensus across different institutions and national settings defining the 'problem' of HCF and potential solutions. This consensus has been achieved through a range of research and training initiatives, project funding, the career movement of individuals, and other forms of collaborative work across higher- and lower-income countries, health economics and public health, and public and private sectors. The global convergence of policy debates since the late 1990s around the need to better identify health priorities, to use economic rationale more directly in priority-setting, and to finance health care through a mixture of public and private sources has been a result of the co-option of policy elites within lower-income countries to a globally defined discourse around HCF.

Thus, in contrast to liberal views of globalisation, which herald the process as opening up decision-making space for a wider range of individuals and groups, this research finds limited evidence of this. Instead, HCF reform supports Cox's concept of a transnational managerial class, with policies strongly shaped by elites involved in research and policy development centred on two countries but with linkages to other countries. Furthermore, specialist technical expertise in economics and public health held by elites suggests the existence of an epistemic community that has gained legitimacy, as well as policy influence, through control of this expertise.

Conclusions and implications for health policy

Analysis of HCF reform is an especially useful illustration of the changing nature of health policy-making in a globalising world. The issue of HCF lies at the heart of health sector reform debates, and embodies many of the fundamental issues concerning the appropriate role of the state and private sector, individual versus collective responsibility for health care, and the difficult task of priority-setting. Moreover, debates about HCF symbolise much larger issues about the importance of social policy within an emerging global order defined by competitive market principles and individualist rights and responsibilities. What are the boundaries of collective responsibility for health that indicate what society should finance, and what should the individual be expected to bear?

However, the purpose of this chapter has not been to argue the positive and negative aspects of particular HCF policies, nor to debate the ethical and ideological dimensions of this policy issue. Rather, the focus has been to draw attention to the process by which policy debates around HCF have been carried out and how this might be linked to globalisation. This chapter has argued that one of the features of HCF policy debates has been the emergence of a global policy network. This network has been, in part, an extension of existing and familiar forms of leadership and dominance in international health. At the same time, it is argued that there are distinct features of this global policy network, namely its transnational nature, mixture of public and private actors, and legitimacy gained from technical expertise, that make it highly influential in defining HCF reform at both the global and national levels. The exclusivity of the policy process surrounding HCF reform since the 1980s raises fundamental concerns about the emerging forms of health governance in a globalising world and, in particular, how this process has contributed to the propagation of particular policies over time.

There are two ways in which this analysis could be extended. First, this chapter has focused on the policy process at the global level, where problem identification and policy formulation largely took place. While some analysis of links to the country level has been carried out, there is a need for more systematic and detailed study of how HCF policies have, in turn, been taken up and implemented in individual countries. The study by Dahlgren (1991) of HCF reform in Kenya is one of the best examples of how individual country case studies should be undertaken that would include analysis of the linkages to the global policy network described in this chapter.

A second potentially fertile area of research would be to apply such analysis to other areas of health and social policy. HCF has been an especially central policy issue in recent decades because of the significance of health spending as a proportion of GDP in most countries. Yet, although there are suspected peculiarities in the sphere of HCF that have lent themselves to transnationally elitist forms of policy-making, such as the technical subject matter, areas such as reproductive health, communicable disease and decentralisation of health services would be worth exploring similarly.

NOTES

The authors would like to thank Gill Walt, Lucy Gilson and Kent Buse for assisting in the interviewing of key informants for this research, and Anne-Marie Foltz for providing insightful comments on an earlier draft of this work. We would also like to thank Sara Bennett for sharing her experiences and insights. Funding for this research was provided by the UK Economic and Social Research Council.
1 GOBI-FFF stands for Growth monitoring, Oral rehydration, Breast-feeding, Immunisation, Food supplements, Family spacing and Female literacy.
2 The health journals searched were: *British Medical Journal, The Lancet, Journal of the American Medical Association, New England Journal of Medicine, Health Policy, Social Science and Medicine, Health Policy and Planning and Health Economics.*
3 Interview with Lee Howard, former Director of Office of Health, USAID, Washington DC, 10 January 1997.
4 Interview with Charlotte Leighton, Deputy for Technical Direction, Partnerships for Health Reform, Abt Associates Inc., Washington DC, 15 January 1997.
5 Interview with Marti Makinen, Vice President, Abt Associates Inc., Washington DC, 15 January 1997.
6 Interview with principal economist, World Bank, Washington DC, 16 January 1997.
7 Interview with Lee Howard, 10 January 1997.
8 Interview with David de Ferranti, Director of PHN, World Bank, Washington DC, 30 March 1995.
9 Interview with Juan Manuel Sotelo, Chief of Analysis and Strategic Planning, PAHO, Washington DC, 17 January 1997.

KEY READINGS

Abel-Smith, B. and Rawall, P. 1992, 'Can the poor afford "free" health care? A case study of Tanzania', *Health Policy and Planning* 7: 329–41.

de Ferranti, D. 1985, *Paying for health services in developing countries: an overview*, World Bank Staff Working Papers no. 721, Washington DC: World Bank.

Gilson, L. 1988, *Government health care charges: is equity being abandoned?*, EPC Publication no. 15, London School of Hygiene and Tropical Medicine.

World Bank 1987, *Financing health services in developing countries: an agenda for reform*, Washington DC.

World Bank 1993, *World development report 1993: investing in health*, Washington DC.

The globalisation of health sector
reform policies: is 'lesson drawing'
part of the process?

Barbara McPake

Introduction

The notion that there is a global pattern to the reforms of health systems in disparate countries is widespread. Ham (1997) argues for the
'convergence' hypothesis, identifying a number of 'common themes':
concern to strengthen the management of health services in order to
reduce variations in performance and to introduce a stronger customer
orientation; interest in making use of budgetary incentives as a way of improving performance; and a move in some countries to introduce market-
like mechanisms into health services. While hedged with caveats about
remaining variation, Ham's view is captured most clearly in Figure 7.1,
which is reproduced from his publication *Management and competition in
the NHS* (Ham 1997).

In developing countries, similar voices can be heard. For example,
Chernichovsky (1995) argues: 'Paradoxically perhaps, developed and developing nations may be closer to similar systemic solutions than the
underlying factors setting them apart might suggest.' Considering Latin
American reform, Londoño and Frenk (1997) conclude that reform initiatives promote convergence on a 'structured pluralism' health system
model in which the parallel sub-systems of 'segmented' health systems
(InterAmerican Development Bank 1996) are reconfigured in order to
achieve a division of system-wide roles.

Marmor (1997) is among those who dispute this view, which he judges
has '*two central misconceptions*':

First ... [convergence advocates] assume that the diagnoses and remedies associated with so-called 'health reform' mean the same things in different settings.
(This view is *a priori* implausible and, as we shall see, empirically unsustainable.)
Secondly, there is the presumption that, since the problems are similar and the
remedies analogous, cross-national learning is largely a matter of 'establishing a
database and information network on health system reform'. This trivializes both
the need to understand the differing contexts of health policy-making and the
real threats to mis-learning that make appeals to easy cross-national transfer of
experience seem so naïve.

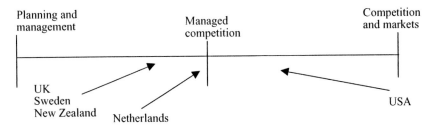

Figure 7.1 The convergence hypothesis (from Ham 1977).

Whichever perspective is deemed more convincing, it is clear that many international actors believe that it is possible to devise 'recipes' for reform with international applicability, albeit with consideration for differences in context. For example, the influential *World development report 1993* (World Bank 1993) argued: 'The policy conclusions of this Report can be tailored to the widely varying circumstances of developing countries.' It proposed a list of ten broad areas of reform that vary in their relevance to three broad groups of countries between 'somewhat relevant', 'relevant' and 'very relevant', with one exception. Zwi and Mills (1995) argue, for example, that: 'There appears to be almost universal acceptance by aid agencies active in health of the desirability of establishing some form of purchaser-provider split.'

The suggestion then is that common policy solutions are emerging, which might be interpreted as a globalised approach to policy-making, though that interpretation would raise as many questions as it would offer diagnoses. It may be argued that the process is one of cognitive globalisation (as defined in the introductory chapter to this volume) or ideological hegemony with roots in neo-liberal values and principles (e.g. Navarro 1999). Alternatively, it may be argued that the common agenda emerges from an analysis of common problems and the identification of common technical solutions (e.g. World Bank 1993). This chapter does not aim to make a contribution to this debate. Rather it considers the extent to which an adequate technical analysis underpins the introduction of policies that seem to be part of the international consensus in particular countries. If shortfalls are identified in this process (as inevitably they are), a number of possible explanations can be put forward ranging from the 'conspiracy' to the 'cock-up'. The evidence considered in this chapter is not very helpful in distinguishing between these, or between gradations between them, and more subtle variants of them.

'Lesson drawing' – a technical approach to policy transfer

In considering the applicability of policies developed in one setting to another, both Rose (1993) and Marmor (1997) identify the opposing fallacies of overlooking context (according to Marmor, the 'World Cup' fallacy which pre-supposes a 'best' health system), and overemphasising context, as equally serious. A rational approach to learning from the burgeoning international debate will rely on an understanding of *how* context matters. This might be tackled through Rose's 'lesson drawing' concept.

According to Rose (1993), 'lesson drawing' in public policy starts with a commonly experienced problem which forces policy-makers to depart from routine and search for potential answers. The process of lesson drawing involves: searching elsewhere, developing a model of how a programme operates, devising a new programme and prospectively evaluating transfer. It is the process of devising a new programme that prevents mere duplication of experience. More sophisticated models build in relevant contextual factors and produce differentiated programme designs, despite agreement that the source policy works in a particular setting. Rose's analysis, however, is not precisely descriptive. In a rational world, this is how policy-makers might set about their task; in a partially rational world it is likely to describe only some aspects of the process.

This chapter aims to review the extent of lesson drawing, thus defined, as it can be discerned in the realms of two commonly introduced health sector reforms: the introduction of user charges for public health services in Africa, and the increasing of managerial and financial autonomy for public sector hospitals globally. Both have been quite widely applied. The former is concluded to be the most common reform component according to a review of health sector reform in developing countries (Creese and Kutzin 1994). The latter was included in a core list of reforms in a 1993 operational review of lending by the World Bank's Population, Health and Nutrition section (Vaillancourt *et al.* 1993), and has been introduced in some form in countries as divergent as the United Kingdom, Thailand, Hong Kong, Tunisia and Zambia (Hanson and McPake 1998).

The reviews of policy development in both areas will attempt to articulate those models which seem to underlie policy proposals and to discern the extent to which a 'lesson drawing' process has occurred.

The case of user charges for public health services in Africa

Can a model underlying the policy be discerned?

A heated debate on this issue has been raging for more than a decade and has spawned not one, but a series of evolving models, which are implicit in the arguments put forward but seldom articulated. The policy of promoting user charges for public health services first came under significant international scrutiny after the publication by the World Bank of the treatise *Financing health services in developing countries: an agenda for reform* (World Bank 1987).

The treatise put forward a model clearly linking policy change to health sector objectives. It argued that by introducing user charges for public health services, improvements in efficiency and equity would be achieved. *Allocative* efficiency (the allocation of resources to those goods and services for which society has the highest values) would be improved because the 'trivial use' of health services would be deterred – hence resources would be concentrated on more valuable interventions. *Internal* efficiency (the use of resources so that outputs are maximised for given use of inputs) would be improved because in the absence of additional resources, the mix of inputs available tended to inefficiently favour staff costs over other costs. In other words, without charges staff time would be wasted on ineffective health services because complementary inputs would not be available. Equity would also be improved by the introduction of the policy because additional resources for the system would enable the health service network to be expanded.

Thus an initial model was put forward proposing a link between policy (introduction of user fees) and common policy objectives (efficiency and equity). Concurrent to the production of the Agenda for Reform, countries were exhorted to devise new programmes introducing fees in their public sectors. Many have argued that very little 'prospective evaluation' of transfer was carried out and, rather, that the international agencies promoting the policy (often through loan conditionality) made little attempt to consider contextual specifics (for example, Dahlgren 1991; Foltz 1994).

Initial experience with the policy tended to contradict the model put forward. Some early studies observed significant utilisation reductions following the introduction of user fees (Waddington and Enyimayew 1989; Yoder 1989), but this was consistent with the model's prediction of reduction in trivial use of health services, and the early studies did not distinguish between trivial and important health service utilisation. Later, however, studies found the introduction of charges to have reduced utilisation for treatment of diseases with important public health implications, suggesting that allocative efficiency had been worsened rather than improved by the policy (for example, Moses *et al.* 1992; Awofeso 1998).

In many but not all cases, revenues raised did not have a noticeable impact on the availability of complementary inputs. For example, in Ghana they accumulated in a non-interest bearing account (Waddington and Enyimayew 1989); in Zimbabwe, they were not retained in the health system at all (Hecht *et al.* 1993); and in a cross-country review they were found to raise an insignificant volume of resources in relation to the overall funding of the health sector in all countries for which information was available to date (Creese 1990). In very few cases were user fee revenues used to expand the health system and improve geographical accessibility with implications for equity.

The Agenda for Reform's model therefore performed poorly against the evidence. By 1992–3 a second model, the 'Bamako Initiative' had come to be seen as an alternative model of user fee policy (World Bank 1993). Cases in which the policy was more successful in raising revenues for complementary inputs tended to involve the retention of user fee revenue in the revenue generating institution. This was one of the guidelines of the Bamako Initiative which were developed in 1992.[1] In the Bamako Initiative model, the issue of complementary inputs was transformed into the broader one of quality of care. Drugs were emphasised as the missing quality component in public services, and an influential paper demonstrated that it was feasible to increase the use of public health services by the poorest quintile of the population if drug supply could be ensured (Litvack and Bodart 1993). This was consistent with the concept of 'relative affordability' introduced by an earlier review of the Bamako Initiative (McPake *et al.* 1993). It was recognised that people of all income levels 'shop around' for health services.[2] If prices are increased while nothing else changes, utilisation (by all groups) will certainly fall. But, if a combination of price and quality changes causes, for any population group, a preferred combination of price and quality to become more widely available than previously, then that group's utilisation of the service in question will increase, and overall – if we accept that people are in the best position to identify their own interests in these circumstances – that group can be concluded to have benefited.

The Bamako Initiative included other components (such as a focus on the primary level and rural environments) that render it not strictly competitive with the model of 'Agenda for Reform' – the models are not mutually exclusive. However, the characteristics of the Bamako Initiative model outlined above have tended to dominate more recent user fee debates. For example, the arguments that user fees will deter 'trivial' users, or that they can be used to extend the health system network, are now more rarely heard and central management of revenues is now not usually assumed.

The rejection of the concern on trivial utilisation has enabled concern with the utilisation impact of user fee policy to take an unambiguous approach. As a simplification, this model can focus on the maximisation of utilisation, recognising that patients' choice among providers depends on price and drug availability, and that drug availability depends on revenue, which depends on some price being charged.

Utilisation maximisation has seldom been articulated, but is implicit, in the Bamako Initiative version. It is generally accepted that falling utilisation means failure, whereas rising utilisation means success (e.g. Litvack and Bodart 1993). It is also consistent with a Paretian perspective,[3] which accepts consumer sovereignty as a guide to welfare. Consider the following categorisation of health service users before and after the introduction of user charges:

1. Those who previously used the public health service before but no longer do so: this group is unequivocally negatively affected since they now choose an alternative (private or self-care) which they judged inferior before.
2. Those who previously used an alternative but now use the public health services: this group is unequivocally positively affected since they must judge the newly available option to be superior to their previous choice.
3. Those who used the public health service before and still do so: the cost–benefit balance for this group is uncertain, they pay more but may receive more – we cannot judge whether they view the marginal change as worthwhile, only that the total package remains their most preferred option out of those available.
4. Those who used an alternative provider and still do so: this group is unaffected.

The focus on utilisation change enables factors 1 and 2 to be compared, while 3 and 4 are not examined. In general, the consumer sovereignty perspective presents well-documented problems in the health sector – we may wish instead to take the perspective of an 'objective expert' to resolve information problems. Assuming that public services are considered an appropriate form of care, the most important information problems may arise under 3. Households may make poor expenditure allocation decisions, favouring health services over more efficient inputs to the household production function (e.g. Coreil 1983). Given the data scarcity inherent in rural African contexts however, and the extreme scarcity of household level information, the model provides as good a 'rule of thumb' as is likely to be available.

It can be shown that the utilisation effect (for any population group) depends on the difference between the disincentive effect of price on utilisation and the positive effect on utilisation of the price increase operating through drug supply. Assuming that the relationship between drug supply and choice is diminishing (anything else would imply unlimited ability to pay for, and believe in, increased drug supply), an 'optimal' fee, from the perspective of utilisation maximisation, exists. This might well be zero. Indeed, assuming that negative fees (payments *to* patients) are not under consideration, zero will capture a wide range of possible results. It might, therefore, be concluded that the introduction of a fee rests on the belief that positive effects of improved drug supply on utilisation outweigh the disincentive effect of price.

This model is largely implicitly rather than explicitly understood and tested. For example, Litvack and Bodart (1993), whose paper is referred to above, did not demonstrate the link between revenue and drug supply. Drug supply improvements were externally funded in the pilot project they report. A small amount of research has been undertaken regarding these relationships (for example, Wouters 1991; Wouters *et al.* 1993; Wouters 1995), and suggests that positive utilisation effects would be very difficult to achieve. In the majority of cases, user fees are set according to best guesses about what is 'affordable' for the majority, which is a judgement of the acceptable disincentive effect, ignoring other considerations.

Evidence of 'lesson drawing' in the Ugandan experience of user fees

If the model as a whole is largely undemonstrated anywhere, it would seem that 'prospective evaluation' of the model in specific contexts remains a scarce commodity. The Ugandan experience with user charges might be viewed as informed by the revised model, based as it was on policy deliberations taking place in the early 1990s. A particular feature of Uganda's environment, suggesting the need to implement other than the 'standard' user charge model, was the background of political instability and the consequences for what seems to be a more pronounced than usual engagement in 'informal survival mechanisms' among Uganda's health sector workers (van der Heijden and Jitta 1993; McPake *et al.* 1999). In 1992, the Ministry of Health Planning Unit produced an unusually thorough consideration of the prospects for financial reform entitled 'The Three Year Plan: financing health for all' (Republic of Uganda 1992) in which, among a range of financing strategies to be pursued, the introduction of user charges was recommended (not for the first time). Some peculiar features of the environment were noted, for example:

The Danish Red Cross donates drugs to health units on the basis of reported volume of out-patients and in-patients. While the objective of this procedure is to introduce equity in the distribution of drugs it provided loop-holes for the manipulation of records, as those units that show a high work load receive a high quota of drugs. (Republic of Uganda: 6)

The medical staff have also responded to a decline in demand and a fall in real wages by spending less time at their work and by engaging in other activities to support themselves and their families, including illicit private practice in government premises. (Republic of Uganda: 10)

[A]lthough the government does not charge user fees, the staff do, and that too without any authority. What is recommended here is not the introduction of user charges but the formalization of already existing . . . charges. (Republic of Uganda: 27–8)

Among the charges proposed in the Three Year Plan are charges at health centre level, which are not to exceed 20 per cent of the cost of treatment, but which are to cover the cost of drugs:

Under the TYP, drug supplies to HSs and HCs will be based on donor assistance. Revenues from the sale of drugs will be used to improve staff welfare, finance repair costs and finance supervision of PHC projects in the vicinity of the health units. In the long run, user charges in HCs and HSs will be used to develop a drug supply system through the uses of revolving funds.

Recognition, therefore, that some of the most important health system failures lay in poor staff welfare and its consequences, and that, for the immediate future, drug supply was ensured through the Danish Red Cross, led the writers of the Three Year Plan to diverge from the Bamako Initiative model and to propose that, for the present at least, revenues should be directed to improving staff morale and performance. This document can be seen as representing the devising of a new programme and the prospective evaluation of its transfer. Unfortunately, its recommendations were ignored.

Similarly, an earlier round of recommendations to government, rejected by parliament (the National Resistance Council: NRC) in 1990, had left in place 'sensitised' health unit management committees (HUMCs) who expected to manage the new user fee system. This group had a clear interest in the new policy since it promised, at the very least, an opportunity for community influence and the right to claim expenses and allowances. Health staff were mainly allied on this – the new policy also promised the possibility of welfare bonus payments – though some staff views dissented from this, perhaps because of the potential effects on the ability to charge informally (McPake *et al.* 1999). In the context of a radical decentralisation, local resistance councils (which later became local councils) deemed themselves entitled to authorise the introduction of user charges and did so in an anarchic manner, at first entirely without the guidance of the centre. It is still the case that user charge policy varies from one health facility to another, although there is now a system of national user charge guidelines in place.

There have been a number of evaluations of user charges as they have been introduced, but these evaluations reveal that few have appreciated as perceptively as the Three Year Plan the crucial differences between the Ugandan context and the generalised Bamako Initiative case. For example, Wamai (1992) reveals that the uses of revenue raised have been 'to pay workers' incentives, to purchase supplementary drugs, to buy fuel and to maintain centre vehicles, to cover cost of stationeries and to cater for incidental expenses'. Another review of experience to date (Jitta *et al.* 1996) comments that: 'Whereas one of the objectives of introducing user charges in government units was to generate funds to purchase additional essential and non-kit drugs to supplement the Uganda Essential Drug Management Programme kit, studies have shown otherwise.' This last comment especially suggests widespread assumption that the main objective from the generalised Bamako Initiative case – improved drug supply – is an appropriate transplant to the Ugandan case.

A research project studying the informal economic activities of public health workers in Uganda – including those alluded to in the Three Year Plan – demonstrates the inappropriateness of this transplant (McPake *et al.* 1999). The study attempted to quantify the extent of such informal activities in ten health centres in two of Uganda's southern districts. Those identified as important were mismanagement of drug supply, informal charging, mismanagement of user charges, offering treatment in health workers' homes, ownership of clinics and drug shops, part-time work in other jobs (most commonly private clinics), agriculture and trade. Crucial for the argument of this chapter is that estimates of drug leakage from health facilities – the proportion of drugs received from the Uganda Essential Drug Management Programme which were not received by patients using the unit – ranged between 40–94 per cent with a median leakage rate of 76 per cent. Whatever the overall adequacy of the initial drug supply – and the research suggests that supplies were adequate for the real utilisation levels of centres if not the ones inflated by the process described in the Three Year Plan – it would seem illogical to charge users in order to further supplement a drug supply which leaks so badly. Given the implicit function of drugs in the system (i.e. to pay health workers), then, unless there are intervening considerations, paying them directly would seem to be more efficient. In practice, intervening considerations would also seem to mediate in the opposite direction; paying health workers through drug supply contributes to a widespread problem of drug misuse in the community as a whole, risking widespread chloroquine and antibiotic resistance and inappropriate and harmful use of injections and drug combinations (Birungi *et al.* 1994; Odoi Adome *et al.* 1996).

Second, understanding the existing informal charging background to user charge implementation implies understanding, as suggested by the Three Year Plan, that to some extent, a formal user charge system implies the formalisation of existing practice. But understood more fully still, it also implies an attempt to redistribute rights and accountability in relation to user charges. Presumably there would be no need to tamper with an informal system if it were felt to be delivering everything that a more formal one might. Therefore, an intention of formalisation can be assumed to be a redistribution among health workers, or between health workers and others (for example, patients), and in addition to either of these purposes, to increase the transparency of the system so that proposed redistributive rules can be monitored (for example, an exemptions policy).

It is hardly surprising in this muddled context that, despite some exceptions (for example, Kamugisha 1993), most evaluations of user charge policy at health centre level[4] in Uganda have concluded negatively (Wamai 1992; Bizimana and Liesener 1993; Mwesigye 1995; Jitta *et al.* 1996). Revisiting the need to devise a new programme in the light of Uganda's specific context, and prospectively evaluating its transfer, would appear indicated. In doing this, the Ugandans could provide countries that have similar default privatisation of their health sectors with a new model that could provide new lesson-drawing opportunities.

The case of hospital autonomy

Can a common problem be discerned?

It may be argued that the policy of granting greater autonomy to public hospitals is 'global' in comparison with that of introducing user fees, in that it is a distinct feature of reform programmes across countries representing all geographical areas and levels of development. Many countries believe that there are significant potential efficiency gains in the hospital area – either because there are substantial new technical possibilities in hospital care which may not be taken up under alternative hospital arrangements, or because there is substantial need to rationalise activity between hospitals or between levels of care. This might seem to provide the basis for a common solution/policy response, hospital autonomy. However, the underlying problems take divergent forms in different countries.

In the UK, the granting of autonomy to, first, a selected cohort of hospitals, and then almost universally, was part of a reform programme premised on allegations of widespread internal inefficiency. This was assumed to underlie the politically charged issue of waiting lists. The analysis of Enthoven (1985) identifying inefficiencies with inappropriate incentives is widely viewed as having been highly influential in the UK policy process. For example, he argued that specialist dominance of hospital decision-making prevented efficiency gains being realised and, as one example, drew attention to the perverse incentives arising from a long waiting list for a specialist. Such long lists could help to enhance reputations on the assumption that long lists would be associated with specialists in high demand, could serve to attract additional resources, and could persuade patients to pay (for treatment from the same specialist, as a 'private patient') rather than wait for free care in the National Health Service (NHS).

In Hong Kong, the pre-reformed public hospital system was characterised by overcrowding and staff attrition and, as in the UK, there were major concerns about waiting times for specialist treatment (Yip and Hsiao 1999). In Indonesia, serious efficiency problems were identified in hospitals, but it appears that the main spur for reform was the wish to increase hospital revenue and reduce hospitals' burden on the central public budget (Bossert *et al.* 1996).

In most poor countries, hospitals, especially at national and regional referral level, are judged to consume an excessive proportion of the public health budget, relative to the importance of the conditions intended to be treated there in terms of their contribution to the burden of disease. This is, in principle, an allocative efficiency problem, and implies that one of the objectives of hospital reform in such countries is to enable resource reallocation (McPake 1996). In practice, the failure of the referral system implies that patients who are actually treated in hospitals, at all levels, present with more important conditions from a burden of disease perspective, but could in principle be treated at lower levels of the system. This is an internal efficiency problem – it means that the cost of treating these patients is higher than it might be.

From a third perspective, the problem is one of resource inadequacy and inequity. The persistent use of hospital services, despite attempts to induce patients to use lower levels of the system, reflects a rejection of inadequate services at lower levels and a determined preference for medically qualified staff and other resources only available at hospitals. Since the health system is incapable of providing those resources for all, the issue becomes one of inequitable access. Usually, access is determined on a geographical basis (those living close to hospitals achieve access, others do not), and sometimes access is determined on the basis of ability to pay or influence.

Reform attempts in such countries therefore aim as much to strengthen lower levels of the system, and the referral system, as at internal efficiency concerns. This is consistent with the arguments for user fees discussed in the previous section – fees at hospital level could allow subsidy to be reallocated to lower levels, and motivate users to use services at lower levels. For example, in Zambia, where a hospital board was attached to the central teaching hospital in 1985, according to an ex-minister (Kalumba 1997):

The UNIP government realized that direct management of Zambia's major hospitals by the Ministry of Health was inefficient, and that these institutions had to be given enough capacity to raise revenues from users, including prescription charges. This was a reversal of the free medical care policy.

Marmor (1997) warns of the dangers of *'commonplace and undifferentiated'* judgements of common ground, which might be tempting in the identification of 'inefficiency' as common to all these descriptions. The nature of the factors deemed to underlie inefficiency appear quite different, even comparing the broad groups of countries 'developed' and 'developing'. Given the differences in the objectives pursued, it is suggested that simply *transferring* the industrialised country version of the policy is likely to have pitfalls.

Can a model connecting policy with desired goals be discerned?

Two models of hospital autonomy can be identified. The first is based on an underlying model of *decentralisation*. Mills *et al.* (1990) have summarised the objectives of decentralisation:

On a philosophical and ideological level, decentralization has been seen as an important political ideal, providing the means for community participation and local self-reliance, and ensuring the accountability of government officials to the population. On a pragmatic level, decentralization has been seen as a way of overcoming institutional, physical and administrative constraints on development.

Since granting hospitals greater financial and managerial autonomy decentralises authority, the policy might be seen in these terms. This is implicit in the quote from ex-Zambian minister of health Kalumba above, and also from the following paragraph from the UK government's White Paper, which launched the reform of health services in the UK:

The government believes that self-ownership for hospitals will encourage a stronger sense of local ownership and pride, building on the enormous fund of goodwill that exists in local communities. It will stimulate the commitment and harness the skills of those who are directly responsible for providing services. Supported by a funding system in which successful hospitals can flourish, it will encourage local initiative and greater competition. All this in turn will ensure a better deal for the public, improving the choice and quality of the services offered and the efficiency with which those services are delivered. (Secretaries of State 1989: 22)

However, the latter quote makes the second model of hospital autonomy equally clear. The policy is intended to bring market forces to bear on hospitals. Although Enthoven (1985) did not himself propose the autonomous hospital component, the market-forces model of hospital autonomy arises from Enthoven's internal market concept. Enthoven argued that the contracting process itself (independent of the competitive environment) produces efficiency gains:

competitive tendering can be the entering wedge for a great deal of management improvement ... It requires management to develop a precise work statement for each department, including quality standards. Avoidable costs in other departments must be estimated ... Information and control systems must be established. Tendering requires a whole new style of management. (1985: 22)

And that greater managerial autonomy in an internal market environment has efficiency advantages:

managers would then be able to use resources most efficiently. They could buy services from producers who offered good value. They could use the possibility of buying outside as bargaining leverage to get better performance from their own providers. They could sell off assets such as valuable land in order to redeploy their capital most effectively. (1985: 22)

Hamblin (1998) suggests that equity goals are absent from the objectives of the competitive environment proposed (which are identified in the above quotation as choice, quality of services and efficiency). However, they can be judged implicitly present in the overall internal market design, as has been argued:

The chosen reform was to maintain tax-financed health care, but to introduce competition between suppliers ... Finance would continue to be raised through general taxation, but would be allocated to agents responsible for purchasing care. Allocation between agents would reflect medical need in local populations ... NHS equity goals of equal access could be maintained whilst introducing incentives provided by competition on the supply side. (Propper 1995)

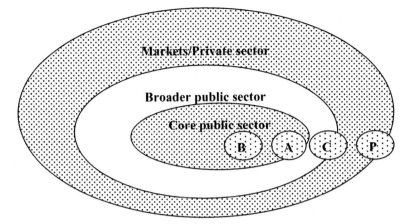

Figure 7.2 Incentive environments (from Harding and Preker 1988).

In a World Bank document, Harding and Preker (1998) develop the market-based conception of the purpose of hospital autonomy in a developing country context, and present the options for hospital arrangements as ranging from 'privatization' to 'corporatization', 'autonomization', and 'budgetary organizations' (labelled P, C, A and B in Figure 7.2). They argue: 'The incentives for efficient production are higher as you move out, and service delivery is often better there' (1998: 3), from which it may be deduced that the rationale for moving from B to A (for example) is to capture incentives associated with market forces.

However, in identifying degrees of privatisation, the model proposed is able to consider *degrees* to which the reform might be able to 'give increased decision making control to management of the organization, and attempt to create new incentives or accountability mechanisms to encourage management to use that autonomy to improve the performance of the facility' (1998: 5). It is argued that hospital arrangements can be classified according to the following scales: (1) the degree to which control is shifted to management; (2) the degree to which revenue is earned in a market; (3) the degree to which the public purse has ceased to be the 'residual claimant' on revenue flows; (4) the degree to which accountability for achieving objectives is based on hierarchy rather than regulation or contracting; and (5) the degree to which social functions delivered by the hospital are implicit and unfunded rather than specified and directly funded (for example, the extent to which catering for the poor is the responsibility of hospital or funder).

This market-forces-based model of hospital autonomy appears now to be the dominant one. It is clear that the model has widespread advocates and that, again, the World Bank is among them. Over and Watanabe (1998) provide a list of 35 World Bank hospital reform projects in 27 countries. These date from 1970 and may not all involve 'autonomy' or 'corporatization' elements but 20 projects post-date 1993, by which time hospital autonomy was clearly considered core to the World Bank's health sector reform agenda. A large number of countries can be identified as having implemented reforms affecting the autonomy of hospital management, including Zambia, Ghana, Kenya, Indonesia, Hong Kong, India, New Zealand and the UK (Hanson and McPake 1998). To what extent is the market-forces model supported by the evidence emerging from these countries?

First, it is important to note that there can be varying degrees to which autonomy is ceded to individual hospital facilities. In both Ghana and Zambia hospital boards are heavily constrained in their activities by central government and evaluations conclude that little real autonomy has been created, suggesting that neither decentralisation nor market-forces models of reform will predict significant effects (Weinberg 1993; McPake 1996; Larbi 1998; Kamwanga *et al.* 1999).

Secondly, the market-forces model of hospital autonomy presents particular theoretical difficulties, which have been most coherently dealt with by Propper (1995) for the British case. The problem is that the policy as implemented is intended to make hospitals behave in a more 'firm-like' way for the advantages of market forces to make themselves felt in the way envisaged. However, an autonomous hospital is not the 'residual claimant' to the surplus generated – thus its interest in profit seeking has to be queried. In addition to this, the financial regime is such that reserves cannot be carried over and profit-seeking pricing and cross-subsidy between activities are precluded. While hospitals are able to evade the pricing rules to some extent (Propper and Bartlett 1997), all this must attenuate the incentives to pursue quality and choice goals with an ultimate profit motivation. Furthermore, 'self-government' is highly circumscribed by the regulatory regime, and 'disinvestment' procedures leave a gap for political rather than market forces to determine outcome. Hence we are left to wonder why we might expect firm-like behaviour and benefits of market forces at all.

Applying these perspectives within the Harding and Preker framework, the mechanisms by which incentives (to efficiency, quality of care and patient choice) get stronger as we move towards the outer ovals of Figure 7.2 remain unarticulated, and it seems at least plausible that there are combinations of scales (1) to (5) which provide weaker efficiency incentives in the case of more autonomous hospitals than the 'budgetary organisation' point of comparison. For example, devolved authority and reliance on a contract basis of payment might entrench inefficient behaviour if not backed up by competent purchasing and monitoring. Harding and Preker (1998) themselves provide an outline of the constraints to good governance (or the match of managers' activities to the objectives of 'owners'– in this case government) in the hospital setting. Without competent purchasing, managers may simply be 'freed' to pursue goals of their choice, which may have little relationship with any of the goals of the reform. From this it might be concluded that the focus on strength of incentives is insufficient, rather the relevant question is: incentives to do what?

Does experience with the policy support the emerging model?

In general, evidence that hospital autonomy can help to achieve the generalised goals of efficiency, quality improvements and patient choice explicitly sought by '*Working for Patients*' in Britain, and implicitly by other countries (McPake 1996), is lacking. In the UK this is at least partly because very little research was done. The Conservative government was hostile to evaluation of the reforms, and hospitals were most able and most likely to make their data inaccessible to those researchers who could secure funds to investigate the issue (Hamblin 1998). In other countries, too, the failure to build an evaluative component into the reform programme is apparent. With respect to efficiency in the UK, there is some agreement that hospital productivity increases did occur following the reforms (Soderlund *et al.* 1997; Maniadakis *et al.* 1999), but dispute over whether these increases can be attributed to autonomous status. With respect to the other goals (quality and choice), there has been virtually no research (Hamblin 1998). In Hong Kong, too, evidence of both efficiency improvement and quality improvement is ambiguous, and there was a failure to collect case-mix controlled, baseline data with which to compare post-reform performance (Yip and Hsiao 1999). Bossert *et al.* (1996) failed to find efficiency improvement or quality trends or differences between autonomous and centrally controlled hospitals in Indonesia, but did find evidence that management systems had improved.

Where there is evidence of effectiveness is where reform has focused on resolving more specific problems. For example, in the UK waiting lists have declined and the introduction of day surgery has accelerated, but it is not clear that this is the effect of the hospital autonomy reform *per se*; more likely, it results from specific initiatives that may have been effective within the old system. In this case, data manipulation may have had some role to play (Harrison 1997). In Hong Kong, the problems of hospital overcrowding and staff attrition from the public sector have been improved, but this may be explained by improved funding to the hospital sector (Yip and Hsiao 1999).

While evidence of efficiency gains remains elusive, perverse incentives with equity implications can be discerned. British evidence gives some further insights into the difficulty. The incentives implicit in the new arrangements were no less capable of aligning in a perverse manner than those ruling previously. Prior to reform there were fears of 'cream skimming' or, more specifically, of attempts to avoid treating patients expected to incur high costs. In the event, perhaps because the reforms did not really imply the imposition of 'firm-like' behaviour on hospitals, there is little evidence of such effects (Hamblin 1998). However, hospitals are argued to have competed more energetically for 'extra-contractual referrals' (mainly patients referred across district boundaries) and for the contracts of general practitioner purchasers – both of which are considered to be exchanged in more competitive markets. As a result, it is alleged that those patients covered by a district health authority contract wait longer for treatment. Although evidence relating to this is anecdotal, it was sufficient to instigate an instruction to hospitals to pool waiting lists (of different purchasers) in July 1997 (Harrison 1998).

The underlying problem is that firm-like behaviour, even in an 'internal' and highly regulated market, may imply internal resource-allocation decisions motivated by revenue (if not profit) seeking rather than equity concerns. Propper and Bartlett (1997) deduce that, at least in the case of one hospital they studied, the dominant objective pursued was employment. This implies a concern with revenue but not cost.

Nevertheless, this degree of inequity is one with which most very poor countries would probably be happy to live with. The problem is that in these countries, public hospitals will often be expected to operate in both an internal and external market after reform. The external market arises from the heterogenous nature of health markets in which patients shop around among public and private, formal and informal providers; and in the concurrent introduction of user fees. Under these circumstances, equity concerns become far more serious.

In Indonesia, post reform, 30–80 per cent of hospital revenues are derived from fee income (Bossert *et al.* 1996). With effective measures to introduce more firm-like behaviour on the supply side and no equity constraint on the demand side, the conclusion that the poor are squeezed out of hospitals is hardly surprising. Even in much more constrained circumstances (in terms of the extent to which arrangements imply 'firm-like' incentives, and the level of income dependent on user fees), for example in Zambia, reallocation of resources towards those able to pay seems likely to be occurring (Kamwanga *et al.* 1999). Here, the incentives to generate surplus would appear strong – constraints to profit-seeking behaviour may be less effectively applied in poor countries. The ability to use revenues to supplement staff salaries, coupled in some cases with the increasing opportunities for corruption arising from higher revenues, may allow hospital autonomy to produce a more unattenuated, profit-driven hospital management strategy in poor countries. If surplus is most easily generated by concentrating hospital resources on those with the ability to pay, 'firm-like' behaviour will not advance equity-focused policy goals. Concerns that autonomy may effectively mean privatisation in such countries need to be taken seriously.

To what extent can 'lesson drawing' be concluded to be evident in the hospital autonomy case? The differences in the implications of the policy for developed and developing countries arise from the differences in the analysis of the problems of the hospital sectors of the two groups of countries. It would appear, again, that insufficient new policy design and prospective evaluation has taken place in transferring the strategy from industrialised to poor countries, and specifically, that the need to pursue the three goals of improving efficiency within hospitals, maintaining equity of access to hospital services, and reallocating public resources from hospitals to the rest of the health sector, has not been adequately recognised. Specifically, the public budget component of funding needs to be used in a manner that creates incentives for hospitals to meet the needs of the poor. This is challenging and requires much more attention.

One country that has aimed to ensure that the needs of the poor are backed by performance-related payment is Colombia (Yepes and Sanchez, in press). In Colombia, the public budget is now channelled through agencies that purchase services for a 'subsidised' population that has been means tested and subsequently targeted. These agencies can reallocate resources among providers and themselves compete for the custom of the subsidised population. However, it is too early to seek evidence as to whether this alternative model has delivered on the promise of its design, especially in the politically unstable context in which it has been applied.

Conclusions

This chapter has not aimed to explain or describe the policy process as policies are adopted by different countries. Rather, it has set itself the more limited objective of seeking to discern the extent of 'lesson drawing' as defined by Rose (1993) in this context. The conclusion reached is that, of the opposing fallacies identified by both Rose and Marmor at the beginning of this chapter (overlooking context and overemphasising context), policy development in developing countries tends to suffer more from the first. The introduction of policies that may be seen to work well elsewhere, but which have been inadequately contextualised imposes serious costs, and in many cases may be worse than 'no change'. In both attempts at 'lesson drawing' reviewed here, failure of contextualisation arose at the first hurdle such a process might present: are the problems tackled by the policy in other contexts, the same as those we identify here? Generalised answers, such as we are all concerned with efficiency, equity, quality and choice, are unhelpful. There is little common ground in the problems faced by the hospital sector in developed and developing countries; and there are key contextual differences between Uganda and the African countries on which models of user fee operation have been developed. Reform models are not adequately tailored to the fullest possible local understanding of potential linkages between policy and desired goals.

As reiterated above, this chapter has not attempted to lay blame or to further elucidate what kind of processes are going on, if 'lesson drawing' is not. The chapter may appear to be blaming such problems on the international agencies, and especially on the World Bank, which has figured prominently in both sections as one agency recommending reform. After all, such institutions might be more likely to be prone to Marmor's 'World Cup' fallacy given their international perspective and more limited familiarity with individual country circumstances than national governments.

In the case of Uganda's inappropriate user charge policy, this would be unfair. Evidence of attempts to base policy on a sensible situation analysis in the form of the Three Year Plan is clear, and an earlier World Bank health sector expenditure review (1991) contains elements of a similar analysis. In fact the Three Year Plan evidences several components of the 'lesson drawing' process. In this case, the problem appears rooted in Uganda's immature political structures and an essentially anarchic policy process (especially in the early 1990s). More appropriate models of reform were available to policy-makers and were rejected. The World Bank was not in the driving seat. Rather, it would seem that local interests – health management committees and health staff – seized on a policy model that suited their interests but had little prospect of meeting desired goals. In such circumstances, failures to articulate a clear and well-founded set of objectives for the policy are unsurprising.

In the case of hospital autonomy, the role of the World Bank and other international agencies associated with enthusiasm for the idea of hospital autonomy in developing countries *may* be more important – but this chapter has not explored that question carefully. Hospitals are complex organisations and industrialised countries are struggling to find ways to govern them effectively. It is clearly premature to seize on a particular model of reform and pronounce its advantages on a global basis – if this has, indeed, occurred.

This is not to argue that poor countries should be wedded to direct public management until industrialised countries find the 'right' way forward. As has been discussed, industrialised countries are not even aiming to solve the same problems that poor countries face. Rather, a plea for greater attention to the stages of new model design and prospective evaluation is being made. In particular, the reconciliation of the goals of increasing private finance, and creating more flexible hospital management without abandoning equity goals, require more creative policy design. What is needed, in developing countries facing the catalogue of problems in the hospital sector described, is reform design based on a revised model. This would ensure that hospitals face as strong incentives to meet the needs of those whose individual ability to pay is insufficient to pay fees, as they do for those who can pay. The first group are usually intended to be priority targets of the public budget. Colombia offers an approach that might provide an initial model. Most developing countries will find Colombia's specific approach too sophisticated, as they are likely to have difficulty means-testing their population and monitoring the activities of multiple purchasing agencies. In devising a new programme, they will need to search for simpler mechanisms for linking public payment to hospitals' performance in targeting the poorest.

NOTES

Barbara McPake is a member of the Health Economics and Financing Programme, which is supported by the UK Department for International Development.

1 The Bamako Initiative itself was launched in 1989 on the basis of pilot projects in Guinea and Benin. However, the model underpinning the Initiative was only fully articulated in retrospect – arguably, significantly changing the original notion.

2 From whatever range of providers is available. Even in remote rural areas this might offer choice between the nearest government clinic or NGO provider, more local drug shops or shops selling ordinary household items who stock some drugs, itinerant drug sellers and traditional practitioners.

3 The perspective of traditional welfare economics: the welfare of society is considered to increase if that of at least one person increases (by own estimation) and no other person's welfare diminishes.

4 Danish Red Cross drug supply support is not available to hospitals and the situation is somewhat different there.

8 Cost-effectiveness analysis and priority-setting: global approach without local meaning?

Lilani Kumaranayake and Damian Walker

The culture of international public health discourse and infectious disease can be characterised in part by the reigning logic of cost-effectiveness.

Henry and Farmer (1999)

Introduction

In recent years there has been a greater focus on the process of priority-setting between competing uses of resources, as many countries face increasing resource constraints in the health sector. For some countries, health care costs have risen rapidly due to the adoption of new and expensive technologies, and ageing populations. For others, fiscal constraints have arisen through a combination of weak economic performance, decreasing public health expenditures, and limited amounts of donor resources going to the health sector. The responses to the scarcity of resources have been varied, but all are encapsulated within a 'global culture of reform' (Yach and Bettcher 1998a).

Health sector reforms of public health service provision have been widely promoted, affecting the organisation, funding and management of health systems (Zwi and Mills 1995). Important components of health sector reform include 'defining priorities, refining policies and reforming the institutions through which those policies are implemented' (Cassels 1995). Limited health care budgets have emphasised the need for providers to use available resources more efficiently. Hence there has been a greater emphasis on explicit priority-setting to determine how resources are allocated between health interventions, as well as a call for improved accountability and transparency of decisions, which is part of both the national and international policy agenda.

Globalisation can be described as the 'process of increasing economic, political, and social interdependence and global integration that takes place as capital, traded goods, persons, concepts, images, ideas, and values diffuse across state boundaries' (Hurrell and Woods 1995). One of the critical implications of globalisation is that the 'link between the lives of individuals and the global context of development' is becoming stronger and the 'domestic and international spheres of public health policy are becoming more intertwined and inseparable' (Yach and Bettcher 1998a).

For more than thirty years, cost-effectiveness analysis (CEA) has been used to evaluate interventions within the health sector. One of the early applications of CEA was its use in looking at alternative ways of achieving similar health outcomes, focusing on those interventions that use the least resources to achieve the greatest gain. A global dimension to CEA and priority-setting, which we refer to as the *global approach to CEA*, is increasingly apparent, presenting a clear example of the growing interface between international and national policy processes. This global approach was spearheaded by the publication of the World Bank's 1993 *World development report* (WDR), and its background studies (Jamison *et al.* 1993; World Bank 1993). This was the first work that attempted comparisons both internationally (involving two or more countries) and globally (broader worldwide comparisons). The work is now being refined by the World Health Organisation (WHO).

The influence of CEA in health policy debates has arisen for a number of reasons. While priority-setting and planning have been emphasised in the health sector since the 1960s, the current prominence of CEA reflects the broader trend of evidence-based planning and priority-setting in the context of health sector reform (Garner *et al.* 1998). Second, the emergence of the World Bank, an institution dominated by economists, as the largest external donor to the health sector has led to a greater emphasis on economic approaches to priority-setting for low- and middle-income countries. The emergence of a global approach to CEA attempts to address the need for evidence where significant gaps in national data exist, or where available data lacks consistency.

While there has been an increased focus on CEA both within and across national settings, there remain questions regarding its appropriateness for policy-making. The global approach to CEA raises issues regarding its methods, the transferability of CEA across different settings, and the importance placed on CEA for local priority-setting. There is a clear concern that, in the push for increased standardisation and comparability of CEA, the global results have little relevance for local settings and policy processes. In this chapter we consider these issues in relation to low- and middle-income countries. We discuss the language of economic evaluation and the development of a global approach. We then consider the wider implications of the global perspective on cost-effectiveness and its meanings for national and local priority-setting.

Cost-effectiveness analysis in priority-setting

Cost-effectiveness analysis is a form of economic evaluation. The methods and tools of economic evaluation are rooted in the fundamental problem by which economists characterise decision-making: making choices between alternatives in the context of scarce resources. Within the scope of international and national public health, these choices are often framed in the debate as to which interventions are/should be a priority and which are considered essential.

The language of economic analysis

Economic evaluations use economic theory to develop a systematic framework by which to assess the relative costs and consequences of different interventions. In practice, this framework can be applied to a whole range of questions such as whether a new drug should be used for a particular treatment or whether freestanding or mobile clinics are the best way to deliver a particular service.

The advantage of such a framework is that it allows clear identification of the relevant alternatives and makes the viewpoint (e.g. whose perspective – the provider? The consumer? Society as a whole?) more explicit. The basic task of any economic evaluation is to identify, measure, value and compare the costs and consequences of the alternatives being considered (Drummond *et al.* 1997). The result of an economic evaluation is a ratio of numbers representing the cost per outcome of a particular alternative. More importantly it gives an idea of the relative magnitude of cost per outcome of the alternatives (e.g. is the difference really hundreds of dollars or a few cents?). Economic evaluation makes the comparisons between alternatives explicit and transparent, and as such, facilitates priority-setting and hence, resource allocation.

There are several types of economic evaluation, which differ in the way that outcomes or consequences are measured (see Box 8.1). In practice, there has been a blurring of the distinctions between CEA and cost-utility analysis (CUA), with the latter seen as an extension of the former (Musgrove 2000); hence, the literature on cost-effectiveness encompasses both these approaches.

It should be noted that the different types of economic evaluation serve different purposes, as described in Box 8.2. Cost-effectiveness analysis, based on 'natural units', primarily addresses technical (or operational) efficiency, in which analysts compare strategies to meet a given goal, i.e. how can you treat a certain number of patients? Cost-utility analysis allows more complex measures of outcomes, has a wider scope and can be

---

Box 8.1   Different types of economic evaluation.

Cost-minimisation analysis: two or more interventions that have identical outcomes (e.g. number of cases treated) are assessed to see which provides the cheapest way of delivering the same outcome.

Cost-effectiveness analysis: measures the outcome of approaches in terms of 'natural units', e.g. for HIV prevention, this could be the number of infections averted.

Cost-utility analysis: these evaluations use a measure of utility (reflecting people's preferences). The outcomes are then expressed in terms of measures such as quality-adjusted life-years (QALYs) or disability-adjusted life-years (DALYs).

Cost–benefit analysis: expresses outcomes (e.g. the number of lives saved) in terms of monetary units.

---

compared over different types of health interventions. However, this approach is still restricted to comparisons of programmes within the health sector. Therefore, within the health sector, the latter analyses can address questions of allocative efficiency, in which comparisons between

---

Box 8.2   Definitions of efficiency and economic evaluations.

Economic evaluation attempts to identify ways in which scarce resources can be efficiently employed. However, efficiency has two meanings.

First, there is *technical or operational efficiency*, which is a narrow definition as it concentrates on maximising the achievement of a given objective within a given budget, e.g. vaccination of children through fixed, outreach or mobile clinics. For this reason it is sometimes dubbed 'low level' efficiency. While all the different types of economic evaluations can be used to assess technical efficiency, this is not true for assessments of allocative efficiency.

Secondly, there is 'high level' efficiency defined as *allocative efficiency*. This describes the search for the optimal allocation of resources across a mix of programmes that cannot all be fully funded, to produce the greatest gain to society. In this broader definition of efficiency, different health care interventions with different objectives and outcomes are compared, and comparisons across sectors can be achieved, e.g. malaria control versus immunisation, health versus education. For this reason, cost-utility analysis can be used to assess allocative efficiency within the health sector, but cannot make comparisons with sectors beyond health, i.e. quasi-allocative assessments. However, cost–benefit analyses are capable of making assessments between different sectors because outcomes are monetised, i.e. allocative efficiency in its purest form.

---

competing programmes are made, i.e. how should the budget of a ministry of health be distributed between different programmes? In theory, cost–benefit analyses have the widest scope of all types of analyses because outcomes are monetised, enabling intersectoral comparisons, i.e. how should a government budget be distributed between different ministries. In practice, the valuation of health benefits is difficult, and preference for CEA over other methods for evaluating health care programmes has been emerging since the late 1970s in both developed and developing countries (Warner and Hutton 1980; Walker and Fox-Rushby, 2000).

A global approach

The development of a global approach to CEA and priority-setting can be characterised in three ways: first, the centralised development of new methods by international agencies, spearheaded by the World Bank, that are then advocated for use in national planning and priority-setting; secondly, the generalisation of CEA between settings, which attempts to use information from one setting or country to generalise to another and so act as a source of input into individual country's priority-setting processes; and, thirdly, the generation of globally applicable cost-effectiveness results, which is done by producing global or regional cost-effectiveness estimates that can then be applied to global priority-setting for international public health resources within and between countries. In this section we discuss the evolution of these different characteristics.

New tools and new approaches: DALY-based CEA

In 1993 the WDR (World Bank 1993) presented a global priority-setting exercise which led to recommendations about essential public health and clinical services packages for low- and middle-income countries. The WDR was sponsored by the World Bank and WHO, and was the follow-up to previous analyses of health sector problems and priorities. The key feature of the exercise was the presentation of a new methodology by which to determine national priorities for resource allocation based on the burden of disease and CEA results.[1]

The WDR applied the concept of disability-adjusted life-years (DALYs), developed by Murray (1994), to measure the burden of various diseases. The WDR methodology was derived in part to improve the transparency and comparability of CEA. A discussion of the DALY is presented in Box 8.3. The WDR advocated a minimum (or 'essential health') package of public health interventions and clinical services that

---

Box 8.3   The DALY (disability-adjusted life-year).

DALYs are constructed from estimates of years of life lost due to premature mortality and of healthy life lost due to disability, weighted for severity
(Murray 1994). The establishment of priorities for low- and middle-income
countries is done by estimating the cost-effectiveness of interventions in
order to obtain a cost per DALY averted for each type of intervention.
Different health care interventions are ranked according to their cost per
DALY averted. Then an estimate of the global burden of the disease is
made in terms of DALYs lost, and the potential health gains associated with
different interventions is calculated as a proportion of this global burden
of disease. These calculations then form the basis of determining priority
interventions.

There has been wide debate on the DALY approach (e.g. Barker and Green
1996; Barendregt et al. 1996; Anand and Hanson 1997). Most substantially,
there was concern that the tables produced a general priority list for developing countries, without taking into account local factors. The background
work for the WDR included the CEA of 50 interventions on 25 major diseases or disease clusters. No consistent approach seems to have been used
across the studies and they vary according to time, context and perspective
(Paalman et al. 1998), such that CEA ratios were reported to vary by two- to
tenfold depending on local factors (Jamison and Mosely 1991). The costing
approach has also been questioned as the costs were considered to be similar
across all low- and middle-income countries. Finally, it is not clear whether
the league table presented average or marginal CEA ratios. This means it is
unclear what happens to these ratios as coverage increases, and more importantly it is unclear what basic public health infrastructure was assumed to be
in place (Mooney and Creese 1993).

---

should be financed by public resources. A 'good buy' is one that is both
cost-effective and addresses a large burden of disease. Table 8.1 presents
the essential package of public health interventions developed for the
WDR.

Ideally, such a priority-setting exercise would use the same methodology for each setting but use country-specific data, allowing more relevant
country-specific priorities to be identified. The legacy of the WDR exercise and its background studies (Jamison et al. 1993) is the DALY, which
is used both as a tool to estimate the relative burden of different illness
and as an outcome measure in CEA analysis. This method of matching
the most cost-effective interventions to deal with those illnesses that contribute the most burdens was then advocated as the means of selecting
priority areas for investment of resources.

There has been some use of these tools in national settings since 1993.
More than twenty country studies have been, or are currently being,
undertaken to quantify national health burdens in terms of DALYs, and

Table 8.1 *Cost-effectiveness of the health interventions (and clusters of interventions) included in the minimum package of health services in low- and middle-income countries*

Country group and component of package	Annual cost US$ (1990) Taken from Table 4.7, 1993 WDR		Annual cost US$ (2000) Using 3.2 per cent inflation rate	
	Cost per DALY	Cost per capita	Cost per DALY	Cost per capita
LOW INCOME				
Public health				
EPI Plus	12–17	0.5	17–24	0.7
School health program	20–25	0.3	27–34	0.4
Other public health programs (including family planning, health and nutrition information)		1.4		1.9
Tobacco and alcohol control program	35–55	0.3	48–68	0.4
AIDS prevention program	3–5	1.7	4–7	2.3
Subtotal	14	4.2		5.8
Clinical services				
Short-course chemotherapy for tuberculosis	3–5	0.6	4–7	0.8
Management of the sick child	30–50	1.6	41–68	2.2
Prenatal and delivery care	30–50	3.8	41–68	5.2
Family planning	20–30	0.9	27–41	1.2
Treatment of STDs	1–3	0.2	1–4	0.3
Limited Care	200–300	0.7	274–480	1.0
Subtotal		7.8		10.7
Total		12.0		16.4
MIDDLE INCOME				
Public health				
EPI Plus	25–30	0.8	34–41	1.1
School health program	38–43	0.6	44–63	0.8
Other public health programs (including family planning, health and nutrition information)		3.1		4.2
Tobacco and alcohol control program	45–55	0.3	62–75	0.4
AIDS prevention program	13 – 18	2.0	18–29	2.7
Subtotal		6.8		9.3
Clinical services				
Short-course chemotherapy for tuberculosis	5–7	0.2	7–10	0.3

Table 8.1 (*cont.*)

Country group and component of package	Annual cost US$ (1990) Taken from Table 4.7, 1993 WDR		Annual cost US$ (2000) Using 3.2 per cent inflation rate	
	Cost per DALY	Cost per capita	Cost per DALY	Cost per capita
Management of the sick child	50–100	1.1	68–137	1.5
Prenatal and delivery care	60–110	8.8	82–151	12.1
Family planning	100–150	2.2	137–205	3.0
Treatment of STDs	10–15	0.3	14–21	0.4
Limited Care	400–600	2.1	548–822	2.9
Subtotal	133	14.7		20.1
Total		21.5		29.4

Source: The US$ 1990 figures are taken from World Bank (1993), US$ 2000 figures are taken from Kumaranayake (2000).
Note: Cost per DALY is rounded to the nearest dollar; cost per capita is rounded to the nearest tenth of a dollar. These are the units in which the original numbers are presented. EPI Plus = Expanded Programme on Immunisation.

to guide national priority-setting (Vos *et al.* forthcoming). Much of this reflects the financial and technical assistance that agencies such as the World Bank have given in promoting the adoption of basic packages of cost-effective interventions (Barillas 1999).

The work of the WDR has also influenced the presentation of cost-effectiveness results in both academic and donor settings. Many of the recent publications dealing with CEA in low- and middle-income countries now attempt to present results in terms of DALYs (e.g. Gilson *et al.* 1997; Goodman *et al.* 1999; Soderlund *et al.* 1999). In addition to the World Bank, other donor organisations are also trying to integrate the use of these CEA concepts in their planning processes: in many recent project memoranda, which are part of the project approval process, the economic and financial appraisal provides information on the cost per DALY saved by the project. For example, a recently approved British project on the prevention and care of HIV/AIDS in China estimated the cost per DALY saved by the project to be between US $5–11 (DFID 1999b).

Generalised CEA

While it is desirable to have country-specific data in order to generate meaningful CEA, the costs of overcoming current data limitations are substantial. Given the paucity of CEA data in the developing world, it is extremely difficult and very expensive to acquire data for each country. Accordingly, there have been attempts to generalise the results of specific studies to other settings. Following the reorganisation of the WHO in 1998, a new programme – 'Choosing Interventions: Costs, Effectiveness, Quality and Ethics' (EQC) – was established as part of the Global Programme on Evidence for Health Policy. EQC aims to collaborate with international organisations to provide international guidelines for CEA intended to provide a more standardised evidence-base, and addressing some of the concerns surrounding the WDR.

Murray *et al.* (2000) describe the development of WHO's international guidelines. Emphasis is placed on promoting a more global approach to CEA, which moves away from considering highly context-specific factors, to a more generalisable CEA that provides information on the relative costs and health benefits of different interventions 'that are meant to contribute through multiple channels to a more informed debate on resource allocation priorities' (Murray *et al.* 2000). They suggest that general perceptions of cost-effectiveness (e.g. which interventions are cost-effective or not) can have far-reaching influence on policy formulation. The focus of this work has now moved squarely into the realm of allocative rather than technical efficiency, centring on resource allocation among competing health sector interventions. Two key propositions underlie the development of the guidelines:

1. CEA should be done based on average rather than marginal approaches,[2] without assuming that there are any existing interventions in place (and thus assumptions regarding the level of infrastructure). This would allow for greater transferability of the results.

2. The results of CEA should be presented in a single global league table, with mutually exclusive interventions.[3] Interventions whose cost-effectiveness ratios are dominated by other interventions (e.g. more expensive and less effective) will not be listed in the league table.

Clearly, there are many context-specific factors that influence the results of CEA. A possible strategy for developing a global league table would be to define a limited set of average health system and epidemiological contexts, allowing comparisons to be more informative (Murray *et al.* 2000). For example, low- and middle-income settings in different regions could be used to characterise different contexts. The results of such an exercise could then be used to derive algorithms that would select interventions subject to budget constraints and the main sources of disease burden in a particular setting (Murray *et al.* 1994). This work, therefore, represents a refinement and extension of the methods used for the WDR. Again, the focus of these priority-setting choices is maximising population health status measured by both the DALY and its variant the DALE – disability-adjusted life expectancy (Murray and Lopez 1997).

There are a number of dangers with this approach. There has been much previous discussion about whether population health status (as measured by DALYs) and the burden of disease are appropriate for use in priority-setting, particularly as the latter emphasises disease reduction as the only goal of health services (Mooney and Wiseman 2000). However, there are further reasons for concern about this type of information if used for global rather than just national policy. First, it assumes that there are interventions that will be exclusively good or bad. In practice, however, factors determining effectiveness vary from context to context. In a study looking at the replication of peer education interventions for HIV prevention, Kumaranayake *et al.* (2000b) found that, even within the same country, there was a 2- to 3-fold difference across different cities, and that the cost-effectiveness varied substantially, reflecting differences in project implementation, motivation of project staff, capacity of staff to reach target populations and heterogeneity of target populations. In reality, there may be very few interventions that are truly 'dominant' in all settings. Secondly, the resource allocation modelling which is advocated, while attempting to cost interventions from first principles, ignores the broader health systems context in which interventions are operating. The ability to shift resources is in itself not cost-less. Ignoring substantial deviations in existing capacity and infrastructure may mean a significant difference between the 'theoretical' CEA based on this global approach and one achievable in any setting. Thirdly, emphasis on such a global league table in order to choose how to allocate resources ignores the very critical investments which must be made to the basic infrastructure of a health system, and which vary according to country and location.

Global priority-setting

In addition to the focus on national priority-setting, there are now greater efforts to prioritise international public health resources as well as raising additional funds for defined priority areas. Global priority-setting has risen to prominence amidst calls for stronger global action and co-operation to address health problems that go beyond the scope of national governments (UNDP 1999). The globalisation of public health risks includes threats of violence, fire-arms, drug-trafficking, communicable diseases and environmental degradation (Berlinguer 1999). A central feature of emerging and re-emerging epidemics such as HIV, malaria and tuberculosis is their transnational nature (Henry and Farmer 1999).

Critics have argued that part of the failure to deal with these epidemics is that, unless there is an urgent local need, the long-term implications of transnational diseases are rarely addressed (Horton 1995).

Concurrently, globalisation is also causing greater interdependence among national health systems: 'No one country can undertake effective public health actions in isolation' (Barillas 1999). There has also been a higher profile for global institutions that are involved in public health, including the World Bank, WHO and the proliferation of institutions with greater global reach such as international health NGOs (Buse and Walt this volume). The lack of progress regarding these global health threats has led to calls for improved global governance and definition of global public goods such as the control of infectious diseases (Turmen 1999). The substantial global problem of malaria and HIV/AIDS has led to the formation of international campaigns such as 'Roll-Back Malaria' and the International Partnership Against AIDS in Africa (Nabarro and Tayler 1998; UNAIDS 1999). Both campaigns are attempting to mobilise resources for their respective diseases and scale-up activity in order to meet ambitious targets for improvement over the next 5–10 years. Against this background, the role of global priority-setting is evident.

In contrast to the previous focus of CEA, where problems were framed in terms of national boundaries, leading to 'localised treatment and localised funding of treatment' (Henry and Farmer 1999), there is now growing discussion regarding the growing utilisation of CEA to determine global priorities. Most notably, in 1996 the WHO's Ad Hoc Committee on Priorities for Health Research and Development used DALY-based CEA as one of two criteria to assess the potential of future R & D efforts.[4] Estimates of the cost per DALY were made for a variety of possible interventions which research might discover, such as an HIV vaccine. Interventions were considered to be excellent buys if the cost per DALY averted by the implemented intervention was less than US $30 and a good buy if less than US $150 (Ad Hoc Committee 1996).

CEAs are also being undertaken in a regional or transnational context, primarily relying on modelling to develop their outcome or effectiveness estimates. Goodman *et al.* (1999) explored the cost-effectiveness of alternative malaria prevention and treatment measures for sub-Saharan Africa using existing data from settings within sub-Saharan Africa. There have also been a number of studies focusing on different interventions to prevent mother-to-child transmission of HIV, which have been produced for sub-Saharan Africa as a whole or a 'typical' country (Mansergh *et al.* 1998; Marseille *et al.* 1998; Marseille *et al.* 1999). Much of this work also attempts to generalise local data from one setting to a broader context.

The global approach to CEA: opportunities and constraints

Given that the rise in prominence of CEA in priority-setting was also synonymous with the DALY-based CEA methodology, there has been an entangling of arguments regarding the methods of the DALY-based approach and the use of CEA in general. In this section we review the use of CEA in priority-setting, considering the opportunities and constraints associated with it. While discussing the global approach to priority-setting and the DALY-based CEA, we will not explore the technical debates regarding the construction and assumptions of the DALY (e.g. life expectancies, discounting, and age-weighting), but rather focus on the policy and priority-setting dimensions.

CEA in health sector decision-making: back to its roots

The possible ways of using CEA in decision-making have been generally described by Power and Eisenberg (1998) as:

1. Health systems policy: using CEA to look at the implementation and delivery of activities within the health sector (e.g. who should deliver and how?).
2. Public policy/priority-setting: using CEA to inform decision-makers about different interventions that are selected for public financing (and/or provision).

In health systems policy, CEA is used to consider how to achieve the best gain for a given set of resources (or the *technical* efficiency of interventions). In the 1970s and early 1980s, the use of CEA in decision-making focused to a large extent on these technical issues – looking at alternative ways of achieving the same outcome. Together with evidence on effectiveness, some of this work has been quite influential in changing methods of delivery of interventions. For example, cost-effectiveness considerations were quite influential in switching from the long-course to the short-course chemotherapy treatment for tuberculosis, despite the fact that the drug cost was substantially higher for the short course (Barnum 1986; Murray *et al.* 1991).

Use of CEA to consider priority-setting became more prominent as the level of resources allocated to the health sector started to stagnate or decline in the early 1980s. During this period, substantial methodological developments were made in common measures such as the QALY in order to be able to compare and choose across different health sector alternatives (*allocative* efficiency). By the early 1990s, there was also substantial debate among economists about how to actually use the CEA results to inform policy-making, i.e. does a cost-effectiveness ratio of US $50 per life-year saved represent 'value for money'? How can this influence policy decisions?

Economists have been searching for systematic ways of identifying, pooling and summing up evidence from different studies (Jefferson *et al.* 1996). A central question remains, however, concerning how a decision-maker actually chooses from a ranking of interventions based on CEA? Do they choose a specific intervention or set of interventions with the lowest CEA ratios? Clearly, how interventions are defined and described is important, and must be viewed in terms of complementary interventions that are also necessary for their success. However, in the absence of formalised tables, implicit comparisons between studies are likely to take place (Mason *et al.* 1993). The danger of league tables is that greater prominence is given to the ranking of results than is justified by the heterogeneity of study methods. Is it useful to make pairwise comparisons between interventions or do we really need to consider the entire package or programme of interventions subject to a specific resource constraint (Drummond *et al.* 1993; Birch and Gafni 1994)? One outcome of this debate was the call to improve the comparability and transparency of economic evaluations, so that CEA ratios generated from different studies were somewhat comparable in the methodology used to derive them. It was also in this environment that the DALY-based CEA approach was derived, emphasising a new way of choosing priorities by looking at both the epidemiological burden as measured by the DALY and the cost-effectiveness of particular interventions.

CEA in policy and priority-setting processes

Concerns have been expressed about the promotion of a mechanistic use of CEAs in priority-setting, using the technical rankings to dominate the decision-making process (whether as a consequence of matching to the burden of disease, or simply by choosing priority interventions from a league table according to some budget constraint).

First, CEA is a tool primarily concerned with efficiency, focusing on specific health interventions rather than population-based interventions. This means that it is not able to explicitly consider equity issues or focus on interventions that give priority to vulnerable groups or the poor (Gilson 1998). Gwatkin and Guillot (1998) contend that: 'the fact that the most efficient interventions tend to specifically benefit the poor is more a result of coincidence than of principle'. The focus on specific health interventions means that CEA does not allow for broader and multi-sectoral action to secure health improvements (Gilson 1998). This runs counter to the growing links between separate health and disease challenges that are presented by the process of globalisation. The focus on specific interventions also underplays the importance of health infrastructure including water and sanitation improvements. A simple ranking of cost-effectiveness ignores the issues of existing infrastructure and capacity, unless the health system can actually 'offer any of the interventions on the list without interfering with the capacity to administer others' (Musgrove 2000). Murray *et al.* (1994) estimated that a model which would also allow improvement and expansion of a health system infrastructure would lead to a 40 per cent higher health gain for a so called 'typical' sub-Saharan African country.

While there is clearly a role for CEA in considering the relative extent of resources and outcomes for different interventions, the DALY-based CEA approach, where interventions are chosen on the basis of the burden of disease as well as CEA, has provoked much ire. The focus on improving overall population health status within a DALY-based CEA system has meant there is greater focus on mortality and morbidity rather than on broader public health goals such as improvement of equity. It is also important to understand that the establishment of priorities is a political process. The DALY-based CEA approach has been labelled 'disease focused, efficiency driven, top-down and technocratic in orientation' (Tollman and Hsiao 1998) with a rather 'naïve view of the policy-making process' (Mills 1997b).

An application of CEA in actual policy-making processes is exemplified by the Oregon experience of priority-setting. In 1994, the state of Oregon introduced explicit rationing for its Medicaid population with a list of 743 rank ordered medical conditions and treatments that would be used to determine the benefit package Medicaid recipients would receive. Initially, the list of conditions was based on a CEA ranking; this list was then revised through a process of community consultations. The final list was very different from the initial CEA ranking. On one hand, the evidence from Oregon suggests that CEA had a very limited impact on priority-setting. However, from a broader perspective, we can see that the process of using CEA brought the concepts of scarcity and choice to the forefront of the debate. These are the basic blocks of economic theory, and the experience from Oregon has shown that the framework for analysis has been used to allocate resources, but the values, rather than coming from economics, have come from the community and political leadership.

So what is the role for CEA in policy-making processes? 'Stripped of its trappings, CEA is in essence a navigational aid, a decision tool that allows for clearer explication of sorting of economic and outcomes information ... Help[ing] decision-makers understand the resources required to achieve the outcomes that may result from alternative decisions and actions' (Power and Eisenberg 1998). Clearly, the use of CEA in policy-making is not straightforward. It raises many ethical and political issues about how CEA is used (Williams 1992). It is clear that CEA processes, while providing a framework by which to consider alternatives, are not value-free when related to priority-setting. The choice of alternatives is a political process and naturally involves a range of stakeholders; techno-cratic approaches are not value-free. Obviously, cost-effectiveness is only one source of information needed for decision-making – factors such as the quality of life in a community, improving equity and reducing poverty can lead to very different choices, relative to interventions chosen solely on the basis of efficiency.

Consideration of a global approach

Given this perspective on the use of CEA in decision-making, what are the issues for a more global approach to CEA? In terms of the new methods, the DALY-based CEA, along with other CEA methods, has 'the potential to make more explicit priority resource allocation choices for improving health status' (Tollman and Hsiao 1998). But there is a clear concern that in the push for increased standardisation and comparability of CEA, the global results have little relevance for local settings.

A key concern remains the ability to generalise or transfer results of CEA between settings. There are a range of technical issues regarding the way that the cost-effectiveness ratios are converted for comparability (e.g. exchange/purchasing power, time units, average rather than marginal approaches), but we will focus on the broader issues of interpretation and use of CEA across different settings.

First, it is very clear that CEA and the resulting ratios are very context-specific, which limits the use of league-tables cross-nationally. Clearly, first one needs data, but secondly one needs to consider how these data are shaped by the context they come from. In particular, factors such as the unit costs or prices of resources, prevalence, incidence and natural history of many diseases, and practices used in one setting, may not be directly relevant from more global scenarios to local national settings (Bryan and Brown 1998). 'Many cost-effective interventions achieve less than their predicted effectiveness because of the limitations imposed by failures of systems or the behaviour of people' (Janovsky and Cassels 1996).

There is a tension between CEA that is general enough to be inter-pretable in a range of settings, and CEA that takes into account the local context and so is useful for particular issues within that context. Moreover, cultural, economic, political, environmental, behavioural and infrastructural differences will also impact on the group of interventions chosen (Paalman et al. 1998). The results of any priority-setting exercise are location- , time- and group-specific (Murray 1994). Attempts at generalising CEA must also be very careful in interpreting application to particular settings. Similarly, regional or global CEA must reflect the uncertainty that is inherent in their structure; a sensible presentation and use of results should present the results in terms of 'realistic ranges rather than simple point estimates' (Goodman et al. 1999). The results of generalised CEA and global/regional CEA should be taken as such, and are valuable in thinking about relative resource allocation from an international context. However, the translation of these results into national policy-making processes requires careful consideration of just how transferable this information is likely to be for each setting.

Conclusions

After reviewing the experiences of priority-setting and CEA, it is clearly important to have 'global methods' but 'local applications' of these methods. The experience from Oregon suggests that: 'innovation is fundamentally a local matter, one of adapting ambitious hopes to local constraints and opportunities' (Jacobs et al. 1999). It also suggests that the real contribution of economic evaluation was in developing a consensus on the need to set priorities in a more transparent fashion. We must also remember that CEA is fundamentally a tool by which to assist decision-making rather than a solution to health problems. There has been discussion that the tools are not mature enough to guide decision-making, hence we must be aware of not expecting too much from the tool in the first place. The experience with CEA suggests that what is important is learning about relative ranges, rather than aiming for precision, which both the data and tool are not designed for. CEA seems to be appropriate for policy development through providing information on particular ways of delivering interventions at a group or disease cluster (e.g. technical efficiency), but it is less precise about allocative efficiency across the sector. We would argue, in particular, that CEA does not take the politics out of policy-making, but rather it provides a framework to consider alternatives. It is an element in the process of overall priority-setting, rather than a mechanistic way to select alternatives. Thus, CEA serves as a guide for decision-makers regarding relative resource requirement for different interventions, and their possible impacts. It is from this perspective that CEA can be generalised across settings and indeed have local meaning.

The global approach to CEA, however, has meant that CEA has moved from a means to consider technical efficiency issues to also considering broader resource allocation issues. In this latter situation, CEA can no longer be used mechanistically to produce results or rankings of interventions, but rather must take into account the wider political processes that are part of the process of priority-setting. To attempt to divorce one from the other will make CEA less, rather than more, relevant for both global and local priority-setting.

NOTES

Lilani Kumaranayake and Damian Walker are members of the Health Economics and Financing Programme that is funded by the Department for International Development of the United Kingdom and based at the London School of Hygiene and Tropical Medicine. Lilani Kumaranayake is also a member of the Centre on Globalisation, Environmental Change and Health. We would like to thank our colleagues in the Health Policy Unit for their comments and suggestions during the drafting of this chapter, and in particular Suzanne Fustukian, Kelley Lee, and Anne Mills who commented on earlier versions of this chapter.
1 Although labelled CEA, strictly the methodology adopts a CUA approach, and is thus capable of comparing outcomes across different health sector interventions.
2 Average cost is calculated by dividing total cost, including capital and recurrent resources, by the total output. Marginal cost is calculated by dividing the cost of the additional (usually only recurrent) resources required to either expand an existing service or introduce a new one, by the total output associated with this investment. Hence the estimation of marginal costs often excludes existing capital outlays, which can result in underestimating the true cost of an intervention.
3 It assumes that interventions are independent of each other.
4 The other criterion was the probability of successful development.

KEY READINGS

Bryan, S. and Brown, J. 1998, 'Extrapolation of cost-effectiveness information to local settings', *Journal of Health Services Research and Policy* 3 (2): 108–12.

Goodman, C. A., Coleman, P. G. and Mills, A. 1999, 'Cost-effectiveness of malaria control in sub-Saharan Africa', *The Lancet* 354: 378–85.

Murray, C. J. L., Evans, D. B., Acharya, A. and Baltussen, R. M. P. M. 2000, 'Development of WHO guidelines on generalised cost-effectiveness analysis', *Health Economics* 9 (2): 235–51.

Paalman, M., Bekedam, H., Hawken, L. and Nyheim, D. 1998, 'A critical review of priority-setting in the health sector: the methodology of the 1993 World Development Report', *Health Policy and Planning* 13 (1): 13–31.

World Bank 1993, *World development report 1993: investing in health*, New York: Oxford University Press.

Part II

Global rhetoric and individual realities: linking violence against women and reproductive health

Susannah H. Mayhew and Charlotte Watts

Introduction

Violence against women (VAW) and poor reproductive health[1] are two issues that place a substantial burden worldwide on the health of women. Both are global in many ways, cutting across national, socio-economic and cultural boundaries. Both VAW and reproductive health have received substantial attention in the increasingly globalised health and development debates of the last decade. There are important connections between the two issues – VAW has a range of reproductive health consequences, and violence is frequently used to control women's sexuality and/or fertility. There have also been a number of similarities in the advocacy processes that resulted in the international recognition of both issues (including the co-ordination between and networking of national and international women's groups). There are also many potential linkages in the delivery of interventions to address both issues (most importantly, the empowerment of women).

This chapter starts by presenting evidence on the global burden of sexual and domestic violence against women, and its relationship to reproductive health. We then chart the evolution of both issues within the United Nations (UN) human rights, health and development agendas. We illustrate how the diversification of actors, the end of the cold war, and the strengthening of networks and linkages between different national and regional women's groups facilitated the development of a strong global women's advocacy movement that was able to influence the global agenda. The opportunities and potential difficulties associated with translating the resulting global rhetoric into an operational reality at the national level are discussed. We compare the actors and processes involved at the national and global level, and discuss how international donor agendas may influence for better or worse the content of national policy. We conclude by highlighting the ongoing importance of the women's movement, and suggest that there may be a key role for some of the regional alliances, which developed as part of the global advocacy initiatives, to play in contextualising and operationalising the gains made at a global level.

The global burden of domestic and sexual violence against women

The term 'violence against women' refers to many forms of harmful behaviour directed at women and girls because of their sex. The UN Declaration adopted by the UN General Assembly in 1993 officially defines violence against women to be:

any act of gender-based violence that results in, or is likely to result in, physical, sexual or mental harm or suffering to women, including threats of such acts, coercion or arbitrary deprivation of liberty, whether occurring in public or in private life. (Article 1, UN Declaration on the Elimination of Violence Against Women)

This definition reflects the increasing consensus that VAW should be considered within a gender framework, because ultimately its origins stem from women's and girls' subordinate status in society. Article 2 of the UN Declaration further clarifies this definition by specifying that it includes acts of physical, sexual and psychological violence in the family and the community, spousal battering, sexual abuse of female children, dowry-related violence, rape (including marital rape), and traditional practices harmful to women, such as female genital mutilation. It also includes non-spousal violence, sexual harassment and intimidation at work and in school, trafficking in women, forced prostitution, and violence perpetrated or condoned by the state, such as rape in war (Heise *et al.* 1999).

There is a range of forms of VAW that are specific to particular cultures or geographic regions. This includes dowry-related murders, honour killings of females, the trafficking of women for sex, and female genital cutting – a procedure prevalent in a number of sub-Saharan African countries, which involves the partial or total removal of the external female genitalia (WHO/FRH 1997).

Although violence affects both males and females, there are important differences between the forms of violence that women and men experience, and their consequences. Men most commonly experience violence outside their homes either from men they do not know, from casual acquaintances or during conflict. In contrast, women and girls are most likely to experience violence from a family member or intimate partner. For example, in Canada women are five to ten times more likely to suffer abuse from family members as compared to men (Statistics Canada

1998). The response of society to the different types of violence is also very different: while street violence is considered a crime and state intervention is seen as legitimate, many governments have been reluctant to legislate or act against violence perpetrated by someone related to or intimate with a woman. This is in part because domestic violence is often considered as being a private matter, out of the realm of state intervention.

This chapter focuses mainly on sexual and domestic violence against women, as these forms of violence are most prevalent. Domestic abuse may take many forms, including physical violence, forced sex, psychological harassment, and economically disempowering forms of abuse. Data on the extent of domestic violence is limited, with different studies using different samples and different working definitions of violence. Nevertheless, population-based studies conducted in fifty countries in both developing and industrialised countries indicate that globally, between 20 and 50 per cent of women have been physically assaulted by an intimate male partner at least once in their lives (WHO/FRH 1997; Heise *et al.* 1999) (Table 9.1). This growing body of evidence illustrates how partner violence occurs in all countries, and transcends socio-economic and cultural boundaries.

Rape is also a common occurrence worldwide. It has been estimated that one in five women worldwide has experienced rape in her lifetime (WHO/FRH 1997; Heise *et al.* 1999). Data on sexual abuse, particularly during childhood, are limited, but there is evidence to suggest that it is common. Although rape is variously defined across cultures, the degree to which young girls are vulnerable to abuse can be appreciated by assessing the extent to which women report that their first sexual experience was unwanted or forced (Table 9.2).

In war, the extent of rape can reach extremes, yet, until recently, it was an under-reported aspect of military conflict. The wars in the former Yugoslavia and Rwanda have focused attention on the use of rape as a deliberate, systematic strategy to undermine community bonds and weaken resistance to aggression. Estimates of the number of women raped during the 1992–5 conflict in Bosnia-Herzegovina vary from 20,000 to 50,000, averaging 1.2 per cent of the total pre-war female population. This is not a new occurrence; rape has also been used as a strategy of war in many previous conflicts, including Korea in the Second World War, the independence war in Bangladesh, and civil war such as in Liberia, Uganda and Rwanda (Swiss and Giller 1993). Conflict often results in refugees, which also places women and children in a situation rendering them vulnerable to increased risk of violence (UNHCR 1995). This risk is likely to persist after the conflict is over, fuelled by the presence of firearms and other weapons. It has been suggested that there is also an

Table 9.1 *Selected studies on the global prevalence of physical violence against women by an intimate male partner*

Country and date of study	Sample	Questions asked	Evidence
Cambodia 1996	Nationally representative sample of 1,374 women and 1,286 men aged 15–49	Modified CTS	16% of women report ever being physically abused by a spouse; 8% report being injured
Canada 1993	National random sample of ever-married women 18 and above ($N = 12,300$)	Multiple questions on specific acts	29% of adult women report ever being physically assaulted by an intimate partner; 3% in past 12 months
Chile 1993	Representative sample of women, aged 22–55, from Santiago, in a relationship for more than two years ($N = 1000$)	Multiple questions on specific acts	26% report at least one episode of violence by a partner, 11% report at least one episode of severe violence and 15% of women report at least one episode of less severe violence
Egypt 1995	Nationally representative sample of ever-married women, aged 15–49 ($N = 7121$)	Gate (screening) question – from the time you were married has anyone ever beaten you? CTS, gate – any experience of battering in previous years	34% of women report being beaten by their husband at some point in their marriage
Korea 1992	National stratified random sample ($N = 707$)	CTS, gate – any experience of battering in previous years	38% of wives report being physically abused by their spouse in the last year.
Mexico 1997	Representative sample of ever married/partnered women from Metropolitan Guadalajara ($N = 650$)	Definitions and questions not stated	27% report at least one episode ever of physical violence by a partner; 15% report physical violence within the last year

Table 9.1 (*cont.*)

Country and date of study	Sample	Questions asked	Evidence
Nicaragua 1996	Representative sample of ever-married women, aged 15–49, from Nicaragua's second largest city, León (N = 360)	CTS	52.2% report ever being physically abused by a partner at least once; 27% report physical abuse in the last year
South Africa 1999 Eastern Cape Mpumalanga Northern Province	Random sample of women 18–49 (N = 403) (N = 428) (N = 475)	Multiple questions on specific acts	26.8% ever physical abuse and 10.9% in last year (Eastern Cape); 28.4% ever and 11.9% last year (Mpumalanga) 19.1% ever and 4.5% last year (N. Province)
Switzerland 1997	National sample of women, aged 20–60, in a relationship (N = 1500)	Modified CTS	12.6% report being physically assaulted ever and 6.3% in past 12 months
Uganda 1997	Representative sample of women aged 20–44 and their partners in two districts, Masaka and Lira (N = 1660)	Questions on beating, slapping, kicking or physically harming	57.9% report being beaten by a partner, or physically harmed by a partner; 41% of men report beating their partner
United Kingdom 1993	Random sample of women in the London Borough of Islington (N = 430)	Multiple questions on specific acts	30% report ever being physically assaulted by partner or ex-partner in lifetime, 12% in the past 12 months
United States of America	National sample of women 18 years and above (N = 8000)	Modified CTS for physical violence	22% reported physical abuse over lifetime, 1.3% in past 12 months
West Bank & Gaza Strip 1998	National sample of Palestinian women (N = 2410) Self-administered	Not defined	48% reported physical assault by an intimate partner during the last 12 months
Zimbabwe 1996	Representative sample of women over 18 years in Midlands province (N = 966)	Multiple questions on specific acts	32% report physical abuse by a family or household member since the age of 16

Source: Garcia-Moreno and Watts (2000).

Notes: CTS = conflict tactics scale.

A 'gate question' is an initial screening question – if the response is affirmative, the respondent is asked more detailed questions.

Table 9.2 *Selected evidence on the global magnitude of coerced sex against girls*

Country	Sample	Evidence of coerced sex
New Zealand 1997	458 women aged 20 to 22	7% of women reported first intercourse as forced; 25% of women sexually active <13 report first intercourse was forced
Barbados 1993	National random survey of 264 women	Nearly one woman in three reported sexual abuse before age 20.
Canada 1990	Population survey of 9,953 men and women aged 15+	13% women, 13% men report child sexual abuse
USA 1995 National Family Growth Survey	National probability sample of 10,847 women aged 15–44	9% of first intercourse not voluntary; 6.9% of 2,042 women aged 15 to 24 years, rated 'wantedness' of their first sexual intercourse at 1 (lowest) on 1–10 scale.
Namibia	Nationally representative sample of 2040 (1020 males, 1020 females) aged 18–25	Ever forced to have sex: 3.6% M, 7.4% F; 1.2% M, 6.2% F with physical force. First sexual encounter forced: M – NA, F 95.2%
Zaria, Nigeria	Female patients seeking treatment for STIs	16% of sample patients were children under 2; 6% were children aged 6–15.
Kabale, Uganda	200 boys and 200 girls between 11–24 years of age (average age 13.9) randomly selected from 40 schools.	19% of girls report having been forced to have sex
Freetown, Sierra Leone	Convenience sample of 144 adult women	31% of respondents reported their first sex was forced
Central African Republic	1307 females nationally representative	22% reported 'rape' (not clearly defined)
Kingston, Jamaica	452 school-girls aged 13–14.	13% experienced attempted rape and 4% completed rape; half before age 12
Switzerland	Randomly selected 9th grade students	20% of girls and 3% of boys 13–17 had experienced sexual assault involving physical contact

Source: Garcia-Moreno and Watts (2000).

increased risk of domestic violence and trafficking in women during or following conflict (Palmer *et al.* 1999).

Feminist discourse has also highlighted the particular aspects of sex-related psychological violence against women and the sexual subjugation of women. This subject has been taken up in much of the family planning literature, which promotes contraception as a means for female empowerment (Hartmann 1987; Dixon-Mueller 1993; Tsui *et al.* 1997) and includes extensive documentation on the negative impact of male domination on reproductive and contraceptive-use decision-making (see for example: Richters 1992; *Population Reports* 1994; Correa 1997; Hollos and Larsen 1997), and psychological, physical and sexual violence (Heise *et al.* 1999; Garcia-Moreno and Watts 2000; IPPF-WHR 2000).

Domestic and sexual violence and women's reproductive health

The reproductive health consequences of domestic violence are numerous (Heise *et al.* 1999). Physical and sexual abuse lie behind unwanted pregnancies, HIV and other sexually transmitted infections (STIs), and complications of pregnancy. A growing number of studies have documented the ways in which violence by intimate partners may substantially limit the degree to which women can refuse sex, control when sexual intercourse takes place, or use contraception or condoms. For example, in Zimbabwe, 25 per cent of ever-married women reported that their partner had forced them to have sex against their will (Watts *et al.* 1998). The prevalence of rape and coercive sex described above clearly illustrates the extent to which violence may limit a girl's or a woman's control over their own sexuality (Garcia-Moreno and Watts 2000). Forced sex may be an important factor contributing to teenage pregnancy; for example, in a study of teenage mothers attending an antenatal clinic in Cape Town, South Africa (mean age: 16.3), 30 per cent reported that their first intercourse was 'forced' and 11 per cent said they had been raped (Wood *et al.* 1998). A history of sexual abuse in childhood can also lead to unwanted pregnancies by increasing sexual risk-taking in adolescence and adulthood (Heise *et al.* 1999).

Worldwide, as many as one woman in every four is physically or sexually abused during pregnancy, usually by her partner. Violence before or during pregnancy is associated with a range of obstetric risk factors. Pregnant women who have experienced violence are more likely to delay seeking prenatal care, or to gain insufficient weight. They are also more likely to have a history of STI, unwanted or mistimed pregnancies, vaginal and cervical infections, kidney infections and bleeding during pregnancy

(Heise *et al.* 1999). Although the findings are inconclusive, several studies suggest that violence during pregnancy contributes significantly to low birth-weight. On the Indian sub-continent, violence may be responsible for a sizeable proportion of pregnancy-related deaths. In such cases, deaths or suicides appeared to be motivated by dowry-related problems, or the stigma of rape and/or pregnancy outside marriage (Heise *et al.* 1999).

Sexual and physical violence also appears to increase women's risk for many common gynaecological disorders, including chronic pelvic pain, irregular vaginal bleeding, vaginal discharge, painful menstruation, pelvic inflammatory disease and sexual dysfunction. For example, a number of studies have found that women suffering from chronic pelvic pain are consistently more likely to have a history of childhood sexual abuse, sexual assault and/or physical and sexual abuse by their partners (Heise *et al.* 1999).

Despite the clear direct and indirect links between the perpetration of violence and adverse reproductive and sexual health outcomes, to date attempts to link these two areas have largely only been made at a global level. Limited effort has been made to bring them together at a local service level. This can in part be understood through an analysis of the evolution of the global debates on reproductive health and VAW and the difficulties of translating these into national action.

The evolution of global debates

The recent recognition of violence against women and reproductive health is the result of more than two decades of activism by individuals and grassroots organisations that coalesced into a global movement for social change in the early 1990s (Heise 1996). Table 9.3 details some of the landmark achievements in the evolution of global debate on reproductive health and VAW (and early opportunities where VAW was not explicitly addressed).

Joachim (1999) describes how international women's organisations placed VAW on the UN agenda. She divides the process into three phases: first, between 1975 and 1985 VAW was first introduced, during the three World Conferences on Women organised within the UN Decade for Women (1975–85). These conferences were organised to identify new and pressing issues concerning women, and were attended by a large number of UN member states (Joachim 1999). The meetings were accompanied by parallel fora for NGOs from around the world. Secondly, from 1985 to 1990 the issue of violence was reflected within other UN debates, including being placed on the agenda of the Commission

Table 9.3 *Landmark events in the evolution of global debate on reproductive health and violence against women*

Key global documents[a]	Significance
1948 Universal Declaration of Human Rights	Served as a basis for the later development of international human rights conventions. No explicit consideration of VAW. However, VAW that is a threat to life, liberty or security, or which could be interpreted as torture, or cruel, inhuman or degrading violates the principle.
1975 Mexico City and Copenhagen 1980 Conferences on Women	First UN conferences seeking to identify new and pressing issues concerning women. Due to influence of regional bloc politics, VAW not identified as a key issue in resulting conference statements.
1976 Tribunal on Crimes Against Women	Alternative forum to Mexico Conference, held by women's movement to provide a forum for women to discuss issues free from governmental interference.
1979 Convention of the Elimination of All Forms of Discrimination Against Women	Most extensive international instrument dealing with the rights of women. VAW not explicitly addressed, except in relation to trafficking and prostitution, although anti-discrimination clauses could potentially be used to protect women from violence.
1984 Mexico Conference on Population and Development	The US Reagan administration pursued a hard right-wing line on population resulting in a realignment of feminist groupings with population planners to safeguard women's right to birth-control.
1985 Nairobi Conference on Women	Violence against women in all its manifestations included in the Forward-Looking Strategies, the final conference document, as a priority issue for the coming decade.
1992 Recommendation 19, 11th Session of CEDAW	The Committee on the Elimination of Discrimination Against Women (CEDAW) that monitors the Convention of the Elimination of All Forms of Discrimination Against Women, formally included gender-based violence under gender-based discrimination.
1993 UN General Assembly Declaration on the Elimination of Violence Against Women	First international human rights instrument to deal exclusively with violence against women. Affirms that violence against women both violates and impairs or nullifies the enjoyment by women of their human rights and fundamental freedoms.
1993 UN World Conference on Human Rights, Vienna	Adoption of Vienna Declaration and Programme of Action. States that gender violence and all forms of sexual harassment and exploitation are incompatible with the dignity and worth of the human person, and calls for its elimination.

(cont.)

Table 9.3 (*cont.*)

Key global documents[a]	Significance
1994 The International Conference on Population and Development, Cairo	Adopted a Programme of Action which emphasises the advancement of gender equality, the empowerment of women and the elimination of all forms of violence against women as cornerstones of population and development-related programmes. Governments called upon to take range of preventive and responsive actions.
March 1994 the Commission on Human Rights appointed the first Special Rapporteur on Violence Against Women	Radhika Coomaraswamy, a Sri Lankan lawyer and activist, was appointed Special Rapporteur. She has the authority to receive and request information from governments, organisations and individuals on violence against women which is gender-specific, and can initiate investigations. The mandate was originally for three years, and was renewed for another three years in 1997.
1995 World Summit for Social Development, Copenhagen	Programme of Action strongly condemns violence against women, and repeats the concerns expressed in the Cairo Programme of Action.
1995 Fourth World Conference on Women, Beijing	Declaration and Platform of Action reaffirmed the importance of improving the status of women to secure their reproductive health. Reproductive health is recognised as a human right and its provision a state obligation. Entire section devoted to violence against women, and recognises that the elimination of VAW is essential to equality, development and peace.
1996 49th World Health Assembly	Adopted resolution WHA49.25 declaring violence a public health priority.
1996 Second United Nations Conference on Human Settlements, Istanbul	Istanbul agenda deals with gender-based violence within the context of shelter and the urban environment. Governments committed themselves to provide shelter and basic education and health support for women and children who are survivors of family violence.
1997 Commission on Human Rights	Condemned all acts of violence against women and emphasised that governments have the duty to refrain from engaging in violence against women, and to prevent, investigate and punish acts of violence against women.

Source: Developed from WHO/FRH (1997), Joachim (1999).
[a]Treaties are legally binding to those states which have ratified or acceded to them, and their implementation is observed by monitoring bodies, such as the Committee on the Elimination of Discrimination Against Women (CEDAW). Declarations reflect the progressive standard of international law. Documents adopted by World Conferences (Conference Statements) reflect an international consensus (WHO/FRH 1997).

on the Status of Women. Thirdly, in the early 1990s the importance of violence against women became further legitimised. In 1993, the Declaration on the Elimination of Violence Against Women was adopted by the UN General Assembly. This was the first international human rights instrument to deal exclusively with violence against women. Later that same year, co-ordinated action by feminist human rights advocates forced domestic and sexual violence on to the international agenda at the World Conference on Human Rights in Vienna. In March 1994, the Commission on Human Rights appointed a Special Rapporteur on Violence Against Women. In 1995, the Beijing Declaration and Platform of Action explicitly recognised the importance of the elimination of violence against women to equality, development and peace, and outlined actions and recommendations for governmental, non-governmental and multilateral organisations.

The evolution of policies on reproductive health and the eventual inclusion of VAW occurred over a similar timeframe. The broadening of the reproductive health concept grew out of the NGO-initiated family planning movement as part of female emancipation in the 1950s. Over the next thirty years, issues of access to birth-control were linked to wider economic and development issues. During the 1970s, initiatives such as the Comision Internamericana de Mujeres (InterAmerican Commission of Women) and the UN Commission on the Status of Women helped put women's development issues, such as economic independence and maternal health needs, on the international agenda (Pettman 1997; Higer 1999; Prugl and Meyer 1999). During the 1980s, women's groups worked to promote broader aspects of maternal health, but economic stringencies of the time resulted in a narrow, more clinical focus on family planning, antenatal care and services ('safe motherhood'). By the late 1980s and 1990s, advocates feared that these more clinical definitions of 'population', 'birth-control' and 'maternal health' divorced reproductive health from its wider context, including individual life styles, gender relations and economic status. The 1994 International Conference on Population and Development (ICPD) in Cairo represented an unprecedented crystalisation of reproductive health by a diverse field of delegates, including over 150 NGOs. The terms 'comprehensive reproductive health' and 'total reproductive well-being' gained currency and the Platform of Action explicitly recognised the importance of social and economic empowerment of women to reproductive rights (United Nations 1994a). The Platform of Action specifically supported the incorporation of VAW as a health issue, and emphasised the advancement of gender equality, and the elimination of all forms of VAW as cornerstones of population and development-related programmes (United Nations 1994a, Principle 4).

Governments were called upon to take full measures to eliminate all forms of exploitation, abuse, harassment and violence against women, adolescents and children.

In the wake of Cairo increased funds were pledged to promote reproductive health activities at national levels. While initiatives addressing VAW were called for, donor demands perpetuated a primary focus on clinical services (especially family planning and management of sexually transmitted diseases) (Lush *et al.* 1999; UNFPA 1999; Mayhew *et al.* 2000). Most recently, in 1995, declarations from the Fourth World Conference on Women in Beijing placed women's sexual and reproductive well-being in the context of basic human rights, 'The human rights of women include their right to have control over and decide freely and responsibly on matters related to ... sexual and reproductive health' and, more significantly, that 'it is the duty of states, regardless of their political, economic and cultural systems, to promote and protect all human rights and fundamental freedoms' (United Nations 1995).

The growth of a global social movement

The advancements described above demonstrate the increasing ability of the coalition of women's health organisations, NGOs and civil rights organisations to shape global policy. Yet, as Heise (1996) states, 'violence against women has emerged as a global issue despite the official indifference of world leaders, not through international leadership'.

During the 1970s and 1980s, women's groups became increasingly involved in international conferences and multilateral agencies (Lane 1994; Krut 1997; Sandberg 1998; Prugl and Meyer 1999). Both the VAW and reproductive health movements were able to draw upon widespread grassroots support. The VAW movement had the support of national initiatives to address VAW in both industrial and developing countries. Many of these organisations were initially founded by a small group of concerned individuals to help women in danger, with a focus on providing services to women experiencing violence (such as counselling, legal support, shelters). Often however, the high levels of demand for services highlighted the failure of social services, the police, courts and health services to respond to women's needs. This led to national-level organisations pushing for systematic reform. For example, during the late 1990s in Malaysia the Joint Action Group Against Violence Against Women sponsored a five-year campaign, consisting of workshops, media campaigns, demonstrations, lobbying, petitions and community organisation. In Mexico in 1988, *Red Nacional contra la Violencia hacia la Mujer* held a National Forum on Sex Crimes, which presented 88 papers and testimonials about rape and domestic violence to the Mexican House of Deputies (Shrader-Cox 1992, cited in Heise 1996).

Similarly, the reproductive health movement could draw upon the early feminist campaigners for contraceptive rights (Ravindran 1995; PANOS 1994; Hartmann 1995; Hardon and Hayes 1997; Petchesky and Judd 1998), and a number of grassroots women's health organisations that had proliferated during the 1970s and 1980s. In particular, organisations such as the Prevention of Maternal Mortality Network and International Women's Health Coalition (IWHC) played a critical role in building consensus on women's reproductive health and rights (Pettman 1997; Higer 1999; Prugl and Meyer 1999).

The development of regional linkages and global consensus increased during the UN Decade for Women, when, for the first time, donor funds became available to support women-focused NGOs. This funding helped to support meetings and exchange programmes that allowed women from different countries to share strategies and build co-ordinated campaigns for reform (Heise 1996; Prugl and Meyer 1999). Building on interactions at the Mexico City and Copenhagen Conferences, national, regional and global networks began to emerge (Joachim 1999). Advocates working on VAW and reproductive health began to develop a shared understanding of women's health concerns, including sexual health and, increasingly, gender violence. They saw the need to make local and regional voices heard at the international level. At the NGO forum in Nairobi, for example, VAW was identified as one of several priority issues in the consensus document. Importantly, advancements in communications technology facilitated scattered groups around the world to communicate and organise to influence global debates.

Despite this grassroots support, the influence of the NGOS only developed over time, as they learned more about the UN system and its methods of operation. At the early UN conferences, a lack of both procedural and substantive experience limited the effectiveness of women's organisations. Few knew how the agenda-setting process worked, how they could gain access to governments, how to present information or how to lobby (Bunch and Reilly 1994; Prugl and Meyer 1999). However, through the early conferences, international women's organisations were able to gain more knowledge about the UN and, in particular, the importance of extensive pre-conference preparation and consensus building. This was critical to the success of NGOs and women's groups in presenting a united and efficient front on women's sexual and reproductive well-being at the ICPD 1994. Women's organisations, spearheaded by the IWHC, arranged three pre-conference 'prepcons', notably the 'Reproductive Health and Justice Conference' at Rio de Janeiro in

1993. This meeting was attended by 218 women who drew up detailed pre-conference material culminating in the Rio Statement, and consolidated networks of sympathetic groupings working in women's health and rights (Higer 1999). Activists for women's rights and sexual and reproductive health also built on the experiences of women's advocacy in other sectors, particularly economic and environmental (Meyer 1999). Of particular importance was the development of the Women's Caucus, introduced at the 1992 UN Conference on Environment and Development, and retained at subsequent UN conferences, including Cairo and Beijing. This group was critical in co-ordinating the lobbying efforts of women's NGOs and acting as a channel for information between activities and intergovernmental conference delegates (Prugl and Meyer 1999).

The success of VAW activism can also be attributed to the strategic decision by activists to employ linkage politics, that is, they sought to gain credibility and funding for the issue of VAW by demonstrating how it relates to issues already high on the international agenda, such as peace, human rights, health and socio-economic development (Heise 1996). In Nairobi, for example, gender violence was framed as an obstacle to peace. This helped place the issue on the agenda of the Commission on the Status of Women (CSW). The commission was important, as it was a subsidiary to the UN Economic and Social Council (ECOSOC) and could thus provide access and make recommendations to this UN body on urgent issues of women's rights. In addition, supporters from within individual CSW member states were able to give outspoken support to VAW activism, and to introduce resolutions on behalf of international women's organisations (Joachim 1999).

One of the most successful of these efforts has been the campaign to frame gender violence as an abuse of human rights. Despite the existence of many international instruments that guarantee an individual's right to life, bodily integrity and security of person, the mainstream human rights discourse had failed to recognise rape or domestic violence by private individuals as an abuse of women's human rights. This was reinforced in the insistence on maintaining a distinction between abuses in the public and private sphere – with traditional human rights theory focusing primarily on violations perpetrated by the state against individuals, such as torture, wrongful imprisonment and arbitrary execution. This public/private distinction is especially prejudicial when it comes to women; for a woman, rape and assault are brutal violations, and it makes little difference whether her assailant is an agent of the state, a stranger or a friend (Heise 1996).

In the late 1980s, women came together to protest the failure of the human rights community to address gender-based forms of persecution.

More than 1,000 women's groups joined the Campaign for Women's Human Rights, an international effort to get the UN to integrate gender into its human rights machinery. The campaign included major initiatives to get human rights law to include rape and domestic violence as violations of human rights, regardless of who is the perpetrator. At the 1993 Second World Conference on Human Rights in Vienna, women presented delegates with almost 500,000 signatures from 128 countries. They held an international tribunal, moderated by an esteemed panel of judges, where women presented well-documented cases of gender-based abuse. This highly organised lobby achieved virtually all of its demands.

A more recent area of activism is to link abuse to health and development concerns, such as unwanted pregnancy, AIDS and sexually transmitted disease. In the late 1980s, a small group of activists worked to frame gender violence as a public health and international development concern. This move to link VAW with public health helps to emphasise the role of prevention, and provides opportunities to work with health and family planning services – institutions that have ongoing contact with women.

Lastly, it is important to recognise that the actions outlined above were taken at a time when changes in the global political economy provided an opportunity for international organisations to work within and influence the UN. In the 1970s and early 1980s, early moves to introduce gender violence to international agendas from the Mexico City and Copenhagen conferences were limited by cold war politics. At these meetings, the three competing blocs dominated the conference with their differing priorities (equality was pushed by the West, increased resources and access to development programmes by the South, and equality and the greater participation by women in the promotion of peace and disarmament by the East). In addition, the tensions between these blocs resulted in highly politicised meetings in which ongoing East–West and North–South tensions were played out in both the UN and governmental fora, and support for resolutions largely reflected bloc politics. In contrast, the third conference in Nairobi was much less politicised, and resulted in the inclusion of gender violence in the 'Forward Looking Strategies'.

Likewise, the political climate strongly influenced global debates on reproductive health. At the 1984 World Population Conference in Mexico City, the US government pursued a hard right-wing line on population. This forced feminist groupings to align with population planners, and to focus their activities on safeguarding women's right to birth-control (Higer 1999). In contrast, at the Cairo Conference in 1994 the Clinton administration provided a relatively favourable climate within which to advance demands for a broader approach to reproductive health, and for a global recognition that VAW is an issue of substantial concern for women's health and well-being.

From global rhetoric to national action

The international debate, and increasing participation of non-state actors, has succeeded in gaining a global consensus on the importance of women's health to development. The framing of both reproductive health and VAW within a human rights context, underwritten by the weight of international law, has also been an important means of legitimising what are traditionally sensitive and marginalised issues. This action has also helped to shift responsibility for women's well-being from civil society to the state, and mobilised funding to address this issue at the national level.

The next challenge is to translate the global rhetoric into meaningful national action. A key question is how, given the implicit links, can reproductive health services explicitly tackle problems of domestic and sexual violence at national and sub-national levels. In some respects the opportunities to do this are substantial. Most women use reproductive health services at some point in their lives (especially for antenatal care and family planning). Reproductive health programmes, particularly family planning, have a long history of dealing with sensitive issues around sexuality, contraception and sex-negotiation, which could be used to good effect to identify and support women experiencing violence. Under their expanded human rights mandate, reproductive health services offer a valuable opportunity to identify and reach women experiencing abuse, with the potential for counselling and referral to specialist services. In addition, both reproductive health services and services for women experiencing violence require a long-term response to the male-dominated gender relations that govern sexual decision-making, gender violence and female rights and autonomy.

Furthermore, it is likely that the clients of reproductive health services would support such initiatives. In South Africa, 88 per cent of women attending a community clinic in Cape Town said they would welcome routine screening for violence (Kim 1999). A study in the United States found that both abused and non-abused women favoured screening, by their health providers, of women patients for experience of violence (McNutt *et al.* 1999). Women emphasised the importance of having providers who were well informed and understanding of domestic violence, willing to listen, and to provide information on the community resources available (Gielen *et al.* 1994). Two important protective support strategies for women experiencing violence during pregnancy, in

Table 9.4 *Operational linkage: reproductive health worker responses to violence*

Reproductive health workers can respond positively to women reporting violence by:

- Being informed about the types and extent of violence, and its underlying causes
- Displaying posters/leaflets on violence
- Supporting women emotionally by validating her experiences, being non-judgemental and willing to listen
- Providing appropriate clinical care (e.g. pregnancy/STI/HIV tests and treatment)
- Documenting the medical consequences of violence
- Maintaining confidentiality
- Referring women to community resources where they exist (e.g. women's groups, NGOs)
- Potentially screening for abuse during reproductive health consultations (highly sensitive)

Source: Heise *et al.* 1999.

a study in the United States, were having a confidante (friend, sister) and community support networks. While community networks in many developing countries are very limited, reproductive health workers could play an important role in providing emotional support to women, and condemning the violence they have experienced. Table 9.4 indicates some of the potential actions that reproductive health providers could take to respond to women using their services who disclose experiencing violence.

There are a number of ongoing initiatives to integrate VAW into re-productive health services. In Europe and North America, for example, guidelines for different health providers have been developed by the professional health organisations. In low- and middle-income countries, initiatives have been supported by international bodies, such as the International Planned Parenthood Federation (IPPF). This includes the development of screening tools for VAW by IPPF, and ongoing pilot ini-tiatives in the Dominican Republic, Peru, Venezuela, Jamaica and Brazil to improve the capacity of sexual and reproductive health services to offer services to victims of gender-based violence.

Although these are important initiatives, it is important to recognise the difficulties that may be associated with attempts to translate global pledges into national action. The changing arena in which policy is being formed affects who is involved in the policy development, the process of policy formulation, the context in which the policy is being implemented, and the potential policy content (see Walt and Gilson 1994). For illustrative purposes Table 9.5 contrasts the actors, processes, context and content of the global initiatives with a potential situation that may arise at the national level.

Table 9.5 *Contrasting situations at global and national levels of action for women's health and rights*

	Global	National
Actors	Women's organisations (e.g. IWHC) Human rights organisations	Ministries of health National planned parenthood associations
	UN agencies Donor agencies International NGOs	Health donors International NGOs
Processes	Growing international women's movement Sustained advocacy Global networks	Limited ownership over concept Lack of recognition and/or information on violence against women Dominance of health donor programme structures and logistics
Context	Ease of communications / travel Increasing knowledge transfer Changing political climate Increased availability of funding for international/national levels	Commitments made at International meetings but reluctance to address private/individual rights Sensitivity of topics Vertical structures of health service delivery Groups addressing violence against women often working outside government structures Resource and capacity constraints Competing priorities Increasing burden of HIV
Content	Holistic view of women's health and rights Intervention experience potentially drawing largely upon Western models	Expanded reproductive health services Separation of strategies to address violence against women and those to address reproductive health

This highlights how the actors at a global level who helped to consolidate the reaffirmation of individual needs and rights within the global rhetoric on reproductive health and VAW are no longer the major players at a national level. Similarly, the contexts in which policy is being formulated differ markedly between the international and national level – with, for example, national-level initiatives having to be delivered within the vertical structures of health service delivery, and with the NGOs most experienced at responding to cases of violence potentially having limited influence on the forms of intervention implemented.

Lessons can be learned about the difficulties of integrating different services from the experiences of reproductive health over the last decade. The dichotomy between the interests and agendas of different players often results in confusion over how reproductive health should be nationally defined; this is manifest in the large number of reproductive health-related policies in sub-Saharan African countries which do not provide clear guidelines on how integrated reproductive health services should be implemented (Lush et al. 1999; Mayhew et al. 2000). VAW is usually addressed at national level within the context of judicial and legal frameworks. National reproductive health policies rarely recognise VAW as a concern within health strategies. The lack of national operational guidelines allows donors and governments to continue with their existing priority programmes and programme structures focusing on measurable, clinical policies (Lush et al. 1999; Mayhew 2000; Mayhew et al. 2000).

In practice, in developing countries the forms of initiative adopted, and the extent to which a more holistic approach to violence can be achieved, are greatly influenced by the existing patterns of health service provision, and the priorities of their main international donors. Reproductive health is a leading donor priority and funds are available for a variety of activities within the reproductive health framework. However, the financial and material support from donors tend to focus on specific, classical components (family planning, safe motherhood, STI/HIV management) (Lush et al. 1999; Mayhew et al. 2000). This has resulted in policy-making for reproductive health often being disparate and uncoordinated, with policies frequently emerging as lists of ideal services in tune with the broad global agenda, but unrealistic given in-country needs, capacities and resources (Rakodi 1996; Lush et al. 1999; Mayhew 1999; Mayhew and Lush 1999).

Donor support also tends to perpetuate existing selective structures of service delivery, by attempting to add on other activities such as STI management (and thus potentially adding violence-related services) to existing family planning and antenatal care, rather than creating the more holistic approach advocated at Cairo and Beijing (Lush et al. 1999; Mayhew et al. 2000). This is perhaps a result of the relative power balance at national level, where donors hold considerably more financial and material sway than do the NGOs who pushed for the all-encompassing international agreements. In addition, international donors (bi- and multilateral) have a range of accountability and transparency requirements which favour more vertical, selective structures for service delivery (Lush et al. 1999); donors are therefore often reluctant to address the broader, less measurable components of Cairo which address women's wider well-being concerns such as living with violence. Such factors tend to result in an over-emphasis of particular activities (Table 9.6), limiting the extent

Table 9.6 *National activity foci for reproductive health and violence against women*

Common components of reproductive health service provision	Common components of violence against women intervention initiatives
Family planning STI screening and treatment Antenatal care Safe delivery Emergency obstetric care Postnatal care Treatment for gynaecological complications (Safe abortion services)	Counselling for women experiencing violence Provision of legal advice, support to women experiencing violence Referral to other support agencies Provision of places of safety for women fleeing violence (including shelters) Public education on the unacceptability of violence/to challenge gender expectations and norms/to inform women of their rights Advocacy with government to reform specific laws, mobilise increased resources Training to public sector organisations coming into contact with women experiencing violence

to which linkage between the two sectors can be made, and polarising the issues from the overriding goal of total reproductive health in the human rights based context of life-experiences, which include violence.

In addition, a key aspect of an integrated response requires that reproductive health and violence groups work together, in partnership with other agencies that may be able to provide support. However, despite the commitments that governments have undertaken to respond to women experiencing abuse, in most cases they do not have explicit programmes responsible for responding to violence against women. Instead, most current action on violence is conducted by small indigenous NGOs (WiLDAF 1995; Njovana and Watts 1996), in a vertical manner, separate to public-sector activities (Table 9.6). While many such organisations are seeking to expand their activities, and to work with a range of public sector organisations (such as health, education, justice and law), inevitably, working with the diverse range of organisations and structures creates many difficulties. Each has its own priorities, institutional cultures and practices, and integrating VAW into their work requires good linkages and in-depth knowledge about the organisation's structure and practices. In addition, many of these agencies are male dominated, and working with them to address gender issues can be slow and frustrating (Stewart 1992). This may inherently limit the extent to which a large-scale initiative can be developed and supported within any one sector.

Such difficulties to date associated with 'integrating' reproductive health service components should sound a note of caution to initiatives seeking to rapidly 'add on' violence issues to reproductive health services. Particularly, since the handling of violence requires a highly sensitive and specialised approach, a rush to respond to women experiencing violence, or to screen for cases of abuse within the health sector, could have serious implications for the safety of women experiencing violence. Instead, it is likely that a more considered, sustainable and context-specific approach can be developed if the pros and cons of different potential forms of intervention are carefully assessed. This must draw upon the experience and expertise of both reproductive health workers and violence activists. In particular, some of the regional alliances that helped propel the issue on to the global agenda may have a key role in the development of appropriate local, national and regional initiatives.

Conclusion

Improvements in access to communications technology and a changing global political climate have increased the numbers of, and enhanced the quality of participation by, civil society groups and NGOs advocating for women's health and rights. Through these changes, a policy 'space' has opened up that has allowed the groups to network, communicate and link more effectively, to share information and to become more active in multinational agencies and global governance structures. These features of globalisation aided the development of a global social movement, around VAW and reproductive health, enabling these issues to be placed higher on the global policy agenda. The achievements made at the global level, in turn, have helped put VAW and reproductive health on to national policy agendas and resulted in increased funds and resources for national activities.

The process of bringing together a global coalition of groups working on women's health and rights, and enabling them to effectively communicate and network, has helped to forge links transnationally among different groups working to address VAW and reproductive health. For the needs of individual women to be met, however, future research and analysis need to focus on the opportunities to develop pragmatic links between services for reproductive health and VAW at the national policy and local service levels. Putting global rhetoric into action will involve different policy groupings, contexts and processes. Experience from initiatives to integrate other areas into reproductive health, however, suggests that in reality this can result in a narrow, activity-specific focus.

In the reality of women's lives, the areas of violence and reproductive health interface. The moves to integrate a variety of reproductive health services create opportunities to develop services that are able to address both reproductive health and violence issues. However, the forms of intervention developed must consider the country-specific contexts in which initiatives are being implemented, and recognise the potential dangers as well as benefits associated with intervening in situations of violence. For this reason, any initiatives must draw upon the experience of national and sub-national women's organisations in providing services to women who have experienced violence. In addition, the regional and global networks and alliances that have facilitated high-level recognition and commitment could potentially play a more central role in contextualising and operationalising policies that tackle the worldwide challenges of VAW and reproductive health.

NOTE

We are grateful for extensive input from Cathy Zimmerman. We would also like to thank the editors for their comments.
1 Reproductive health is defined as 'complete physical, mental and social well-being in all matters related to the reproductive system' United Nations (1994b). Reproductive care essentially includes 'family planning, pre- post-natal and delivery care, prevention and treatment of sexually transmitted diseases and reproductive tract infections and safe abortion services'.

10 The globalisation of DOTS: tuberculosis as a global emergency

John Porter, Kelley Lee and Jessica Ogden

> The tubercle bacillus is an index by inversion of the real
> progress of the human race. By it the claim of civilisation
> to dominate human life may fairly be judged.
>
> J. B. Huber (1907)

Introduction

In 1993, one hundred and eleven years after the causative organism for tuberculosis (TB) was identified, and half a century after the introduction of clinically effective therapy, the World Health Organisation (WHO) declared the disease a global emergency (WHO 1994). This recognition that the public health community had effectively failed to control such a long-understood and treatable infection is unprecedented. The global strategy in response to the current emergency has centred on the development and implementation of directly observed therapy, short course (DOTS). In a few short years, DOTS has become the dominant strategy in the widely supported, global campaign against the disease, and has proven effective in treating many individual cases around the world.

While the battle against TB is one spanning many centuries, there are notable features of the current crisis that closely link it to the impacts of globalisation on health. Indeed, TB control is a useful case study for understanding how health policy is being shaped by globalisation and, in turn, how globalisation in its current form is being reinforced by such health policies. Globalisation in the late twentieth and early twenty-first centuries is a process changing human societies in complex ways, 'as capital, traded goods, persons, concepts, images, ideas, and values diffuse across state boundaries' (Hurrell and Woods 1995). The links between globalisation and TB are threefold.

First, the chapter begins by locating tuberculosis in its historical context, and the well-documented link between tuberculosis and poverty. The resurgence of TB in the late twentieth century has taken place within the context of contemporary forms of globalisation that are widening the gap between haves and have nots. Inequities being created within and across countries are providing fertile ground for the tubercle bacillus to thrive, creating distinct challenges for TB control programmes.

Secondly, it is within this global context that the strategy of DOTS has been introduced and promoted worldwide. The DOTS strategy can be seen as an extension of the biomedical approach that has dominated disease-control programmes for many decades. This medical paradigm has become globalised as the 'gold standard' for all countries to follow. Thirdly, the promotion of DOTS raises issues concerning how we can define 'global'. While taken up by over one hundred Member States of WHO, this chapter asks to what extent can the strategy be considered truly global? Criteria are explored that could be used to define a 'global control strategy', and applied to assessing how the process of developing and implementing DOTS has been carried out. The chapter concludes that a truly global strategy for TB may need to include efforts to promote alternative forms of globalisation and public health strategies that more directly address the intimate relationship between global inequities and the alarming spread of TB.

Tuberculosis and the global burden of disease

Tuberculosis is a devastating illness on both an individual and global scale. Historically, TB accounted for a heavy burden of disease, for example being responsible for about one-quarter of deaths in the US and England in the mid-nineteenth century, and the chief cause of death in the US until 1909 (Spink 1995). Tuberculosis has long been recognised as a disease closely associated with socio-economic disadvantage and deprivation, thriving in the often crowded, damp and unsanitary living conditions of the urban poor. As Porter and Ogden (1998) write:

In the late eighteenth century, the onset of the Industrial Revolution and the decline of agricultural employment together created the conditions for large-scale migration into the cities . . . the majority of the population were living in appalling, overcrowded conditions and . . . areas with the greatest poverty suffered the highest mortality rates. The overcrowded conditions in the urban slums undoubtedly contributed to the transmission of infection. It was recognized in 1899 that 'the most powerful factors in producing tuberculosis are: (1) air contaminated by the so called tubercle bacillus, (2) food inadequate in purity, quality, quantity, (3) confined and overcrowded dwellings, (4) a low state of general health and resisting power of the body' (Weber 1899).

From the 1860s, however, incidence rates steadily declined in industrialising countries where there were gradual improvements in socio-economic factors such as housing and nutrition, and to a lesser extent health care

(McKeown and Record 1962; McKeown *et al.* 1975). With the advent of effective antibiotic and chemotherapy treatment in the 1940s, further progress on controlling and treating TB was made. Indeed, given declining mortality from TB, it was believed in these countries, that TB could no longer be considered a major threat to public health.

In large parts of the world, namely in lower-income countries, where these improvements did not take place or where drug treatments were not available or widely accessible, TB has continued to account for a major burden of disease to the present day. The country with the highest burden of disease from TB is India, where there are a reported 1.83 million new cases and 437,000 deaths each year (Chakraborty 1997). The second most affected country is China with 1.4 million new cases and 258,000 deaths each year (WHO 2000c). Table 10.1 lists the twenty countries with the highest burden of disease from tuberculosis. In higher-income countries, where TB was no longer seen as a public health priority, and within international organisations and bilateral aid agencies supported by these countries, this persistently high incidence of TB in developing countries began to be overlooked by the 1970s (Walt 1999).

The resurgence of TB in the late twentieth century has challenged the characterisation of the disease as one confined to the developing world. Indeed, the epidemiology of TB now appears to be changing, from a North–South to an increasingly complex global issue. The reasons for this are multiple and seemingly linked to particular features of the emerging global political economy. First, it is increasingly argued that current forms of globalisation are contributing to a widening of socio-economic inequalities within and across countries (UNDP 1999). There is growing evidence that conditions of inequality, in turn, are leading to changes in the burden of communicable diseases including TB. As discussed above, historically TB has been strongly associated with deprivation and poor living conditions. The resurgence of the disease in the late twentieth century has continued to follow this pattern worldwide. Taking advantage of what Chossudovsky (1996) calls the 'globalisation of poverty', TB has spread more readily among disadvantaged individuals and groups, across both rich and poor countries, including the urban poor, substance abusers, homeless, unemployed, migrant labour and newly arrived immigrants (Spence *et al.* 1993). For example, in England and Wales between 1980 and 1992, TB incidence showed a 35 per cent increase among the poorest 10 per cent of the population, a 13 per cent increase among the next poorest 20 per cent, but no increase among the remaining, relatively more affluent 70 per cent (Bhatti *et al.* 1995). Data from the US similarly confirm that TB rates are highest among the poor and marginalised. Such groups face a higher burden of disease in

Table 10.1 *The twenty highest burden countries from tuberculosis*

COUNTRY	Estimated new cases (000 per year)	Estimated deaths (000 per year)	Number of cases notified in 1998	Prevalence of MDRTB in cases not previously notified	DOTS population coverage (per cent)
Bangladesh	305	68	72 256		90
Brazil	124	19	84 194	0.9	3
Cambodia	58	9	16 946		100
China	1414	258	457 349	2.8–10.8	64
Congo (DR)	130	39	58 869		60
Ethiopia	160	49	69 472		64
India	1828	437	1 130 038	3.4	9
Indonesia	591	140	40 497		80
Kenya	86	28	48 936		100
Nigeria	259	69	20 249		45
Pakistan	268	64	89 599		8
Peru	66	7	43 723	3.1	100
Philippines	224	48	159 866		17
Russian Federation	156	26	121 434	6.5–9.0	5
South Africa	172	72	128 415		22
Tanzania	99	31	51 231		100
Thailand	85	17	15 850	2.1	32
Uganda	68	24	29 228	0.5	100
Vietnam	147	20	87 449		96
Zimbabwe	64	33	47 277	1.9	100

Source: Compiled from WHO (2000c).

relation to conditions of homelessness, substance abuse, psychological stress, poor nutritional status and congregate residence in shelters or in-carceration facilities (Brudney and Dobkin 1991; Gittler 1994; Bayer and Dupuis 1995). Also, WHO (1998c) estimates that as much as 50 per cent of the world's refugees may be infected with TB. Overall, a global profile of TB is emerging that suggests a resurgence of the disease in association with the growth worldwide of poverty and inequality.

A second feature of the resurgence of TB is its close association with the HIV/AIDS pandemic. Because of the close interaction between TB and HIV infection, the effect of the HIV/AIDS pandemic on TB has been significant. In 1994 it was estimated that 5.4 million people were infected with both HIV and *Mycobacterium tuberculosis*, the majority of cases occurring in sub-Saharan Africa. By 1996, this number had risen to over 6 million (WHO 1996b). WHO estimated that, by 2000, 14 per cent of TB cases would be HIV-related, accounting for 1.4 million cases worldwide and 600,000 cases in Africa alone (Dolin *et al.* 1994). Like TB, the pattern of HIV/AIDS infection can be closely associated with a particular world order of transnational liberalism that has created fertile ground for the disease to spread worldwide. The emerging structure of global economic and political power, for example, has led to an unequal vulnerability to HIV/AIDS among the poor and disadvantaged (Lee and Zwi 1996). Coupled together, the global pattern of spread of TB and HIV/AIDS epitomises the ways in which winners and losers are being created by globalisation.

Thirdly, globalisation is contributing to the spread of multi-drug resistant TB (MDRTB). The emergence of MDRTB is largely due to the decline in effective control programmes within public health systems around the world and also to the decreased support for marginalised population groups through withdrawal of state welfare, public housing, support for asylum seekers etc. As numbers of TB cases began to drop, particularly among the more affluent sections of society, the TB control structures began to be dismantled (Reichman 1991). While drug resistance in the 1940s and 1950s was seen in roughly 1–2 per cent of cases, this had risen to 3–5 per cent in the United States by the 1970s. Since then this figure has been steadily rising. Today in New York City, 33 per cent of TB strains have been found to be resistant to at least one drug, and 19 per cent to two or more drugs. In other parts of the world, so-called 'hot zones' of drug resistance have emerged in countries as widespread as Russia, Dominican Republic, Argentina and the Ivory Coast (WHO 1999d). It is estimated that up to 50 million people may be infected with drug-resistant TB (WHO 1997a,b). This more recent rise in MDRTB has been facilitated by political and economic instability in those so-called 'hot zones', resulting in a deterioration in public health infrastructure, greater human mobility and increased poverty and deprivation. Furthermore, there is evidence that adjustment to fundamental social changes in these countries has been worsened by the introduction of particular policies by the aid community, such as structural adjustment and other forms of liberalisation, without sufficient consideration of the social impacts. Finally, the greater mobility of people worldwide on a greater scale and at a faster pace also risks spreading MDRTB, and TB in general, across national and continental boundaries. The scattered, but growing incidence, of MDRTB in many higher-income countries suggests the importation of the disease through human mobility.

Finally, the interconnectedness of national economies, and consequent vulnerability to global movements of capital and investment, may be adversely affectin efforts to control the spread of TB. In Asia, described as the 'epicentre of the world's TB emergency', there are concerns that TB will rise in the wake of the global economic crisis as a result of pressures on public health expenditure on disease prevention, control and treatment (WHO 1998d). In Thailand, for example, there is some evidence that the economic crisis of the late 1990s has been accompanied by a rise in incidence of some infectious diseases, although not mortality rates as yet (Wilbulpolprasert 2000).

Overall, TB is killing more people than at any other time in history, with one-third of the world's population infected with the tubercle bacillus (WHO 1998e). It is estimated that the disease is responsible for between 2.2 and 3 million deaths annually, including at least 100,000 children for whom it is the fourth leading cause of mortality after malaria, acute respiratory infections and gastrointestinal disease. Among infectious agents, TB is the single most important cause of youth and adult deaths (7 per cent of all adult deaths and 26 per cent of preventable adult deaths), killing more people than AIDS, malaria and other tropical diseases combined (Grange 1999). This resurgence of a well-understood disease, against which a relatively strong arsenal of drug treatments exists, can be seen to have been facilitated by specific features of globalisation. Historically, TB exacted a heavy toll on general populations because of the absence of public health systems, chemotherapy and knowledge about the disease, although it was a greater risk to the poor and deprived. As these improved, the disease gradually came to be defined along North–South lines, concentrated in the poor within the developing world. Today, what is enabling TB to move from a disease of the developing world to one of global dimensions are the widening inequalities being created by globalisation, greater human mobility, and the structural instability of many states that has led to a weakened capacity to provide effective control and treatment programmes. As Rangan and Ogden (1997) write, TB is a 'barometer of social justice and equity' across countries, resulting in more complex and transborder patterns of incidence that reflect the nature of current forms of globalisation. It is this feature that can be described as a 'global TB emergency'.

The development of TB control policy: 'Getting the bugs to the drugs'

Since the discovery of the tubercle bacillus by Robert Koch in 1882, great strides have been made in understanding the infectious agent of

TB and how to treat it. The 1940s brought developments in effective antibiotics and chemotherapy treatment.[1] Accompanying these advances were public health infrastructure and control strategies to deliver them, as well as tools for diagnosis and treatment. By the 1970s, short-course chemotherapy (6–8 months of treatment) was developed and, in higher-income countries, provided through a well-supported public health system. The effectiveness of these advances was such that, during this period, TB was believed to be a disease under control and perhaps even on the brink of eradication (Henderson 1998).

WHO was central to the promotion of TB control strategies internationally, beginning in the early 1950s with the establishment of the WHO Tuberculosis Programme (encompassing the then existing Tuberculosis Research Office). The programme focused on a worldwide campaign to control the spread of TB through the use of the BCG (Bacille Calmette–Guérin) vaccine. From 1951 until the late 1950s, WHO and UNICEF worked together on a mass campaign to vaccinate children and adolescents. While the programme proved successful at dramatically reducing the number of cases in Europe, tens of millions of cases continued to occur in the developing world. Indeed, by 1957 doubts began to be raised as to the efficacy of this mass campaign approach.

The concept of a comprehensive control programme, implemented on a nationwide scale through existing health services, was developed in the 1960s. This concept was formulated in the Eighth Report of the WHO Expert Committee on Tuberculosis (WHO 1964) and reaffirmed in the Ninth Report in 1974 (WHO 1974). Its main principles are that a TB programme should be national, permanent and specifically adapted to the expressed needs of local populations in order to be acceptable and accessible to them (i.e. appropriate to the context in which it is applied). Initially, vertical TB control programmes were again created. This was followed by efforts, soundly based on empirical data and operational experience, to integrate them into comprehensive primary health care (PHC) as later advocated by the Alma-Ata Declaration in 1978 (WHO 1982, 1988).

By the 1970s, however, there was declining political and, as a consequence, financial support for TB control programmes, particularly in the north. TB programmes became victims of their perceived success as TB was no longer seen as an urgent public health priority. Nationally, public health infrastructure (e.g. isolation sanitoriums, health workers) in many countries was dismantled. Internationally, financing of research waned and the number of TB-related staff at WHO headquarters dwindled to a single person (WHO 1996c; Walt 1999). Because of inadequate political and financial commitment, and concomitant pressures to support high-profile vertical programmes, the notion of TB programmes as an integrated part of PHC waned (Banerji 1990).

As reported cases of TB began to rise from the mid 1980s, notably in many higher-income countries but also in low-income countries, international concern returned. In 1989, WHO began to re-build its TB programme and staffing increased from one person at headquarters (Walt 1999) to a forty-person team, with additional staff at regional and country offices, by the late 1990s. Funding for TB control activities also grew once again (e.g. Global Tuberculosis Research Initiative), accompanied by efforts to develop new strategies with technical assistance from the International Union against Tuberculosis and Lung Disease (IUATLD).

In 1993, WHO declared TB a 'global emergency' in an effort to rally public attention and support. A WHO Global Tuberculosis Programme was formed in 1995 to consolidate and take forward a wide range of activities, including efforts to build closer links with NGOs, private industry, community groups and activist organisations. The Stop TB Initiative, a partnership hosted by WHO, was established in 1998 to strengthen the networking approach further in recognition that a global movement involving many countries and organisations was needed. This relationship has led to a proposed Global Partnership Agreement introduced at a Ministerial Conference on TB and Sustainable Development in March 2000. The focus of such an agreement, to be developed and implemented through 'close consultation with governments and organizations' by autumn 2000, would be the securing of strong commitment on the part of diverse parties to prepare and implement National Action Plans on TB control (Amsterdam Declaration 2000).

Underpinning much of this work was the launch in 1993 of a WHO strategy known as DOTS. The main elements of the DOTS strategy are:

1 government commitment to a national programme;
2 case detection through 'passive' case finding (sputum smear microscopy for pulmonary tuberculosis suspects);
3 short-course chemotherapy for all smear-positive pulmonary TB cases (under direct observation for at least the initial phase of treatment);
4 regular, uninterrupted supply of all essential anti-TB drugs; and
5 a monitoring system for programme supervision and evaluation (WHO 1994; Harries and Mayer 1996).

Importantly, the 'global targets' for TB control, as endorsed by the World Health Assembly and set out by WHO (1994), were to detect 70 per cent of existing cases and cure 85 per cent of the detected new smear-positive TB cases by the year 2000. WHO has actively pursued efforts to globalise

DOTS as the centrepiece in its strategy to raise the profile of TB on national health agendas. Since 1990, the number of countries using DOTS has increased from less than 10 countries in 1991 to 119 in 1998. By the end of 1997, 85 per cent of all TB cases were living in the 102 countries that had adopted the DOTS strategy. WHO (1999d) estimates further that the number of new smear-positive TB cases reported (notified) by DOTS programmes have increased by an average of 100,000 per year since 1994, with DOTS reaching 21 per cent of cases in 1998.

The notable emphasis placed on the global dimensions of the disease, and the need for a rapid and broadly based response by the public health community in all countries, has been a defining feature of the 1990s. In a letter to the *Lancet*, the Director of the WHO Global Tuberculosis Programme, Dr A. Kochi (1994), wrote:

The Tuberculosis Programme at WHO has worked since 1990 to form a worldwide coalition of member states, national tuberculosis programme managers, international agencies, such as the World Bank, non-governmental agencies, and foundations, in the recognition that tuberculosis will not be eradicated in industrialised countries without considerable reductions in the disease in their less-industrialised neighbours.

Referring to the staggering global burden of disease from TB despite the existence of a 'cost-effective intervention' (Murray *et al.* 1990), Kochi called on the 'global village to get its act together'.

Achieving the global through the local: putting partnerships into practice

As described above, there is a clear emphasis in current TB initiatives on the global, both in terms of the nature of the disease and the strategies advocated to control the disease. In an effort to reinvigorate and mobilise political support for control programmes, WHO and other organisations have emphasised the global risks from TB and MDRTB. How well the 'fit' will be, however, between controlling the disease and current and planned control programmes, hinges on a number of issues.

One important issue is the strong promotion of DOTS as the successful centrepiece of the 'global control strategy'. There is evidence that DOTS itself may be leading to questionable practices that challenge the reported success of the strategy. Research of practices at two chest disease clinics in New Delhi, India shows that TB health workers were screening patients attending their clinics to assess their likelihood of complying with DOTS. This pre-selection process resulted in the majority of patients (57 per cent combined average for the two chest clinic areas) being rejected for treatment (Sarin *et al.* 1998; Singh *et al.* 1998a, 1998b). Importantly, those turned away tended to be individuals with no fixed address, migrant workers and new and poorly connected migrants; indeed, the very categories of people DOTS was designed to support (Voelker 1996). Thus, DOTS has been found to fail to support the most vulnerable TB patients.

The gap between nationally and globally aggregated statistics, and the treatment of individuals, raises the challenge of appropriately adapting broadly encompassing strategies at the global level to the particular conditions and needs of local contexts. The adoption of DOTS as the 'global standard' was strongly influenced by the experience of TB control in the 1980s in a number of lower-income countries including Tanzania, Mozambique and Nicaragua. The strategy was then developed and applied in New York City in the 1990s where relatively large volumes of resources and a well-developed public health infrastructure is available. The New York programme was further supported by a broad partnership of social support (Klein *et al.* 1994; Klein and Naizby 1995; Freudenberg 1995). In countries such as India and China, the introduction of DOTS without sufficient understanding of social, economic and cultural context can bring unexpected practices, as described in the Indian context.

The slow and difficult uptake of the strategy in many countries, with 21 per cent of smear-positive TB cases worldwide treated under a DOTS programme (WHO 1998c,e; 1999d), might suggest that much greater attention needs to be given to local contexts. Notably, a WHO TB guide on advocacy (1998e) has consistently recognised the need to consider local context in advocating DOTS, stating that 'obviously, political protocol, media etiquette and social values vary widely from country to country: advocacy tactics that work in London might not be appropriate for Jakarta'. The guide provides specific examples and ideas for how to apply DOTS in different settings. None the less, DOTS has been advocated as an intervention, some might even say a solution, to the increasing cases of TB in all countries around the world. There is an acceptance that the context for each programme will be different, but that the systems and structures that need to be established are the same. In this sense, DOTS is seen as an essentially technical intervention that, in and of itself, is value-neutral. DOTS, it is claimed, provides a 'common language' through which to develop national and local strategies.

There is growing evidence, however, that DOTS as advocated by the international community through WHO, may not be appropriate to all settings, and that more flexibility is required in the way TB services are administered (Klein and Naizby 1995; Bayer *et al.* 1998; Heymann *et al.* 1998; Zwarenstein *et al.* 1998). At a global level, TB policy has been driven by the desire to find 'gold standards' for disease control. These gold standards focus on biological and technical solutions, but, when applied in varied national and community level contexts, can take inadequate account of the wide range of influences that affect policy implementation, such as cultural acceptability, medical pluralism, the impact of health reforms on resources, and health systems management (Porter *et al.* 1999a). Although the WHO DOTS strategy stresses the importance of flexibility in the implementation of the strategy, it does not appear to accept that the strategy itself has been created with concepts and values that are inherent within western industrialised democracies, and is being introduced into countries, in particular in Asia and Africa, which may have different concepts and values. Hence, the package still has not been accepted and incorporated into many national health care systems. One of the principal reasons for this is that the health structures, which are needed to support a DOTS programme, are often insufficiently resourced and poorly maintained. As the Indian literature indicates, TB control programmes cannot and should not be developed unless there is a strong health care infrastructure to support them (e.g. Banerji 1990; Uplekar and Rangan 1995).

It can be argued that there is a global concept of how TB should be controlled, but there is little understanding of *what* happens at the national or local levels or *how* it should happen. What happens when the DOTS package is introduced into a ministry of health and *how* does the ministry administer 'the package' to the regions, districts and communities (i.e. locally)? Inaccuracies in the reporting of data are one area for which WHO is able to see quite vividly that there may be problems at the periphery. The 1999 global report on tuberculosis, for example, notes that 'Even in DOTS programmes, detection rates ... do not concur with the practical experience of some TB control workers' (WHO 1999d). WHO is not as clear, however, about the extent to which these inconsistencies are due to staff failures or the failure of the programme to adequately meet and address the needs of those implementing and reporting it.

A further issue lies in the strong belief that 'Curing TB is really about getting the drugs – TB medication – to the bugs' (Holmes 1996), without sufficient understanding and attention to the broader socio-economic factors that contribute to the spread of the disease. To the extent that DOTS pays attention to structural issues, the focus remains on supply chains and health care infrastructure to deliver drugs and monitor patient compliance. However, this remains a limited view of the importance of socio-economic determinants of health. The profound effects of poverty and/or economic inequity, racism, gender inequalities, drug use, homelessness, political violence, civil disturbance and war are all key factors in, for example, the inability of patients to obtain, maintain and complete therapy (Farmer 1997). In relation to MDRTB, it is these structural factors (what Farmer refers to as *structural violence*) that will influence the presence or absence of monotherapy, regular or erratic drug supplies, and better or worse access to adequate care facilities. Farmer concludes that 'throughout the world, those least likely to comply are those least able to comply ... [T]hese settings are crying out for measures to improve the quality of care, not the quality of patients' (Farmer 1997: 353).

The heavy emphasis on DOTS has also raised concerns that the strategy is being promoted too heavily at the expense of other interventions. With finite resources for TB control worldwide, many believe that the key challenge lies in getting drugs of proven effectiveness to patients, rather than in the development of other control tools (Styblo and Bumgarner 1991; Snider 1994). Similar arguments are beginning to be made for 'DOTS-plus' for MDRTB. As Portaels *et al.* (1999) indicate, all five elements of the DOTS strategy may need to be modified, again with treatment needing to be individualised rather than standardised, according to local needs and conditions.

These concerns around the appropriateness and effectiveness of current global TB control strategies have been recognised to some extent in current policy discussions that seek to take forward new initiatives. As noted above, 'The Stop TB Initiative' has proposed the adoption of a Global Partnership Agreement to Stop Tuberculosis, although details on the precise nature of such a partnership remain to be defined.[2] While the desire to work in a broader coalition of stakeholders is a laudable one, the detail of how this will be achieved has not been agreed. Among the questions raised are: what is meant by a 'global partnership'? What will it look like in practice? Who will be members of this partnership? What will be the rights and responsibilities of the private sector and civil society? What will be the institutional means of governance? How will authority be distributed and wielded? Who will contribute intellectual, financial and human resources? Who will control the allocation of resources?

The process of building such a 'global partnership' will be the focus of considerable effort in coming years and, it is argued here, how these kinds of questions are addressed will strongly influence the effectiveness of such a partnership (see Buse and Walt, chapter 3). It is proposed that an alternative global TB control strategy would begin with the principles of equity and social justice (Porter and Ogden 1997; Porter *et al.* 1999a,b). It would then seek to link the local and global together, rejecting a top-down and standardised approach to DOTS. Such an alternative strategy would have the following features (Ogden 2000):

- Participatory – in the process of decision-making, involving, in particular, currently vulnerable or disadvantaged groups affected by TB.

- Multi-pronged – in its approach to the complex, largely socio-economic, causes of TB infection, rather than focused primarily on biomedical treatment, linking TB initiatives with those directed at poverty alleviation, equitable access to health care, improved housing, employment, nutrition etc.

- Inclusiveness – in availability and effectiveness to all who are affected by TB regardless of country or socio-economic status.

- Understanding – of the importance of balancing globally defined and standardised strategies with local needs and contexts.

Conclusion: tuberculosis control in a world of global inequality

This chapter has been concerned with the links between globalisation and tuberculosis. Currently, the dominant motif of globalisation is one of growing interconnectedness, of shared and mutual interests among individuals and communities throughout the world. In infectious disease control policy, globalisation has led to a focus on the enhanced potential for infectious agents to spread across national borders. In the case of TB, renewed attention to the disease within higher-income countries and international organisations has arisen because of such fears. The key strategy put forth for addressing this 'new' threat has been DOTS.

However, this chapter considers the link between globalisation and TB control from a broader perspective. Challenging the notion of globalisation as a neo-liberal utopia, not only may globalisation be integrating individuals and groups more closely together, it is also widening divisions between haves and have nots within and across countries (Amin 1997). It is these divisions that have contributed to the global resurgence of TB and that have created the key challenges to developing effective control strategies.

It is in this context that DOTS has been advocated worldwide as a global strategy, but, as discussed in this chapter, a number of issues can be raised concerning the truly global nature of this strategy. The need for greater sensitivity to local contexts and needs, the problems of a narrow biomedical focus, insufficient attention to social and economic determinants of health, and exclusion of significant groups from accessing DOTS suggest that the strategy is falling short of being truly global. In discussions on ways forward, it will be critical to avoid worsening the present distance between the governed and governing, between the powerful and the powerless, and between those who make, and those affected by, policies. Until a global TB strategy is adopted that is based on principles of social justice and equity, that directly addresses the underlying socio-economic causes of TB, TB will continue to grow as a global emergency.

NOTES

1 During the 1940s a series of drugs were developed and clinically tested as effective, including isoniazid, pyrazinamide and ethambutol (streptomycin). A fourth drug, rifampicin, was introduced in the 1970s.
2 However, see the Amsterdam Declaration to Stop TB, signed and agreed at the 20–24 March 2000 Ministerial Conference on TB and Sustainable Development, Amsterdam. Available to view at <www. stoptb.org>.

KEY READINGS

Bayer, R., Stayton, C., Desvarieux, M., Healton, C., Landesman, S. and Tsai, W. Y. 1998, 'Directly observed therapy and treatment completion for tuberculosis in the United States: is universal supervised therapy necessary?', *American Journal of Public Health* 88 (7): 1052–8.
Farmer, P. 1997, 'Social scientists and the new tuberculosis', *Social Science and Medicine* 44 (7): 347–58.
Grange, J. M. 1999, 'The global burden of tuberculosis', in Porter, J. D. H. and Grange, J. M. (eds.) 1999, *Tuberculosis – an interdisciplinary perspective*, London: Imperial College Press, pp. 3–31.
Porter, J. D. H. and Ogden, J. A. 1997, 'Ethics of Directly Observed Therapy for the control of infectious diseases', *Bulletin of the Institute Pasteur* 95: 117–27.
Walt, G. 1999. 'The politics of tuberculosis: the role of process and power', in Porter, J. D. H. and Grange, J. G. (eds.) *Tuberculosis – an interdisciplinary perspective*, London: Imperial College Press, pp. 67–98.

11 Ageing and health policy: global perspectives

Peter Lloyd-Sherlock

Introduction

Accelerated population ageing is now a global trend: it is already a significant issue for developed countries and is becoming one in many poorer parts of the world. Different aspects of globalisation may have potential relevance for the health and well-being of older people. Globalisation has influenced the emergence of international policy debates about population ageing, particularly through the diffusion of a negative cultural paradigm of old age largely of western origin. Also, global orthodoxies of health care financing and management have become increasingly prominent, and many of them have important, and often detrimental, impacts on elders. This chapter examines these issues, paying particular attention to possible implications for health policy.

Definitions, meanings and trends

There is general dissatisfaction with defining old age in purely chronological terms, but there would appear to be no universally appropriate alternatives to this approach. Old age is perceived and understood in a multitude of different ways, often with important cultural variations. These may refer to biological processes and physical appearance, key life events or social roles (Knopoff *et al.* 1991; Derricourt and Miller 1992; Apt 1997). Since old age can cover a span of over three decades, most cultures distinguish between the 'old old' and 'young old', and it is usually more meaningful to think in terms of a gradual change, rather than a sharp cut-off between adulthood and later life.

Demographic ageing (defined as an increase in the percentage of a population aged sixty-five years or over) is now an established trend in most world regions, with the exception of Africa (Table 11.1).[1] Data aggregated at the level of world regions hide important internal variations. Table 11.2 shows the proportion of older people at the individual country level, selecting countries that represent the extreme range for each

Table 11.1 *Estimated medium variant projection of total population aged 65 years or more by world region (percentage)*

	1950	1970	1990	2010	2030
Europe	8.2	10.5	12.6	15.5	21.4
Africa	3.2	3.1	3.1	3.3	4.6
Asia	4.1	4.0	4.9	6.5	10.7
Latin America and Caribbean	3.5	4.1	4.8	6.5	11.2

Source: United Nations (1994b).

world region. Population ageing is usually a consequence of a country passing into the final stage of demographic transition, when sustained drops in fertility occur (Chesnais 1992). As the number of children being born in the younger cohorts falls, the relative size of the elderly population increases. This effect is compounded by significant reductions in adult mortality, which contribute to extended life expectancy. Many sub-Saharan African countries are yet to enter the final stage of transition, and it remains uncertain if they ever will (Kirk 1996). However, high rates of mortality from HIV/AIDS among younger groups may cause a sudden surge in demographic ageing, which is not factored into most current projections (Mupedziswa 1997).

Table 11.2 *Countries with highest and lowest proportions of population aged 65 or over by world region, 1990*

Region	Country	Percentage of population aged 65+
Africa	South Africa	4.3
	Botswana	2.3
Asia	Japan	12.0
	Cambodia	2.6
Europe	Sweden	17.8
	Albania	5.3
Latin America	Uruguay	11.6
	Nicaragua	3.0

Source: United Nations (1994b).

Ageing and international policy development

Before the 1990s, population ageing was not seen as a significant global development issue. Many developing countries had not yet reached the final stage of demographic transition, and fertility rates remained high. As such, there was more concern about total rates of population growth (the population 'time bomb') and the policy implications of bottom-heavy population pyramids, including maternal and child health needs (Ehrlich 1971; Stanford 1972).

Attempts to include older peoples' well-being in the international development agenda date back to 1948, when a draft 'Declaration of Old Age Rights' was proposed at the United Nations General Assembly (Gorman 1999a). However, it was not until 1982 that a major international conference addressed the subject, when the UN hosted a 'World Assembly on Ageing' in Vienna and adopted an International Plan of Action on Ageing.[2] This long delay reflects the low priority given to ageing issues during the intervening period. The International Plan of Action was followed by the designation of an annual UN Day for Older Persons. During the 1980s the response to these initiatives was minimal. Several agencies, such as WHO and the UN Division for Social Policy and Development, established ageing programmes, but these were small scale and under-resourced. Indeed, it was not until 1991 that the UN adopted a legally binding charter of rights: the UN Principles for Older Persons.

The lack of concern about ageing in global development discourses was echoed in international health policy debates. The emergence of primary health care (PHC) as the dominant health policy discourse during the 1980s was largely derived from the perceived failures of curative, hospital-centred models, particularly in developing countries. A central tenet of the new approach was a shift away from expensive treatment for chronic diseases towards basic services and essential drugs, particularly for mothers and young children (WHO 1978; Rifkin and Walt 1986). Whilst age discrimination was never an explicit goal of PHC, it inevitably entailed a reduced prioritisation of services which principally benefited older age groups. In fact, many older people in developing countries also lacked access to basic health services, and there is no reason why aspects of PHC, such as health promotion and community participation, could not have taken particular account of this group's needs (Dinotshe Tou and Sandberg 1994; Durán-Arenas et al. 1996). However, the prominence of mother and child health needs, with a particular emphasis on child health, within PHC discourse has largely precluded this possibility.

During the early 1990s, it was increasingly recognised that population ageing had become a global trend, giving rise to a wide range of policy challenges. These concerns were fuelled by events in different parts of the world: recognition of the ultimate demographic impact of one-child policies in China; the increasing cost of old-age health care and social services in OECD countries; multi-billion dollar bankruptcies of state pension funds across Latin America; and the plight of older people in Former Socialist Economies (Banister 1987; Mesa-Lago 1991; Moon 1993; Rush and Welch 1996). At the same time, fertility rates in most developing countries had started to decline rapidly. This gave demographers and population policy-makers time and space to consider new issues, and past worries about a population 'time bomb' gave way to new ones about an 'old age crisis' (World Bank 1994b).

Concerns about population ageing might have been expected to feature prominently in the 1994 Cairo International Conference on Population and Development. In fact, the issue was largely overlooked, given that the central thrust of the meeting was to replace population control programmes with a broader, rights-based approach to reproductive health care (Lane 1994; McIntosh and Finkle 1994). Although reaching global consensus on the latter issue was a considerable achievement, with widespread ramifications for population policy, health policy and social development, reproductive health care is closely linked with PHC and thus reinforces the emphasis on mother and child health.

Two developments in international health policy during the 1990s potentially had significant implications for older people. The first was an increased recognition of adult health problems, many of which, such as smoking and diet, could be directly addressed by policy interventions. Under-pinning this concern was the view that adult populations were economically and socially productive, and therefore improving their health would benefit development in general (Feachem *et al.* 1992; Reich 1995). The principal form of economic evaluation of health interventions advocated by the World Bank, the disability-adjusted life year (DALY), explicitly incorporates these considerations, by affording the health gains of 'productive populations' (curiously defined as those aged 9 to 55 years) a higher DALY value than for other groups (Paalman *et al.* 1998). However, the possibility that many older people in developing countries might also be both economically and socially productive was overlooked. As such, rather than extend its reach to older people, the adult health initiative led to further discrimination against the aged.

The second health policy change has been the adoption of neo-liberal inspired health sector reforms in most developed and developing countries. The global diffusion of these new health care models, incorporating

inter alia privatisation, decentralisation, cost recovery and new management structures, may have many effects on the access of older people
to health services (Lloyd-Sherlock 2000). Some of these issues are considered in more detail below. However, when ageing is mentioned by
proponents of sectoral reform, it is primarily in terms of a pressure on
health spending, and is used as a justification for change (van der Gaag
and Precker 1997). Conversely, the health needs of elders have received
little if any specific attention in the development and diffusion of these
models, nor has their impact on older people been evaluated.

Despite recognition that population ageing is a significant global phenomenon, it remains largely peripheral to international development and
health policy discourse. Recent years have seen a number of international
meetings linked to the designation of 1999 as the UN International Year
of the Older Person, and the United Nations plans to hold a major global
conference on ageing in Madrid in 2002. These initiatives succeeded in
raising the profile of population ageing at the national level in a number of
countries. However, at the international level, rather than radically shift
agendas, these initiatives have simply thrown into relief a continued lack
of interest in this field. For example, of the seven major international development reports published in 1998 only two gave significant coverage
to ageing issues (Help Age International 1999).[3]

The failure to raise the international policy profile of population ageing can be attributed to a number of causes. A key difficulty is the global
predominance of a negative paradigm of old age. This draws on western experiences, which equate old age with withdrawal (from both economic and social spheres), dependency, physical frailty and pensioner
status. The applicability of these stereotypes in the context of developed
countries is highly contestable, but in most developing countries they
are largely meaningless. Older people are seen as marginal to economic
activity and development, and are usually excluded from labour-force
statistics, yet empirical research from around the world challenges this
view (Kaiser 1994; Gorman 1999b). This negative paradigm of old age
is reinforced through media imagery in both developed and developing
countries (Hazan 1991). Reflecting this paradigm, the 'policy market' for
older people may present a relatively unattractive 'product', compared
to that for other issues and other groups (Barnett and Lloyd-Sherlock
2000). Similar observations have been made by Michael Reich (1995)
in his account of international agenda setting around child and adult
health.

As part of this global paradigm, older peoples' health needs are characterised as requiring high-cost, long-term treatments. Elders are therefore
seen as part of the 'problem' of overly curative health care, low technical

efficiency (narrowly defined) and mounting costs. In an extreme form, this has given rise to statements that adding years to later life simply brings closer the bankruptcy of schemes such as Medicare.[4] These views lose sight of the fact that, whilst the very old are more likely to suffer from chronic illnesses, there is still considerable scope to improve their health through promotion and education programmes (Fletcher *et al.* 1998). The relationship between population ageing and health expenditure is unclear, especially for developing countries (see below). Moreover, access to basic services remains a key issue for poor older people in poorer parts of the world.

A second barrier to the emergence of a clear international policy agenda is the absence of an influential global policy community whose principal concern lies with the health and well-being of older people. Whilst many international agencies may have some interest in ageing issues, for none is it a high priority. Only one international NGO, Help Age International, has a primary interest in ageing and development issues. Although organisations such as the World Bank and the International Labour Organisation (ILO) have taken a greater interest in recent years, this has tended to serve as a justification for existing ideological preferences, rather than a concern with addressing fundamental issues around ageing, development and well-being. In the area of international health policy, even this has not happened.

Other obstacles to developing a strong global agenda include the fact that population ageing is a gradual, and largely predictable process, not a sudden event which might do more to capture the attention of policymakers, the media and public opinion. Moreover, the timing and the intensity of the process vary between countries. This may in part account for the absence of an influential international interest group representing older people: 'grey power' is largely a phenomenon of the US and a handful of developed countries. Finally, the lack of interest shown by the scientific community, particularly social scientists, has compounded these problems. Population ageing as a research agenda is mainly framed as a developed country issue, rather than a global concern.

Consequences of population ageing for health policy

When considering health policies for older people, and the impact of ageing on health expenditure, the associated epidemiological changes would seem to be a logical starting point. Unfortunately, there is little available information on which to base such an analysis. In the developed world there is still disagreement about whether increased longevity means an extension of healthy active lives or an extension of morbidity (Fries 1980;

Sidell 1995; Manton *et al.* 1997). For other regions, available data do not even allow for an informed debate.

It should not be assumed that the epidemiology of older populations in developing countries will match that of their counterparts in richer ones. The developed world has gone through an 'epidemiological transition' similar to, and associated with, the demographic one. This has seen the main causes of death and illness shift from infectious diseases, under-nutrition and inadequate hygiene to a post-transition phase, where 'diseases of wealth' (including chronic disease, road accidents and stress) are now prominent (Frenk *et al.* 1991; Caldwell 1993). In developing countries the situation is often more complex, and is sometimes referred to as 'incomplete epidemiological transition' (Londoño and Frenk 2000). On the one hand, easily preventable diseases and poverty-related problems still continue to account for a high share of mortality and morbidity. On the other, emerging 'diseases of wealth' have seen rapid increases. Often distinct epidemiological scenarios can be identified between different geographical zones (rural/urban, rich/poor region) and between different socio-economic groups. As such, many developing countries face a double health challenge.

Given the differences in the broader epidemiological contexts of developed and developing regions, it is to be expected that the health problems of older people will vary between the two. Those living in developing regions face both pre- and post-transition risk factors. For relatively wealthy older people living in cities, the latter set of factors may be most significant. However, for poorer old people, particularly in rural districts, both sets of risk factors can be important. As such, it is dangerous to generalise about the health problems of older people across a single country. For example, in the largely poor rural state of Oaxaca in Mexico, intestinal infections were the second most important cause of death among elders in 1990, whereas, in the richer, more urbanised state of Baja California, they occupied only twelfth place (Ham-Chande 1996).

The conventional wisdom that the health needs of older people are expensive to treat and require complex interventions is challenged by the widespread problem of cataract-induced blindness. In 1990, it was estimated that there were 38 million blind people globally, and a further 110 million had low vision and were at high risk of becoming blind (Thylefors *et al.* 1995). Of these, a disproportionate number (58 per cent) were over sixty years old. Age-specific prevalence rates show that levels of blindness will increase sharply over the decades to come, unless appropriate policies are developed. The majority of cases are caused by cataracts, for which cheap and effective treatment is available (Venkataswamy and Brilliant 1981).

Even if population ageing is associated with a global increase in the incidence of certain forms of chronic disease, its impact on health services may not be as direct as is widely claimed. Rather than driving up health spending, the main impact of ageing may be a shifting of priorities. Any society is faced by a far higher demand for health services than it can meet, and therefore some form of rationing is always present. The gap between demand and provision is especially wide in lower-income countries, highlighted by failures such as the lack of access of most AIDS sufferers to effective drug therapies. The likelihood that changing demographics will lead to a health care cost explosion in these contexts is remote.

Even in developed countries there is clear evidence that health care spending is not directly affected by population ageing *per se* (McGrail *et al.* 2000). A range of other factors, such as technological change, the organisation of services and general levels of material wealth have been found to be more significant (van der Gaag and Precker 1997). Although health spending is usually above average for older people, this is mainly due to the cost of treating patients close to death. The 'costs of dying' may indeed be lower for older people than for other age groups, where they receive less treatment because of ageist bias.

Rather than formal health service provision, the main financial impact of population ageing may result from the more general care needs of some older people. These long-term care requirements are not usually seen as a core responsibility for health care systems. However, the division between the two is often quite arbitrary, both in theory and in practice. Meeting these care needs is now recognised as a major financial challenge in developed countries. In the UK, around 14 per cent of women and 7 per cent of men aged over 65 years require daily help to maintain independent living, at an estimated cost of £500 million a year (Lloyd-Sherlock 2000). In low- and middle-income countries, assumptions about the strength of informal family support systems have largely kept this issue off the policy agenda. However, this belief should be questioned. For example, in Uruguay, despite a Latin culture which stresses family solidarity, a higher proportion of older people live in residential care than is the case in the USA. Where families' support is not forthcoming and where residential care is not available (or is stigmatised), the only option may be to hospitalise older people. This is a widespread problem in many countries, and it is likely to worsen, unless more direct policy responses are developed.

Older people and access to health care

Older people may face particular problems of access to health services, and these may be affected by the global diffusion of new models of health care. As well as the obvious barriers of mobility, elders in many parts of the world suffer from high levels of illiteracy, which is recognised as a major influence on access to services. Moreover, the negative paradigm of old age is often apparent in the attitudes of providers, as well as older people themselves and their families. A study of the uptake of cataract services in India and sub-Saharan Africa found that older people were less likely to seek treatment than other age groups (Fletcher and Donoghue 1998). The main barriers to uptake were found to be the low status of elders in some communities and the misconception that poor vision was a natural consequence of the ageing process. Similar problems of cataract uptake, albeit on a smaller scale, have been observed in the UK.

Changes in the financing and organisation of health services may increase problems of access for the aged. To date, no single approach to old-age health financing has been accepted at the global level. It is unlikely that the US model of Medicare will be exported to developing and transitional countries with the same vigour as, for example, health care maintenance organisations (HMOs). The undoubted failings of Medicare are well recognised even beyond the USA. Between 1967 and 1984 Medicare expenditures grew at over 9 per cent annually in real terms. Only a small part of this can be accounted for by growing affiliation or by an increase in members' average ages (Garber 1994). Since the 1980s, levels of coverage provided by Medicare have been eroded, and the scheme now incorporates incentives for members to take out additional insurance with HMOs or other private organisations (Moon 1993). Attempts by the first Clinton administration to radically overhaul and upgrade Medicare were thwarted by a well-orchestrated and well-funded campaign of resistance led by medical practitioners. The only obvious parallel to this approach is the Programa de Asistencia Medica Integral (PAMI) old-age health fund in Argentina.[5] This fund was initially successful in extending a range of health and other social services to insured older people (about two-thirds of the total elderly population), but by the mid-1990s it had begun to accumulate substantial deficits: these had reached US $1.5 billion by 1995 (Lloyd-Sherlock 1997). PAMI's financial crisis has deepened since then, despite a US $200 million bale-out loan from the World Bank.

The experiences of Medicare and PAMI are not encouraging. Whether similar programmes are appropriate to the needs of other countries depends on the broader context of health care financing and organisation. In countries with unitary, universal social insurance schemes, such as the UK, there would seem to be little point in creating separate programmes. Indeed, such a move might ghettoise health care for the aged, prevent intergenerational solidarity and create an institutional logic of cost escalation. However, in countries where health care programmes are fragmented and non-universal, and where private insurance is a major component, there may be little alternative. This is because market mechanisms and individually contracted health insurance often discriminate against the aged through cream-skimming. For example, in Chile, where private HMOs have become a major component of health care financing, only 3 per cent of their patients are aged sixty or more, compared to 12 per cent in public hospitals and clinics (Stocker *et al.* 1999). Similarly, surveys of newly formed private insurance companies in Russia indicate a strong tendency to discriminate against the aged (Twigg 1999). In most countries with private insurance, attempts to prevent cream-skimming through regulation have proved to be largely ineffective. Access to insurance is particularly limited for those older people with pre-existing conditions. Also, firms may be discouraged from employing older people because they are unable to find moderately priced health insurance for them.

As such, the growing global prominence of private health insurance and schemes such as HMOs is likely to further marginalise health care for elders, unless specified old age funds *à la Medicare* are in place (Chollet and Lewis 1997). The apparent problems of such funds and the lack of alternatives to them should be considered as an intrinsic cost of shifting away from unitary public programmes, and, where possible, these costs should be passed on to private insurers.

For publicly financed health services, the increased global emphasis on cost-recovery may have specific impacts on the aged. Whilst user fees and co-payments may sometimes be helpful in generating additional revenue or 'rationalising' usage, they are often inequitable, even where exemptions are theoretically in place for vulnerable groups (Russell and Gilson 1997). A recent survey of older people in Ghana found that most were unaware that they were exempt from paying user fees for services from public hospitals, and that this had greatly reduced access (Ahenkora 1999).

The dominant global principles of health care management place considerable emphasis on increasing the technical efficiency of health services. This, combined with growing pressures to ration provision, often on the basis of age, may have serious consequences for elders (Binstock and Post 1991; Paalman *et al.* 1998). The introduction of an internal market in the UK's National Health Service (NHS) led to fears that high-cost older patients would be less attractive to independent hospital trusts. These fears were supported by several surveys, which found that some health authorities were indeed reducing their numbers of long-term beds and geriatric care (Walker and Maltby 1997). Similar concerns that risk rating would not deter GP fund-holders from discriminating against older people would seem to be less well founded (Le Grand 1998). Both of these models are now being actively exported and marketed in developing countries, where the capacity of state regulation to mitigate their potential effects on older people may not be so strong.[6]

Overseas residence is likely to grow significantly over the next few decades, making health provision for older people an increasingly global issue. Large numbers of northern European and North American retirees now reside in more southerly climes (Warnes *et al.* 1999). In other cases, overseas residence may entail return migration from countries such as the UK back to the Caribbean and South Asia. Living abroad can create problems of access in the host country if services are financed through an insurance scheme to which the expatriate lacks entitlement. This has been identified as a particular problem for British returnees in Jamaica (Goulbourne 1999). In the USA, such concerns have led to calls for Medicare to fund providers in Mexico and Costa Rica (countries where large numbers of US senior citizens are resident) – a strategy which might actually reduce Medicare costs if overseas providers are cheaper than their US counterparts. As well as immigration, older people may opt to travel overseas in order to receive health care which is unavailable or more expensive in their own countries. Indeed, meeting the health needs of US and Canadian senior citizens has now become a significant source of funding for the Cuban health service (Garfield and Holz 2000).

Older people's access to good-quality informal care may be strongly influenced by rapid processes of socio-economic change associated with globalisation, including migration and changing family compositions. For example, a shift towards smaller households is thought to weaken the bases of informal support and caring (Contreras de Lehr 1989). These issues are of particular concern for developing countries where change is often abrupt and where compensatory social services are less extensive. However, empirical research has revealed that relationships between living arrangements and informal care are complex, and cannot be inferred from crude demographic data (Varley and Blasco 2000). Studies from East Asia have found cases where intergenerational exchange has stood up well to social change (Thailand) and cases where it has been less resilient (Hong Kong) (Phillips 2000). As such, it is dangerous to generalise about global trends in informal care arrangements, and attention should be paid to the role of local factors.

Conclusion

Population ageing is now a global demographic trend. It will have important consequences for all aspects of health policy, although these may not be as obvious as is often claimed. The development of effective strategies has been hampered by a lack of international policy focus on the well-being of older people, and by the predominance of a negative global paradigm of old age. This characterises elderly populations as economically unproductive and a growing financial burden on the social sectors. There is little indication that this view is changing. As a result, most international health policy initiatives ignore the needs of elders, and many may worsen existing problems of access.

Population ageing creates many challenges for health policy, but the current tendency to reduce the issue to one of an 'old age cost explosion' is both misleading and prejudiced. The impact of changing demographics on health spending can only be understood with reference to a range of other considerations, many of which may carry greater weight than any effect of old age. The health status of elders may be significantly improved through health promotion and education campaigns (Fletcher *et al.* 1999). In developing countries guaranteeing universal access to basic provision is as important for older people as it is for other age groups. The relationship between ageing, population health and health care systems is now being reshaped by the global spread of new models of financing and provision, particularly private insurance funds.

A global response to population ageing should be based on a much deeper understanding of these issues. A particular challenge will be the development of long-term care services, as these are likely to be considerably more expensive than any other area of health care. Health policy responses must be located in an inter-sectoral framework, which recognises the interrelationships between different aspects of older people's well-being and the central importance of intergenerational bargaining.

NOTES

1 In much of Africa, accelerated life-cycle transitions mean that standard chronological thresholds of old age (population aged 65 years or over) understate the true importance of the ageing process (Apt 1996).
2 The International Plan was adopted by 124 UN member states and the General Assembly, but is not a legally binding document. It outlines principles and recommendations to governments in the areas of health, nutrition, income security, education and research. The full text is available at <www.un.org/esa/socdev/ageing.html>.
3 These reports are *The state of the world population, 1998* (UNFPA/Australian National University 1998), *The world health report* (WHO 1998f); *World Bank development indicators 1998* (World Bank 1998a); *The world disasters report 1998/9* (IFRC 1999); *The world development report 1998* (World Bank 1998b); *The human development report 1998* (UNDP 1998); *Social Watch NGO coalition* (Social Watch 1998).
4 Medicare is a US, federally financed, health insurance fund for people aged sixty-five years and over. By the 1990s, it was accounting for over 40 per cent of total US federal health care spending.

5 The PAMI fund provides comprehensive health insurance and various other so-cial services to older Argentines who previously worked in the formal economy (about 65 per cent of those aged over sixty-five). Its main source of funding is a 1 per cent levy on all formal sector wages.

6 For example, the UK government Department for Trade and Industry has been particularly active in promoting the export of British health care models to other countries, working closely with professional bodies such as the Royal Colleges of Physicians, and regional trade promotion agencies such as the Latin American Trade Advisory Group (LATAG).

KEY READINGS

Fletcher, A., Breeze, E. and Walters, R. 1999, 'Health promotion for older people: what are the opportunities?', *Promotion and Education* 6: 4–7.

Gorman, M. 1999, 'Development and the rights of older people', in Help Age International, *The ageing and development report*, London: Earthscan.

Londoño, J. and Frenk, J. 2000, 'Structured pluralism. Towards an innovative model for health system reform in Latin America', in Lloyd-Sherlock, P. (ed.) *Healthcare reform and poverty in Latin America*, London: Institute of Latin American Studies.

McGrail, K., Green, B., Barer, M. L., Evans, R. G., Hertzman, C. and Normand, C. 2000, 'Age, costs of acute and long term care and proximity to death: evidence for 1987–88 and 1994–95 in British Columbia', *Age and Ageing* 29 (3): 249–54.

World Bank, 1994, *Averting the old age crisis: policies to protect the old and promote growth*, Oxford University Press for the World Bank.

12 Workers' health and safety in a globalising world

Suzanne Fustukian, Dinesh Sethi and Anthony Zwi

When wages less than the minimum are imposed on female garment workers in Bangladesh, that is a violation of the minimum wage law. When the workplace is put under lock and key with workers inside, that is a violation of human rights. When hundreds of these women die in a fire because they cannot get out, that is a human tragedy. When 27 million workers in the world's export processing zones are not allowed to organize in unions, that is a violation of workers' rights as well as human rights.

UNDP (1999)

Introduction

Recent public health debate has focused attention and action on the health issues linked to the global trade of commodities such as tobacco (Yach and Bettcher 1998a,b; Baris and McLeod 2000; Bettcher *et al.* 2000), and the distribution of communicable diseases with global impact such as HIV/AIDS, cholera and tuberculosis (Lee and Zwi 1996; Lee and Dodgson 2000; Porter *et al.* this volume). However, a significant gap in the discourse around globalisation and health has been an analysis of the impact of global trade and production on the direct producers of global wealth – the workforce. In the current climate of intense global competition and mobility, many industries have shifted production to countries with lower labour costs, poorly organised and protected workers, and minimal environmental and safety regulations. Although such strategies may lead to short-term financial and employment gains, the longer-term consequences of damage to health and the environment are generally overlooked. A shift in agendas can be noted, however, with a growing consensus among international agencies and civil society organisations that workers' rights, including occupational health and safety provisions, need to be urgently addressed as part of a global social contract (ICFTU

1999; Deacon 2000). Transnational companies (TNCs) are also increasingly concerned about the 'triple bottom line', highlighting concerns not only with economic, but also social and environmental achievements.

The following review focuses attention on this important but neglected public health issue. We first discuss why workers' health is a significant global issue, using Lee's concept of global health risk (Lee 2000). This is followed by an analysis of the pressures and consequences of globalised production on the working population in low and middle income economies and communities. Current debates and strategy proposals by international agencies and civil society organisations responding to the higher profile of labour rights are briefly surveyed, as is evidence of occupational health and safety risks in workplaces worldwide. Lastly, we examine the prospects for improving health and safety in the workplaces of low- and middle-income countries (LMICs) and consider proposed mechanisms for doing so.

Workers' health – a global issue

Clarifying whether a specific health issue is 'global' as opposed to 'international' has implications for how policies are constructed and which stakeholders are engaged in this process (Lee 2000). International issues need to be addressed by governments, often working with multilateral organisations such as the United Nations, whereas 'global' issues require a broader range of stakeholders to be involved in addressing them.

Lee (2000) suggests a number of defining features of 'global' health issues: 'a health issue may be considered global in that it occurs ... in populations located geographically throughout the world'; there is 'inequality of risk creation and distribution resulting in an increased vulnerability of certain individuals and groups, or the creation of new patterns of vulnerability'; there is 'blurring of the creation of risk (cause) and its immediate experience (effect) across time and space'; it has 'the capacity to affect relatively large populations rather than single individuals'; and, finally, a wide range of stakeholders is necessary to effectively address it. While many of these features can be applied to national and international issues, the responsibility for identifying the need for formulating a response, and for developing interventions, can no longer be left to national- and international-level organisations: it is this which ultimately defines an issue as 'global'.

Work-related ill health is present to varying degrees in all settings and is an issue of worldwide occurrence. The risks and hazards associated with work are largely experienced by, but not confined to, low-income groups as well as by other vulnerable groups, such as women, children and minorities. Where wealthier and better-informed workers are at risk, they may be able to negotiate a trade-off between extra risk and extra remuneration: such options are unavailable to poorly informed and organised workers. According to the International Labour Organization (ILO), an estimated 1.2 million people die from work-related diseases and injuries annually, equivalent to annual mortality from malaria but capturing only a fraction of the attention. There are estimated to be 160 million new cases of work-related diseases each year, while a further 250 million workers experience work-related injuries (ILO 2000a). As much as 10 per cent of non-fatal injuries may lead to some form of permanent impairment, yet prevention strategies receive a tiny fraction of donor funds (Kjellstrom *et al.* 1992). Unlike malaria, which is geographically concentrated in specific climatic zones, work-related ill health is experienced in every part of the globe.

The global burden of occupational diseases and injuries is expected to increase over the next fifty years, due to the greater transfer of industrial processes to the developing world (WHO 1999e) as well as to increases in the size of the employed workforce across the globe, particularly in LMICs (World Bank 1995). Currently, 318 million DALYs[1] are estimated to be lost each year from occupational disease and injuries, whether from acute injurious or toxic exposures, or longer-term chronic disorders, including cancers and various forms of organ dysfunction, resulting from exposure to toxic chemicals, noise, stress and physically debilitating work patterns (World Bank 1993). The chronic nature of much occupational disease, the multiple exposures to a variety of hazards, and the long latency period, suggest that future work-related ill health will dramatically increase (WHO 1999e).

There are several ways in which 'inequality of risk creation and distribution' are displayed in relation to workers' health. First, while workers worldwide are at risk of exposure to a range of physical, chemical, biological, psychosocial and ergonomic hazards in their work environments, occupational diseases and injuries are more common in poor countries where most workers do not benefit from equivalent occupational health and safety standards. Deaths from occupational injuries, for example, are estimated to be ten times higher in LMICs than in developed countries (Kjellstrom *et al.* 1992). Injuries, both fatal and non-fatal, commonly occur in occupations related to agriculture, transportation, construction and primary industries such as mining. Agriculture, in which 'over 60 per cent of the economically active population' in LMICs is engaged (Wesseling *et al.* 1997), is regarded as one of the most dangerous occupations. (Kjellstrom *et al.* 1992). Specific agricultural hazards include falls, injuries from cutting instruments and machinery, transport-related injuries, drowning and exposure to disease-carrying animals and pesticides.

Secondly, inequalities are manifest in the global movement of workers. In particular, 'migrants tend to be concentrated in sectors of economic activity with no health and safety protection, and little or no legal protection, where they are particularly vulnerable to human rights abuses' (United Nations 1999a). For decades, migrant workers have performed the most dangerous and least profitable jobs, whether in the South African mines, the agricultural sector on the US–Mexico border, the South and East Europeans providing cheap labour for Western Europe, or the Asians providing domestic labour for the oil-rich Middle Eastern countries. Associated with migrant status is impermanence, reflected in temporary status, limited rights and least recourse when ill health occurs. Irregular or unofficial migrant workers are particularly vulnerable to exploitation (United Nations 1999a).

Thirdly, we increasingly witness the transfer of technology from highly regulated to less-regulated or even totally unregulated settings. Production processes common to specific industries, such as agriculture, microelectronics, and clothing and textiles, are found worldwide. However, while processes specific to each industry may be considered hazardous to human health, the degree of risk will vary according to the setting. The transfer of technology to LMICs may pose additional risks to workers in these settings. As Schenker (1992) points out, 'movement of "high tech" industries to less industrialised countries may not be accompanied by the same degree of attention to the control of workplace exposures'. The risk to workers from chemical and other hazards is particularly problematic in LMICs where standards for exposure are non-existent, not enforced or set too low (Michaels *et al.* 1985; Satterthwaite *et al.* 1992). Even in the US, standards for exposures to chemicals in the dynamic semiconductor industry are hotly contested, as 'little is known about the long-term health consequences of exposure to chemicals by semiconductor workers' (Chepesiuk 1999). A key issue arises in determining who bears the burden of risk where the consequences of exposure are currently unknown: is it the industry which should be forced to ensure minimal exposure given potential risk, or is it the workers who must work in uncontrolled environments because the actual risk has yet to be determined? All too often it is the workers rather than the manufacturers who bear the risks associated with uncertainty.

Box 12.1   The globalisation of the workforce in the microelectronic industry.

The microelectronic industry is highly competitive and innovative and raises particular concerns for workers' health worldwide. Large amounts of toxic chemicals are routinely used in the production of microchips, the core of the modern electronics industry, often as many as 300 different types (Chepesiuk 1999). Unlike older industries, such as mining or construction, where a significant level of health and safety research exists (Schenker 1992), little is known about the long-term health consequences of exposure to many of the chemicals used in semiconductor manufacturing (Geiser 1986; Chepesiuk 1999). As Schenker (1992) explains, 'there are numerous highly toxic materials used in the industry as well as several chemicals for which the toxicity in humans is unknown'. The combination of chemicals used includes known or suspected carcinogens, teratogens or mutagens (Geiser 1986), and includes 'metals such as arsenic, cadmium, and lead; volatile solvents such as methyl chloroform, toluene, benzene, acetone, and trichloroethylene; and toxic gases such as arsine' (Chepesiuk 1999).

The little evidence that does exist is based on acute exposures to high concentrations of these substances (Geiser 1986; Schenker 1992); almost nothing is known about the health effects of long-term exposure to low levels of many of these chemicals, nor about their synergistic effects (Geiser 1986; Chepesiuk 1999). Systemic poisoning, or 'multiple chemical sensitivity', may occur through low-level exposure to multiple, rather than single, toxic chemicals (Geiser 1986; Theobald 1999), about which 'absolutely nothing is known' (LaDou, quoted in Chepesiuk 1999). LaDou and others predict a significant rise in the cancer rate among workers in the semiconductor industry in the near future (Chepesiuk 1999).

Besides the chemically intense nature of the production process (Schenker 1992), the highly competitive and experimental nature of the industry also adds to raised levels of health risk (Geiser 1986; Chepesiuk 1999; Theobald 1999). Innovation means the introduction of new chemicals into the production process on an accelerating basis (Chepesiuk 1999); for example, Chepesiuk (1999) reports that Intel 'makes an average of 30–60 significant changes each year in its operations in order to ramp up production of new types of computer chips'. Toxicology assessments of many of these innovations involving new chemicals are either inadequate or non-existent as long as 'competitive advantage means that such chemical inputs, quantities and methods are closely guarded trade secrets' (Geiser 1986). As Theobald (1999) found, 'workers' testimonies' are often the only source of evidence in this environment, but only after their exposure to a range of hazards.

The chemical hazards in the new 'high tech' industries (see Box 12.1) are paralleled by increased chemical use in more traditional occupations, such as agriculture. Of worldwide concern is the increased use of toxic agrochemicals in all types of agriculture, with the exception of organic farming. The positive and negative effects of pesticide use have in recent years attracted attention (Forget *et al.* 1993). Although studies on the health consequences of long-term pesticide exposure are limited (Baris and McLeod 2000), these have been shown to include 'cancers, reproductive effects, peripheral neuropathies, neurobehavioural disorders, impaired immune functions, respiratory effects, and skin disorders' (Wesseling *et al.* 1997: 286).

New vulnerabilities: The incorporation of women and children into a globalised informal sector

Women and children are particularly vulnerable members of the global workforce, in part because they are less likely to be formally organised and more likely to be employed in the informal sector (Delahanty 1999a). This exposes them to more hazardous working conditions in unregulated settings. Many women in the informal sector are employed as maids, labourers, street vendors, workers in small-scale manufacturing and homeworkers undertaking sewing and assembly work (Barten 1993). With the growing 'feminisation' of the workforce in low-wage, export-oriented industries, women are increasingly exposed to new hazards (see Boxes 12.1 and 12.2), while being exposed also to age-old hazards of physical, economic and sexual coercion.

With the deterioration of economic conditions and growing poverty in many countries, the number of working children has also increased in recent years (UNDP 1999). Child labour is broadly defined by the ILO (1996) as economic activities carried out by children under the age of fifteen years, excluding household work. International concern, however, is concentrated on those children working in excessively abusive and exploitative conditions (Kent 1998): the ILO estimates that, of the 250 million working children under the age of fifteen years, 70 per cent work in hazardous conditions (in WHO 1999f). International campaigns have focused mainly on export industries such as carpet weaving, textiles and footwear production, although there are substantial numbers of children undertaking hazardous work for domestic consumer markets (PRIA 1992; Satterthwaite *et al.* 1992). In an effort to address this situation, an ILO Convention (Number 182) was adopted in 1999 focusing on the elimination of the 'worst forms of child labour' (ICFTU 1999). Additional hazards to both children and women relate to slavery, trafficking and incorporation, often against their will, into sex-work.

Children, in general, are extremely vulnerable to chemical and physical hazards in the work environment. Child garbage pickers in the

---

Box 12.2   Export processing zones.

An estimated 27 million workers work in approximately 850 export process-ing zones (EPZs) around the world (Jones 1999; UNDP 1999). EPZs are industrial zones specialising in manufacturing, particularly processing and assembly, of textiles, clothing and footwear, electronics, toys and other com-modities for export. Governments offer significant incentives to TNCs to set up in these specially deregulated enclaves: provision of physical infrastruc-ture and services offered at low cost; trade concessions, including exemption from taxes and customs duties; and exemptions from national labour laws, including minimum wage or health and safety regulations (Dicken 1998; Jones 1999; Scholte 1997a). The waiver of labour rights and standards ap-pears to be the pivotal factor in competition between EPZs set up in different countries. In many EPZs, unions are banned or severely circumscribed; for example, the Government of Bangladesh advertises that 'Bangladesh offers [a] most inexpensive but productive labour force. [The] law forbids forma-tion of labour unions in the [export processing] zones and strikes are illegal' (Alexander in Delahanty and Shefali 1999). Violations of workers' human rights in EPZs are frequent: factories patrolled by armed guards, with the workers locked in; enforced overtime without payment or release from the factory site until quotas completed; physical and sexual abuse; enforced pregnancy testing or sacking of women who become pregnant; and use of forced labour and child labour (Abell 1999; Jones 1999; Seyfang 1999).

Women increasingly form the 'bulk of the cheap and flexible labour force which is sought on the global labour market' (Delahanty 1999a). Women form 80 per cent of the workforce in EPZs (Jones 1999), 90 per cent in the textile, clothing and electronic assembly plants (ICFTU 1999). The pref-erence for female labour is based on a perception that women are more likely to be docile and non-militant, that they will more readily put up with repressive working conditions in order to keep their jobs. Some of the early EPZs, such as the *maquiladoras* on the Mexico/US border, were es-tablished when industry was, by and large, dominated by a unionised, male workforce; the EPZs were a means of bypassing a militant, male workforce (Abell 1999).

While such zones may bring some positive benefits to the largely female workforce in the form of employment and other social gains, the overall contribution is a denial of workers' human rights and the potential under-mining of their physical and mental health.

Philippines, for example, are at risk of lead and mercury poisoning, vi-olence, serious infections, skin disorders and skeletal deformities. In the agricultural sector, children are at risk from exposure to toxic agrochem-icals, and injuries from implements and machinery. Another concern is the many children who are caught up in the bonded-labour system, no-tably in South Asia and Latin America. This occurs when an advance payment is given to the bonded labourer, who is then trapped into paying the debt off with future (sometimes indefinite) earnings. In Pakistan, of the 20 million bonded labourers, 7.5 million are children (Kent 1998).

Worker exposure to the negative externalities of globalising industries

Negative externalities are created worldwide by industrial and agricultural processes that rely on, or produce as by-products, hazardous chemicals and processes, including pesticides, solvents, acids and toxic gases. All have the potential for contributing to environmental damage or posing a risk of industrial accidents (Geiser 1986; Cooper Weil *et al.* 1990; Satterthwaite *et al.* 1992; LaDou and Rohm 1998). Hazardous waste substances may be produced by agriculture and mining, nuclear power production, chemical processing, steel making, oil refining, metal working and the electronics industry. The hazardous effects of all the substances are not known, but many have been identified as mutagenic, teratogenic or carcinogenic. Other than dumping and landfills, the alternatives to waste management are incineration, recycling, detoxification and biological treatment. The methods are costly, sites for their treatment are scarce, and such methods are not always effective in removing potential hazards. These toxins not only have long-term environmental and health impacts if disposed of inappropriately, but will also pose health risks to handlers and workers, particularly if safety standards are lax or absent, and if knowledge of the hazards is scarce, as is often the case in LMICs (Castleman and Navarro 1987; LaDou 1992; Unwin *et al.* 1998).

Numerous reports confirm the practice of double standards by TNCs when comparing safety performance in their home countries with that pertaining in their LMIC operations (see Box 12.3) (Castleman and Navarro 1987). Hazardous technology has routinely been transferred without the concomitant transfer of engineering controls and expertise to protect workers and communities. These double standards were dramatically illustrated by the most disastrous industrial 'accident' in history: the Union Carbide disaster in Bhopal, India, in December 1984, which led to 3,000 deaths and 300,000 injuries (Shrivastava 1987). The number of people left with permanent lung damage is unknown. Investigations revealed that the sudden release of methylisocyanate gas into the surrounding community resulted from numerous shortcomings, including substandard design, poor equipment and maintenance, and operational deficiencies, many of which related to the indiscriminate economy drives by the Indian subsidiary of Union Carbide and its parent company. As victims of the explosion streamed to medical centres, neither government nor Union Carbide officials could provide information

---

Box 12.3   Double standards in occupational health.

- Exposure to recognised hazards in the South that would not be accepted in the North
- Lack of warning to those exposed
- Poor notification to employees of medical conditions discovered by industrial physicians
- Inadequate compensation of injured worker as employee
- Inadequate compensation of injured worker as consumer of industrial and agricultural products
- Exposure to technologies which have been replaced by safer alternatives

---

on which gas had been responsible or on how to treat those affected (Shrivastava 1987).

The tragedy has led to changes in practice by some large TNCs, with lesser volumes of toxic and potentially explosive substances being stored, and safety checks more rigorously undertaken. However, workers in LMICs remain at risk from many forms of hazard export (LaDou 1992) and are still at risk of chronic exposure to substances for which strict safety standards exist in the North. Through financing, licensing of technology, supply of raw materials and international marketing arrangements, TNCs preside over the nature and form of much industrialisation of the Third World. Governments and local organisations are dwarfed by these companies both economically and in terms of their technical know how.

The global crisis in work-related health

Occupational diseases and injuries are more prevalent in LMICs, including the so-called transitional economies in eastern and central Europe and the former Soviet Union, than in developed countries (Kjellstrom *et al.* 1992). While this may be partly explained by the fact that only 5–10 per cent of workers in LMICs have access to occupational health services, compared with 20–50 per cent of workers in industrialised nations (WHO 1999f), even these figures underestimate the real crisis of work-related ill health. First, reporting of most work-related deaths, illnesses and/or injuries seriously underestimates the scale of the problem. Data collection is notoriously incomplete, and few countries have comprehensive surveillance systems in place. Even in high-income countries, reporting systems are fragmented and depend on a variety of sources, ranging from worker's compensation claims, vital registration data, cancer registries and health service records. The situation in LMICs is worse, with reliable data almost non-existent. For example, WHO estimates that only between 1 and 4 per cent of the occupational diseases in Latin America are reported (WHO 1999f). Misdiagnosis of occupational diseases is also common (WHO 1992). Theobald (1999) reports that, in Thailand, this may be considered politically expedient by the government to ensure the continuing presence of the electronics industry in northern Thailand. Small, officially recognised, economic enterprises are often exempt from most existing labour laws (Reverente 1992), while economic activities in the informal sector are unrecorded in official statistics since the sector is largely unrecognised by official definitions of employment (Portes *et al.* 1989). Even in industrialised countries there may be under-reporting because of the liability of companies in paying compensation (Leigh *et al.* 1999).

Secondly, how occupational health has been defined limits a fuller appreciation of the potential impact that work has on people's health. Recent studies on occupational health indicate that there are important connections between work, the living environment and social factors, which contribute to positive or negative health among workers (Shukla *et al.* 1991; PRIA 1992; Delahanty and Shefali 1999; Theobald 1999). A narrow focus on 'occupational disease or injury' may overlook the potential for working conditions to aggravate other health and/or social problems of workers (Schenker 1992) and, in the opposite direction, that environmental and socio-cultural factors may present as risk factors in the work environment (Packard 1989; Jeyaratnam 1992). Work-related health risks are also compounded by the overwhelming neglect of public infrastructure and services, and decline in healthy living environments, particularly in urban areas (LaDou 1992; Satterthwaite *et al.* 1992). In addition to acute or chronic diseases, poor working conditions may also lead to higher levels of stress and despair, which, in turn, may result in increased injuries, mental illness and domestic and/or community violence (WHO 1991b; Jeyaratnam 1992; Theobald 1999).

The health of workers and the global economy: a symbiosis

The broad overview above highlights the ways in which workers can be exposed to serious health risks in performing tasks that are integral to current forms of economic globalisation. While rapid change has occurred in the nature and location of production processes, provisions for the protection of workers from risks arising from these changing work conditions have lagged far behind. As WHO points out, work-related health issues are consistently given low priority on the health policy agenda (WHO 1995: 31). We argue below, however, that globalisation has presented opportunities to redefine and respond to work-related ill health. By taking advantage of globalised forms of communication and organisation around workers' human rights, workers and their advocates could achieve significant improvements in workers' health and safety.

Work-related health problems need to be considered within a wider spectrum of issues regarding global economic and corporate restructuring, the dismantling of institutions of social protection, deregulation and/or non-enforcement of environmental and health and safety regulations, and a denial of workers' human rights in organising to protect themselves (Delahanty and Shefali 1999; Theobald 1999). With deregulation and the decreased influence of the state, the pressures of global competition have led many LMICs to seek a 'comparative advantage' from exploiting the low-wages and relatively unprotected work environments which characterise work in many LMICs (Delahanty and Shefali 1999; ICFTU 1999; Deacon 2000). In the presence of high global unemployment, particularly in LMICs (ILO 1999), intense market competition and global mobility of capital and industry, the pressures on LMICs to keep wages down and workplaces unregulated remains high.

In an increasingly integrated global economy, Deacon (2000) argues that 'systems of global production are replacing trade as the major means of international economic integration'. As Scholte (1997a: 435) explains, 'in globally integrated production . . . no country hosts all stages of manufacture. Each of the various links in the transborder chain specializes in one or several functions, thereby creating economies of scale and/or exploiting cost differentials between locations.' In a process that began in the 1960s, many Northern-based manufacturers strategically relocated various aspects of production to the South in order to take advantage of a low-waged workforce, attractive tax incentives, a comparative absence of trade unions and the absence of minimal environmental and health and safety regulations (Scholte 1997a; Dicken 1998; Deacon 2000). TNCs have developed a variety of strategies to ensure that they achieve the most competitive production costs in order to maximise profits. Dicken (1998), for example, describes a strategy involving the positioning of factories in a variety of different countries around which production can be shifted as costs in each location vary. Scholte (1997a) describes a situation of 'country hopping' by which firms, such as the sportswear company, Nike, 'relocate certain stages of production several times in short succession in search of profit maximization'.

Most global corporations rely extensively on decentralised global production chains (Scholte 1997a; Dicken 1998), many of which can be invariably traced through various subcontracting firms to a low-waged, unorganised and unprotected workforce (Delahanty and Shefali 1999;

ICFTU 1999; Deacon 2000). TNCs in certain industries, such as microelectronics, have transferred the bulk of the labour-intensive production process to LMICs, while locating the value-added elements – research and development, design, marketing – in their home country or in other industrialised countries (Scholte 1997a; Dicken, 1998). In the clothing industry, Delahanty and Shefali (1999) describe how 'buyer-driven' chains, formed by large retailers and brands, focus only on design and marketing, subcontracting the manufacturing process to 'local firms which subcontract to middle people, which further subcontract to small commodity producers and homeworkers'.

Flexibility in responding to the global market is much prized by TNCs, hence the preference for out-sourcing labour-intensive aspects of production to subcontractors (Delahanty and Shefali 1999). The demand for flexibility is found in both producer-driven chains, linked with 'capital- and technology-intensive industries' (Dicken 1998: 9), and buyer-driven chains in that both 'frequently adjust the number of workers in their labour force to meet changes in market conditions' (Dicken 1998: 438). Such 'casualisation' not only results in a lack of security for workers but also contributes to a downward pressure on wages as TNCs seek out countries or firms with the lowest labour costs (Scholte 1997a; Dicken 1998; Delahanty and Shefali 1999; Deacon 2000). Flexibility also means greater intensification of work – longer working hours and/or higher productivity targets (Delahanty and Shefali 1999; Theobald 1999).

In Theobald's study of northern Thailand's electronics firms, pressure to work overtime and bonuses for speed gradation were part of company policy (Theobald 1999), while in the Bangladesh garment industry, women routinely worked between '11–16 hours per day, seven days a week' (Delahanty and Shefali 1999). Such workplace policies are commonly found across a range of industries (Dicken 1998), generating an array of health hazards: women in the Thai firms complained of exhaustion, not being able to sleep, irregular menstrual cycles and loss of appetite. In order to maintain the pace of work, some workers used amphetamines to keep going, while many made little use of protective equipment in order to work at greater speed or risked injuries through exhaustion (Theobald 1999). In the Bangladesh clothing industry, research by Delahanty (1999b) found that women 'often had no access to even basic utilities, toilet facilities, and clean drinking water. They endure such workplace hazards as poor ventilation, cramped conditions, and risk of fire – in 1997 many workers were killed during a garment factory fire in Dhaka because the exit doors were locked.'

Poor conditions cannot be blamed solely on globalisation; however, the declining capability or willingness of the state in regulating labour standards, the intensification of competition operating across the globe, and the global reach of TNCs, combine to contribute to exacerbating pre-existing phenomena. The growing level of health risk faced by many low-income workers, whether in the North or South, for example, may be seen as a significant by-product of a decentralised production process. Company policies commonly emphasise long hours, minimal breaks and days off, and extremely high production targets, yet when injuries or toxic exposures occur due to exhaustion or stress, the individual is generally blamed (Theobald 1999). As Moure-Eraso (1999: 314) comments, 'not only can production be the direct cause of pathologies, e.g. the manufacturing of asbestos products, but even the manufacturing of 'healthy' products can involve inhuman exploitation of workers – witness manufacturing of apparel for US consumption in countries where sweatshop conditions prevail'. To many critics, TNCs and related firms are engaged in a 'race to the bottom' in terms of wage levels and working conditions; countries, even entire regions, are being 'pitted against each other' in competition for the roving eye of industry (Deacon 1997; ICFTU 1999; Wallach and Sforza 1999; Deacon 2000). From the workers' perspective, there is often little choice between the prospect of employment in potentially hazardous conditions and unemployment. Theobald (1999) comments that women workers in the Thai electronics factories were well aware that while 'protests may serve to improve conditions . . . they could also initiate the dismissal of troublemakers, or even the possibility of the departure of the employers to more desirable, less stringent locations'.

TNCs tend to avoid regions with active labour unions as organised workers are in a better position to ask questions, as well as to negotiate higher wages and safer working conditions. Dicken (1998: 190) observes that this is 'demonstrated by their tendency to relocate from such regions or to make new investments in places where labour is regarded as being more malleable'. Many governments have responded to TNC preferences for a 'flexible', low-waged and unorganised workforce by setting up export processing zones (EPZs) (see Box 12.2). Without unions, Geiser (1986) suggests, worker protection must depend on government enforced regulations. Yet in today's global economy, government standards, where they exist, are vague or ignored (Cooper Weil *et al.* 1990; Chen and Chan 1999). Industrialisation has clearly been given priority by many LMICs with little regard for the harsh social costs paid by workers engaged in the production process (Theobald 1999; Deacon 2000). The competitive advantage gained through this strategy has led to an increased 'informalisation' of work: 'newly industrialized countries informalize themselves *vis-à-vis* their competitors as well as *vis-à-vis* their own formal laws, so as to obtain a competitive advantage for their production relative to more regulated areas of the world economy' (Castells and Portes 1989). In China, for example, Special Economic Zones, usually covering a territory much larger than most EPZs, have been set up to attract foreign investment and manufacturing, offering similar incentives, including a controlled workforce. Many factories in these zones – both foreign and domestic – routinely violate China's own labour standards and laws (National Labor Campaign 2000), including those concerned with health and safety. In a study of the footwear industry in China, Chen and Chan (1999) found that, once foreign factories were established, occupational health and safety problems in the industry became much worse, even in the state-owned enterprises, in efforts to be more competitive. Collusion between foreign firms and local government is reported to be widespread. High-level officials in one city admitted that 'they had not and would not enforce OSH standards in the foreign-run footwear firms for fear of driving away investments' (Chen and Chan 1999: 806).

Core labour standards

The willingness of many governments in the South to seek to preserve their 'comparative advantage', i.e. a low-waged and unprotected workforce, is one reason for their reluctance to support the proposal to incorporate core labour standards into World Trade Organization (WTO) rules and regulations (Nyerere 1999; Khor 2000). First identified as basic standards at the Copenhagen Summit in 1995 (ILO 2000a), the standards are based on seven existing ILO Conventions already ratified by many of its Member Countries (ICFTU 1999). These were also adopted by the International Labour Conference in 1998 in the 'Declaration on Fundamental Principles and Rights at Work', which was supported by governments, employers and trade unions. The core standards emphasise recognition of: 'freedom of association and the effective recognition of the right to collective bargaining, the elimination of all forms of forced or compulsory labour, the effective abolition of child labour, and the elimination of discrimination in respect of employment and occupation' (ICFTU 1999: 42). Although health and safety standards are not specifically mentioned in the proposed core standards, the protection afforded to work-related health and safety would be significantly enhanced by recognition of workers' rights in these areas (World Bank 1995).

Many argue that integrating workers' rights and labour standards into global trade rules is necessary to ensure that globalisation broadly benefits workers and their communities (ICFTU 1999; UNDP 1999; Wallach and Sforza 1999). Global 'integration' has concentrated wealth and power – both economic and political – in the hands of the few (Tooze 1997;

UNDP 1999), while, for the vast majority, the process has been one of fragmentation, the loss of hard won economic and social gains, growing global inequality, and poverty (Deacon 1997; Scholte 1997a). As Labonte (1998: 247–8) argues, 'by allowing the increased strength of globalized capital to "discipline" wages downwards ... health-compromising internal income inequalities' have increased dramatically. This imbalance has been further exacerbated by current WTO rules and dispute mechanisms, which strongly favour TNCs, giving them greater freedoms and rights (UNRISD 1995). Wallach and Sforza (1999: 174) outline several rules that potentially undermine advocating and enforcing workers' rights:

First, the WTO rules generally prohibit distinguishing among non-product-related Production and Processing Methods (PPMs). PPMs are defined as distinctions between products based not on their physical characteristics or end uses, but on the way they are produced. This makes it nearly impossible for citizens and consumers to hold corporations and governments accountable to human rights standards. Second, under the Most Favored Nation rule, one WTO country cannot treat other WTO countries differently. That means that the treatment provided any WTO Member country must be provided to all WTO Member countries, regardless of their labor or human rights records. Third, the WTO Agreement on Government Procurement (AGP) prohibits noncommercial considerations in governments' purchasing decisions. These provisions make procurement rules giving environmental or social preferences or banning the purchase of goods produced in violation of ILO labor or U.N. human rights conventions – a violation of WTO rules. Finally, the WTO dispute settlement body can be used to challenge worker safety safeguards as technical barriers to trade.

Despite support from a spectrum of mainly Northern governments (Elliott 1999; Jenkins 1999) and civil society organisations, notably trade unions (ICFTU 1999) and workers' rights campaigns (Corporate Watch 1998a), the move to incorporate these standards into WTO rules has not been widely supported. LMICs are particularly antagonistic, seeing the position of Northern governments as cynically protectionist of their own labour markets, giving them an excuse to refuse imports from LMICs (Fleshman 1999; Khor 2000). At the April 2000 summit meeting in Havana, Cuba, the Group of 77[2] countries strongly opposed the 'application of all disguised protectionist measures such as labour standards' (Khor 2000: 13). Supporters of the core standards argue, however, that 'observing core labour rights would not ... remove the legitimate comparative advantage of developing countries' in that they 'do not set levels of pay or working conditions' but 'simply give the workers in the global economy the right to form unions to negotiate wages. They give children the right to a childhood and they outlaw forced labour, prison labour and discrimination' (TUAC 1999). This perspective is also shared by the ILO, which has indicated that 'the fundamental rights of workers have to be respected independently of levels of economic development and strength', which would allow them to 'freely participate in negotiating the support levels which are economically and socially viable' (Tapiola 1999a) in their respective countries.

Most LMICs are satisfied, however, with leaving the responsibility for workers' rights and labour standards with the ILO (Fleshman 1999; Raghavan 1999). The main drawback with this position is the ILO's negligible ability, compared with that of the WTO, to enforce the adoption of desirable practice by governments or corporations (Dicken 1998; Jones 1999; Seyfang 1999). Wallach and Sforza (1999) suggest this is why business groups also prefer that the ILO retains the principal mandate for labour standards. The ILO Declaration of 1998 on Fundamental Principles and Rights, for example, which contains the core labour standards, is 'strictly promotional in nature and [does] not involve any punitive aspect' (Kellerson 1998: 226). Although the follow-up mechanism emphasises implementation, the method relies on governments' self-reporting their progress in meeting standards; a global progress report from the Director-General is also to be published annually (Kellerson 1998).[3] Others, such as the Trade Union Advisory Committee (TUAC) of the OECD (TUAC 1999), recommend that the Declaration be observed across the UN system and, at the very least, that organisations such as the WTO do not 'contradict' the ILO's efforts at promoting standards (Tapiola 1999b).

Alternative strategies – negotiating with corporate interests

Both strategies – incorporating core labour standards in WTO rules and the ILO 1998 Declaration – are aimed at ensuring and/or encouraging governmental regulation of working conditions and workers' rights. But, as has been shown above, legislation is not free of corporate pressure: TNCs, in particular, penalise countries for promoting labour standards by relocating to countries without regulations or enforcement (Dicken 1998; Wallach and Sforza 1999). Given that the scope for policy action by governments in this area is extremely limited, even for those states committed to protecting workers' rights (ICFTU 1999), and the limited enforcement capability of the ILO and other UN agencies, alternative strategies and alliances have become necessary. This reflects the critical shift in power from the state to non-state actors brought about by the globalisation process (Held et al. 1999). Besides the TNCs and the host of subcontracting firms associated with a global production chain, non-state actors also include civil society organisations such as trade unions, workers' organisations, activist campaigning groups, consumer advocacy groups, NGOs, women's organisations and the media (North–South Institute 1998). All of these groups have, or could, become key actors in demanding higher labour standards from TNCs.

While TNCs often argue that poor standards and working conditions are not their responsibility but that of their subcontractors, it is clear from the evidence that buyers or contractors are in a position to demand higher standards from their subcontractors (UNRISD 1995; ICFTU 1999; Seyfang 1999). A range of strategies is being promoted and piloted in a number of industries and countries, including framework agreements, a variety of codes of conduct and social labelling. Framework agreements are largely based on the core labour standards discussed above and are negotiated between International Trade Secretariats (ITS) and TNCs concerning the international activities of a specific company (ICFTU 1999). The agreement between IKEA[4] and the International Federation of Building and Wood Workers (IFBWW), for example, assures that IKEA will demand that its subcontractors recognise: national standards of employment as a minimum protection; child labour and forced labour are not acceptable; workers are free to join trade unions and bargain collectively; working time is reasonable; and conditions must be 'safe, hygienic and the best health and safety conditions must be promoted' (IFBWW–IKEA 1998). Unfortunately, very few companies have signed such comprehensive (or even more limited) agreements with ITSs.

Codes of conduct represent voluntary self-regulation by specific firms to ensure that specified working conditions and rights will be met (Seyfang 1999; Deacon 2000). The impetus for the codes has come from civil society actors pressing for greater social responsibility and accountability by TNCs. For industry, the concern is to avoid negative publicity that might affect profitability (Deacon 2000). According to Seyfang (1999), the codes, which are growing rapidly in number, display significant variation in content. For example, in a survey of 18 codes of conduct by Ferguson (quoted in Seyfang 1999), all included health and safety measures, while many excluded the more contentious right to trade union organisation and collective bargaining. In a separate study of 20 different codes, 19 precluded child labour, 16 included the right to organise and bargain collectively, and 15 included health and safety standards, no forced labour, no discrimination and minimum wages (Seyfang 1999). Very few codes were initiated by the state, while the majority were instigated by NGOs and workers' organisations. Codes initiated by industry were generally weaker but more likely to be adopted. However, only half of the codes surveyed extended to subcontractors and a third to homeworkers (Seyfang 1999), hence their value and relevance to the workers who need protection at the lower ends of the production chain is doubtful.

Some codes have been extended to subcontractors. Nike, the global sportswear manufacturer, improved its existing code of conduct in May 1998, after significant pressure from anti-sweatshop activists.[5] Following revelation of poor working conditions in supplier firms located in countries such as Indonesia and other LMICs in the 1990s, Nike became the target of negative media coverage and consumer boycotts. As a result, Nike decided to integrate economic, social and environmental concerns within its own organisation (Elkington and Fennell 1998). The revised Nike code applies to its numerous subcontractors in LMICs and includes adopting the American Occupational Safety and Health Administration (OSHA) indoor air-quality standards, and accelerating the replacement of petroleum-based solvents with safer water-based compounds and other substitutions for water-based primers, degreasers and cleaners (Corporate Watch 1998a). Other important developments in assessing compliance with their own code include: NGO participation in the monitoring system, commitment to make audit summaries public (Corporate Watch 1998a), and revealing their factory locations (*The Guardian*, 4 July 2000), thus opening them to further scrutiny. Unfortunately, workers' rights to organise and bargain collectively were not included (Corporate Watch 1998b).

As indicated above, a number of voluntary codes aimed at improving labour standards have been developed in recent years. Seyfang (1999: 23) outlines the following key factors that together, she suggests, make up an effective and relevant code:

[The code] should emerge from the concerns of workers themselves, be negotiated locally, and be supported by NGO campaigns in consumer markets, rather than being imposed from above by an image-conscious parent company. A code should be founded on the ILO core conventions, but have scope to reflect local needs ... Crucially, the firm must be prepared to internalise the code of conduct and respond to it appropriately at all levels of management. And to ensure credibility and transparency, the firm must be subject to external, independent monitoring and verification.

These features represent a benchmark for codes of conduct; clearly, significant effort will be needed to ensure their adoption and compliance. It is clear also that at least some TNCs are increasingly concerned about what they call the 'triple bottom line': financial, social and environmental accountability. McIntosh (1998) indicates the rationale for this:

Some companies have acknowledged that there is enhanced corporate reputation to be gained through recognising that capitalism will be most successful when it cares for its customers, its producers, the environment, and the communities in which it operates.

A recent development in this direction has been to establish a credible, verifiable and certifiable standard that can be audited by independent parties to indicate that work standards have been maintained. SA8000 has been proposed as such a standard. It covers nine essential areas: child labour, forced labour, health and safety, freedom of association, freedom from discrimination, disciplinary practices, work hours, compensation and management practices (Marlin 1998). Although the standard may have limitations (Seyfang 1999), it does begin to place a set of objectives against which accountability can be assessed in the public domain, and through which consumer and other groups can exert pressure for the promotion of good practices. Labour standards, as well as broader human rights principles and environmental protection, are also included in the Global Compact, initiated by the UN Secretary-General, Kofi Annan, in January 1999 (United Nations 1999b). This initiative aims to enhance 'global corporate citizenship' by increasing corporate adherence to the fundamental principles enshrined in UN Declarations. However, as Kofi Annan highlighted: 'the Global Compact is not a code of conduct. Neither is it a disguised effort to raise minimum standards, nor a vehicle for special interest groups. It is a Compact to help markets deliver what they are best at ... while at the same time contributing to a more humane world' (in Corporate Watch 1999). This approach signals not only a shift in UN relations with the private sector (see chapter by Buse and Walt, this volume) from confrontation to co-operation (Corporate Watch 1999), but is also a response to the gap in global governance identified by civil society pressure groups active in these areas.

Conclusion

Globalisation, accompanied by deregulation, marketisation, technology transfer and new working practices, has presented new challenges for protecting workers' health and working conditions. This problem is particularly urgent in countries undergoing rapid industrialisation with poor existing safety standards and where weak labour organisations are unable to advocate for worker's health. In the absence of a global framework for protecting workers' health as well as other global social responsibilities (UNDP 1999; Deacon 2000), alliances of civil society actors have proved necessary in building direct pressure on TNCs. Many of these coalitions have promoted innovative solutions, such as codes of conduct and social labelling. Civil society coalitions have also been crucial in building sustained pressure on governments and multilateral agencies regarding the need for broad frameworks for the global regulation of trade, production and investment (ICFTU 1999; Oxfam 1999; Wallach and Sforza 1999).

However, there is no substitute for governmental action in providing strong legal and regulatory frameworks, on codes for conducting commerce and production and for enforcement through monitoring and punishing violations (UNDP 1999; Deacon 2000). As Deacon (2000) argues, globalisation has raised the need for greater social protection by governments, not less. However, the discussion concerning social standards has been dominated by those with less to lose; LMICs may be more willing to support common global labour and social standards if the Northern countries 'shared part of the burden . . . since they also benefit from the reduction of these "international public bads"' (Lee, in Deacon 2000: 27). In this way, workers in the domestic economy, not only in the export-oriented sector, would also benefit.

A system of global governance is also urgently needed to ensure that global labour standards are followed by TNCs. Stronger mechanisms need to be developed to ensure that awareness of workers' health problems and working conditions builds on current advocacy and leads to long-term action and change. For example, rather than diverse campaigns targeting different sectors, a global workers' health watch could be established as a tool for advancing global health awareness and vigilance. Efficient surveillance systems are therefore a priority. Whereas gains have been made in the area of emerging infectious disease and surveillance, workers' health has lagged behind. Efforts are needed to establish warning systems about the export of hazardous processes and work practices, to monitor the health consequences, to formulate international standards of good practice and to bring liability to bear upon corporations and individuals that abuse these standards. The opportunities offered by globalisation to increase public accountability by transnational and national actors need to be more rigorously employed in protecting workers' health and human rights. These global warning systems are urgent – we cannot continue to destroy poor peoples' health for an increment of profit.

NOTES

1 DALYs include both years of life lost due to premature mortality and years of life lived with disability, thus capturing more fully the importance of non-fatal outcomes. These are an improvement on traditional measures such as mortality and life expectancy. For a fuller explanation, see Murray (1994).
2 The G77 was formed in 1964 at the UN Conference on Trade and Development and is the 'umbrella body of the developing world dealing with economic and social matters' (Khor 2000: 5).

3 Both follow-up reports have been produced for the first time in 2000. The first set of annual reports received from governments was reviewed by seven expert-advisors in the Declaration's four categories of principles and rights (ILO 2000b). The first annual ILO Global Report – Your Voice at Work – has also been published (ILO 2000c), reporting on 'freedom of association and the right to collective bargaining', one of the four categories. The other three categories will be the subject of the next three annual reports.

4 IKEA is a home furnishing company, with procurement of products and supplies from up to 70 countries, and retail outlets in approximately 30.

5 Coalitions and information about anti-sweatshop activities can be found on a number of web-sites, including Corporate Watch <http://www.corpwatch.org/> and the National Labor Campaign <http://www.nlcnet.org/>.

KEY READINGS

Deacon, B. 2000, Globalization and social policy: the threat to equitable welfare, Occasional Paper 5, March 2000, Geneva: UNRISD <http://www.unrisd.org/engindex/cop5/forum/opgs.htm>.

Dicken, P. 1998, *Global shift: transforming the world economy*, 3rd edition, London: Paul Chapman Publishing Ltd/Sage Publications Company.

ICFTU, 1999, 'Building workers' human rights in the global trading system', Geneva: International Confederation of Free Trades Unions.

Labonte, R. 1998b, 'Healthy public policy and the World Trade Organization: a proposal for an international health presence in future world/trade investment talks', *Health Promotion International* 13 (3): 245–56.

Wallach, L. and Sforza, M. 1999, *Whose trade organization? Corporate globalization and the erosion of democracy; an assessment of the World Trade Organization*, Washington, DC: Public Citizen.

13 Globalisation, conflict and the humanitarian response

Anthony Zwi, Suzanne Fustukian and Dinesh Sethi

> In the twentieth century, the idea of human universality rests less on hope than on fear, less on optimism about the human capacity for good than on dread of human capacity for evil, less on a vision of man as maker of his history than of man the wolf towards his own kind.
>
> Michael Ignatieff (1998)

Introduction

Collective violence confronts daily tens of millions of people living in zones of conflict, as well as those displaced within their own countries or across national borders. For those previously living in conditions of peace and security, collective violence and its effects were somewhat removed: the terrorist attacks in America on 11 September 2001 shattered that perception. Yet, with such violence regularly splashed across our television screens and newspapers, we are acutely aware of the need for appropriate collective security and humanitarian responses. Nobel peace prizes for the Office of the United Nations High Commissioner for Refugees (1981), International Physicians for the Prevention of Nuclear War (1985), International Campaign to Ban Landmines (1997) and Médecins sans Frontières (1999) have given recognition to the vital role played by humanitarian agencies and the United Nations itself (Nobel Peace Prize 2001) in the challenge of preventing or mitigating these crises. However, despite increasing knowledge of the detrimental effects of violent political conflict, our ability to prevent such conflicts, and to take appropriate action while they are ongoing or in their aftermath, remains poorly developed.

Ignatieff (1998) argues that new technologies have created 'new' types of wars, crimes and victimhood. But they have also stimulated a new form of response, what he terms modern moral universalism, borne from the failure to prevent the Holocaust and built upon the need to respond to crimes against humanity. Using characteristically graphic language, he argues that modern conflicts, sometimes manifested in genocide, 'pulverize' people into equal units of 'pure humanity', 'sever' them from social relations that would normally protect them, destroy the 'capillary system' of social support structures, and create the 'pure victim'. Such victims are stripped of social identity and thus bereft of the specific moral audience that would in normal times be there to hear their cry. In so doing, 'human brotherhood', a residual moral system of obligations when all other social relations capable of protecting an individual have been destroyed, comes into force. This is exhibited through the provision by the international community of military, political, economic and/or humanitarian assistance.

While illuminating in many respects, Ignatieff's analysis narrowly focuses on the event of war itself, overlooking the failure by the international community to anticipate the potential for collective violence in fragile states, or to identify and respond to inappropriate policies that may exacerbate the descent into violence (Cliffe and Luckham 1999). He also does not recognise that insufficient action has been taken early enough in recent conflicts to prevent or mitigate significant human rights abuses or the exacerbation of organised violence. Moreover, the links between external and internal non-state actors, such as private companies and diaspora communities, that can play a major role in supporting violence, are glossed over (Collinson 1999; Duffield 1999).

This chapter considers key linkages between current forms of globalisation and recent experiences of, and responses to, complex political emergencies (CPEs) in many parts of the world. We argue that keeping a watch on the downsides of globalisation, notably those features that threaten peace and security, is critical to the realisation of its benefits.

Current trends in conflict

The twentieth century witnessed immense loss of life and widespread destruction of societies from war and other forms of collective violence. Few countries avoided the experience of war in the last century. The number of deaths that resulted directly from war, and indirectly through disease and starvation, exceeded 110 million people, with civilians accounting for about 60 per cent of these deaths (Sivard 1996). Approximately 75 per cent of these deaths occurred in Europe, largely from the First and Second World Wars. This changed from 1945 to the end of the cold war when almost all major conflicts took place in the developing regions of Africa, the Middle East, Asia and Latin America.

The end of the cold war, including the break-up of the Soviet Union, and the pace and intensity of globalisation, have contributed to more recent conflicts since the mid 1990s. Many of these conflicts are described as CPEs, defined by Goodhand and Hulme (1999) as conflicts that occur within but also across state boundaries; have political antecedents often relating to competition for power and resources; are protracted in duration; are embedded in existing social, political, economic and cultural structures and cleavages; and are often characterised by predatory social formations. Often termed 'new wars' (Cliffe and Luckham 1999; Kaldor 1999), CPEs result from a dynamic interaction between changing local and global conditions. Kaldor (1999) describes the features of new wars as entailing a blurring between war (usually defined as violence between states or organised political groups for political purposes), organised crime (violence undertaken by privately organised groups for private purposes, usually financial gain) and large-scale violations of human rights (violence undertaken by states or politically organised groups against individuals and minorities). Many recent conflicts reveal an element of 'identity politics' involving claims to power on the basis of a particular national, clan, religious or linguistic identity. Strategies are deployed, such as forced resettlement, mass killings and intimidation, which aim to control or get rid of groups of a different identity. New linkages bridging local, decentralised conflicts with a 'globalised war economy' are included in a process described by Duffield (1999) as the 'privatisation' of violence, which includes the increased involvement of non-state actors in issues of international and national security.

Cliffe and Luckham (1999) argue that these new wars are transforming 'liberation, separatist or reformist rebellions into warlord insurgencies'. 'Old' conflicts in countries such as Angola, formerly a site of cold war stand-off, have been rekindled as the elites of opposing forces jostle for control of diamond and oil resources, fuelled by the replacement of superpower rivalry with competition by private companies in a global economy (Global Witness 1998, 1999; Duffield 1999). Elsewhere, such as in the former Yugoslavia, Indonesia and Rwanda, historical animosity has resurfaced in the post-cold war power vacuum, whipped up by economic and political competition among ethnic groups. Indeed, Lipschutz and Crawford (1999) argue that so-called ethnic conflicts are reflections of failing social contracts between different groups as global economic forces place governments under immense pressure to promote greater economic efficiencies and exploitation of local resources. In such situations, ethnicity has been a lever used by new elites to mobilise the constituencies needed to grasp economic and political power.

Every conflict has winners and losers (Le Billon 2000). However, the losses are typically disproportionately felt by those who have little material resources and influence to stop the fighting or change the status quo, since those who benefit from the conflict, through manipulating scarcity or seizing assets, also have an interest in perpetuating it. Humanitarian aid itself has become a resource over which groups compete, and such assistance and resources may directly or indirectly stoke the conflict (Anderson 1996). This has presented a major challenge to the international humanitarian system – how to ensure that aid reaches those already made vulnerable through a longer-term pre-conflict process of impoverishment (Macrae and Zwi 1994).

The impact of conflict on health and health systems

The impact of conflict on health status varies with the nature and background of the conflict, its geographic extent, intensity, type of military technology used, organisation and development of the health system, and prior health status of the population. Impacts may be direct or indirect, and manifest in both health and other societal systems.

Refugees and internally displaced persons typically experience high mortality, especially in the period immediately after their migration (Toole *et al.* 2000). Deaths from malnutrition, diarrhoea and infectious diseases especially occur among children, while some communicable diseases such as malaria, tuberculosis and HIV infection, as well as a range of non-communicable diseases, injuries and violence, typically affect adults. Prior health status and access to food, shelter, water and sanitation, and health services, as well as the level of resource availability, all affect health prior to and as a result of conflict.

Existing health problems may also be greatly exacerbated in wartime. Infant mortality often rises in association with reduced access to health services, impairment of the basic infrastructure necessary to promote health, poorer nutrition of children and their mothers, and population displacement. The occurrence and transmission of communicable diseases increases due to reduced access to clean water and sanitation, reduced immunisation coverage, increased population movement with exposure to new agents of infection, and reduced public health campaigns and outreach activities. High-risk situations for HIV transmission are created in conflict settings for women in particular, who may be raped or forced to engage in unsafe sex in order to maintain livelihoods. In many conflicts soldiers with high rates of HIV infection can buy or force sex, with sexually transmitted infections poorly controlled. The results from the decline in the necessities to promote health can be horrifyingly severe. In Rwanda, epidemics of water-related disease (shigella dysentery and cholera) led to the death, within a month, of 6–10 per cent of the refugee population arriving in Zaire (Goma Epidemiology Group 1995). The crude death rate of 20–35 per 10,000 population *per day* was two to three times higher than that previously reported in refugee populations (Goma Epidemiology Group 1995).

The mental health impact of conflict may be extensive, reflecting the nature of the conflict, the form of trauma experienced or directly inflicted (as in the case of torture and other repressive violence), the individual and community response, cultural context, and the psychological health of those affected prior to the event. Adverse effects may be experienced in the form of psychosocial distress, with manifestations in depression and anxiety, psychosomatic ailments, intra-familial conflict, alcohol abuse and antisocial behaviour (Summerfield 1991). Silove *et al.* (2000) draw attention to the variety of forms of mental health response needed.

The impact of conflict on health services is wide-ranging and can often result in significantly reduced access to material and human resources, as these are diverted elsewhere to sustain the conflict. Declines in outreach and community-based activities, reductions in strategic planning and consultation around policy issues, and the cessation of previously planned health system developments are usually immediate consequences. The specific targeting of food production and distribution activities during periods of conflict is extensive: supply routes may be disrupted, supplies destroyed or looted, and scarcity manipulated in order to raise prices, or used to control populations and their movement (Macrae and Zwi 1994). In seeking to fill the gaps left by the state, an increase in NGO activity is noted, as is a marked rise in the privatisation of health care provision. Damage to infrastructure, including water supplies, electricity and sewage disposal further exacerbates the determinants of health and the operation of health services. While evidence from El Salvador (Ugalde *et al.* 2000) indicates that it is possible, with selective health care interventions and major resource inflows, to improve certain health indices during ongoing conflict, such reports are exceptional. The impact of conflict on community participation may occasionally be positive, although this seems to occur particularly when 'liberation' struggles, with a high ideological content, are waged, as was more frequent in the 1970s and 1980s before the end of the cold war.

One consequence of the targeting by warring factions of entire communities and their livelihoods has been the large numbers of displaced people. Refugee (those seeking refuge across international borders) numbers have risen from 2.5 million in 1970, to 11 million in 1983, 18.2 million in 1992 and 23 million in 1997 (Reed *et al.* 1998; Deacon 2000). Added to these numbers is an increase in internally displaced people, of whom, in the decade following the end of the cold war, there were an estimated 30 million (Reed *et al.* 1998), the vast majority fleeing conflict zones.

Those displaced within countries have less access to resources and support from the international community, and may be at ongoing risk from violence perpetrated by the state and other local actors (Hampton 1998; Collinson 1999). Moreover, established agencies such as the United Nations High Commission for Refugees (UNHCR) are mandated to deal with refugees and not specifically with those internally displaced.

The attention of the global mass media is increasingly important in drawing attention to the impacts of conflict on populations. The so-called 'CNN factor' has a significant influence on whether a given crisis receives domestic political attention in high-income countries, as well as the nature and extent of resources made available to the UN and humanitarian agencies. While some CPEs attract a substantial response, others fail to do so, despite substantial loss of life, population displacement and infrastructure destruction (Munslow and Brown 1997). For instance, the amount of funds made available for humanitarian assistance per Kosovar Albanian affected has been many more times that made available to those in equivalent, if not greater, risk in countries such as Sierra Leone, Sudan, Burma, Colombia, Algeria and the Democratic Republic of Congo. This disparity in available funds clearly has implications for the quantity and quality of services available to address health and related needs, and for longer-term development in these settings.

In what ways are globalisation and conflict linked?

How we understand the linkages between globalisation and conflict rests on how we conceptualise the process and consequences of globalisation. In this, we are confronted with ongoing debates concerning the defining features and dynamics of globalisation (Clark 1997; Scholte 1997a; Held *et al.* 1999; Deacon 2000). There is, however, broad agreement that globalisation is a multi-faceted process affecting economic, political, social and cultural spheres of activity (see chapter 1). Many would also agree that at the core of the debate is the changing relationship between the state, state authority and global capital (Strange 1996; Clark 1997; Scholte 1997a; World Bank 1997b). Collinson (1999) defines globalisation, for example, as a 'set of processes that are global in scope, that transcend the territorial borders of states and which, as a consequence, profoundly affect the nature and functions of state governance in the world political economy'. She cites Scholte (1997a) as remarking that 'there is a notable change in the character of the state: its capacities; its constituencies; its policy-making processes; its policy content; and so on'. The functions and authority of the state are undergoing major transformations in reacting to and managing the dynamics of globalisation; states with either strong or weak capabilities and authority differentially adapt to these evolving conditions.

The capacity of many states, particularly low and middle-income countries (LMICs), is particularly weak 'in the fundamental matters of providing security against violence, stable money for trade and investment, a clear system of law and the means to enforce it and a sufficiency of public goods like drains, water supplies, infrastructures for transport and communications' (Strange 1996, in Collinson 1999). The *World development report 1997* (World Bank 1997b) highlights the incapacity of many of these states to fulfil essential functions. The report differentiates low-, intermediate- and strong-capacity states in terms of their ability to undertake and promote collective actions efficiently, such as those related to law and order, public health and basic infrastructure. Collinson (1999) further argues that, 'while the authority of *all* states is diminishing', inequity is rapidly developing between stronger states with structural power 'who retain some control over their destinies' and weaker states 'who are effectively incapable of exercising any such controls' (Strange 1996, in Collinson 1999). Hurrell (1999) highlights similar concerns: 'Whilst globalization erodes the power and viability of many states, it also increases the power of those states that are best able to adapt and to exploit its new opportunities. Globalization then, involves not only a shift in power from states to markets, but also from weak states to strong states.'

The processes associated with globalisation have contributed to state weakness or failure in a number of ways. First, one of the core objectives of much macroeconomic policy since the early 1980s was to produce a residual state, whose functions and roles were drastically scaled down and replaced by the 'operations of the market' (Woodward 1999), a goal achieved through structural adjustment policies (SAPs), supported by the IMF, the World Bank, global capital and many high-income governments. Globalisation has helped promote neo-liberal perspectives and has ensured the hegemony of such discourse through the global mass media, global financial institutions and the UN. Akokpari (1998) cogently argues, in relation to sub-Saharan Africa, that: 'by severely curtailing its distributional powers, SAPs undermined the capabilities of the African state further, including its ability to contain conflicts'. Cliffe and Luckham (1999) also point to failing state capacity, emphasising that 'systemic crises', such as those provoked by SAPs, have led to a situation where the 'effective absence of the state or the loss of its monopoly of violence allows societal conflict to escalate and take violent forms'.

A state's limited authority and capacity to confront intra-state conflict, other than with repression and violence, is partly a consequence of the '"structural violence" of maldevelopment' (Rupesinghe 1998; Cliffe and

Luckham 1999). Galtung (cited in Rupesinghe 1998) describes structural violence as manifested in 'the inequalities of societal structures', that include 'uneven resource distribution, access to medical supplies, hygiene, education, income and . . . political power'. Other examples of structural violence include 'the inefficient or unfair administration of justice', 'repression of free speech and thought', 'institutional violence' and 'sexual, religious, racial, linguistic, economic or age-based discrimination'; these are clearly linked to state incapacity and capability as referred to by Strange (1996), Collinson (1999) and the World Bank (1997b). Strong states, too, that have no counter-power within the private sector and civil society, are also at risk of perpetrating violence against their own citizens. Hurrell (1999) asserts, however, that, while 'the state can certainly be a major part of the problem', it 'remains an unavoidable part of the solution'. Debate about the nature of any post-Taliban government in Afghanistan highlights such challenges.

Secondly, the World Bank continues to advocate strongly that state economic policies must be responsive to 'the parameters of a globalized world economy' amplifying the state's changing role from provider to facilitator and regulator (World Bank 1997b). Many, however, doubt the Bank's fundamental assertion that living standards will improve overall if countries opt for integration with, rather than remain 'outside', the global economy. Duffield (1999) argues, for example, that the growing economic and political marginalisation of many developing countries is a salient and intrinsic feature of globalisation. It is evident that the convergence of 'advanced economic activity' and ensuing benefits is concentrated within the advanced industrialised states (Hirst, in Clark 1997; World Bank 1997b). As Tooze (1997) indicates, countries of North America, Western Europe, Japan and Southeast Asia are increasingly at the centre of wealth creation, with strong interdependence among these countries and regions. Those outside of these areas are disadvantaged, while 'with this process of economic concentration comes also the political domination of the management of the world political economy' (Tooze 1997; see also chapter 2 in this volume).

Thirdly, global disparity across the economic and political spectrum, experienced differentially by rich and poor states, reflects other aspects of global inequality. It is increasingly apparent that 'the opportunities and rewards of globalization [are] spread unequally and inequitably – concentrating power and wealth in a select group of people, nations and corporations, marginalizing the others' (UNDP 1999). As Collinson (1999) asserts, the 'relative marginalisation of these countries from the global economy does not mean that they are in any way protected from it. Indeed, because of the usually very narrow base of their economies and the increasingly narrow margins within which many people subsist, they are, if anything, the most vulnerable of all to any changes and instability in the global economy.' It is notable that in more than 80 countries, per capita income is lower than it was a decade or more ago. Since 1990, 55 countries, mostly in sub-Saharan Africa, Eastern Europe and the Commonwealth of Independent States, have had declining incomes. Inequalities in many countries have been rising since the early 1980s, a trend all too apparent in China and Eastern Europe, as well as the UK, Sweden and the US. The income gap between the best off one-fifth of the world and the worst off one-fifth has increased from 30:1 in 1960 to 60:1 in 1970 and 74:1 in 1997. By the late 1990s, the fifth of the world's population living in the countries with highest income possessed 86 per cent of global GDP (compared with the lowest fifth's 1 per cent), 82 per cent of global exports (versus 1 per cent), and 68 per cent of foreign direct investment (versus 1 per cent). In the past decade, wealth has become increasingly concentrated in fewer countries and, within countries, in fewer hands. The world's 200 richest people have assets in excess of US $1 trillion; the assets of the three wealthiest individuals in the world are more than the combined GNP of all the least-developed countries and their 600 million people (UNDP 1999).

Inequality and exclusion

Thus, while globalisation has brought about integration on some levels, it has contributed to fragmentation on others (Clark 1997), dividing communities, nations and regions into those that are integrated and those that are excluded. Income and wealth gaps are much wider in the developing world than the developed, as material inequalities are 'more entrenched' and increasing faster (Pakulski 1999). As Akokpari (1998) writes, 'economic crisis exemplified in long periods of recession, unemployment, and inflation, exacerbate scarcity and intensify distributional conflicts'. Status divisions around gender, ethnicity and race are also typically greater in these settings, contributing to an increased likelihood of violent social conflict (Rupesinghe 1998). Hurrell and Woods (1999) decry the fact that 'globalization is exacerbating inequalities of resources, capabilities, and perhaps most importantly, the power to make and break rules in the international arena'.

Inequalities, especially those based on ethnic, religious or cultural affiliation, are a potentially important cause of conflict (Box 13.1). These are exacerbated in the presence of risk factors such as intense resource constraints or competition, features of current forms of globalisation where shelter or isolation from the global market and its impact is increasingly difficult.

Box 13.1   Features of globalisation that increase risks and negative outcomes of collective violence.

Economic
- Engagement of global capital, trade and industry in natural resource extraction in conflict zones
- Speed and magnitude of changes in capital flows and investment
- Globalising trade in illicit commodities to and from conflict zones (e.g. drugs, weapons, natural resources)
- Global production and trade in arms
- Emergence of privatised armed forces willing to be contracted for military-security operations but lack of accountability other than to the contractor
- Increased polarisation in distribution of wealth

Political
- Diminished capacity of the state in low- and middle-income countries to guarantee basic levels of social welfare
- Decreased systems of global governance to control weapons production and distribution
- Declining commitment to asylum policies and support to international refugee regime
- Inequitable response by the international community to different CPEs

Cultural
- Use of global communications technologies to incite hatred for political gain
- Increasing role of diaspora communities who provide funds and promote more extreme solutions to economic and political crises
- Personal and economic aspirations dominated by perception of availability of life styles and wealth present in the richest of countries and promoted through globalised media

Social
- Increased vulnerability and marginalisation of populations on the periphery of the globalised economy
- Heightened ethnic identity and intolerance – inflamed by political leadership which plays on such identities to consolidate personal and group economic and political power
- Promotion of an individual vs. a social ethic

Environmental
- Acceleration and intensification of resource depletion
- Increased local competition for control of natural resources sought by global economy

Source: This box uses a framework by Lee (2000) that identifies the spheres and dimensions of globalisation. The box contents are those of the authors.

Duffield's (1994a) argument that complex political emergencies are deeply politicised conflicts 'characteristic of areas of protracted economic crisis and growing social vulnerability' has significant resonance in conflict settings such as Afghanistan, Angola, Serbia and Sierra Leone. While state failure is a critical element, conflict is an integral response to the process of marginalisation of countries, regions and populations from the dynamics of the global economy (Akokpari 1998), in which 'violence has become an important adjunct of economic and political survival in landscapes increasingly lacking alternatives' (Duffield 1994b). Social tensions and conflicts ignite in the presence of extreme inequality, not only of income and wealth, but also in political participation, access to economic assets (such as land, human capital and communal resources) and social conditions (education, housing and employment). Trends in recent years have demonstrated the rapidity and magnitude of global financial instability, with massive capital outflows occurring in seconds leaving countries to deal with social problems associated with rapid currency devaluation, social expenditure cuts, and mass unemployment. The 'new wars' described earlier occur in situations where state revenues have declined, reflecting economic constraints as well as the spread of criminality, corruption and inefficiency; violence is privatised as a result of organised crime and the emergence of paramilitary groups which pillage and plunder, and political legitimacy is eroded (Duffield 1999; Kaldor 1999). The net effect is a blurring between barbarity and civility, combatants and non-combatants, and the soldier, policeman and criminal (Kaldor 1999).

Other features of new wars also interface with globalisation, including the development of 'particularist identities', the 'changed mode of warfare', the growing importance of non-state actors, and the emergence of a 'globalized war economy' (Kaldor 1999). The use of global communication technologies assists those who are excluded, or perceive themselves to be, from the dividends of globalisation in the construction of new ethnic identities by drawing together local and diaspora communities. Such connections provide political and economic support to emerging group identities (Clark 1997; Collinson 1999). It had been thought that trends in global interconnectedness would reduce nationalist claims, but it is increasingly apparent that nationalism can be fostered by: loss of control to foreign investment, hostility to immigration, fears of unemployment, resentment of international institutions, fears of terrorism and subversion, hostility to global media, and the attractions of secession (Halliday 1997). Seaton (1999) comments that 'the process of elaborating and allocating characteristics to groups of people defined as the enemy, and disseminating a view of them, is critical in the internal mobilization of opinion that is required to move populations towards war with each other'. Collinson (1999) suggests that 'ethnic affiliation represents one of the few remaining bases for mobilising political support at the state level'. Alternatively, she suggests, communities alienated by and from the state may continue to periodically 'rise up' against a 'moribund and irrelevant' state.

Modes of warfare are increasingly focused on destabilisation and terror, specifically to undermine community structures in opposing groups through massacres of civilians, destruction and looting of neighbours, and systematic rape. Among those immediately targeted are those who espouse a different politics, who try to maintain social relations between groups, and who have some sense of public morality. Kaldor (1999) writes that some conflicts can be understood in terms of 'exclusivism and cosmopolitanism', a reflection of a globalising world. In contrast to traditional wars between states, funded through national taxation and other financial instruments (e.g. war bonds), current wars are often decentralised systems in which a degree of dependence on external support and resources (from diaspora communities and neighbouring governments) may be present, fighting units are financed through plunder (including of humanitarian aid) and the black market (including trade in arms, drugs and valuable resources such as diamonds, oil and timber) (Global Witness 1998; Duffield 1999; Kaldor 1999).

The declining capacity of many states to enforce legitimate order has led to the increased privatisation of the means and conduct of conflict. Non-state actors have, in this process, become increasingly important as direct sources of challenge to the state and as alternative authorities (Duffield 1999). This has resulted in a growth of vigilantism, formation of paramilitary groups, and the 'purchase of security within an expanding commercial marketplace' (Hurrell 1999). As such, modes of warfare draw more extensively on paramilitary groups, local warlords, criminal gangs, mercenaries, private armies and breakaway units of the police and army. Military companies and mercenary armies train government, corporate and other armies to protect their respective interests, and can be contracted themselves to secure particular strategic interests. This has been further facilitated by the globalised nature of the arms trade, which has led to widespread availability of weaponry and private armies to deploy them (Duffield 1999; Held *et al.* 1999). Shearer (1998) has recently explored the potential positive and negative roles of such a military 'business', highlighting the lack of means to govern their activities. For instance, private armies may stoke up conflict while offering services for conflict resolution. Private military companies may help win time and space, but also enable heinous crimes against civilian populations.

Table 13.1 *Indicators of states at risk of violent political conflict*

Indicator	Manifestation
Inequalities	Widening inequalities, especially those manifest between, rather than within, groups.
Demographic pressures	High infant mortality; rapid changes in population including massive refugee movements; high population density; youth bulge; insufficient food supply or access to safe water; ethnic groups sharing and disputing land, territory or environmental resources.
Lack of democratic processes	Criminalisation or delegitimisation of the state; human rights violations; kleptocratic and corrupt processes of governance.
Regimes of short duration	Rapid changes of regimes.
Ethnic composition of the ruling elite differing from the population at large	Political and economic power exercised (and differentially applied) through ethnic and religious identity; desecration of ethnic symbols by opposing sides.
Deterioration or elimination of public services	Reduction in the size and performance of social safety nets that ensure a minimum standard of service available to all.
Sharp and severe economic distress	Uneven economic development; differential benefits or losses to one or other group or geographic zone as a result of significant changes in economy; massive economic transfers or losses over short periods of time.
Legacy of vengeance-seeking group grievance	History of inter-group rivalry with disputes settled through violence.
Massive, chronic or sustained human flight	Sufficiently adverse social, political, economic or environmental conditions to propel large numbers of the population into displacement within or across borders.

Source: Adapted from Carnegie Commission on Preventing Deadly Conflict (1997) and from Stewart (2000).

The Carnegie Commission on Preventing Deadly Conflict (1997) identified a range of factors that contributes to the occurrence of violent political conflict (Table 13.1). It is argued here that many risk factors are being exacerbated by current processes of globalisation. Figure 13.1 presents a framework in which linkages between globalisation and conflict can be envisioned, highlighting widening inequities in the presence of increased competition, widespread availability of weapons, and a declining or worsening capacity of states to manage the political challenges

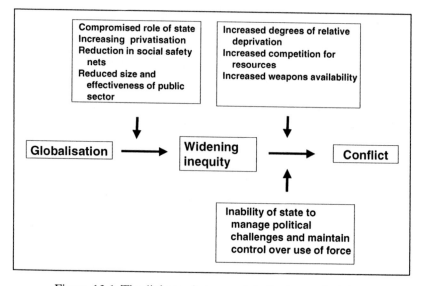

Figure 13.1 The linkages between globalisation and violent political conflict.

inherent in such unstable situations and, ultimately, to maintain control over the exercise of force.

The globalised humanitarian response

While the processes of globalisation have contributed to changing the nature and form of conflicts, so, too, have they affected the response to such crises. The humanitarian community has been transformed into a global industry, attracting high levels of global media interest and funding for favoured causes from donor agencies. The number of agencies operating in these complex settings has increased dramatically from a small handful in the 1970s to many hundreds two to three decades later. Agencies have to respond immediately if they are to attract international funding while media interest is still high – activities are thus sometimes structured around what will attract global media attention and visibility. Key agencies simultaneously compete for a 'market share' while promoting professional and regulatory frameworks for operating in the increasingly blurred interfaces between the social, economic, political and military dimensions of conflict.

The award of the Nobel Peace Prize in 1999 to Médecins sans Frontières (MSF) highlights the 'value' accorded to humanitarian agencies. Such agencies are increasingly called upon to mitigate the effects of CPEs, and are a key element of the 'moral universalism' referred to earlier. Humanitarian agencies are expected to provide a moral and humane face despite adversity, to demonstrate commitment to the plight of others, and to alleviate the most negative features of their experience. At a global political level, in developing the 'international community' response to the 11 September 2001 terrorism, leaders such as George Bush, President of the USA, and Tony Blair, Prime Minister of the UK, were challenged to accord equal weight to the military, diplomatic and humanitarian responses. The poet Seamus Heaney, addressing an East Timor protest meeting, said 'Everybody has felt the pity and the terror of the tragedy but I think we have also experienced something more revealing, which is a feeling of being called upon, a feeling of being in some way answerable' (quoted by Robinson 1999).

The level of funding committed to humanitarian crises rose dramatically immediately after the end of the cold war, but reduced in the years preceding the Kosovo and East Timorese crises of 1999. In 1989, non-food emergency and distress relief amounted to US $809 million; this rose to a peak of US $3,468 million in 1994, before declining to US $2,163 million in 1997 and US $2,786 million in 1998 (IFRC 1999, 2000). Along with such high levels of funding have come expectations, notably from the donor community, but also from politicians and the media, for value-for-money. The donor community has expressed an increased desire for humanitarian responses to fit in with other conflict management strategies. Powerful states seek to ensure that humanitarian assistance is present, effective and visible, as part of their response to crises. Demands for accountability have emerged from recent evaluations, such as that of the humanitarian response to the Rwandan genocide, which revealed numerous shortcomings (Millwood 1996). These included short-termism among some of the less-established agencies, lack of application of best-practice standards, inefficiencies, duplication of effort and poor co-ordination. A particularly visible response has been the pressure on hundreds of humanitarian agencies to sign up to an international code of conduct, and to strive to employ best-practice standards in undertaking their humanitarian tasks (Sphere Project 1999).

Alongside attempts to increase the accountability of humanitarian agencies have been debates about the changing mandates of such agencies, critiques of their traditional values of impartiality and neutrality in the presence of new types of conflict, debate over their interface with the military in its response to humanitarian crises, and attempts to maintain a degree of independence amidst increasing attempts by government to co-opt humanitarian agencies into their conflict management strategies. Humanitarian workers and resources have increasingly been targeted in recent conflicts leading to increased efforts to collaborate with the military and security sector. Despite notable benefits such as improving logistics and the potential protection of affected communities, such involvement may also bring negative consequences, and threaten the neutrality and impartiality that many agencies aspire to.

In some cases, the military may be competing directly for contracts to deliver assistance; for the armed forces, identifying new markets for their skills and resources is one way of maintaining government and public support and resources. At the same time, resource constraints on the non-governmental sector in many countries has made them more reliant on government and UN contracts for survival, presenting risks of a loss of independence by some agencies. In the United States in particular, a number of humanitarian agencies are increasingly seen as part of the State Department's response to crises.

Can we take advantage of globalisation to improve humanitarian responses to conflict?

While the above paints a gloomy scenario, trends in globalisation also present opportunities to improve humanitarian responses to conflict (Box 13.2). The so-called 'CNN factor', for example, has both positive and negative features. The positive is the potential to initiate widespread awareness of some conflicts and their contributory causes and the human misery they produce. The negative relates to the 'dumbing down' of the complexity of these situations, often focusing on tribal or inter-ethnic enmity and the 'goodies' (e.g. the USA) and 'baddies' (e.g. Bin Laden, the Saudi Arabian terrorist sheltered by the Taliban regime in Afghanistan). Little attention is devoted to understanding the underlying structural causes of CPEs and the contributing factors of the global arms trade, widening social inequalities and, in some cases, the role of transnational corporations in bolstering corrupt regimes or profiting from instability in resource-rich settings. The challenge to ensure that all such conflicts are given attention, and to sustain this attention, may need to be the responsibility of other actors and means.

New information and communication technologies offer one key means of broadening our awareness and understanding of, and improving our responses to, CPEs. Hurrell (1999) argues that the definition of a security threat remains dominated by the interests of high-income countries. Such threats are traditionally defined in terms of military threats, originating externally from the country, to the integrity of the state as a political entity and the domestic population within it. More recently, this concept of national security has widened to include non-military threats such as organised crime, infectious agents and environmental degradation. None the less, threats to national security continue to be seen as

---

Box 13.2   Globalisation and the development of appropriate public health responses.

Economic
- Highlight inequalities and marginalisation of groups as potential contributors to collective violence
- Highlight negative impact of ongoing conflict for markets, development and social capital
- Demonstrate global civil society responsiveness to humanitarian needs and to ethical behaviour by transnational corporations

Political
- Monitor trends in socio-economic and social indicators in high-risk areas
- Reform the United Nations and the Security Council
- Place states and multilateral agencies under scrutiny through civil society and global legal action
- Develop global mechanisms to promote standards and accountability for humanitarian action
- Monitor movement of armaments and sale to states in which increasing inequities and potential for conflict are present

Cultural
- Use new technologies to give voice to those most marginalised and affected by conflict
- Develop methods to control hate media and to inform general media of complexities

Social
- Highlight need to promote a more humane form of globalisation
- Promote state and multilateral agency accountability through public action
- Facilitate agency–academic linkages and public debate and critique of performance

Source: This box uses a framework by Lee (2000) that identifies the spheres and dimensions of globalisation. The box contents have been developed by the authors.

---

originating externally, potentially impacting across national borders to threaten the state. The shortfall of this perspective lies in the failure to understand the contradictions in the nature of the emerging global system itself (of which all countries are increasingly a part) that contribute to collective violence including CPEs and which conspire to make countries such as the USA a target for terrorism.

One means of improving understanding of the links between globalisation and conflict may be through technologies like the Internet which allow us to be alerted earlier to detrimental developments, such as increases in relative inequality or increased inter-group tensions and human rights abuses, within and between groups. Civil society groups, local communities and scholars around the world continue to raise contentious issues that could be shared more widely in the public domain. Information from those affected by conflict is also more available, although users of such data need to approach them with caution given the value placed by parties to conflicts on having their views presented to the world (e.g. NATO). Nevertheless, they offer insights into the perspectives, concerns, claims and objectives of contesting groups. Identifying mechanisms for eliciting viewpoints from those most affected by conflict requires particular attention. Access to the new technologies, if this can be expanded for marginalised groups, will be one mechanism for projecting viewpoints and experiences into the public domain.

Information shared in this way can also increase the accountability of the 'humanitarian industry'. The trend towards demanding better evidence of the effectiveness and efficiency of humanitarian interventions could contribute to improvements in practice. As 'good practice' needs to be context-sensitive, drawing insights from a variety of settings and clarifying their specificities will be essential (Fustukian and Zwi 2001). Debates on key concerns, such as effective mechanisms for working with the military in delivering humanitarian assistance (Weiss 1997) and a humanitarian ombudsman to ensure that neglected communities can articulate their concerns (Christoplos 2000; Mitchell and Doane 2000), could be facilitated in this way. Lessons regarding the use of health-based interventions to promote peace-building similarly require rigorous assessment if their claims of contributing to building peace are to be replicated in other settings (WHO 1999g). Importantly, mechanisms for bolstering the resilience of individuals, communities and systems to the ill-effects of violent political conflict need to be developed and promoted. At the same time, efforts to better understand the determinants and contributors to violent political conflict, and to address them, are essential. Failure to identify and address root causes prior to, and in the aftermath of, conflict is likely to set up a new cycle of violence and retribution.

Towards a more humane globalisation

Globalisation continues apace and our present abilities to shape its processes, and monitor its impacts, remain limited. Accelerating globalisation reveals winners and losers at the global, national and local levels. Most notably, wealth is increasingly concentrated in fewer hands, and there are fewer safety nets to assist those who benefit least. The exacerbation of such inequalities within and across societies appears to be worsening inter-group tensions and conflicts. Current forms of globalisation appear to be inherently conflict-producing rather than conflict-diminishing.

UNDP has called for a more humane globalisation that includes improving systems of global governance, reversing the most extreme forms of marginalisation, and seeking more actively to eradicate widespread poverty (UNDP 1999). These and related interventions are necessary if the most negative effects of globalisation, many of which are associated with collective violence between states, but more particularly within states, are to be reduced. There is widespread recognition of the human consequences of such forms of violence, the impact on health, human security and health systems, and of the limitations of the international humanitarian response. More action needs to be taken earlier and more effectively if such crises are to be avoided.

The humanitarian response can be improved through better information and structures that help identify countries and regions at risk of collective violence, encourage earlier intervention where appropriate, ensure ethical practices by the humanitarian industry, and hold to account those guilty of crimes against humanity. The globalising mass media has drawn attention to many conflicts worldwide, and made the work of organisations like UNICEF, ICRC and MSF more familiar to us all. Furthermore, there are greater opportunities for hearing the voices of those most marginalised and adversely affected by global instability and conflict. The question remains whether we are willing to listen and learn from these voices.

KEY READINGS

Deacon, B. 1997, 'Nongovernmental organizations and global social policy in conditions of conflict', in *Global social policy, international organizations and the future of welfare*, London: Sage, pp. 153–94.

Duffield, M. 1999, 'Globalisation and war economies: promoting order or the return of history?', *The Fletcher Forum of World Affairs*, 23 (2): 12–36.

Global Witness, 1998, *A rough trade; the role of companies and governments in the Angolan conflict*, London: Global Witness.

1999, *A crude awakening; the role of oil and banking industries in Angola's civil war and the plunder of state assets*, London: Global Witness.

Kaldor M. 1999, *New and old wars: organized violence in a global era*, Oxford: Polity Press.

Pearson, F. S. 1994, *The global spread of arms*. Boulder, CO: Westview Press.

14 Globalisation and health policy: trends and opportunities

Kent Buse, Nick Drager, Suzanne Fustukian and Kelley Lee

Introduction

In this concluding chapter, we focus on key lessons from the preceding chapters concerning the potential impacts of globalisation on the making of health policy, particularly policy affecting the health of populations in low- and middle-income countries (LMICs). The contested nature of the globalisation and health policy debate was touched upon in the introductory chapter. The political left and right, as well as groups in the North and South, among others, advance divergent claims, counter-claims and speculation regarding the impact of globalisation on health policy. Regrettably, these claims are too rarely based on empirical analysis. This book represents an attempt to infuse into the debate analysis on a selected range of health policy issues.

In light of our understanding of globalisation, as a set of processes that are transforming the nature of human interaction across a wide range of spheres (e.g. social, political, economic and technological) and along three dimensions of change (spatial, cognitive and temporal), we begin with the assumption that globalisation has altered the world of policy-making in tangible ways. Evidence of this is manifest in the answers to a range of questions that this concluding chapter seeks to explore. In what ways, and to what extent, can health issues be considered global? How is globalisation changing the nature of the challenges faced by policy-makers? How do determinants of health that are transnational in nature affect the type of issues on the health agenda? To what extent are transnational forms of policy-making emerging or being strengthened as a consequence of globalisation? Who is and who is not represented in these globalising policy apparatuses? How is globalisation affecting the distribution of power and influence among relevant actors involved in health policy-making? How, and to what extent, are globalising forces particularly impacting on the national health policies of LMICs?

This chapter is structured according to a framework by Walt and Gilson (1994) introduced in chapter 1. They suggest that there are four components of policy that need to be analysed: (a) policy actors (i.e. what individuals and social groups make policy and how have power relationships changed); (b) policy process (i.e. what forms of interaction and relationships determine policy outcomes); (c) policy context (i.e. what are the broader contextual factors characterising globalisation which affect health policy); and (d) policy content (i.e. what substantive or content issues are on the health policy agenda and how has this changed). We begin by establishing the contextual background against which globalising health policy is taking place. Thereafter we examine, in turn, the policy content, actors and processes involved. The chapter concludes with an agenda for research and action that seeks to further understand the changing nature of health policy and how policy-making could be strengthened in a globalising world.

The policy context: a blurring of boundaries

When considering the ways globalisation may be changing the nature of the policy context for health, it is important to bear in mind that the concept of globalisation represents a set of processes, rather than a fixed endpoint. These complex processes are subject to varied and sometimes contradictory forces. Consequently, the costs and benefits of globalisation will be experienced differently by different individuals, socio-economic classes, genders, communities, countries, and ecological and economic regions. Indeed, the current phase of globalisation of recent decades has witnessed a profound widening of inequalities in income and wealth, both within and between countries. Although average income per capita has tripled in the past fifty years, inequality has also increased (Milanovic 1998; UNDP 1999). Globalisation, therefore, impacts variably on individuals and population groups, with many excluded from its benefits and vulnerable to its costs.

The differentiated and multifaceted impacts that globalisation is having, therefore, pose a conceptual challenge in attempting to ascribe changes to the policy context. It remains true that health policy continues to be beset by the familiar challenges of poverty, inequality and resource constraints. None the less, a 'global spin' on these challenges is increasingly apparent, arising from the geographical reach (extensity), density and intensity of interconnectedness that marks globalisation of recent decades (Held *et al.* 1999).

This unprecedented interconnectedness is leading to the blurring of a variety of boundaries, perhaps led foremost by the changing role of the state. From a period of relative symmetry between the territorial boundaries of the state and its capacity to exert sovereign authority over its domestic population, it is widely argued that the increasing porousness of national boundaries is eroding the power of the state (Elkins 1995). According to Reinicke and Witte (1999), the impact has not been felt so much on formal or 'external' sovereignty (i.e. the entitlement to rule over a defined territory) as 'internal' sovereignty (i.e. the ability to articulate and pursue domestic policy). The 'global shift' towards a world economy, described by Dicken (1998) and briefly discussed in chapter 12, has perhaps been the leading driver of this redefinition of state capacities. The emergence of transnational forms of human interaction and, with them, newly defined constituencies and interests, such as the cosmopolitan human rights culture (Linklater 1998), means that state authority 'has leaked away, upwards, sideways, and downwards. In some matters, it seems even to have gone nowhere, just evaporated' (Strange 1995). Scholte (2000) similarly argues that the growth of transborder capital movements means that state sovereignty is no longer about defending a physical 'place' but rather a more modest attempt to retain 'state influence in a given area of regulation'. The relationship between globalisation and the state is thus marked by both continuity and change. States remain the primary actor in international relations with clear responsibility for public policy-making including health policy. None the less, pressures arising from globalisation are changing the capacity of the state to formulate and implement health policy.

One of the major consequences of the changing role of the state in health policy has been the blurring of the respective roles, responsibilities and jurisdictions of the public and private spheres (Cutler et al. 1999a). The period with which this book is concerned (i.e. from the late twentieth century) has been marked by ideological disagreement over the appropriate role of the state and other institutions in the so-called social sectors. For many of the policy issues examined in the preceding chapters, this debate has been largely won by those who support a minimal role for the state, one of basic social support as a last resort to those most in need. The main engine and provider of economic wealth should come from the private sphere, with the state 'filling gaps' only when markets and other private initiatives fail. Based on this perspective, the relative size of the public and private spheres has shifted towards the latter. Lloyd-Sherlock (chapter 11), for example, writes that, despite the challenges of accelerated population ageing, the promotion of privately managed individual pensions has gained ground over policies of collective social responsibility for the aged. Lee and Goodman (chapter 6) describe how, in health care financing reform, the agenda has strongly focused on enhancing private sources of financing. Buse and Walt (chapter 3) analyse public–private partnerships as a means by which private actors have become more involved in areas traditionally perceived as public.

One consequence of this 'privatisation' of health policy is the trend in some parts of the world towards what Cerny (1995) calls the residual state. Residual states are those that lose to private sources of authority, to varying degrees, their monopolies over certain functions traditionally fulfilled by the state, notably peace and security and the financing and delivery of social services. A number of chapters in this book examine the effects of this trend on health. Zwi et al. (chapter 13), for example, explore the links between globalisation, particularly the 'structural violence of maldevelopment' (Cliffe and Luckham 1999) that exacerbates inequalities within and between states, and the troubling rise in the frequency and spread of complex humanitarian emergencies. Where the state can no longer maintain peace and security, uses violence against domestic populations to retain power, or loses exclusive control over collective force to non-state actors, the effectiveness of public policy-making in other spheres (including health) breaks down.

Even in relatively stable environments, an increasingly residual state means a weak role in regulating the correspondingly growing private sector. In their analysis of private health care providers in LMICs, Brugha and Zwi (chapter 4) conclude that the public sector's willingness and ability to regulate private providers is woefully inadequate. Similarly, Kumaranayake and Lake (chapter 5) note that the growth in global health markets has been unaccompanied so far by effective public regulation, exposing health systems to potential market failures and their human consequences. Moreover, as Fustukian et al. (chapter 12) argue, where regulation does exist, it tends to leave ultimate authority in private hands, relying on self-regulation through self-administered and enforced voluntary codes. Similarly, Buse and Walt (2000c) raise a range of issues about the circumscribed governance of public–private partnerships. Overall, effective regulation to protect and promote human health lags behind the proliferating role of the private sector in health. What should be the appropriate balance between the public and private spheres remains a key point of policy debate. Many argue, however, that there must be a reassertion of the state's role, not least to mediate the adverse effects of globalisation and to facilitate the sharing of its benefits (Kaul et al. 1999; Deacon 2000).

As well as a blurring of the public and private sectors, the context for health policy-making is being shaped by a greater interconnectedness between health and other sectors (e.g. environment, trade, labour). With the determinants of health increasingly diffuse, the integration of previously distinct policy domains is becoming essential. The need for closer intersectoral co-operation, of course, has been called for over many decades within the development aid community. Globalisation, however, is bringing the interconnectedness of different policy areas into sharper focus, prompting policy-makers to find win–win situations that improve policy outcomes for all concerned sectors.

Of particular note is the emerging global economy with its increased volume and speed of trade in goods, services and capital (Dicken 1998). The potential for conflict between the policy objectives of free trade, on the one hand, and the protection and promotion of public health and safety, on the other, have existed from at least the nineteenth century. However, as Ranson *et al.* observe (chapter 2), health considerations to date have been dealt with as limited exceptions in trade agreements, allowable only under narrowly defined conditions. Recent trade disputes over hormone-treated beef, genetically modified organisms and antiretroviral drugs reveal the intensifying tensions between public health policy and multilateral trade agreements arising from globalisation. The settlement of such disputes in the World Trade Organization (WTO) represents greater efforts to reconcile trade and other areas of policy including health (Drager 1999). None the less, as Ranson *et al.* argue, considerably more integration of policy communities will be required in future. This includes the need for the public health community to build bridges with non-traditional sectors, such as trade and finance, and to engage more directly and substantively in trade negotiations and dispute resolution. More challenging still is the need to effectively tackle the global economy, as it is presently emerging, as a structural determinant of ill health. Porter *et al.* (chapter 10) argue that the global tuberculosis strategy focusing on 'getting the drugs to the bugs' needs to be accompanied by initiatives to address the root causes of the disease's re-emergence – increased poverty and health inequalities. Again, this requires a paradigmatic shift – putting health within the context of sustainable and equitable economic development – and engaging in those policy forums that impact on global economic policy (e.g. Group of Seven, OECD, IMF).

Finally, one of the key contextual features confronting health policy-makers is how to balance the heterogeneity of human societies, which remains a striking feature of a globalising world, with the intensifying and accelerating interconnections among them. Many writers on globalisation have pondered the prospects of a global community emerging, 'signalled by the development not just of global common interests but also of a worldwide consciousness of common identity' (Brown 1995). This is not to say that we are sceptical of the very phenomenon of globalisation (Hirst 1997), but that we need to be cognisant of its many different faces. At the same time, one myth of globalisation is that local or national context matters less as we move increasingly towards shared identities and, therefore, that policies adopted in one part of the world can be easily and successfully transferred to others. For instance, McPake (chapter 7) argues that the impact of user fees on public services will vary depending on how they are implemented in different contexts. Others have found that highly effective interventions, such as 'syndromic management' for the control of sexually transmitted infections (Grosskurth *et al.* 1995), may not be very effective where different social, economic and epidemic conditions prevail (Hawkes *et al.* 1999). Kumaranayake and Lake (chapter 5) draw attention to differences in national capacity to regulate emerging global markets in health care, with the increasingly transborder nature of finance, production and marketing particularly challenging LMICs. As diseases, such as TB and HIV, become globalised in a territorial sense, they create worldwide risks, but not all population groups are put at similar risk. The poor and socially marginalised face far greater vulnerability to these and other communicable diseases (Farmer 1997; Gilks *et al.* 1998; Maniar 2000). Overall, individuals and population groups vary considerably in their abilities to adapt to the exigencies of globalisation. Any effective policy response must thus recognise and address this inequity. Similarly, states differ markedly in their capabilities and capacities to articulate and implement such policy (World Bank 1997b).

Policy content and the contented: an unhealthy myopia of alternatives

One of the key findings that emerges from this volume is the impact that globalisation is having on the content of health policies worldwide. As described in chapter 1, policy content concerns the substance of actual policies. It ultimately reflects what health issues are given priority by decision makers and, equally important, what issues are not. It concerns the universe of possible options for addressing issues that make it on to the policy agenda, the agreed goals to be pursued through them, and the means by which they are to be achieved. The chapters in this book argue that policy content has been closely aligned with global shifts in power and influence among key policy actors. For students of politics, the link between policy and power is hardly a revelation. In international health, where science and evidence-based practice are keenly upheld, analysis of the role of power in influencing what policies gain and lose currency remains neglected. Yet, it is reflexiveness that is needed to explain how certain policies have emerged and spread worldwide, even in the face of insufficient or contrary evidence of their appropriateness and effectiveness.

One theme linking many chapters in this volume is whether or not there is a convergence of policy content occurring across countries and, if there is, the reasons for this convergence. On the one hand, convergence can be seen as progressive, reflecting an increased sharing of knowledge, ideas, standards and technology across different policy contexts. As Rose (1993) writes, 'the volume of activity with the objective of cross-national learning is evidence of the globalisation process in the exchange of information, ideas and ideology across the themes which are usually grouped under the health sector reform heading'. Mayhew and Watts (chapter 9), for example, describe how the policy issues of reproductive health and violence against women (VAW) have benefited from transnational sharing of information and collaborative advocacy among NGOs, largely facilitated by the advent of global communications. Their efforts, in turn, have led to greater recognition of the importance of these issues irrespective of national, cultural and socio-economic differences. This trend towards policy convergence can also be found in the adoption of global targets for a range of indicators related to health status and the determinants of health, most notably through a series of major international conferences including the World Summit on the Rights of the Child (UNICEF, 1989), the International Conference on Population and Development (1994), the World Summit for Social Development (1995) and International AIDS Conferences (biannually). Undoubtedly, these meetings have made an invaluable contribution to strengthening commitment to a range of laudable causes, such as human rights, workers' health and safety, and reproductive health, and have sought to globalise higher standards of health care and status. The agreements reached have also been significant for reinvigorating, in many cases, tired policy agendas and garnering high-level support in the form of development aid and technical expertise.

On the other hand, convergence may result from inequities in power whereby the ideas, values and beliefs of the more powerful are spread either coercively (e.g. policy conditionality) or consensually (e.g. intellectual leadership). Power is a core concept in the study of politics and the substantial literature on its theory and definition cannot be reviewed in detail in the context of this chapter. A discussion of how power can influence the policy process is provided below. However, many chapters in this book suggest the need to better understand how power, in its varied forms, has contributed centrally to defining the parameters of health policy debates in many issue areas. Foremost is the wider acceptance of the commodification of health care provision and financing through more competitive and private markets, as described in chapter 7, McPake (autonomous hospitals), chapter 6, Lee and Goodman (user fees) and chapter 4, Brugha and Zwi (private health service providers). Acceptance of the greater need for market forces in the health sector has been accompanied by the promotion of certain analytical tools such as cost-effectiveness analysis (CEA) and the disability-adjusted life-year (DALY) (see chapter 8, Kumaranayake and Walker). Collectively, such policies have been packaged under the heading of 'health sector reform'. Yet, Ranson *et al.* (chapter 2) describe the wider context of multilateral trade agreements within which policy convergence has taken place and how this may further reinforce behind-the-border convergence in the health sector.

The worldwide adoption of such policies, crudely categorised as neo-liberal, by countries at many levels of wealth and on widely varying positions on the political spectrum, of course may be attributable to the soundness of the policies themselves in achieving improved health care for relevant population groups. However, McPake (chapter 7) draws attention to the failure to sufficiently balance global policies with local contexts before user fee policies were introduced to parts of Africa from the late 1980s. Kumaranayake and Walker (chapter 5) argue that the use of certain analytical tools has proceeded apace despite limitations in data quality and methodology. Even a relatively technical intervention such as DOTS, according to Porter *et al.* (chapter 10), needs careful reflection on its particular impacts on local populations. In short, whether or not health policy convergence has been sufficiently evidenced-based or informed by cross-national learning has been a subject of intense debate. The policies analysed in this book offer limited evidence of their transferability to widely differing social contexts, particularly to address the health challenges faced by LMICs. Moreover, the salience given to efficiency over equity in the propagation of health policy has led to concerns (Gilson 1998; Gwatkin and Guillot 1998). Another feature of globalised health policy is that it is essentially western in terms of experience, expertise and solutions. As Makinda (2000) argues, globalisation requires that the 'values, institutions, interests and norms of some peoples and societies have to be sacrificed' and it is power that determines whose standards become 'global'.

In summary, the health policy agenda from the late twentieth century is seeing a struggle between the need for collective efforts to address global health challenges, and the difficulties of formulating and disseminating policies that are relevant and effective for diverse population groups and environments. Undoubtedly, there is great potential for globalisation to revitalise neglected policy issues and to mobilise resources to tackle them. Global linkages among governmental and non-governmental organisations are being facilitated, and scientific knowledge and technical expertise is being shared across countries on an unprecedented scale. None the less, this book also finds that this convergence of policy content is occurring within a circumscribed ideological universe, yielding a narrow set of policies inextricably linked to inequities in power relations.

Globalisation and health policy actors: the many and the few

The question of who makes policy in a globalising world remains contested in both the scholarly and popular literature. For some, the answer is straightforward – globalisation is 'a convenient term to indicate American hegemony' (Sur 1997). Phillips and Higgott (1999) advance a more nuanced interpretation in describing the 'two-tiered' nature of globalisation: interests that participate meaningfully in processes of social change and those largely excluded from it. Among the former Slaughter (1997) identifies as the legions of civil servants working behind the scenes across national borders, as well as 'bankers, lawyers, business people, public-interest activists, and criminals'. Similarly, Barnett and Finnemore (1998) point to the proliferation of international organisations[1] and their bureaucratic workings as critical to understanding how the global system works.

In relation to the health sector, it is widely observed that the number and variety of actors engaged in health policy has rapidly expanded. Where ministries of health and the World Health Organisation, largely staffed by medical professionals, once dominated policy-making at the national and international levels respectively, today they are joined by other professionals (e.g. social scientists, trade lawyers, economists, insurance adjusters, information technology specialists) and other institutions. At the national level, policy actors might include other ministries (e.g. trade, finance, foreign affairs, education), NGOs (e.g. Save the Children Fund, Médecins sans Frontières), foreign aid donors, regional and multilateral development banks, other UN organisations (e.g. UNFPA, UNICEF), private companies and industry associations, consultancy firms, charitable foundations, research institutions and criminal organisations. The number and diversity of actors directly or indirectly concerned with health has led to the conclusion by some that a more pluralist policy environment has emerged (Frenk 1995), characterised by the diffusion of power among many interest groups who compete (more or less equitably) for policy influence (Walt 1994).

A number of chapters support the observation that there has been, and by extension should be, a greater pluralism of policy actors. A useful starting point for conceptualising types of actors is the work of UNDP (1997) on governance, which classifies actors into three spheres: the state, private sector and civil society. Broadly speaking, the role of the state is to create a political and legal environment conducive for policy-making. The private sector generates wealth, primarily in the form of economic resources. Civil society[2] facilitates political and social interaction, mobilising groups to participate in economic, social and political activities. Globalisation has impacted upon the roles of each of these sectoral actors (and the interdependencies among them) in a number of ways.

First, as described above, the changing role of the state has been a defining feature of the policy context for health in a globalising world. In relation to specific actors, changes to the roles of certain state-defined institutions (i.e. national governments, intergovernmental organisations) can be observed. National governments, in general, are increasingly constrained in their capacity to mediate many of the determinants of health of their domestic populations. The intensification of transnational flows of capital, people and ideas, as well as the migration of authority upwards (supranationally) to organisations like the World Trade Organization, have challenged all states. In large part, this has been due to policies that support a minimalist state, resulting in a reduced sphere of authority in which states are accepted as legitimate players.

At the same time, of course, capacity remains highly variable among different states. The familiar difference between rich and poor countries remains valid. Since the end of the cold war, the United States has enjoyed unrivalled political and economic power. In stark contrast, LMICs as a whole have experienced diminished influence because of their inability to play off superpower rivalries. This is, of course, a simplistic assessment of the complexities of world politics and the shifting 'balance of power' among states. Yet, the analyses in this volume suggest a reinforcement and even exaggeration of power differences among states to influence the policy environments around them. Thus, while dominant states, it is argued, have 'catalysed' globalisation (Scott 2000), increased transborder activities have 'severely constrained the bargaining positions of smaller and weaker states, mainly in the south' (Scholte 1997b). The constraints faced by LMICs in intergovernmental relations have been well documented (Oloka-Onyango and Udagama 2000). In the health sector, understanding of the workings of key organisations like the WTO, let alone the capacity to influence its decision-making, is woefully inadequate among LMICs (chapter 2, Ranson *et al.*). LMICs played a minimal role in policy debates on health financing reform except as targets of such reforms (chapter 6, Lee and Goodman). The weakness of regulatory frameworks in LMICs in the face of emerging global health markets leaves their populations especially vulnerable to inappropriate practices (chapter 5, Kumaranayake and Lake). Where LMICs have acted effectively, such as to protect the 'comparative advantage' of employing low-waged and unprotected labour forces from being undermined by WTO provisions (chapter 12, Fustukian *et al.*), economic interests seeking to integrate these countries into the global economy have taken precedence over efforts by public health interests to raise health and safety standards.

Secondly, many of the chapters point to a marked ascendance of private (for profit) sector actors in health policy in recent decades within the context of a 'global shift' in the world economy. The relative increase in the proportion of economic activity and trade generated and controlled by the private sector and, in particular, transnational corporations has been well documented elsewhere (Dicken 1998). The number of firms that are transborder in nature grew phenomenally from the 1960s; this was followed in the 1980s and 1990s by similarly spectacular growth in transborder business mergers and strategic alliances (Scholte 1997b). These trends have resulted in increased concentration of ownership and power in many areas of production and industrial sectors (Garten 1999). Increasing concentration characterises, for example, the pharmaceutical industry (Tarabusi and Vickery 1998). Indeed, horizontal acquisitions and mergers within the industry and vertical concentration resulting from the take-over of biotechnology companies by all of the major research-based pharmaceutical companies during the 1990s has, according to Mytelka and Delapierre (1999) resulted in a global 'networked, knowledge-based biopharmaceutical oligopoly'. Oligopolies and increasing concentration empowers individual mega-companies in relation to both state and intergovernmental organisations, but also increases the possibilities for industry-wide association and organisation (e.g. IFPMA in the case of pharmaceuticals). In the context of an increasing polycentric political system and concentrated economic system, TNCs have gained some powers formerly monopolised by the state (Held *et al.* 1999: 281).

What is notable, and relevant in relation to the theme of this book, is the translation of this economic power into greater influence over policy-making that has hitherto been seen as the realm of the public sphere (Cutler *et al.* 1999a: 16). Lee *et al.* (1997), for example, document the participation of private sector actors in the formal negotiations of three UN organisations – the International Telecommunications Union (ITU), International Maritime Organisation (IMO) and International Timber Treaty Organisation (ITTO). Sell (1999) describes how twelve chief executive officers of US-based transnational corporations (TNCs) organised themselves in 1986 into the Intellectual Property Committee for the Uruguay Round of the General Agreement on Tariffs and Trade (GATT) negotiations, and 'succeeded in getting most of what they wanted from an intellectual property agreement, which now has the status of public international law'. Dunoff (1998) has documented the extent to which private sector interests have been highly influential in the dispute settlement procedures of the WTO. In the health sector, the rapid growth of public–private partnerships in recent years has given the private sector unprecedented entrée into policy-making circles in national governments and key organisations such as WHO, UNICEF and the World Bank (chapter 3, Buse and Walt). Lloyd-Sherlock (chapter 11) discusses efforts to increase private insurance to fund the health costs associated with population ageing. The general trend toward the privatisation of health finance and delivery (chapter 4, Brugha and Zwi) also decreases the influence of the state over health policy.

Thirdly, this book finds that civil society actors have also gained greater prominence over health policy in recent decades. Conceptual writing about civil society is a rich literature that has generated a varied range of definitions. In brief, civil society is used here to denote the social sphere that operates above the individual and below the state. It is, as Walzer (1995: 7) writes, 'the space of uncoerced human association and also the set of relational networks – formed for the sake of family, faith, interest and ideology – that fill this space'. The role of civil society as policy actor in an evolving global order has been widely explored by other authors. Salamon (1994) predicts that 'a global "associational revolution"... may prove to be as significant to the latter twentieth century as the rise of the nation-state was to the latter nineteenth' (1994: 109). Keck and Sikkink (1998) describe how transnational advocacy groups, characterised by the centrality of principled beliefs and values, have been highly successful in terms of reframing global debates, shaping policy agendas and gaining leverage over big business and big government. The consumer boycott of Nestlé over the promotion and marketing of breast-milk substitutes is a significant example of this (Sikkink 1986). Wapner (2000) offers a theoretical account of how civil society 'provides a terrain on which actors can organise material and ideational resources to shift the institutional matrix that shapes widespread human behaviour'. In particular, certain transnational social movements organise to directly pressure states and intergovernmental organisations to undertake specific actions or assert mechanisms of governance beyond the state sphere in an effort to initiate or articulate public policy. As this sector lies beyond the self-interests pursued by states and the market, it holds some normative promise of a progressive nature. He warns, however, that there are dangers of accountability and transparency. Similarly, Scholte (1999) suggests caution in that civil society can also be 'uncivil' (e.g. undermine social justice as in the case of transborder criminal networks), offer flawed policy prescriptions, be internally governed by poor democratic criteria, or provide inadequate representation of relevant interests.

This book finds evidence of greater policy influence by civil society actors in the health sector. Mayhew and Watts document the evolution of global debates on reproductive health and VAW as a gradual growth and expansion of transnational women's networks that, in turn, have succeeded in giving a higher profile to these issue areas. Fustukian *et al.* (chapter 12) argue that civil society organisations have been influential in drawing attention to poor workers' health and safety standards in the emerging global economy. They contend that the trend towards voluntary codes of practice within the commercial sector is largely due to the activities of civil society. Zwi *et al.* (chapter 13) note the increased 'privatisation' of conflict situations in the form of increased NGO involvement in the delivery of humanitarian assistance. The influence of NGOs such as MSF and Health Action International (HAI) in campaigning for access to essential drugs and against liberalised trade policy has also been critical. In other health policy domains, such as health care financing reform, civil society organisations have been notable in their absence (chapter 6, Lee and Goodman).

In addition to changes in state, private sector and civil society actors, this book finds an increase in policy influence by individuals without traditional biomedical expertise. Several chapters point to the prominence of health economists in setting and promoting the health agenda from the late twentieth century (chapter 8, Kumaranayake and Walker; chapter 6, Lee and Goodman). Ranson *et al.* (chapter 2) draw attention to the importance of expertise in international trade law on health policy, with the traditional public health community playing 'catch up' in understanding this complex policy area. This is supported by Alston (1997) who describes international lawyers as the 'handmaidens' of globalisation regardless of issue area, with policy options available to states increasingly constrained 'as a matter of international law'.

From the analysis above, therefore, it would seem that there is ample evidence that greater pluralism is indeed occurring within the realm of health policy. The changing yet reaffirmed role of the state, and the increased importance of private sector and civil society actors attest to the diversity of actors shaping and influencing health policy. However, an important qualification to this vision is necessary and indeed central to understanding the nature of globalisation as it is currently evolving. Although some of the drivers of globalisation, notably communication technologies, are opening up the political space for policy influence to a wider spectrum of actors, this book finds that new forms of elitism and exclusivity are also being created. Lee and Goodman (chapter 6) trace the actors involved in the genesis and propagation of health care financing reform policies during the 1980s and 1990s to a circumscribed 'epistemic community' of about twenty key individuals. This transnational policy network of state and non-state actors linked a small number of influential institutions (the World Bank, WHO, USAID, ODA/DFID), as well as three universities and consultancy firms located in western industrialised countries. Importantly, this 'transnational managerial class' was perceived to hold the needed technical expertise on health financing reform, thus enabling it to define the nature of the policy problem (i.e. how to generate greater resources for health care other than through the state) and the universe of policy options (i.e. user fees, private insurance).

This development of policy networks across the spheres of the state, private sector and civil society is also evident in other areas of health policy. Buse and Walt (chapter 3) document numerous examples of global public–private partnerships that bring together diverse actors, notably large pharmaceutical companies and multilateral organisations, to focus on specific health issues, notably research and development for infectious disease control. Efforts to create a Global Partnership Agreement to Stop Tuberculosis, for example, seek to bring together a wider range of interests through the greater engagement of civil society at local levels (chapter 10, Porter *et al.*). Overall, Kaczmarski and Cooperider (1999: 57–58) describe this trend as a reflection of the 'relational age' that is upon us, one that is drawing together people from the local to the global level through various forms of partnerships aimed at solving problems.

For these reasons, health policy might be described as characterised by 'elite pluralism' in that a new form of elitism, cutting across the state, private sector and civil society, is emerging as a result of globalisation. In a sense, a 'top' slice of the most powerful actors in each sphere has become increasingly influential in decision-making. Thus, for example, the organised pharmaceutical industry, a powerful actor in its own right (i.e. the IFPMA), has gained additional influence in multilateral settings through its affiliation with the Director General of WHO through periodic 'round tables'. Similarly, major philanthropists, such as George Sorros and Bill Gates, through financial support, play key roles with respect to global tuberculosis and immunisation policy respectively.

In summary, globalisation is changing each of the three spheres of actors traditionally involved in health policy, in large part opening up a political space for potential democratisation of policy-making to a broader range of interests. At the same time, the relational and operational boundaries of these three spheres are blurring, resulting in unclear mandates at worst and innovative partnerships at best. Finally, the potential for greater democratisation is being circumscribed by elite pluralism; there are clear inequities persisting in who has power and influence over health policy. The prospect for realising this potential lies largely in the nature of global governance that emerges in coming decades, a subject closely related to the process of health policy described below.

Globalisation and the health policy process: in need of better governance

That specific, and often very limited numbers of, individuals and institutions are making global health policy might not be of any great consequence if these institutions and actors were adequately representative and accountable to the various relevant interests that their policy affects. If these conditions held, one could be sanguine that policies were fashioned that were relatively legitimate, appropriate and feasible in terms of implementation. Regrettably these conditions do not always hold in global health policy-making. A number of the authors in the book have signalled the need for increased participation, improved accountability and transparency in global health policy-making. The changing nature and mix of actors involved in global health is important in that the particular interests which they represent, and values they hold, will forcefully condition how 'health problems' are defined and framed, the universe of possible solutions, and the legitimation of possible policy approaches. As we have argued in the global health agenda section, globalisation is not devoid of specific content or values.

Governance, in both theory and practice, is concerned with each of these and how they interact together. Key challenges arise when private, public and civil society actors hold different interests resulting in relationships that can be unstable, often to the detriment of health. The task for governance is to make these relations more smooth and productive. As UNDP (1997) reports: 'Because each has weaknesses and strengths, a major objective of our support for good governance is to promote constructive interaction among all three.' Yet, this entails a major challenge where inequities of material, intellectual and other resources exist. Importantly, the concept of hegemony does not necessarily imply conspiratorial intent or collusion by the powerful over the less powerful. The distinction between true and hegemonic consensus lies in the nature of the exchange process and its openness to critically assess the appropriateness of policies to specific contexts. The former can be assessed by who participates in the policy process, how power is wielded etc., while the latter can be assessed by the appropriateness of different health policies in various settings, the outcomes of policy convergence and the capacity of relevant stakeholders to adapt global policies to local realities.

The cases in this book suggest that a number of trends regarding health policy process and governance may be emerging. The first regards accountability. Critics of globalisation have argued that it is an alienating process which removes power from common people and relocates it to a distant 'global' realm. With greater distance between the governors and the governed, accountability appears to be diminished. For example, in their analysis of the global promotion by the World Bank and USAID of private markets for health, Brugha and Zwi highlight the fact that there was no reciprocity of accountability between national and global actors for the consequences of what, in retrospect, appears to have been questionable policy advice. Consequently, these analysts argue that global policy advocates have a responsibility to promote only those policies that have been proven effective and to assume responsibility when unanticipated events transpire.

Secondly, inadequate accountability of globally powerful actors may be exacerbated by perceptions of insufficient transparency in the policy process. Referring to the establishment of the multilateral trade regime, Ranson *et al.* (chapter 2) conclude that 'negotiations... lacked the transparency required for a balanced incorporation of civil society views, and have been strongly influenced by specific industries and commercial interests'. The tendencies, however, towards fragmentation of power and some relocation of authority to non-state (often commercial) actors complicate the process of assigning responsibility and reinforce the perception of alienation from the policy process.

The latter brings us to the third problem, which Kaul *et al.* (1999) dub, in relation to global governance, the 'participation gap'. They suggest that this gap may be filled by democratising international institutions as well as by developing new forms of policy-making. The current approach to dealing with the participation gap appears to be the formation of global networks (Reinicke *et al.* 2000) and public–private partnerships for global policy-making within the context of the shift towards a 'network society' (Castells 1996). Networks and partnerships open up the policy process to non-state interests and thereby pluralise the arena. Above, we have referred to the role of a variety of networks (advocacy, epistemic, private interest, etc.) in health policy-making. Through networks and partnerships, the influence of non-state actors goes beyond efforts directed at influencing the formal processes of government decision making to, in some cases, becoming part of the decision-making structure formerly reserved as a public sphere. Contributions in this text have hypothesised that global policy networks may be necessary to garner sufficiently broad support to get issues on to the global health policy agenda. The presence of a global network might, for example, explain the success of introducing a particular approach to health care financing reform globally (see chapter 6, Lee and Goodman) and the relative failure to get ageing on to the health policy agenda (see chapter 11, Lloyd-Sherlock). However, the chapters in this book dealing with networks (chapter 6, Lee and Goodman) and partnerships (chapter 3, Buse and Walt) argue that the problems of legitimate representation, effective accountability and transparency have yet to be seriously addressed in these novel approaches to global heath policy-making.

The fourth characteristic of globalised policy-making appears to be the promotion and propagation of what are assumed to be globally relevant policy models that are imposed largely from the 'top-down'. Cases in this book deal with the promotion of specific financing instruments (chapter 6, Lee and Goodman, and chapter 7, McPake), methods of service delivery (chapter 7, McPake on hospital autonomy; chapter 10, Porter *et al.* on DOTS; chapter 4, Brugha and Zwi on regulation of the private for-profit sector) and methods for priority-setting (chapter 8, Walker and Kumaranayake on the DALY). One common finding from these case studies suggests that there has been insufficient lesson drawing on what works and for what reasons in successful global transfers of health sector reform policies. Dahlgren (1991) and Foltz (1994) drew attention to the importance of understanding contextual specifics in relation to the introduction of user fees in the early 1990s. And, despite globalising processes, context remains too heterogeneous for a cookie-cutter approach. One of the issues to which McPake (chapter 7) draws attention is that policies that might be described as seeking similar objectives (e.g. hospital autonomy) might in fact be attempting to achieve very specific and distinct objectives given the particular context in which they are introduced. However, evidence continues to accrue that the promotion and propagation of global policy models has often preceded systematic attempts to generate evidence on whether or not policies work, under which conditions and what their impacts are likely to be on the public health of vulnerable communities. In contrast, it appears that these global policy models are often conceived from predetermined ideological preferences and introduced through top-down approaches that often fail to take adequate cognisance of local realities and preferences. Fortunately, it would appear that some actors in global policy circles have come to appreciate this. Lee and Goodman (chapter 6), for example, cite a senior World Bank official as remarking that the Bank was somewhat naïve in basing its health financing policy on a prototype African country, rather than recognising the diversity among countries, and that there may have been 'better ways to get to better places'.

The fifth finding pertinent to health policy process, and alluded to above, concerns the variable extent to which states retain an autonomous capacity to make health policy or, alternatively, are influenced by trans-global forces. Kumaranayake and Lake (chapter 5), for example, draw attention to the differences between Thailand and South Africa in resisting attempts of the Office of the US Trade Representative and the White House to impose a TRIPS-Plus interpretation of the multilateral trade agreement. For their part, Fustukian *et al.* (chapter 12) have illustrated that the global pressures to roll-back health-and-safety regulations have been far less successful among Northern countries in comparison with their Southern counterparts. It would appear that the influence of global policy actors and networks on public policy development is magnified when LMICs suffer from capacity and resource constraints, or find that their public expenditure programmes are overly dependent on donor agencies that provide them with development assistance. In this regard, the increasing number of actors involved in health policy, and the interest of the global health community in seeking to propagate a relatively narrow and homogenous health policy agenda, goes some way to explaining the emphasis placed on aid and donor co-ordination at the national level during the 1990s and, in particular, the interest expressed by powerful donors in the sector-wide approach (Buse and Walt 1997; Walt *et al.* 1999). However, even if some states face a 'crisis of legitimacy' arising from the fact that external, and sometimes global, forces dictate domestic policy, the crisis of legitimacy in many LMICs may equally arise from their capture by indigenous elites whose power has been further entrenched through globalisation (Baviskar undated). Yet, to reiterate, the common thread affecting all states, but to varying degrees, is reflected in the 'jurisdictional gap' – or what Kaul *et al.* (1999) define as 'the discrepancy between a globalised world and national, separate units of policy-making'.

A further dimension of globalised health policy-making which bears drawing out is the extent to which non-governmental instruments form de facto health policy. The past decades have witnessed the rise in voluntary codes of conduct, social labelling and other forms of private authority that have complemented, pre-empted or superseded public regulation of the health sphere. Kumaranayake and Lake (chapter 5) argue that informal approaches to the regulation of emerging global, private health markets (i.e. sales of drugs over the Internet) might work better than the use of formal regulatory measures. Others argue for a more balanced approach that is tripartite in nature. For example, in relation to pharmaceutical promotion, where many governments are either unwilling or unable to regulate industry, Lexchin and Kawachi (1996) have proposed that public interest groups be provided with all information made available to the regulator and with participation rights in all committees that monitor and enforce industry self-regulation; thereby making them 'credible watchdogs'. In this regard, the amount of informal policy-making is also noteworthy. Kumaranayake and Lake (chapter 5), for example, have drawn attention to the webs of informal relationships that can influence provider behaviour in relation to regulating the emerging global markets in health. However, it would be misleading to suggest that informal, non-state policy and regulation have become the norm. The importance (which is hard to overstate) of governmental and intergovernmental regulation of (legal) trade through binding WTO treaty arrangements provides a case in point.

In summary, health policy-making is increasingly marked by a number of characteristics that differentiate it to varying degrees from processes that preceded this epoch. These include, in some cases, increasing distance between the governors and those whom they govern, which has heightened existing problems of accountability and participation in the health policy process. Another consequence of this distance between those making health policy and those affected by it has been the rash of globalised policies which have proven inappropriate *in situ*. Attempts to pluralise the policy process (for purposes of both legitimation and effectiveness) through global networks and partnerships are widespread, but many of these initiatives suffer from their own shortages of accountability, legitimate representation and transparency. Finally, while all countries are affected by the jurisdictional gap, countries vary widely in the extent to which they are vulnerable to transglobal forces on their autonomous capacity to develop effective health policy.

Understanding the global dimensions of health policy: an agenda for research

In the writing of this book, we remain much aware that we are only beginning to understand the impact of globalisation on health policy and how to analyse this impact. Health policy, as a field of study, is traditionally located within public policy, defined as 'policies developed by governmental bodies and officials, and thus focus[es] on purposive action by or for governments' (Walt 1994: 41). At the same time, however, there is a recognition that 'the set of institutions, organizations, services and funding arrangements of the health care system...goes beyond health services...and includes actions or intended actions by public, private and voluntary organizations that have an impact on health' (Walt 1994: 41). The analysis of public policy including health policy, in turn, is approached in different ways by various authors including studies of policy content, process and outputs; evaluation studies; information for policy-making; process advocacy; and policy advocacy (Hogwood and Gunn 1984: 26–8). The extension of policy analysis to study the emerging processes of globalisation may pose an additional challenge to all of these approaches, as well as require the development of new approaches, theorising, methodologies and data-sets. We are thus only too conscious of the limitations that beset the analyses of this book, but hope that new veins of research can be opened by questions raised in these chapters (see Box 14.1).

The foremost challenge is the need to define the analytical boundaries of global health more clearly in terms of the particular policy issues raised by globalisation. Indeed, if the analysis of global health is to be recognised as a distinct and legitimate endeavour, it must avoid the tendency towards fuzzy conceptualisation and thus the danger of being overly encompassing. In chapter 1, it is argued that international health becomes global health when the causes or consequences of a health issue circumvent, undermine or are oblivious to the territorial boundaries of states and, thus, beyond the capacity of states to address effectively through state institutions alone. Thus, issues such as food safety, drug regulation and infectious disease control remain *international* health policy issues if they are effectively addressed through strengthened state action. However, it is when the causes and consequences of these issues circumvent states and their authority that they become *global* health policy issues. Hence, when food safety is threatened by global environmental change, drug regulation is undermined by the illicit drug trade, or the control of infectious diseases is weakened by human hypermobility and spreading drug resistance, these policy issues have extended to the global sphere.

A useful task, therefore, would be to reconsider for all major areas of health policy whether, and how, processes of globalisation may be creating new features for analysis. In this volume, we have touched on a range of policy issues – infectious diseases, reproductive health and violence against women, occupational health and safety, collective violence, ageing, health sector reform – and have sought to explore some of the global aspects of policy-making around them. This is a far from comprehensive list of policy areas; similar analyses could be undertaken on such topics as non-communicable diseases, nutrition, mental health, human resources, environmental health, maternal and child health, and health information systems. Each of these invites a 'global spin' to be put on them.

Box 14.1   A research agenda for global health policy.

International versus global health policy
- Categorisation of issues in specific areas of health policy as international (causes or consequences within territorial boundaries of states) or global (causes or consequences circumvent, undermine or are oblivious to the state)

Global–local health interface
- Comparative case studies that document the impact of globalisation and policy responses for particular population groups within and across communities, countries and regions
- Case studies of policy transfer between different levels of health policy-making

New approaches, methods and tools for global health policy
- Reinterpretation of existing data-sets to understand cross-border nature of health determinants and status
- Development of analytical methods and tools that capture the cross-border cause and effects of globalisation
- Application of tools and methods to identify needs and priorities of specific population groups in addition to states

Cross sectoral policy studies
- Descriptive analysis of policy content, actors, contexts and processes of key policy-making institutions in other sectors (e.g. trade, environment, labour, peace and security) and their impact on health
- Case studies of the intersection of policy-making in health with other policy areas

Global health governance
- Mapping of change in key actors and their respective roles in health policy as a consequence of globalisation
- Development of criteria and measures to assess 'good governance' in the health sector at different levels and within different institutions of policy-making
- Case studies of 'best' and 'bad' practice in global governance using above criteria and measures
- Analysis of relationship between nature of policy issue and type of governance mechanism deemed effective for achieving agreed goals

---

A second aim of a research agenda for global health policy is to understand better the highly variable nature of the impacts that globalisation is having on specific individuals and population groups. Whether globalisation is good or bad for health is far too crude a question, and even misleading in the monolithic image that it portrays of highly complex cause and effects. As Fidler (1999: 2) writes, 'Analyzing the health–globalization relationship proves, however, to be a very complex business because both "health" and "globalization" are complicated concepts.' It is the diversity of settings from which global forces are being generated, and in which the consequences of global forces are being played out, that remains so poorly understood by those seeking to mediate the effects of globalisation. The poor record of policy transfer described in this book by Kumaranayake and Walker (chapter 8), Brugha and Zwi (chapter 4), Mayhew and Watts (chapter 9), McPake (chapter 7) and others points to the need for research that illuminates the cause-and-effect links between the global and the local. At a minimum, more systematic evidence of how particular policies work under specific conditions should precede the wider transfer of policies set at the global level to the national and sub-national levels. Marmor (1997) goes as far as to doubt the 'one size fits all' policy prescriptions generated in increasing numbers in a globalising world, warning of the dangers of trying to find the 'best' model from around the world and transplanting it elsewhere. Globalisation, in short, is not the homogenisation of policy needs, and research that illuminates the diversity of needs remains of foremost importance. Comparative country case studies are called for to establish the impact of differing public policies and the respective roles of state and non-state actors in making policy coherent and feasible.

Thirdly, the study of health policy in a globalising world requires innovative conceptual thinking, and methods of data collection and analysis, that recognise the reconfiguration of the boundaries that define the world around us. By this we mean that globalisation is changing a host of political, economic, social, cultural, environmental and other boundaries. As Friedman (2000) writes, globalisation is distinguished from the cold war system by its own demographic pattern, dominant culture, defining technologies, emphasis on speed, anxieties (i.e. rapid change) and structure of power. Furthermore, he writes that the emerging global system is built around three overlapping balances – the traditional balance among states, between states and global markets, and between states and individuals. It has been because of these features that this new system has 'come upon us far faster than our ability to retrain ourselves to see and comprehend it' (2000: 15).

Health policy analysis has traditionally defined the needs of individuals and societies in terms of states, either as aggregates of sub-national data or as whole units of analysis. Regional and international data, in turn, are aggregates of national data from two or more states. While state and interstate relations remain centrally important to the analysis of health policy, what is presently missing are means for understanding the links that are forming within and across states, creating patterns of health status and determinants whose dynamics are not necessarily captured by state-centric analyses. For example, all major sources of health data (e.g. *World health report*, *World development report*, *Human development report*) use the state as the defining unit of analysis. States are variably ranked according to geographical region, high, middle and low income, or high, medium or low human development. Similarly, the global burden of disease and injury initiative represented an unprecedented effort to address the need for comprehensive and comparable data on the epidemiological conditions and burden of disease in all countries. Putting aside criticism of the validity, rigour and ethical underpinnings of its methodology, the approach drew attention to the difficulties of identifying health needs and priorities in individual countries and groups of countries because of weaknesses in data (Murray and Lopez 1994). Despite its use of the term, however, the method does not provide global measures, in the sense that transborder (within and across communities, countries, regions) patterns of disease are not discernible. As such, it is not possible to see if certain diseases are occurring within population groups, not conforming to national boundaries, in different parts of the world as a consequence of global trends in capital flows, trade, conflict or environmental change.

The analysis of health policy in a globalising world, in other words, requires conceptual and methodological approaches that capture the particular features and processes of globalisation, and the transborder impacts that they may be having on health – that is reflecting the notion of 'globality-as-supraterritoriality' (Scholte 2000). In some cases, the disaggregation of existing data-sets and reassessment in innovative ways may yield fresh insights. An example is a study by Milanovic (1998) that uses intra- and inter-national data to estimate global trends in income distribution. Eschewing state-centric measures, the study divides world population into income quintiles and finds that the average income of the top 5 per cent increased from 78 to 114 times greater than the bottom 5 per cent between 1988 and 1993. New ways of seeing and measuring health determinants, status and trends, therefore, need to be developed. Other areas of policy analysis that have already begun to grapple with globalisation, such as the environment, finance and criminology, may offer ways forward.

Fourthly, and following from the last point, globalisation is bringing together different areas of policy-making and challenging policy researchers to better appreciate the growing interdependence of different issue areas. This volume, for example, points to the need for the health policy community to grapple more directly with trade and finance, peace and security, and labour and gender issues. Others include telecommunications and the environment. On the one hand, concerted efforts are needed in the health sector to understand the policy content, actors, contexts and processes of these areas, and how they intersect with health. Detailed study, for instance, of the key ideas informing policies in each field, the power and influence of major actors, and specific decision-making procedures can explain, in particular, why there may be a lack of policy coherence with other policy areas and at different levels of policy-making. As Ranson *et al.* (chapter 2) write, for example, TRIPS may make sense according to international economic theory, but are sometimes contrary to the health interests of low-income population groups. Such a task is preliminary, on the other hand, to the health community engaging more effectively with other policy agendas. The capacity to promote and protect health interests through these policy areas requires an ability to understand and use specialist language and terminology, to be familiar with formal procedures and 'culture' of policy-making in other sectors, and to identify opportunities to exert leverage when they become available.

Fifthly and finally, changes in policy actors have been a key theme across many of the previous chapters. As described above, traditional boundaries have blurred among state institutions, private for-profit actors (including those engaged in illicit activities) and the heterogeneous organisations known as civil society. Some of the shifts in their respective roles in health policy have been highlighted in this volume, but there is need for more systematic mapping of these actors, their interests and their relative power and influence in specific areas of health policy. In particular, more emphasis should be given to the innovative nature of interaction among them and the emergence of new forms of relationships. Buse and Walt (chapter 3) describe the growth of global public–private partnerships as one example of new relationships in health policy. Other writers have written about global social change organisations (Kaczmarski and Cooperider 1999), global social movements (O'Brien *et al.* 2000), transnational managerial class (Cox 1987) and global civil society (Walzer 1995). Many of these actors, but also organised commercial and criminal actors, as well as those more familiar to us, are contributing to policy-making across national boundaries in the form of global public goods and 'bads' (Kaul *et al.* 1999), global public policy (Reinicke 1998) and global social policy (Deacon 1997). A critical exercise for policy research would be to understand who these actors are, what they are doing and how they are influencing health policy.

As well as descriptive analysis, there is a prescriptive dimension to such policy research. The need for improved means of health governance, including global health governance, is a subject of increasing debate. As described in chapter 1, the diverse and uneven impacts of globalisation on human health have been accompanied by efforts to explore the implications of these challenges to existing institutions and practices of health governance – how should collective action be taken to mediate the positive and negative impacts of globalisation on human health? Assessment of how 'good' particular forms of health governance are is invariably a normative exercise, informed by implicit or explicit values. In this volume, we suggest that governance in a number of areas, including health financing reform, trade, humanitarian assistance, and occupational health and safety, do not sufficiently comply with UNDP-defined criteria of legitimacy, transparency and accountability, competence and respect for human rights and the rule of law. This seems to be changing somewhat for reproductive health and violence against women, with greater access by civil society groups to global communications. Efforts to build broader links to civil society groups and the private sector to support a global TB strategy also offer an opportunity for improved governance according to the above principles.

Policy research is needed to inform, in concrete terms, what forms of governance are appropriate to tackle specific policy issues. Blanket criteria of what health governance should look like needs to be given more nuance, with different forms of governance needed for particular purposes. A health emergency, for example, that requires rapid action may not be effectively governed by mechanisms that require time-consuming consultation with a broad range of stakeholders. Policies that concern culturally sensitive or potentially controversial moral issues, such as reproductive health, would be more appropriately governed by mechanisms that allow broader representation. Any criteria that are used to assess health governance should be defined in measurable terms, with methods and tools developed to assess their attainment. With this established, examples of 'best' and 'bad' practice from the health and other sectors could be documented in terms of how they are governed (i.e. membership, rules of decision-making, mandate, distribution of power), how effective they have been in achieving agreed goals, and what lessons they might offer for managing global health issues.

Managing globalisation for health policy: an agenda for action

The challenges of globalisation, both its risks and opportunities, elicit a sense of urgency, because of the profound changes faced and their consequences, and inertia, because of the difficulties of grasping what effective action is needed. As Weick (1999: 39) writes:

Global issues that involve organizing on a massive scale have been described as contested, nonlinear metaproblems with long lead times, unintended side effects, unclear cause–effect structures, and consequences that are often irreversible. Issues demanding change on a global scale are like an onrushing wall of fire and are just as tricky to manage.

We find this in the health field where, alongside vital recognition that broader determinants of health (e.g. poverty, inequity, environmental degradation) are equally, if not more, important than traditional biomedical concerns (e.g. disease agents), the challenges are to address these macro-level factors effectively, through appropriate means, and within a suitable timeframe (see Box 14.2).

One starting point for policy action might be the interconnectivities that globalisation is bringing to health policy. Intensifying linkages across different countries and population groups, levels of policy-making, types of policy actors and sectors are the defining features of the emerging policy environment. Extending the Gaia concept[3] from environmental studies, human health might be approached in more holistic terms as inextricably tied to the social and natural environment. Just as it is now recognised that we have a common interest in protecting the natural environment that sustains all life, so we gain mutual benefit from supporting conditions for the health and well-being of the human population. It makes little sense from this perspective, therefore, to protect and promote only the health of certain population groups (i.e. higher-income countries, wealthy)

Box 14.2   An action agenda for global health policy.

- Health sector aid to strengthen basic health and health-related infrastructure (including surveillance) across all countries
- Health sector aid to build complementary infrastructure at regional and global levels that address the transborder determinants of health
- Support for enabling appropriate participation in global health governance by disadvantaged or excluded population groups through training programmes, information dissemination, technical support and financial aid
- Establishment of a process of peer review of health policies (similar to WTO trade policy reviews and OECD development policy reviews) that enables countries to understand what may or may not work in a given context
- Representation of health interests at all levels of policy-making on trade, investment, development, environment and other policy areas
- Use of communication technologies to improve health information needs for policy-making and to improve transparency of health policy-making

separately from humankind as a whole. Global health means that the health of the poorest and most vulnerable has direct relevance for all populations because of the many interconnectivities that increasingly bring us together.

From this perspective, the underlying basis of health sector aid should shift from providing charitable handouts, to ensuring appropriate and sufficient resources for a global health system that meets the common needs of the human species (Lee and Mills 2000). At a minimum, targetted investment to provide for the basic needs of clean water and sanitation, housing, food and health care are building blocks at the local level towards an essential infrastructure through which better health is achievable. In the early twenty-first century, we are still far from achieving universal access to these minimal requirements. Failure to address these basic needs raises the prospect that health problems (e.g. antibiotic resistance, multi-drug tuberculosis, contaminated drinking water) and other types of risk (e.g. political and economic instability) may impact on other population groups.

The prospect of 'contagion effect' in the financial sector has led to widespread calls for improved global governance of capital markets (Chang and Majnoni 2000). The literal manifestation of such risk in the health sector has led to similar efforts to strengthen global governance to address health risks and opportunities of a global nature (Jayaraman and Kanbur 1999). One useful framework is offered by Kaul *et al.* (1999) who argue that there is a need for greater investment to control global public health bads, such as the spread of infectious diseases, through the increased provision of global public goods, notably disease surveillance, immunisation programmes and health information systems. The emphasis of global public goods/bads on health risks and benefits that directly spill over national boundaries is perhaps more narrowly focused than the holistic approach described above. In the context of globalisation, Yach and Bettcher (1998a,b) categorise the determinants of health as distal and proximal. All health determinants, in this sense, have potential spill-over effects that need to be addressed through an integrated and coherent health system. Systems need to be developed to identify these determinants and ensure that domestic and external resources are allocated accordingly.

An essential feature of such a system is the need to strengthen global health governance, notably by improving the means by which relevant population groups can participate appropriately in decision-making. As argued in previous chapters, the 'elite pluralism' of health governance continues to be exclusive to the relatively well-resourced, mobile, experienced and informed. Representation in multilateral trade negotiations, under the auspices of the WTO, for example, is starkly skewed in favour of higher-income countries and large corporate interests. This situation does not benefit anyone if those who feel excluded find alternative means to express their dissatisfaction. The development of social cohesion and building of social capital demands more systematic approaches to including civil society and the commercial sector in global governance. This means further specification of appropriate roles and responsibilities of these actors. Assistance to ensure 'good governance' at all levels of health policy-making is thus needed through, for instance, training of prospective delegates to major meetings, financial aid for travel costs, and innovative use of communication technologies (e.g. virtual conferences, on-line discussion groups).

A further challenge is improved policy coherence across sectors to ensure that the promotion and protection of health is not unduly compromised by other policy agendas. The public health community has, until recently, been noticeably absent from key discussions about the emerging structure and governance of the global political economy. Traditionally, health has been firmly located within the realm of social policy and 'low politics',[4] with policy-making largely governed by medical and technical expertise. The ascendance of health economics analysis in the 1980s, the high-level linking of the health agenda with the environment, population, gender and social development from the early 1990s, and the further association with trade, and peace and security issues from the late 1990s, have moved aspects of health policy into the 'high politics' realm. Recently, and without precedent, for example, health has found its way into the UN Security Council agenda (United Nations 2000) and into US national security strategy (White House 1999). Consequently, on the one hand, public health has an unprecedented opportunity to assert the importance of health development. On the other hand, advancing the health policy agenda requires informed representation in a wider range of fora. There is a need to expand and share knowledge on the effects of globalisation on health and the appropriate policy responses that should be taken to protect and promote health, particularly of the poorest population groups. This should include the support of a process of peer review of health policies (along the lines of WTO trade policy reviews and OECD development policy reviews) to better enable countries to understand what works and what may not, given their country-specific context. Many health administrations also need to strengthen their capacity to actively and effectively educate, network, negotiate and influence their colleagues if they are to ensure that their health and social objectives are represented on trade, investment and development agendas.

For WHO, and its broad coalition of partners for health action, there is a need to support common efforts to integrate populations and countries into the world economy through policies to promote accelerated debt relief, support to market access and increased financing for areas that increase human security. Moreover, WHO should continue to function as an independent provider of knowledge and evidence so as to assist policy-makers, regulatory authorities and authorities in health and other sectors (e.g. international trade bodies) to reach informed judgements as to the consequences of their actions upon health. This role should extend to the provision of technical support to enable health ministries to make effective inputs to their government's negotiating positions in regional and global development negotiations, and to enable them to identify potential effects of globalisation and respond quickly and effectively to promote and protect health.

Conclusion: globalisation with a human spin

The primary aim of this book has been to explore the impacts that globalisation is having on the making of health policy. As part of the growing attention to the social dimensions of global change, the contributors share a common concern that the forces that currently drive globalisation take insufficient account of their implications for protecting and promoting human health. The need to take fuller account of these implications, we argue, is not of secondary importance to the long-term sustainability of any global system that emerges. Indeed, widespread challenges to present forms of globalisation threaten to undermine its trajectory, and suggest the need to take account of risks, for example, to human security, social cohesion, and political and economic stability.

The desire to shape globalisation, in a manner that provides optimal human welfare benefits to the greatest numbers, rejects the view that processes of global change are irreversible or inevitable in nature. The authors, in this sense, are aligned with writers such as Amin (1997) and Falk (1999) who argue for alternative approaches to global policy that can result in improvements in human security and justice. Only by managing the process of globalisation can it be inclusive of those presently being left behind in the development process. More specifically, contributors have advocated for improved mechanisms to respond to collective violence, to govern labour standards, to structure multilateral trade agreements, to regulate emerging global health markets, to provide for ageing populations, to control infectious disease and to govern policy-making in these and other areas.

As well as throwing up new challenges for achieving these, globalisation offers opportunities for moving the policy agenda forward. There is now widespread awareness of the shared fate of the human species and the interconnectedness of the many spheres of our lives. Whether motivated by moral principles, enlightened self-interest or profit-seeking, the mutual interest we have in improving global health could be harnessed through research and action that contributes to informed, inclusive and timely policy debate. In achieving this, we must be prepared to shed traditional boundaries that define our thinking and action about health.

NOTES

1 In 1860 there were five international governmental organisations (IGO) and one international nongovernmental organisation (INGO). By 1940 this had grown to 61 IGOs and 477 INGOs, and by 1996 there were 260 IGOs and 5472 INGOs (Barnett and Finnemore 1998).

2 It is recognised that the term civil society is variably defined in the literature and is sometimes defined as encompassing the private sector. In the context of this book, we have found it useful to maintain a distinction between the two spheres.

3 The Gaia hypothesis was put forth by James Lovelock, a British atmospheric scientist, who posits that 'the components of the Earth's biosphere – comprising all living organisms, the geosphere, and the cycles of water, gases, nutrients and energy – make up a global homeostatic mechanism that ensures constancy of the environment. Gaia (from the Greek goddess "Mother Earth") thus acts as a coordinated, self-regulating superorganism, using feedback mechanisms to counter externally imposed disturbances' (McMichael 1993: 48–9).

4 According to Evans and Newham (1992: 184): 'A term used in the analysis of foreign policy. Issues are held to be low politics if they are not seen as involving fundamental or key questions relating to a state's national interests, or those of important and significant groups within the state. Low politics issues tend to be dealt with by the bureaucracy employing standard operating procedures.'

References

Abell, H. 1999, 'Endangering women's health for profit: health and safety in Mexico's maquiladora', *Development in Practice* 9 (5): 595–600.

Abel-Smith, B. 1986, 'The world economic crisis. Part 1: Repercussions on health', *Health Policy and Planning* 1 (3): 202–13.

Abel-Smith, B. and Creese, A. (eds.) 1988, *Recurrent costs in the health sector – problems and policy options in three countries*, Geneva: WHO/USAID.

Abel-Smith, B. and Rawall, P. 1992, 'Can the poor afford 'free' health care? A case study of Tanzania', *Health Policy and Planning* 7: 329–41.

Adam, C., Cavendish, W. and Mistry, P. 1992, cited in Bennett, S., McPake, B. and Mills A. (eds.) 1997a, pp.1–18.

Ad Hoc Committee on Health Research Relating to Future Intervention Options. 1996, *Investing in health research and development*, Document TDR/Gen/96.1, Geneva: World Health Organisation.

Agha, S., Squire, C. and Ahmed, R. 1997, 'Evaluation of the Green Star Pilot Project', Washington DC: Population Services International/Social Marketing Pakistan, April.

Ahenkora, K. 1999, 'The contribution of older people to development. The Ghana study', London: Help Age International and Help Age Ghana.

Akokpari, J. K. 1998, 'The state, refugees and migration in sub-Saharan Africa', *International Migration* 36 (2): 211–31.

Aljunid, S. 1995, 'The role of private medical practitioners and their interactions with public health services in Asian countries', *Health Policy and Planning* 10 (4): 333–49.

Alston, P. 1997, 'The myopia of the handmaidens: international lawyers and globalisation', *European Journal of International Law* 8 (3): 435–48.

Amin, S. 1996, 'The challenge of globalisation', *Review of International Political Economy* 3 (2) 216–59.

1997, *Capitalism in the age of globalisation: the management of global society*, London: Zed Press.

2000, 'Democratising globalisation', *Al-Ahram Weekly*, 20–26 April, issue 478.

Anand, S. and Hanson, K. 1997, 'Disability-adjusted life years: a critical review', *Journal of Health Economics* 16 (6): 685–702.

Anderson, J. E. 1975, *Public policy making*, London: Nelson.

Anderson, M. 1996, *Do no harm. Supporting local capacities for peace through aid*, Cambridge, MA: The Collaborative for Development Action.

Annan, K. 1999, United Nations Secretary-General address to the United States Chamber of Commerce, Washington DC, 9 June.

Apt, N. 1996, *Coping with old age in a changing Africa: social change and the elderly Ghanaian*, Aldershot, USA: Avebury.

1997, *Ageing in Africa*, Geneva: World Health Organisation.

Asian Development Bank, 1999, *Health sector reform in Asia and the Pacific. Options for developing countries*, Manila: Asian Development Bank.

Awofeso, N. 1998, 'Implementing tuberculosis control programmes in Kaduna State, Nigeria', *International Journal of Tuberculosis and Lung Disease* 4: 336–7.

Bale, H. 1999, 'The globalisation of the fight against disease', advertisement sponsored by Pfizer written by the Director General of the International Federation of Pharmaceutical Manufacturers Association, *The Economist*, 24 April, p. 26.

Banerji, D. 1990, 'People's felt needs, health services and the commodification of medicine', in Banerji, D. 1990, *A sociocultural, political and administrative analysis of health policies and programmes in India in the eighties: a critical appraisal*, New Delhi: Lok Prash.

Banister, J. 1987, *China's changing population*, Stanford University Press.

Banta, D. 2000, 'Increase in global access to essential drugs sought', *Journal of the American Medical Association* 283 (3): 321, 323.

Barber, B. 2000, 'Jihad vs. McWorld' in Lechner, F. and Boli, J. (eds.), *The globalisation reader*, London: Blackwell, pp. 21–26.

Barendregt, J. J., Bonneux, L. and van der Maas, P. J. 1996, 'DALYs: the age-weights on balance', *Bulletin of the World Health Organisation* 74 (4): 439–46.

Barillas, E. 1999, 'The global transformation of national health systems', *Development* 42 (4): 76–8.

Baris, E. and McLeod, K. 2000, 'Globalization and international trade in the twenty-first century: opportunities for and threats to the health sector in the South', *International Journal of Health Services* 30 (1): 187–210.

Barker, C. and Green, A. 1996, 'Opening the debate on DALYs', *Health Policy and Planning* 11 (2): 179–83.

Barnett, M. and Finnemore, M. 1998, 'The politics, power and pathologies of international organizations', Paper presented at the ACUNS/ASIL Summer Workshop on Global Governance and Nonstate Actors, Yale University, August 1998.

Barnett, T. and Lloyd-Sherlock, P. 2000, 'The impact of HIV/AIDS on inter-generational exchange: orphans and older people – the missing generation' (mimeo).

Barnum, H. N. 1986, 'Cost savings from alternative treatments for tuberculosis', *Social Science and Medicine* 23: 847–50.

Barten, F. 1993, 'Workers pay with their health', *Health Action* 5 (June–August): 4–5.

Bauman, Z. 1998, *Globalization, the human consequences*, Cambridge: Polity Press.

Baviskar, A. (undated), 'A grassroots movement and globalisation: the campaign against the Narmada Dam in India', Unpublished monograph on file with the author.

Bayer, R. and Dupuis, L. 1995, 'Tuberculosis, public health and civil liberties', *Annual Review of Public Health* 16: 307–26.

Bayer, R., Stayton, C., Desvarieux, M., Healton, C., Landesman, S. and Tsai, W. Y. 1998, 'Directly observed therapy and treatment completion for tuberculosis in the United States: is universal supervised therapy necessary?', *American Journal of Public Health* 88 (7): 1052–8.

Bellamy, C. 1999, 'Public, private and civil society', Statement of UNICEF Executive Director to Harvard International Development Conference on 'Sharing responsibilities: public, private and civil society', Cambridge, MA, 16 April.

Bennett, S. 1991, *The mystique of markets: public and private health care in developing countries*, PHP Departmental Publication no. 4, London School of Hygiene and Tropical Medicine.

1997, 'The nature of competition among private hospitals in Bangkok', in Bennett, S., McPake, B. and Mills A. (eds.) 1997a, pp. 102–23.

Bennett, S., McPake, B. and Mills, A. (eds.) 1997a, *Private health providers in developing countries: serving the public interest?*, London: Zed Books.

1997b, 'The public/private mix debate in health care', in Bennett, S., McPake, B. and Mills A. (eds.) 1997a, pp. 1–18.

Bennett, S. and Ngalande-Banda, E. 1994, *Public and private roles in health: a review and analysis of experience in sub-Saharan Africa*, Geneva: World Health Organisation.

Berkley, S. and Lenton, C. 1999, 'The International AIDS Vaccine Initiative', Paper presented at the Third Global Forum for Health Research, Geneva, 8–10 June.

Berlinguer, G. 1999, 'Health and equity as a primary goal', *Development* 42 (4): 17–21.

Bettcher, D. and Yach, D. 1998, 'The globalisation of public health ethics', *Millennium Journal of International Studies* 27: 469–96.

Bettcher, D. W., Yach, D. and Guindon, G. E. 2000, 'Global trade and health: key linkages and future challenges', *Bulletin of the World Health Organisation* 78 (4): 521–34.

Bhat, R. 1996, 'Regulation of the private sector in India', *International Journal of Health Planning and Management* 11: 253–74.

1999, 'Characteristics of private medical practice in India: a provider perspective', *Health Policy and Planning* 14 (1): 26–37.

Bhatti, N., Law, M. R., Morris, J. K., Halliday, R. and Moore-Gillon, J. 1995, 'Increasing incidence of tuberculosis in England and Wales: a case study of the likely causes', *British Medical Journal* 310: 967–9.

Binstock, R. and Post, S. 1991, 'Old age and the rationing of health care', in Binstock, R. and Post, S. (eds.) *Too old for health care? Controversies in medicine, law, economics and ethics*, London: Johns Hopkins University Press Ltd.

Birch, S. and Gafni, A. 1994, 'Cost-effectiveness ratios: in a league of their own', *Health Policy* 28: 133–41.

Birdsall, N. 1986, *Cost recovery in health and education: bank policy and operations*, PHN Technical Note 86–24, Washington DC: World Bank.

Birungi, H., Asiimwe, D. and Whyte, S. R. 1994, *Injection use and practices in Uganda*, Geneva: World Health Organisation.

Bizimana, D. and Liesener, L. 1993, *Financing of health services in Kapchorwa, Mbale and Pallisa*, Kampala: Care International Uganda.

BMS, 1999, 'Bristol–Myers Squibb commits $100 million for HIV/AIDS research and community outreach in five African countries', Press Release, Washington DC, 6 May.

Bond, P. 1999, 'Globalisation, pharmaceutical pricing, and South African health policy: managing confrontation with US firms and politicians', *International Journal of Health Services* 29 (4): 765–92.

Bossert, T., Kosen, S., Harsono, B. and Gani, A. 1996, *Hospital autonomy in Indonesia*, Boston, MA: Harvard School of Public Health.

Braithwaite, J. and Drahos, P. 1999, 'Ratcheting up and driving down global regulatory standards', Paper presented at the International Roundtable on 'Responses to globalisation: rethinking equity and health', Geneva, 12–14 July.

Brown, C. 1995, 'International political theory and the idea of world community', in Booth, K. and Smith, S. (eds.) *International relations theory today*, London: Polity Press, ch. 4.

Brudney, K. and Dobkin, J. 1991, 'Resurgent tuberculosis in New York City', *American Review of Respiratory Diseases* 144: 745–9.

Brugha, R. and Varvasovszky, Z. 2000, 'Stakeholder analysis: a review', *Health Policy and Planning* 15 (3): 239–46.

Brugha, R. and Zwi, A. B. 1998, 'Improving the delivery of public health services by private practitioners in low and middle income countries', *Health Policy and Planning* 13 (2): 107–20.

1999, 'Sexually transmitted disease control in developing countries: the challenge of involving the private sector', *Sexually Transmitted Infections* 75: 283–5.

Brundtland, G. H. 1999a, 'Public health for a new era', Presentation to a seminar at The King's Fund, London, 14 January.

1999b, 'Global partnerships for health', *WHO Drug Information* 13 (1): 1–2.

Bruyere, J. 1999, 'MMV goes independent: it's a new world', *TDR News* 61, <http://www.who.int/tdr/kh/rres_link.html>.

Bryan, S. and Brown, J. 1998, 'Extrapolation of cost-effectiveness information to local settings', *Journal of Health Services Research and Policy* 3 (2): 108–12.

Bunch, C. and Reilly, N. 1994, *Demanding accessibility: the global campaign and tribunal for women's human rights*, New Brunswick, NJ: Centre for Women's Global Leadership.

Buse, K. and Walt, G. 1997, 'An unruly melange: coordinating external resources to the health sector: a review', *Social Science and Medicine* 45 (3): 449–63.

2000a, 'Global public–private partnerships: Part 1 – a new development in health?', *Bulletin of the World Health Organisation* 78 (5): 549–61.

2000b, 'Global public–private partnerships: Part II – what are the issues for global governance?', *Bulletin of the World Health Organisation* 78 (4): 699–709.

2000c, 'The United Nations and global public–private health partnerships: in search of 'good' global health governance', Paper presented at the Workshop on Public–Private Partnership in Public Health, Dedham, MA, 7–8 April 2000, available at <http://www.hsph.harvard.edu/partnerships/>.

Caldwell, J. 1993, 'Health transition: the cultural, social and behavioural determinants of health in the third world', *Social Science and Medicine* 36 (2): 125–35.

Carmichael, A. 1997, 'Bubonic plague: The Black Death', in Kiple, Kenneth (ed.) *Plague, pox and pestilence: disease in history*, London: George Weidenfeld and Nicolson: 60–7.

Carnegie Commission on Preventing Deadly Conflict, 1997, *Preventing deadly conflict. Final report*, New York: Carnegie Corporation of New York.

Cassels, A. 1995, 'Health sector reform: key issues in less developed countries', *Journal of International Development* 7 (3): 329–48.

Cassese, A. 1986, *International law in a divided world*, Oxford: Clarendon Press.

Castells, M. 1996, *The rise of the network society*, London: Blackwell.

Castells, M. and Portes, A. 1989, 'World underneath: the origins, dynamics, and effects of the informal economy', in Portes, A., Castells, M. and Benton I. A. (eds.) *The informal economy: studies in advanced and less developed countries*, Baltimore: Johns Hopkins University Press.

Castleman, B. and Navarro V. 1987, 'International mobility of hazardous products, industries and wastes', *Annual Review of Public Health* 8: 1–19.

Cattaui, M. S. 1998a, 'Business and the UN: common ground', *ICC Business World*, Paris, 3 August.

1998b, 'Business partnership forged on global economy', ICC press release, Paris, 6 February.

1999, 'Business community takes up Kofi Annan's challenge', press release, Paris: International Chamber of Commerce, 15 March.

CEO, 1998, *The Geneva business dialogue. Business, WTO and UN: joining hands to deregulate the global economy?*, Corporate Europe Observatory web site, <www.globalpolicy.org/socecon/trncs/maucher.htm>.

2000, 'Citizen's Compact on the United Nations and Corporations', posted on January 27, 2000 at <http://www.xswall.nl/~ceo/untnc/citcom.html>.

Cerny, P. G. 1995, 'Globalization and the changing logic of collective action', *International Organization* 49 (4): 595–625.

Chakraborty, A. K. 1997, *Prevalence and incidence of TB infection and disease in India: a comprehensive review*, WHO/TB/97.231, Geneva: WHO.

Chambouleyron, A. 1995, 'La nueva ley de patentes y su efecto sobre los precios de los medicamentos. Análisis y propuestas', *Estudios*, Año XVIII, no. 75 (October/December): 156–68.

Chaparro, E. and Gevers, C., undated, 'The new corporate citizens: Investing in communities makes for sound business', <http://www.worldbank.org/bdp/achives/article/htm>.

Chapman, J. 1999, 'The response of civil society to the globalisation of the marketing of breast milk substitutes in Ghana', *Development* 42 (4): 103–8.

Chen, M. and Chan, A. 1999, 'China's "market economics in command": footwear workers' health in jeopardy', *International Journal of Health Services* 29 (4): 793–811.

Chepesiuk, R. 1999, 'Where the chips fall: environmental health in the semiconductor industry', *Environmental Health Perspectives* 107 (9): A452–7.

Chernichovsky, D. 1995, What can developing economies learn from health system reforms of developed economies? in Berman, P. (ed.) *Health sector reform in developing countries: making health development sustainable*, Boston, MA: Harvard University Press.

Chesnais, J. 1992, *The demographic transition: stages, patterns and economic implications*, Oxford University Press.

Chicago Tribune, 1999, Editorial, 15 June.

Chollet, D. and Lewis, M. 1997, 'Private insurance: principles and practice', in Schieber, G. (ed.) *Innovations in health care financing: proceedings of a World Bank conference, 10–11 March 1997*, World Bank Discussion Paper no. 365, Washington, DC: World Bank.

Chossudovsky, M. 1996, *The globalisation of poverty, impacts of IMF and World Bank reforms*, London: Zed Books.

CI 1994, 'Ensuring food safety: a question of standards – the work of the Codex Alimentarius Commission', *Briefing Paper* (September 1994), London: Consumers International.

Clark, I. 1997, *Globalization and fragmentation: international relations in the twentieth century*, Oxford University Press.

Cliffe, L. and Luckham, R. 1999, 'Complex political emergencies and the state: failure and the fate of the state', *Third World Quarterly* 20 (1): 27–50.

Coburn, D. 2000, 'Income inequality, social cohesion and the health status of populations: the role of neo-liberalism', *Social Science and Medicine* 51: 135–46.

Collinson, S. 1999, 'Globalisation and the dynamics of international migration: implications for the refugee regime', *New Issues in Refugee Research*, Working Paper no. 1, Geneva: Centre for Documentation and Research, UNHCR, <http://www.unhcr.ch/refworld/pubs/pubon.htm>.

Consumer Project on Technology, undated, <http://www.cptech.org/ip/health/sa/pharmasuit.html>.

Cook, J. 1999, Personal correspondence with J. Cook, Executive Director, International Trachoma Initiative, 20 May.

Cooper Weil, D. *et al.* 1990, *The impact of development policies on health: a review of the literature*, Geneva: WHO.

Coreil, J. 1983, 'Allocation of family resources for health care in rural Haiti', *Social Science and Medicine* 17: 709–19.

Corporate Watch 1998a, 'Nike CEO Philip H. Knight announces new labor initiatives', May 12, 1998 <http://www.corpwatch.org/trac/nike/announce/nikes.html>.

   1998b, 'Global Exchange's public response to Nike's new labor initiatives' <http://www.corpwatch.org/trac/nike/announce/globex.html>.

   1999, 'The Global Compact: the UN's new deal with 'global corporate citizens', October 1999 <http://www.corpwatch.org/trac/globalization/un/globalcompact.html>.

Correa, S. 1997, 'From reproductive health to sexual rights: achievements and future challenges', *Reproductive Health Matters* 10: 107–16.

Cottier, T. 1998, 'The WTO and environmental law: three points for discussion', in Fijalkowski, A. and Cameron, J. (eds.) *Trade and the environment: bridging the gap*, The Hague: Cameron May International Law & Policy.

Cox, R. W. 1987, *Production, power and world order: social forces in the making of history*, New York: Columbia University Press.

Creese, A. 1990, *User charges for health care: a review of recent experience*, Geneva: World Health Organisation.

Creese, A. and Kutzin, J. 1994, *Lessons for cost recovery in health*, Geneva: WHO.

Creese, A. and Parker, D. 1991, *Cost analysis in primary health care. A training manual for programme managers*, Geneva: WHO.

Cross, P., Huff, M., Quick, J. and Bates, J. 1986, 'Revolving drug funds: conducting business in the public sector', *Social Science and Medicine* 22 (3): 335–43.

Cutler, A. C., Haufler, V. and Porter, T. (eds.) 1999a, *Private authority and international affairs*, New York: State University of New York Press.

Cutler, A. C., Haufler, V. and Porter, T. 1999b, 'Private authority and international affairs', in Cutler, A. C., Haufler, V. and Porter, T. (eds.), 1999a, pp. 3–30.

Dahlgren, G. 1991, 'Strategies for health financing in Kenya – the difficult birth of a new policy', *Scandinavian Journal of Social Medicine*, suppl. 46: 67–81.

Dartnall, E., Schneider, H., Hlatshwayo, Z. and Clews, F. 1997, *STD management in the private sector: a national evaluation*, Johannesburg: Centre for Health Policy, University of the Witwatersrand.

Deacon, B. 1997, *Global social policy, international organizations and the future of welfare*, London: Sage Publications.

2000, 'Globalization and social policy: the threat to equitable welfare', Occasional Paper 5, March 2000, Geneva: UNRISD <http://www.unrisd.org/engindex/cop5/forum/opgs.htm>.

de Ferranti, D. 1985, *Paying for health services in developing countries: an overview*, World Bank Staff Working Papers no. 721, Washington D.C: World Bank.

Delahanty, J. 1999a, 'A common thread: issues for women workers in the garment sector'. Prepared for the Women in Informal Employment: Globalizing and Organizing (WIEGO), Global Markets Program, Garment Sub-Sector. Toronto, North–South Institute.

1999b, 'Global industry, global solutions: options for change in the garment sector'. Conference Report, 21 September 1998. Toronto, North–South Institute.

Delahanty, J. and Shefali, M. K. 1999, 'From social movements to social clauses, assessing local, national and international strategies for improving women's health and labour conditions in the garment sector', Paper presented at the International Roundtable on 'Responses to globalization: rethinking equity in health', Geneva, 12–14 July.

Derricourt, N. and Miller, C. 1992, 'Empowering older people: an urgent task in an ageing world', *Community Development Journal* 27 (2): 117–21.

Deutsch, C. H. 1999, 'Unlikely allies join with the United Nations', *New York Times*, 10 December.

DFID 1999a, *International development target strategy paper, better health for poor people, November 1999, consultation document*, London: Department for International Development.

1999b, 'Project memorandum China HIV/AIDS prevention and care project', East Asia and Pacific Department, UK Department for International Development <http://www.dfid.gov.uk/public/news/china_hivaids.pdf>.

Diaz, D. and Hurtado, M. 1994, 'International trade in health services: main issues and opportunities for the countries of Latin America and the

Caribbean', *Technical Report Series* no. 33, Washington DC: Pan American Health Organization.

Dicken, P. 1998, *Global shift: transforming the world economy*, 3rd edition, London: Sage Publications.

Dinotshe Tou, S. and Sandberg, E. 1994, 'The elderly and their use of the health care system', in Bruun, F., Mugabe M. and Coombs Y. (eds.) *The situation of the elderly in Botswana. Proceedings from an international workshop*, Gabarone: National Institute for Development and Research Documentation.

Dixon-Mueller, R. 1993, 'The sexuality connection in reproductive health', *Studies in Family Planning* 24 (5): 269–82.

Dodgson, R., Lee, K. and Drager, N. 2000, 'Global health governance: a conceptual review', in Lee, K. (ed.) *Key issues in global health governance*, Geneva: WHO.

Dolin, P. J., Raviglione, M. C. and Kochi A. 1994, 'Global tuberculosis incidence and mortality during 1990–2000', *Bulletin of the World Health Organization* 72: 213–20.

Donald, A. 1999, 'Political economy of technology transfer', *British Medical Journal* 319: 1298.

Drager, N. 1999, 'Making trade work for public health', *British Medical Journal* 319: 1214.

Drummond, M. F., Mason, J. M. and Torrance, G. W. 1993, 'Cost-effectiveness league tables: more harm than good?' *Social Science and Medicine* 37 (1): 33–40.

Drummond, M. F., O'Brien, B., Stoddart, G. L. and Torrance, G. W. 1997, *Methods for the economic evaluation of health care programmes*, Oxford Medical Publications.

Duckett, M. 1999, 'Compulsory licensing and parallel importing: what do they mean?', Paper prepared for International Council of AIDS Service Organisations.

Duffield, M. 1994a, 'The political economy of internal war: asset transfer, complex emergencies and international aid', in Macrae J. and Zwi A. (eds.) 1994.
1994b, 'Complex emergencies and the crisis of developmentalism', *IDS Bulletin* 25 (4): 37–45.
1999, 'Globalisation and war economies: promoting order of the return of history?', Paper prepared for the *Fletcher Forum of World Affairs* issue on 'The geography of confidence: environments, populations, boundaries', mimeograph.

Dukes, G. 1997, 'The contribution of the private sector: an introduction', *Australian Prescriber* 20 (suppl. 1): 74–75.

Dunoff, Jeffrey 1998, 'The misguided debate over NGO participation and the WTO', *Oxford Journal of International Economic Law* 1 (3): 433–56.

Durán-Arenas, L., Sánchez, R., Vallejo, M., Carreón, J. and Franco, F. 1996, 'Financiamiento de la atencíon a la salud de la población de la tercera edad', *Salud Pública de México* 8 (6): 501–12.

Ebrahim, G. J. and Ranken, J. P. 1988, *Primary health care*, London: MacMillan.

The Economist, 1999, 'Corporate hospitality: companies and health', *The Economist*, November 27: 100.

2000, 'Business ethics: doing well by doing good', *The Economist*, 22 April: 83.

Ehrlich, P. 1971, *The population bomb*, New York: Ballantine Press.

Elkington, J. and Fennell, S. 1998, 'Can business leaders satisfy the triple bottom line?', *Visions of Ethical Business* 1, October: 34–36.

Elkins, D. 1995, *Beyond sovereignty: Territory and political economy in the twenty-first century*, University of Toronto Press.

Elliott, L. 1999, 'Workers' rights row divides rich and poor', *The Guardian*, 2 December <http://www.guardianunlimited.co.uk/Archive/Article/ 0,4273, 3937210,00.html>.

Enthoven, A. 1985, *Reflections of the management of the NHS*, London: Nuffield Provincial Hospitals Trust.

Esty, D. 1994, *Greening the GATT. Trade, environment, and the future*, Washington, DC: Institute for International Economics.

Evans, P. 1994, *Unpacing the GATT*, London: Consumers International.

Evans, G. and Newnham, J. 1992, *The dictionary of world politics*, London: Harvester Wheatsheaf.

Falk, R. 1999, *Predatory globalization: a critique*, Cambridge: Polity Press.

FAO/WHO 1999, *Understanding the Codex Alimentarius*, Rome: Food and Agriculture Organisation and World Health Organisation.

Farmer, P. 1997, 'Social scientists and the new tuberculosis', *Social Science and Medicine* 44 (3): 347–58.

Feachem, R., Kjellstrom, T., Murray, C., Over, M. and Phillips, M. (eds.) 1992, *The health of adults in the developing world*, Oxford University Press.

Fidler, D. 1999, 'Neither science or shamans: globalization of markets and health in the developing world', *Indiana Journal of Global Legal Studies* 7: 1–34.

2000, *International law and public health: materials on and analysis of global health jurisprudence*, Ardsley, New York: Transnational Publishers.

Fleshman, M. 1999, 'WTO impasse in Seattle spotlights inequities of global trading system', *Africa Recovery* 13 (4): 1, 30–35.

Fletcher, A., Breeze, E. and Walters, R. 1998, 'Health promotion for elderly people: recommendations for the European Union', London School of Hygiene and Tropical Medicine.

1999, 'Health promotion for older people: what are the opportunities?', *Promotion and Education* 6: 4–7.

Fletcher, A. and Donoghue, M. 1998, 'Barriers to the up-take of cataract services and proposed strategies to address these', London School of Hygiene and Tropical Medicine.

Foltz, A. 1994, 'Donor funding for health reform in Africa: is non-project assistance the right prescription?', *Health Policy and Planning* 9 (4): 371–84.

Forget, G., Goodman, T. and de Villiers, A. 1993, 'Impact of pesticide use on health in developing countries', Proceedings of a symposium held in Ottawa, Canada, 17–20 September 1990, Ottawa: International Development Research Centre.

Foster, S. 1989, 'A note on financing of health services: some issues and examples', Briefing Note prepared for DANIDA, WHO Action Programme on Essential Drugs, Geneva, March.

Frederickson, G. and Wise, C. (eds.) 1977, *Public administration and public policy*, Lexington, MA: Lexington-Heath.

Frenk, J. 1995, 'Comprehensive policy analysis for health system reform', *Health Policy* 32 (1): 255–77.

Frenk, J., Bobadilla, J., Stern, C., Frejka, T. and Lozano, R. 1991, 'Elements for a theory of the health transition', *Health Transition Review* 1: 21–38.

Freudenberg, N. 1995, 'A new role for community organisations in the prevention and control of tuberculosis', *Journal of Community Health* 20 (1): 15–28.

Freudman, A. and Maggs, J. 1997, 'Bankers, insurers celebrate WTO pact: deal puts financial-services markets under global rules for the 1st time', *Journal of Commerce*, 16 December.

Friedman, T. 2000, *The lexus and the olive tree*, New York: HarperCollins.

Fries, J. F. 1980, 'Aging, natural death, and the compression of morbidity', *New England Journal of Medicine* 303 (3): 130–5.

Frost, L. and Reich, M. 1998, *Mectizan® donation program: origins, experiences, and relationships with co-ordinating bodies for onchocerciasis control*, Department of Population and International Health, Boston: Harvard School of Public Health.

Fustukian, S. and Zwi, A. (2001), 'Balancing imbalances: facilitating community perspectives in times of adversity', *Bulletin of the National Association of Practising Anthropologists* 21: 17–35.

Garber, A. 1994, 'Financing health care for elderly Americans in the 1990s', in Noguchi, Y. and Wise, D. (eds.) *Aging in the United States and Japan. Economic trends*, University of Chicago Press.

Garcia-Moreno, C. and Watts, C. 2000, 'Violence against women: its importance for HIV/AIDS prevention', *AIDS* suppl. 2000.

Garfield, R. and Holz, T. 2000, 'Health system reform in Cuba in the 1990s', in Lloyd-Sherlock, P. (ed.) *Healthcare reform and poverty in Latin America*, London: Institute of Latin American Studies.

Garner, P., Kale, R., Dickson, R., Dans, T. and Salinas, R. 1998, 'Implementing research findings in developing countries', *British Medical Journal* 317: 531–5.

Garten, L. E. 1999, 'Op-ed: mega-mergers, mega-influence', *The New York Times*, 26 October.

Geiser, K. 1986, 'Health hazards in the microelectronics industry', *International Journal of Health Services* 16 (1): 105–20.

Gielen, A. C., O'Campo, P. J., Faden, R. R. *et al.* 1994, 'Interpersonal conflict and physical violence during the childbearing years', *Social Science and Medicine* 39 (6): 781–7.

Gilks, C., Floyd, K., Haran, D., Kemp, J., Squire, B. and Wilkenson, D. 1998, *Sexual health and health care: care and support for people with HIV/AIDS in resource-poor settings*, DFID Health and Population Occasional Paper, London: DFID.

Gilson, L. 1988, *Government health care charges: is equity being abandoned?*, EPC Publication no. 15, London School of Hygiene and Tropical Medicine.

1998, 'In defence and pursuit of equity', *Social Science and Medicine* 47 (12): 1891–6.

Gilson, L., Mkanje, R., Grosskurth, H. *et al.* 1997, 'Cost-effectiveness of improved treatment services for sexually transmitted diseases in preventing HIV-1 infection in Mwanza Region, Tanzania', *The Lancet* 350: 1805–9.

Gilson, L., Russell, S. and Buse, K. 1995, 'The political economy of user fees with targeting: developing equitable health financing policy', *Journal of International Development* 7 (3): 369–401.

Gittler, J. 1994, 'Controlling resurgent tuberculosis: Public health agencies, public policy and law', *Journal of Health Politics, Policy and Law* 19: 107–43.

Gleick, J. 1999, *Faster, the acceleration of just about everything.* New York: Little, Brown & Co.

Global Witness, 1998, *A rough trade: the role of companies and governments in the Angolan conflict,* London: Global Witness.

 1999, *A crude awakening: the role of oil and banking industries in Angola's civil war and the plunder of state assets,* London: Global Witness.

Godlee, F. 1994, 'The World Health Organisation: WHO in crisis', *British Medical Journal* 309: 1424–8.

Goma Epidemiology Group, 1995, 'Public health impact of Rwandan refugee crisis: what happened in Goma, Zaire, in July 1994?', *The Lancet* 345: 339–44.

Goodhand, J. and Hulme, D. 1999, 'From wars to complex political emergencies: understanding conflict and peace-building in the new world disorder', *Third World Quarterly* 20 (1): 13–26.

Goodman, C. A., Coleman, P. G. and Mills, A. J. 1999, 'Cost-effectiveness of malaria control in Sub-Saharan Africa', *The Lancet* 354: 378–86.

Gordenker, L., Coate, R., Jonsson, C. and Soderholm, P. 1995, *International cooperation in response to AIDS,* London: Pinter.

Gorman, M. 1999a, 'Development and the rights of older people', in Help Age International, *The ageing and development report,* London: Earthscan.

 1999b, 'Reinforcing capability: informal community-based support schemes for older people in the developing world', in Help Age International, *The ageing and development report,* London: Earthscan.

Goulbourne, H. 1999, 'Exodus? Some social and policy implications of return migration from the UK to the Commonwealth Caribbean in the 1990s', *Policy Studies* 20 (3): 157–72.

Govindaraj, R., Murray, C. and Chellaraj, G. 1995, *Health expenditures in Latin America,* World Bank Technical Paper 274, Washington DC: World Bank.

Grange, J. M. 1999, 'The global burden of tuberculosis', in Porter, J. D. H. and Grange, J. M. (eds.) *Tuberculosis – an interdisciplinary perspective,* London: Imperial College Press, pp. 3–31.

Grindle, M. and Thomas, J. 1991, *Public choices and policy change: the political economy of reform in developing countries,* Baltimore: Johns Hopkins University Press.

Grosskurth, H., Mosha, F., Todd, J. *et al.* 1995, 'Impact of improved treatment of sexually transmitted diseases on HIV infection in rural Tanzania: randomised control trial', *The Lancet* 346: 530–6.

Gwatkin, D. R. 1999, 'Poverty and inequalities in health within developing countries (1999)', Paper prepared for the ninth annual Public Health Forum of the London School of Hygiene and Tropical Medicine, 19–23 April.

Gwatkin, D. and Guillot, M. 1998, 'The burden of disease among the global poor: current situation, trends and implications for research and policy', Paper prepared for the Global Forum for Health Research, Geneva, Washington DC: World Bank.

Haas, P. M. 1989, 'Do regimes matter? Epistemic communities and Mediterranean pollution control', *International Organization* 43 (3).

1992, 'Introduction: Epistemic communities and international policy coordination', *International Organization* 46 (1): 1–18.

Halimi, S. 2000, 'When market journalism invades the world', in Lechner, F. and Boli, J. (eds.), pp.17–20.

Halliday, F. 1997, 'Nationalism', in Baylis, S. and Smith, S. (eds.) *The globalization of world politics: an introduction to international relations*, Oxford University Press, pp. 359–73.

Ham, C. 1997, *Management and competition in the NHS*, Abingdon, Oxon: Ratcliffe Medical Press.

Hamblin, R. 1998, 'Trusts', in LeGrand, J., Mays, N. and Mulligan, J. A. (eds.) *Learning from the NHS internal market*, London: King's Fund Publishing.

Ham-Chande, R. 1996, 'Envejecimiento: una nueva dimensión de la salud en México', *Salud Pública de México* 38 (6): 409–18.

Hammer, J. 1996, 'Economic analysis for health projects', Policy Research Working Paper, no. 1611, May, Washington DC: World Bank.

Hampton, J. 1998, *Internally displaced people: A global survey*, London: Earthscan.

Hancock, T. 1998, 'Caveat partner: reflections on partnership with the private sector', *Health Promotion International* 13 (3): 193.

Handy, C. 1993, 'On the work of the organization and its design', in *Understanding organizations*, Harmondsworth: Penguin, 4th edition 253–90.

Hanson, K. and Berman, P. 1998, 'Private health care provision in developing countries: a preliminary analysis of levels and composition', *Health Policy and Planning* 13 (3): 195–211.

Hanson, K. and McPake, B. 1998, 'Country experiences with implementing autonomous hospitals policies', London School of Hygiene and Tropical Medicine.

Harding, A. and Preker, A. 1998, 'Chapter 1: Conceptual framework', in Harding, A. and Preker, A. Innovations in health care delivery: organisational reforms within the public sector, Washington DC: World Bank, draft.

Hardon, A. and Hayes, E. (eds.) 1997. *Reproductive rights in practice: a feminist report on Quality of Care*. London: Zed Books.

Harries, A. D. and Mayer, D. 1996, *Tuberculosis/HIV: a clinical manual*, Geneva: World Health Organisation (TB/96.200).

Harrison, A. 1997, 'Hospitals in England: impact of the 1990 National Health Service reforms', *Medical Care*, suppl. 35 (10): OS50–61.

1998, *Health care UK 1997/8. The King's Fund annual review of health policy*, London: King's Fund.

Harrison, P. and Lederberg, J. 1997, *Orphans and incentives: developing technologies to address emerging infections*, Washington DC: Institute of Medicine, National Academy Press.

Hartmann, B. 1987, *Reproductive rights and wrongs*, New York: Harper and Row. 1995, *Reproductive rights and wrongs: the global politics of population control.* Boston, MA: South End Press.

Hawkes, S., Morison, L., Foster, S., *et al.* 1999, 'Managing RTIs in women in low prevalence, low income situations; an evaluation of syndromic management in Matlab, Bangladesh', *The Lancet* 354: 1776–81.

Hazan, H. 1991, 'Victim into sacrifice: the construction of the old as a symbolic type', *Journal of Cross-Cultural Gerontology* 5 (1): 77–84.

Hecht, R., Overholt, C. and Homberg, H. 1993, 'Improving the implementation of cost recovery for health: lessons from Zimbabwe', *Health Policy* 25: 213–42.

Heise, L. 1996, 'Violence against women: Global organizing for change', in Edleson, J.L. and Eisikovits, Z.C. (eds.) *Future interventions with battered women and their families*, London: Sage Publications: 7–33.

Heise, L., Ellsberg, M. and Gottemoeller, M. 1999, 'Ending violence against women', *Population Reports* Series L, no. 11, Baltimore, MD: Johns Hopkins University School of Public Health, Population Information Program.

Held, D., McGrew, A., Goldblatt, D. and Perraton, J. 1999, *Global transformations: politics, economics and culture*, Cambridge: Polity Press.

Help Age International, 1999, 'International agencies sideline older people', *The Ageing and Development Report*, issue 3, May.

Henderson, D. 1998, 'The siren song of eradication', *Journal of the Royal College of Physicians*, London 32 (6): 580–84.

Henry, C. and Farmer, P. 1999, 'Risk analysis: infections and inequalities in a globalising era', *Development* 42 (4): 31–4.

Heymann, S. J., Sell, R. and Brewer, T. F. 1998, 'The influence of programme acceptability on the effectiveness of public health policy: a study of directly observed therapy for tuberculosis', *American Journal of Public Health* 88 (3): 442–45.

Higer, A. J. 1999, 'International women's activism and the 1994 Cairo Population Conference', in Meyer, M. K. and Prugl, E. (eds.) *Gender politics in global governance*, Lanham, MD: Rowman and Littlefield Publishers Inc.: 122–41.

Hirst, P. 1997, 'The global economy: myths and realities', *International Affairs* 73 (3): 409–25.

Hogwood, B. W. and Gunn, L. A. 1984, *Policy analysis for the real world*, Oxford University Press.

Hollos, M. and Larsen, U. 1997, 'From lineage to conjugality: the social context of fertility decision among the Pare of northern Tanzania', *Social Science and Medicine* 45 (3): 361–72.

Holmes, C. 1996, 'DOTS: Getting the drugs to the bugs', *TB Observer*, London, 5 November, p. 1.

Hongoro, C. and Kumaranayake, L. 2000, 'Do they work? Regulating for-profit providers in Zimbabwe', *Health Policy and Planning* 15 (4): 368–77.

Horton, R. 1995, 'Towards the elimination of tuberculosis', *The Lancet* 34: 790.

Hsiao, W. C. 1994, 'Marketisation – the illusory magic pill', *Health Economics* 3 (6): 351–8.

Huber, J. B. 1907. 'Civilisation and tuberculosis', *British Journal of Tuberculosis* 1: 156–9.

Huff-Rouselle, M., Shepherd, C. and Trisolini, M. 1993, 'Improved diagnostics, more bitter medicine, user fees', in Morgan, R. and Rau, B. *Global learning for health*, Washington DC: National Council for International Health.

Hurrell, A. 1999, 'Security and inequality', in Hurrell, A. and Woods, N. (eds.) *Inequality, globalization and world politics*, Oxford University Press, pp. 248–72.

Hurrell, A. and Woods, N. 1995, 'Globalization and inequality', *Millennium Journal of International Studies* 24 (3).

1999, 'Introduction', in Hurrell, A. and Woods, N. (eds.) *Inequality, globalization and world politics*, Oxford University Press.

IAVI, 1996, *Intellectual property rights: Summary report and recommendations of an international meeting*, 13 August 1996, New York: IAVI.

ICC, 1998, 'UN and private sector need each other – Kofi Annan', *ICC Business World*, 23 September.

2000, 'Business supports Kofi Annan's Global Compact but rejects "prescriptive rules", ICC Press Release, Budapest, 4 May.

ICFTU 1999, *Building workers' human rights in the global trading system*, Geneva: International Confederation of Free Trades Unions.

IFBWW–IKEA 1998, 'IFBWW–IKEA Agreement on Rights of Workers', 25 May 1998   <http://www.ifbww.org/~fitbb/TRADE_UNION_RIGHTS/IKEA/IFBWW-IKEA_eng.htm>.

IFRC 1999, *World disasters report 1999*, Geneva: International Federation of Red Cross and Red Crescent Societies.

2000, *World disasters report 2000*, Geneva: International Federation of Red Cross and Red Crescent Societies.

Ignatieff, M. 1998, *The warrior's honour. Ethnic war and the modern conscience*, London: Chatto and Windus.

ILO 1996, 'Child labour: what's to be done' <http://www.ilo.org/public/english...... documentation/etexts/what/index.htm>.

1999, *World employment report, 1998–1999*, Geneva: International Labour Organization.

2000a, 'Decent work and poverty reduction in the global economy', Paper submitted by the International Labour Office to the Second Session of the Preparatory Committee for the Special Session of the General Assembly on the Implementation of the Outcome of the World Summit for Social Development and Further Initiatives, April 2000 <http://www.un.org/esa/socdev/geneva2000/docs/ilo.pdf>.

2000b, 'Review of annual reports under the follow-up to the ILO Declaration on Fundamental Principles and Rights at Work' <http://www.ilo.org/public/english/standards/relm/gb/docs/gb272/pdf/d1-intro.pdf>.

2000c, *Your voice at work. The ILO global report, 2000*, Geneva: International Labour Organization <http://www.ilo.org/public/english/standards/decl/vaw/pdf/fullreport/introduction.pdf>.

Institutes of Medicine 1997, *America's vital interest in global health*, Washington DC: IOM.

InterAmerican Development Bank 1996, *Economic and social progress in Latin America, 1996 Report: making social services work*, Baltimore, MD: Johns Hopkins University Press.

International Herald Tribune, 2000, 'Canadian asbestos case', 16 June.

Jacobs, L., Marmor, T. and Oberlander, J. 1999, 'The Oregon health plan and the political paradox of rationing: what advocates and critics have claimed and what Oregon did', *Journal of Health Politics, Policy and Law* 24 (1): 161–79.

Jamison, D. T. and Mosley, W. H. 1991, 'Disease control priorities in developing countries: health policy responses to epidemiological change', *American Journal of Public Health* 81: 15–22.

Jamison, D. T., Mosley, W. H., Measham, A. R. and Bobadilla, J. L. (eds.) 1993, *Disease control priorities in developing countries*, Oxford Medical Publications.

Janovsky, K. and Cassels, A. 1996, 'Health policy and systems research: issues, methods and priorities', in Janvosky, K. (ed.) *Health policy and systems development: an agenda for research*, Geneva: WHO.

Jayaraman, J. and Kanbur, R. 1999, 'International public goods and the case for foreign aid', in Kaul, I., Grunberg, I. and Stern, M. (eds.).

Jefferson, T., Mugford, M., Gray, A. and Demicheli, V. 1996, 'An exercise on the feasibility of carrying out secondary economic analysis', *Health Economics* 5: 155–65.

Jeyaratnam, J. 1992, 'Occupational health services in developing nations', in Jeyaratnam, J. (ed.) *Occupational health in developing countries*, Oxford University Press.

Jitta, J., Kawesa-Kisitu, D., Tereka, S., Babikwa, D. and Magezi, A. 1996, 'Evaluation of health financing reforms in Uganda: a document review of user fees', Child Health and Development Centre, Makarere University, Kampala.

Joachim, J. 1999, Shaping the human rights agenda: the case of violence against women', in Meyer, M. K. and Prugl, E. (eds.) *Gender politics in global governance*, Lanham, MD: Rowman and Littlefield Publishers Inc.: 142–60.

Johnston, T. and Stout, S. 1999, 'Investing in health. Development effectiveness in the health, nutrition and population sector', Washington DC: World Bank.

Jones, R. 1999, 'New dimensions of international trade. Addressing the challenges ahead: the role of labour standards', Trade Union Advisory Committee, OECD <http://www.tuac.org/statemen/communiq/labstand99.htm>.

Jonnson, C. 1993, 'International organization and co-operation: an interorganizational perspective', *International Social Science Journal* 138: 463–77.

Kaczmarski, K. M. and Cooperrides, D. L. 1999, 'Constructionist leadership in the global relational age: the case of the mountain forum', in Cooperrides, D. L. and Duttor, J. E. (eds.) *Organizational dimensions of global change, no limits to cooperation*, London: Sage, 57–87.

Kaiser, M. 1994, 'Economic activities of the elderly in developing countries: myths and realities', *UN Bulletin on Ageing* 2 (3).

Kaldor, M. 1999, *New and old wars. Organized violence in a global era*, Cambridge: Polity Press.

Kale, O. O. 1999, 'Review of disease-specific corporate drug donation programmes for the control of communicable diseases', Paper presented at the

Symposium: Drugs for Communicable Diseases – Stimulating development and availability, Paris, 15 October 1999.

Kalumba, K. 1997, 'Towards an equity oriented policy of decentralization in health systems under conditions of turbulence: the case of Zambia', Discussion Paper no. 6, Division of Analysis, Research and Assessment, Geneva: World Health Organisation.

Kamugisha, J. 1993, 'Health cost sharing in Kabarole District', Kampala: Tropical Health Consult.

Kamwanga, J., Hanson, K., McPake, B. and Mungule, O. 1999, 'Autonomous hospitals in Zambia and the equity implications of the market for hospital services. Phase 1 report: a description of hospital autonomy policy', London School of Hygiene and Tropical Medicine.

Kanter, R. M. 1994, 'Collaborative advantage – the art of alliances', *Harvard Business Review* 72 (4): 96–108.

Kasongo Project Team, 1984, 'Primary health care for less than a dollar a year', *World Health Forum* 5 (3): 211–15.

Kaul, I., Grunberg, I. and Stern, M. (eds.) 1999, *Global public goods: international co-operation in the 21st Century*, Oxford University Press.

Keck, M. E. and Sikkink, K. 1998, *Activists beyond borders: advocacy networks in international politics*, Ithaca: Cornell University Press.

Kellerson, H. 1998, 'The ILO Declaration of 1998 on fundamental principles and rights: a challenge for the future', *International Labour Review* 197 (2): 223–7.

Kent, G. 1998, 'Children', in Snarr, M. T. and Snarr D. N. (eds.) *Introducing global issues*, London: Boulder.

Khor, M. 2000, 'Reform WTO and financial architecture, says action plan', *Third World Resurgence* 117, May: 12–19.

Kickbusch, I. 1999, 'Global public health: revisiting healthy public policy at the global level', *Health Promotion International* 14 (4): 285–8.

    2000, 'The development of international health policies – accountability intact?', *Social Science and Medicine* 51: 979–89.

Kickbusch, I. and Quick, J. 1998, 'Partnerships for health in the 21st century', *World Health Statistics Quarterly* 51: 69.

Killick, T. 1998, *Aid and the political economy of policy change*, London: ODI–Routledge.

Kim, J. 1999, 'Health sector initiatives to address domestic violence against women in Africa', Proceedings of the Health Care Strategies for Combatting Violence Against Women in Developing Countries meeting, Ghent, Belgium, August 1999.

Kirk, D. 1996, 'Demographic transition theory', *Population Studies* 50: 361–87.

Kjellstrom, T., Koplan, J. P. and Rothenberg, R. B. 1992, 'Current and future determinants of adult ill-health', in Feacham, R. G. A., Kjellstrom, T., Murray, C. J. L., Over, M. and Phillips, M. A. (eds.) *The health of adults in the developing world*, Oxford University Press, pp. 209–59.

Klein, N. 1999, 'UN pact with business masks real dangers', *Toronto Star*, 19 March.

Klein, S. J., DiFernando, G. T. and Naizby BE. 1994, 'Directly observed therapy for tuberculosis in New York City' [Letter], *Journal of the American Medical Association* 272 (6): 435–6.

Klein, S. J. and Naizby, B. E. 1995, 'Commentary: New linkages for tuberculosis prevention and control in New York City: innovative use of non-traditional providers to enhance completion of therapy', *Journal of Community Health* 20 (1): 5–13.

Knight, W. A. 1995, 'Beyond the UN system? Critical perspectives on global governance and multilateral evolution', *Global Governance* 1: 229–53.

Knopoff, R., Golbert, L. and Feldman, J. 1991, *Dimensiones de la vejez en la sociedad argentina*, Buenos Aires: Centro Editor de América Latina.

Kochi, A. 1994, Letter, *Lancet* 344: 608–9.

Koivusalo, M. and Ollila, E. 1997, *Making a healthy world*, London: Zed Books.

Korten, D. 1997, 'The United Nations and the corporate agenda', text circulated on the Internet, July 1997. Internet communication at <http://www.igc.org/globalpolicy/reform/korten.htm>.

Kumaranayake, L. 1997, 'The role of regulation: influencing private sector activity within health sector reform', *Journal of International Development* 9 (4): 641–9.

1998, *Economic aspects of health sector regulation: strategic choices for low and middle income countries*, PHP Departmental Publication no. 29, London School of Hygiene and Tropical Medicine.

2000, 'The real and the nominal: making inflationary adjustments to cost and other economic data', *Health Policy and Planning* 15 (2): 230–4.

Kumaranayake, L. and Lake, S. 1998, 'Regulation in low and middle-income country context', Working Paper, Health Economics and Financing Programme, London School of Hygiene and Tropical Medicine.

Kumaranayake, L., Lake, S., Mujinja, P., Hongoro, C. and Mpembeni, S. 2000a, 'How do countries regulate the health sector? Evidence from Tanzania and Zimbabwe', *Health Policy and Planning* 15 (4): 357–67.

Kumaranayake, L., Watts, C. and Mangtani, P. *et al.* 2000b, 'Replication of interventions working with sex workers and their clients: generalisability of costs and effectiveness', *XIII International AIDS Conference*, Durban, July 2000, Abstract (ThPeC5431).

Labonte, R. 1998, 'World trade and investment agreements: implications for public health', *Canadian Journal of Public Health* 89 (1): 10–12.

LaDou, J. 1992, 'The export of industrial hazards to developing countries', in Jeyaratnam, J. (ed.) *Occupational health in developing countries*, Oxford University Press.

LaDou, J. and Rohm, T. 1998, 'The international electronics industry', *International Journal of Occupational and Environmental Health* 4 (1): 1–18.

Lane, S. 1994, 'From population control to reproductive health: an emerging policy agenda', *Social Science and Medicine* 39 (9): 1303–14.

Larbi, G. 1998, 'Institutional constraints and capacity issues in decentralizing management in public services: the case of health in Ghana', *Journal of International Development* 10: 377–85.

Le Billon, P. (with Macrae, J., Leader, N. and East, R.) 2000, 'The political economy of war: what relief agencies need to know', Humanitarian Practice Network, Paper no. 33, London: Overseas Development Institute.

Lechner, F. and Boli, J. (eds.) 2000, *The globalization reader*, London: Blackwell.

Lee, K. 2000a, 'An overview of global health and environmental risks', in Parsons, L. and Lister G. (eds.) *Global health: a local issue*, London: The Nuffield Trust.

2000b, 'Globalisation and health policy: a review of the literature and proposed research and policy agenda', in Bambas, A., Casas, J. A., Drayton, H. and Valdes, A. (eds.), *Health and human development in the new global economy*, Washington DC: Pan American Health Organization, pp. 15–41.

2001, 'Globalisation – a new agenda for health?' in McKee, M., Garner, P. and Stott, R. (eds.) *International co-operation and health*, Oxford University Press, ch. 2.

Lee, K. and Dodgson, R. 2000, 'Globalization and cholera: implications for global governance', *Global Governance* 6 (2): 213–36.

Lee, K., Humphreys, D. and Pugh, M. 1997, "Privatisation' in the United Nations System: patterns of influence in three intergovernmental organisations', *Global Society* 11 (3): 339–57.

Lee, K. and Mills A. 2000, 'Strengthening governance for global health research', *British Medical Journal* 321: 775–76.

Lee, K. and Walt, G. 1995, 'Linking national and global population agendas: case studies from eight developing countries', *Third World Quarterly* 16 (2): 257–72.

Lee, K. and Zwi, A. 1996, 'A global political economy approach to AIDS: ideology, interests and implications', *New Political Economy* 1: 355–73.

Le Grand, J. 1998, 'The National Health Service: crisis, change or continuity?' in Evans M. *et al.* (eds.) *The state of welfare II: the economics of social spending*, Oxford University Press.

LeGrand, J. and Bartlett, W. 1993, cited in Mills 1997a.

Leichter, H. 1979, *A comparative approach to policy analysis: health care policy in four nations*, Cambridge University Press.

Leigh, J., Macaskill, P., Kuosma, E. and Mandryk, J. 1999, 'Global burden of disease and injury due to occupational factors' *Epidemiology* 10 (5): 626–31.

Leppo, K. 1997, 'Introduction', in Koivusalo, M. and Ollila, E. *Making a healthy world: agencies, actors & policies in international health*, London: Zed Books.

Lexchin, J. and Kawachi, I. 1996, 'The self-regulation of pharmaceutical marketing: initiatives for reform', in Davi, P. (ed.) *Contested ground: public purpose and private interest in the regulation of prescription drugs*, Oxford University Press.

Lindbeck, A. 1997, 'Incentives and social norms in household behaviour', *American Economic Review* 87 (2): 370.

Linklater, A. 1998, *The transformation of political community: ethical foundations of the post-Westphalian Era*, Cambridge: Polity Press.

Lipschutz, R. and Crawford, B. 1999, ' "Ethnic" conflict isn't', from Policy Brief no. 2, March 1995, Institute on Global Conflict and co-operation, reprinted in Sneden, L.E. (ed.) *Globalization and conflict*, Dubuque, Iowa: Kendall Hunt, pp.189–93.

Litvack, J. and Bodart, C. 1993, 'User fees plus quality equals improved access to health care: results of a field experiment in Cameroon', *Social Science and Medicine* 37 (3): 369–83.

Lizza, R. 2000, 'The man behind the anti-free-trade revolt, Silent Partner', *The New Republic* 10 January.

Lloyd-Sherlock, P. 1997, 'Healthcare provision for elderly people in Argentina: the crisis of PAMI', *Social Policy and Administration* 31 (4): 371–89.

2000, 'Population ageing in developed and developing regions: implications for health policy', *Social Science and Medicine* (forthcoming).

Londoño, J. and Frenk, J. 2000, 'Structured pluralism. Towards an innovative model for health system reform in Latin America', in Lloyd-Sherlock, P. (ed.) *Healthcare reform and poverty in Latin America*, London: Institute of Latin American Studies.

Lush, L., Cleland, J., Walt, G. and Mayhew, S. 1999, 'Integrating reproductive health: myth and ideology', *Bulletin of the World Health Organization* 77 (9): 771–7.

Mach, E. and Abel-Smith, B. 1983, *Planning the finances of the health sector*, Geneva: WHO.

MacKintosh, M. 1997, 'Informal regulation: a conceptual framework and application to decentralised mixed finance in health care', Paper presented at conference on Public Sector Management for the Next Century.

Macrae, J. and Zwi, A. B. (eds., with Duffield, M. and Slim, H.) 1994, *War and hunger: rethinking international responses to complex emergencies*, London: Zed Books.

Mahoney, R. T. and Maynard, J. E. 1999, 'The introduction of new vaccines into developing countries', *Vaccine* 17 (7–8): 646–52.

Makinda, S. 2000, 'Recasting global governance', Paper presented at 'On the threshold: the UN and Global Governance in the New Millennium', New York, 19–21 January 2000, United Nations.

Mandil, Salah H. 1998, 'Telehealth; what is it? Will it propel cross-border trade in health services?' in UNCTAD, *International trade in health services: a development perspective*, Geneva: WHO.

Maniadakis, N., Hollingsworth, B. and Thanassoulis, E. 1999, 'The impact of the internal market on hospital efficiency, productivity and service quality', *Health Care Management Science*: 75–85.

Maniar, J. K. 2000, 'Health care systems in transition III. India, Part II. The current status of HIV–AIDS', *India Journal of Public Health Medicine* 22 (1): 33–7.

Mansergh, G., Haddix, A., Steketee, R. and Simonds, R. J. 1998, 'Cost-effectiveness of zidovudine to prevent mother-to-child transmission of HIV in sub-Saharan Africa', *Journal of the American Medical Association* 280: 30–1.

Manton, K., Corder, L. and Stallard, E. 1997, 'Chronic disability trends in elderly United States populations: 1982–1994', *Proceedings of the National Academy of Sciences* 94: 2593–8.

Marceau, G. and Pedersen, P. 1999, 'Is the WTO open and transparent? A discussion of the relationship of the WTO with non-governmental organisations and civil society's claims for more transparency and public participation', *Journal of World Trade* 33 (1): 5–49.

Marek, T., Diallo, I., Ndiaye, B. and Rakotosolama, J. 1999, 'Successful contracting of preventive services: fighting malnutrition in Senegal and Madagascar', *Health Policy and Planning* 14 (4): 382–91.

Marlin, A. T. 1998, 'Visions of social accountability: SA 8000', Visions of Ethical Business, no. 1, October, London: *Financial Times*, pp. 39–42.

Marmor, T. R. 1997, 'Global health policy reform: misleading mythology or learning opportunity', in Altenstetter, C. and Bjorkman, J. W. (eds.) *Health policy reform, national variations and globalization*, London and New York: Macmillan, pp. 348–93.

Marseille, E., Kahn, J. G., Mmiro, F. *et al.* 1999, 'Cost effectiveness of single-dose nevirapine regimen for mothers and babies to decrease vertical HIV-1 transmission in sub-Saharan Africa', *The Lancet* 354: 803–9.

Marseille, E., Kahn, J. G. and Saba, J. 1998, 'Cost-effectiveness of antiviral drug therapy to reduce mother-to child HIV transmission in sub-Saharan Africa', *AIDS* 12: 939–48.

Mason, J., Drummond, M. and Torrance G. 1993, 'Some guidelines on the use of cost effectiveness league tables', *British Medical Journal* 306: 570–2.

Maucher, H. O. 1997, 'Ruling by consent', *The Financial Times*, 6 December, *FT* Exporter, p. 2.

1998, *The Geneva Business Declaration*, Geneva: ICC, 24 September.

Mayhew, S. H. (2000) 'Integration of STI services into FP/MCH services: health service and social contexts in rural Ghana', *Reproductive Health Matters*, 8 (16): 112–24.

Mayhew, S. H. and Lush, L. 1999, 'Double speak on reproductive health: triumph of politics over science?', *Development Research Insights* 32: 3–4.

Mayhew, S., Lush, L., Cleland, J. and Walt, G. 2000, 'Integrating component services for reproductive health: the problem of implementation', *Studies in Family Planning* 31 (2): 151–62.

Maynard, A. 1982, 'The regulation of public and private health care markets', in McLachlan, G. and Maynard, A. (eds.) *A public/private mix for health: the relevance and effects of change*, London: Nuffield Provincial Hospitals Trust.

McCombie, S. C. 1996, 'Treatment seeking for malaria: a review of recent research', *Social Science and Medicine* 43 (6): 933–45.

McGrail, K., Green, B., Barer, M. L., Evans, R. G., Hertzman, C. and Normand, C. 2000, 'Age, costs of acute and long-term care and proximity to death: evidence for 1987–88 and 1994–95 in British Columbia', *Age and Ageing* 29 (3): 249–54.

McGregor, A. 1999, 'Compulsory drug licensing for countries hit by HIV is mooted', *The Lancet* 353: 1165.

McIntosh, M. 1998, 'Introduction', Visions of Ethical Business, no. 1, October, London: *Financial Times*.

McIntosh, A. and Finkle, J. 1994, 'The Cairo Conference on Population and Development: a new paradigm', *Population and Development Review* 21 (2): 223–60.

McKeown, T. and Record, R. G. 1962, 'Reasons for the decline of mortality in England and Wales during the nineteenth century', *Population Studies* 16: 94–122.

McKeown, T., Record, R. G. and Turner, R. D. 1975, 'An interpretation of the decline of mortality in England and Wales during the twentieth century', *Population Studies* 29: 391–422.

McMichael, A. J. 1993, *Planetary overload: global environmental change and the health of the human species*, London: Canto.

McMichael, A. J. and Beaglehole, R. 2000, 'The changing context of public health', *The Lancet* 356 (9228): 495–9.

McNeil, D. G., Jr. 2000, 'Move could speed wider availability in third world nations', *International Herald Tribune*, 12 May.

McNutt, L., Carlson, B. E., Gagen, D. *et al.* 1999, 'Reproductive violence screening in primary care: perspectives and experiences of patients and battered women', *Journal of the American Medical Association* 54 (2): 85–90.

McPake, B. 1993, 'Can health care user fees improve health service provision for the poor?', *The Health Exchange*, International Health Exchange, June/July 1993.

1996, 'Public autonomous hospitals in sub-Saharan Africa: trends and issues', *Health Policy* 35: 155–77.

McPake, B., Asiimwe, D., Mwesigye, F. *et al.* 1999, 'Informal economic activities of public health workers in Uganda: implications for quality and accessibility of care', *Social Science and Medicine* 49: 849–65.

McPake, B., Hanson, K. and Mills, A. 1993, 'Community financing of health care in Africa: an evaluation of the Bamako Initiative', *Social Science and Medicine* 36 (11): 1383–95.

Mejia, A., Pizki, H. and Royston, E. 1979, *Physician and nurse migration: analysis and policy implications*, Geneva: WHO.

Mesa-Lago, C. 1991, 'Social security: ripe for reform', in Inter-American Development Bank, *Economic and Social Progress in Latin America. The 1991 Annual Report*, Washington DC: IADB.

Michaels, D., Barrera, C. and Gacharna, M. G. 1985, 'Economic development and occupational health in Latin America: new directions for public health in less developed countries', *American Journal of Public Health* 75 (5): 536–42.

Milanovic, B. 1998, *Income, inequality and poverty during the transition from planned to market economy*, Washington DC: World Bank.

Mills, A. 1997a, 'Contractual relationships between government and the commercial private sector in developing countries', in Bennett, S., McPake, B. and Mills A. (eds.) 1997, pp. 189–213.

1997b, 'Leopard or chameleon? The changing character of international health economics', *Journal of Tropical Medicine and International Health* 2 (10): 963–77.

Mills, A., Vaughan, J. P., Smith, D. L. and Tabibzadeh, I. 1990, *Health system decentralization: concepts, issues and country experience*, Geneva: World Health Organisation.

Millwood, D. (ed.) 1996, *The international response to conflict and genocide: lessons from the Rwanda experience*, Copenhagen: Steering Committee of the Joint Evaluation of Emergency Assistance to Rwanda.

Mirza, Z. 1999, 'WTO/TRIPS, pharmaceuticals and health: impacts and strategies', *Development* 42 (4): 92–7.

Mitchell, J. and Doane, D. 1999, 'An ombudsman for humanitarian assistance?', *Disasters* 23 (2): 115–24.

Mitchell, V. S., Philipose, N. M. and Sanford, J. P. 1993, *The Children's Vaccine Initiative*, Washington DC: Institute of Medicine, National Academy Press.

Moon, M. 1993, *Medicare now and in the future*, Washington DC: Urban Institute Press.

Mooney, G. and Creese, A. 1993, 'Priority-setting for health service efficiency: the role of measurement of burden of illness', Appendix C in Jamison *et al.* (eds.) 1993.

Mooney, G. and Wiseman, V. 2000, 'Burden of disease and priority-setting' *Health Economics* 9 (3): 69–372.

Moses, S., Manji, F., Bradley, J. E., Nagelkerke, N. J. D., Malisa, M. A. and Plummer, F. A. 1992, 'Impact of user fees on attendance at a referral centre for sexually transmitted diseases in Kenya', *The Lancet* 340: 463–6.

Moure-Eraso, R. 1999, 'The convergence of labor and public health: a natural and critical alliance', *Journal of Public Health Policy* 20 (3): 310–7.

Mujinja, P., Mpembeni, R. and Lake, S. 2001, 'Awareness and effectiveness of regulations governing private drug outlets in Dar es Salaam: perceptions of key stakeholders', in Soderlund, N. and Mendoza-Arana, P. (eds.) *The new public–private mix in health: exploring changing landscapes*, Geneva: Alliance for Health Policy and Systems Research, WHO.

Munslow, B. and Brown, C. 1997, 'Complex emergencies and institutional complexes', *Contemporary Politics* 4 (3): 307–20.

Mupedziswa, R. 1997, 'AIDS and older Zimbabweans: who will care for the carers?', *South African Journal of Gerontology* 6 (2): 9–12.

Murden, S. 1997, 'Cultural conflict in international relations: the West and Islam', in Baylis, J. and Smith, S. (eds.) *The globalization of world politics: an introduction to international relations*, Oxford University Press.

Murray, C. J. 1994, 'Quantifying the burden of disease: the technical basis for disability-adjusted life years', *Bulletin of the World Health Organisation* 72 (3): 429–45.

Murray, C. J. L., DeJonghe, E., Chum, H. J., Nuangulu, D. S., Salomao, A. and Styblo, K. 1991, 'Cost effectiveness of chemotherapy for pulmonary tuberculosis in three sub-Saharan African countries', *The Lancet* 338: 1305–8.

Murray, C. J. L., Evans, D. B., Acharya, A. and Baltussen, R. M. P. M. 2000, 'Development of WHO guidelines on generalised cost-effectiveness analysis', *Health Economics* 9 (2): 235–51.

Murray, C. J. L., Kreuser, J. and Whang, W. 1994, 'Cost-effectiveness analysis and policy choices: investing in health systems', in Murray, C. J. L. and Lopez, A. D. (eds.) 1994.

Murray, C. and Lopez, A. (eds.) 1994, *Global comparative assessments in the health sector: disease burden, expenditures and intervention packages*, Geneva: WHO.

Murray, C. J. and Lopez, A. D. 1997, 'Regional patterns of disability-free life expectancy and disability-adjusted life expectancy: Global Burden of Disease study', *The Lancet* 349: 1347–52.

Murray, C. J. L., Styblo, K. and Rouillon, A. 1990, 'Tuberculosis in developing countries: burden, intervention and cost', *International Journal of Tuberculosis and Lung Disease* 65: 6–24.

Muschell, J. 1995, 'Privatisation in health', WHO Task Force on Health Economics, Geneva: WHO.

Musgrove, P. 2000, 'A critical review of "A Critical Review"', *Health Policy and Planning* 15 (1): 110–5.

Mytelka, L. K. and Delapierre, M. 1999, 'Strategic partnerships, networked oligopolies and the state', in Cutler, A. C., Haufler, V. and Porter, T. (eds.) 1999a, pp. 3–30.

Nabarro, D. N. and Tayler, E. M. 1998. 'The "Roll Back Malaria" Campaign', *Science* 280: 2067–8.

Nagarajan, V. 1999, 'Thailand to negotiate with Bristol–Myers Squibb for production of generic ddI', *Reuters-Health* <http://HIV.medscape.com/reugers/prof/1999/11/11.16/rg11169c.html>.

Nandraj, S., Khot, A., Menon, S. and Brugha, R. 'A stakeholder approach towards hospital accreditation in India', *Health Policy and Planning*, forthcoming.

National Labor Campaign 2000, 'Made in China. The role of U.S. companies in denying human and worker rights' <http://www.nlcnet.org/report00/>.

Navarro, V. 1999, 'Health and equity in the era of "globalization", *International Journal of Health Services* 29 (2): 215–26.

New, W. 2000, 'Special report: NGOs wary of UN corporate links', *UN Wire Business Weekly* 1 June 2000, accessed 14 June 2000 on the Internet at <www.unfoundation.org/>.

Njovana, E. and Watts, C. 1996, 'Gender violence in Zimbabwe: a need for collaborative action', *Reproductive Health Matters* 7, May: 45–53.

North–South Institute 1998, 'Civil society: the development solution?' Draft working paper, Civil Society and the Aid Industry <http://www.nsi-ins.ca/civil/csdp01.html>.

Nyerere, J. K. 1999, 'Are universal social standards possible?', *Development in Practice* 9 (5): 583–7.

O'Brien, R. J. *et al*. 2000, *Contesting global social governance: multilateral economic institutions and global social movements*, Cambridge University Press.

The *Observer*, 1999, 'The century that murdered peace', quoting Fred Halliday, Sunday, 12 December.

ODI 1999, 'Global governance: an agenda for the renewal of the United Nations?', ODI Briefing Paper 1999(2) July, London: Overseas Development Institute.

Odoi Adome, R., Whyte, S. R. and Hardon, A. 1996, *Popular pills: community drug use in Uganda*, Amsterdam: Het Spinhuis.

OECD 1996, *Globalization of industry: overview and sector reports*, Paris: OECD.

Ogden, J. 2000. 'Improving tuberculosis control: social science inputs', *Transactions of the Royal Society of Tropical Medicine and Hygiene* 94: 135–40.

Ogunbekun, I., Ogunbekun, A. and Orobaton, N. 1999, 'Private health care in Nigeria: walking the tightrope', *Health Policy and Planning* 14 (2): 174–81.

Ogus, A. 1994, *Regulation – legal form and economic theory*, Oxford: Clarendon Press.

Oloka-Onyango, J. and Udagama, D. 2000, *The realization of economic, social and cultural rights: globalization and its impact on the full enjoyment of human rights*, Report of the UN subcommission on the Promotion and Protection of Human Rights, Geneva: UNHCHR.

Over, M. and Watanabe, N. 1998, 'Evaluating the impact of organizational reforms in hospitals', in Harding, A. and Preker, A. *Innovations in health care delivery: organisational reforms within the public sector*, Washington DC: World Bank, draft.

Oxfam 1999, 'Loaded against the poor: World Trade Organisation', Oxfam Policy Paper: Oxfam GB Position Paper, November 1999 [http://www.oxfam.org. uk/policy/papers/wto2a.htm].

Paalman, M., Bekedam, H., Hawken, L. and Nyheim, D. 1998, 'A critical review of priority setting in the health sector: the methodology of the 1993 World Development Report', *Health Policy and Planning* 13 (1): 13–31.

Packard, R. 1989, 'Industrial production, health and disease in sub-Saharan Africa', *Social Science and Medicine* 28 (5): 475–96.

Pakulski, J. 1999, 'Social equality and inequality', in Kurtz, L. (ed.) *Encyclopedia of violence, peace and conflict*, San Diego and London: Academic Press, pp. 311–28.

Palmer, C. A., Lush, L. and Zwi, A. B. 1999, 'The emerging international policy agenda for reproductive health services in conflict settings', *Social Science and Medicine* 49 (12): 1689–703.

PANOS (1994), *Private decisions, public debate: women's reproduction and population*, London: PANOS.

Pecoul, B., Chirac, P., Trouiller, P. and Pinel, J. 1999, 'Access to essential drugs in poor countries: a lost battle?', *Journal of the American Medical Association* 281 (4): 361–7.

Petchesky, R. P. and Judd, K. (eds.) 1998, *Negotiating reproductive rights*. London: IRRAG, Zed Books.

Pettman, J. J. 1997, 'Gender issues', in Baylis, J. and Smith, S. (eds.) *The globalization of world politics; an introduction in international relations*, Oxford University Press, ch. 25.

Phillips, D. 2000, 'Family support for older persons in East Asia: durability or demise', unpublished background paper for United Nations Social Division Expert Group Meeting on sustainable social structures in a society for all ages, Addis Ababa, Ethiopia, 2–5 May 2000.

Phillips, N. and Higgott, R. 1999, *Global governance and the public domain: collective goods in a 'Post-Washington Consensus' era*, CSGR Working Paper no. 47/99, Warwick: Centre for the Study of Globalisation and Regionalisation.

Portaels, F., Rigouts, L. and Bastian, I. 1999, 'Addressing multi-drug resistant tuberculosis in penitentiary hospitals and in the general population of the former Soviet Union', *International Journal of Tuberculosis and Lung Disease* 3 (7): 582–8.

Porter, J. D. H. and Ogden, J. A. 1997, 'Ethics of directly observed therapy for the control of infectious diseases', *Bulletin of the Institute Pasteur* 95: 117–27.

1998, 'Re-emergence of infectious disease', in Strickland, S. S. and Shetty, P. S. (eds.) *Human biology and social inequality*, Cambridge University Press, pp. 96–113.

Porter, J. D. H., Ogden, J. A. and Pronyk, P. 1999a, 'The way forward: an integrated approach to tuberculosis control', in Porter, J. D. H. and Grange, J. G. (eds.) *Tuberculosis – an interdisciplinary perspective*, London: Imperial College Press, pp. 359–78.

1999b, 'Infectious disease policy: towards the production of health', *Health Policy and Planning* 14 (4): 322–8.

Portes, A., Castells, M. and Benton, L. A. 1989, *The informal economy: studies in advanced and less developed countries*, Baltimore, MD: Johns Hopkins University Press.

Power, E. J. and Eisenberg, J. M. 1998, 'Are we ready to use cost-effectiveness analysis in health care decision-making?' *Medical Care* 36 (5): MS10–7.

Prassad, H. A. C. 1997, 'Health care exports under consumption abroad mode; opportunities, obstacles and challenges for developing countries in general and in India in particular', New Delhi: Indian Institute of Foreign trade, Unpublished document, cited in Orvill, Adams and Kinnon, Colette 1997, 'Measuring trade liberalisation against public health objectives: the case of health services', Health Economics Technical Briefing Note, WHO Task Force on Health Economics, Geneva: WHO.

PRIA 1992, 'Stark realities beyond the mist of fragrance', *Bulletin of Participatory Research in Asia* 26, August: 10–12.

Price, D., Pollock, A. M. and Shaoul, J. 1999, 'How the World Trade Organisation is shaping domestic policies in health care', *The Lancet* 354 (9193): 1889–92.

Propper, C. 1995, 'Agency and incentives in the NHS internal market', *Social Science and Medicine* 40: 1683–90.

Propper, C. and Bartlett, W. 1997, 'The impact of competition on the behaviour of NHS trusts', in Flynn, R. and Williams, G. (eds.) *Contracting for health: quasi-markets and the National Health Service*, Oxford University Press, pp. 115–34.

Prugl, E. and Meyer, M. K. 1999, 'Gender politics in global governance', in Meyer, M. K. and Prugl, E. (eds.) *Gender politics in global governance*, Lanham, MD: Rowman and Littlefield Publishers Inc.: 3–16.

Raghavan, C. 1999, 'Developing countries reject labour issues in WTO', Third World Network <http://twnside.org.sg/souths/twn/title/reject2-cn.htm>.

Rakodi, C. 1996, 'The opinions of health and water service users in Ghana', The Role of Government in Adjusting Economies, Paper 10, June 1996, DAG/LSHTM/ODG.

Rangan, S. and Ogden, J. 1997, *Tuberculosis control in India: a state of the art review*, New Delhi: Department for International Development (DFID).

Ravindran, S. 1995, 'Women's health policies: organising for change', *Reproductive Health Matters* 6: 7–11.

Raymond, S. (ed.) 1997, *Global public health collaboration: organizing for a time of renewal*, New York: New York Academy of Sciences.

Reed, H., Haaga, J. and Keely, C. (eds.) 1998, *The demography of forced migration*, Summary of a workshop, Washington DC: National Academy Press.

Reich, M. 1995, 'The politics of agenda-setting in international health: child health versus adult health in developing countries', *Journal of International Development* 7 (3): 489–502.

1996, 'Applied political analysis for health policy reform', *Current Issues in Public Health* 2: 186–91.

Reich, M. R. and Govindaraj, R. 1998, 'Dilemmas in drug development for tropical diseases: experiences with praziquantel', *Health Policy* 44: 1–18.

Reichman, L. B. 1991, 'The U-shaped curve of concern' (Editorial), *American Review of Respiratory Disease* 144: 741–2.

Reinhardt, U. 1996, 'A social contract for 21st century health care: three-tier health care with bounty hunting', *Health Economics* 5: 479–99.

Reinicke, W. 1998, *Global public policy: governing without government?*, Washington DC: Brookings Institution.

Reinicke, W. H., Deng, F. M. *et al.* 2000, *Critical choices: The United Nations, networks, and the future of global governance*, Ottawa: IDRC.

Reinicke, W. H. and Witte, J. M. 1999, 'Interdependence, globalisation and sovereignty: the role of non-binding international legal accords', in Shelton, Dinah H. (ed.) (forthcoming) *Commitment and compliance: the role of non-binding norms in the international legal system*, Oxford University Press, ch. dated July 1999.

Republic of Uganda, 1992, *The three year health plan: Financing health for all*, Entebbe: Ministry of Health Planning Unit, p. 86.

Reverente, T. 1992, 'Occupational health services for small-scale industries', in Jeyaratnam, J. (ed.) *Occupational health in developing countries*, Oxford University Press.

Richters, A. 1992, 'Introduction', *Social Science and Medicine* 35 (6): 747–51.

Rifkin, S. and Walt, G. 1986, 'Why health improves: defining the issues concerning comprehensive primary health care and selective primary health', *Social Science and Medicine* 23 (6): 559–66.

Robinson, M. 1999, 'We can end this agony', *The Guardian*, 23 October.

Rockefeller, 1999, 'Meeting on public–private partnerships in biotech/pharma', The Rockefeller Foundation, 28–29 January 1999, New York, unpublished.

Roemer, M. I. 1991, *National health systems of the world, Vol. 1*, Oxford University Press.

1993, *National health systems of the world, Vol. II*, Oxford University Press.

Rose, R. (ed.) 1975, *The dynamics of public policy: a comparative analysis*, London: Sage Publications.

Rose, R. 1993, *Lesson drawing in public policy: a guide to learning across time and space*, Chatham, NJ: Chatham House.

Rosenau, J. N. 1995, 'Governance in the twenty-first century', *Global Governance* 1 (1): 13–43.

Rosenthal, F. and Newbrander, W. 1996, 'Public policy and private sector provision of health services', *International Journal of Health Planning and Management* 11: 203–16.

Rupesinghe, K. 1998, *Civil wars, civil peace. An introduction to conflict resolution*, London: Pluto Press.

Rush, D. and Welch, K. 1996, 'The first year of hyperinflation in the former Soviet Union: nutritional deprivation among elderly pensioners, 1992', *American Journal of Public Health* 86: 790.

Russell, S., and L. Gilson. 1997, 'User fee policies to promote health service access for the poor: a wolf in sheep's clothing?', *International Journal of Health Services* 27 (2): 359–79.

Salamon, L. M. 1994, 'The rise of the nonprofit sector', *Foreign Affairs* 73 (4).

Sandberg, E. 1998, 'Multilateral women's conferences: the domestic political organisation of Zambian women', *Contemporary Politics* 4 (3): 271–83.

Sarin, R., Singh, V., Jaiswal, A. *et al.* 1998. 'Obstacles to TB treatment for women in Delhi', *International Journal of Tuberculosis and Lung Disease 2*

(11): S350 (Abstract no. 598-PC, Global Congress on Lung Health, 29th World Conference of the International Union Against Tuberculosis and Lung Disease).

Satterthwaite, D., Hardoy, J. E. and Mitlin, D. 1992, *Environmental problems in Third World cities*, London: Earthscan Publications.

Schenker, M. 1992, 'Occupational lung diseases in the industrializing and industrialized world due to modern industries and modern pollutants', *Tubercle and Lung Disease* 73: 27–32.

Scholte, J. A. 1997a, 'Global trade and finance', in Baylis, J. and Smith, S. (eds.) *The globalization of world politics; an introduction to international relations*, Oxford University Press.

1997b, 'Global capitalism and the state', *International Affairs* 73 (3): 427–52.

1999, *Global civil society: changing the world?*, CSGR Working Paper no. 31/99, Warwick: Centre for the Study of Globalisation and Regionalisation.

2000, *Globalization: a critical introduction*, London: Macmillan Press.

Scott, S. V. 2000, 'International lawyers: handmaidens, chefs or birth attendants?', *European Journal of International Law* 9 (4).

Sell, S. K. 1999, 'Multinational corporations as agents of change: the globalization of intellectual property rights', in Cutler, A. C., Haufler, V. and Porter, T. (eds.) 1999a.

Sen, A. 2000, 'Freedom's market', *The Observer*, 25 June, London.

Seyfang, G. 1999, 'Private sector self-regulation for social responsibility: mapping codes of conduct', Working Paper no. 1, 'Ethical trading and globalisation: self-regulation and workers' experience'. Social Policy Research Programme, funded by the Social Policy Division, UK Department for International Development.

Shearer, D. 1998, 'Outsourcing war', *Foreign Policy* Fall.

Shretta, R., Brugha, R., Robb, A. and Snow, R. W. 2000, 'Sustainability, affordability, and equity of corporate drug donations: the case of Malarone®', *The Lancet* 355 (9216): 1718–20.

Shrivastava, P. 1987, *Bhopal: anatomy of a crisis*, Cambridge, MA: Ballinger.

Shukla, A., Kumar, S. and Ory, F. G. 1991, 'Occupational health and the environment in an urban slum in India', *Social Science and Medicine* 33 (5): 597–603.

Sidell, M. 1995, *Health in old age: myth, mystery and management*, Buckingham: Open University Press.

Sikkink, K. 1986, 'Codes of conduct for transnational corporations: the case of the WHO/UNICEF code', *International Organization* 40: 815–40.

Silove, D., Eklad, S. and Mollica, R. 2000, 'The rights of the severely mental ill in post-conflict societies', *The Lancet* 355: 1548–9.

Singh, V., Jaiswal, A., Jain, R. C. *et al.* 1998a, 'Social vulnerability and the treatment of tuberculosis in Delhi: can DOTS fill the gap?', *International Journal of Tuberculosis and Lung Disease* 2 (11): S364 (Abstract no. 368-PC, Global Congress on Lung Health, 29th World Conference of the International Union Against Tuberculosis and Lung Disease).

1998b, 'Patient experiences with the Revised National Tuberculosis Programme, India', *International Journal of Tuberculosis and Lung Disease* 2 (11): S354 (Abstract no. 367-PC, Global Congress on Lung Health, 29th

World Conference of the International Union Against Tuberculosis and Lung Disease).

Singkaew and Chaichana 1998, cited in Janjaroen, Wattana S. and Supakankunti, S., 'Health services systems and the consequences for the GATS', presentation at the Regional Consultation on WTO Multilateral Trade Agreements and their implications on health – TRIPS, 16–18 August 1999, Bangkok, Thailand.

Sivard, R. L. 1996, *World social and military expenditures*, 16th edition, Washington DC: World Priorities.

Skaar, C. M. 1998, *Extending coverage of priority health care services through collaboration with the private sector: selected experiences of USAID cooperating agencies*, Bethesda, MD: Partnerships for Health Reform, Abt Associates.

Slaughter, A. M. 1997, 'The real new world order', *Foreign Affairs* 76: 183.

Snider, D. 1994, 'Tuberculosis: the world situation. History of the disease and efforts to combat it', in Porter, J. D. H. and McAdam, K. P. W. J. (eds.) *Tuberculosis: back to the future*, Chichester: John Wiley & Sons.

Social Watch 1998, *Social Watch NGO coalition*, Social Watch, Monteoideo.

Soderlund, N., Csaba, I., Gray, A., Milne, R. and Raftery, J. 1997, 'Impact of the NHS reforms on English hospital productivity: an analysis of the first three years', *British Medical Journal* 315: 1126–9.

Soderlund, N., Zwi, K., Kinghorn, A. and Gray, G. 1999, 'Prevention of vertical transmission of HIV: analysis of cost effectiveness options available in South Africa', *British Medical Journal* 318: 1650–5.

Spence, D. P. S., Hotchkiss, J., Williams, C. S. D. and Davies, P. D. O. 1993, 'Tuberculosis and poverty', *British Medical Journal* 307: 759–61.

Sphere Project 1999, 'The Humanitarian Charter and Minimum Standards in Disaster Response', also available online at <http://www.sphereproject.org>.

Spink, W. 1995, *Infectious diseases, prevention and treatment in the nineteenth and twentieth centuries*, Dawson, MN: University of Minnesota Press.

Stanford, Q. 1972, *The world's population: problems of growth*, Oxford University Press.

Stares, P. 1996, *Global habit, the drug problem in a borderless world*, Washington DC: Brookings Institution.

Statistics Canada 1998, 'Family violence in Canada: a statistical profile 1998', Report (Cat. 85–224-XPE), Ottawa.

Stenson, B., Tomson, G. and Sihakhang, L. 1997, 'Pharmaceutical regulation in context: the case of Lao PDR', *Health Policy and Planning* 12 (4): 329–40.

Stewart, F. 2000, 'The root causes of humanitarian emergencies', in Nafziger, E. W., Stewart, F. and Väyrynen, R. (eds.) *War, hunger and displacement: the origin of humanitarian emergencies*, Oxford University Press.

Stewart S. 1992, 'Working the system: sensitising the police to the plight of women', in Schuler M. (ed.) *Freedom from violence: women's strategies from around the world*, New York: United Nations Development Fund for Women.

Stocker, K., Waitzkin, H. and Iriart, C. 1999, 'The exportation of managed care to Latin America', *New England Journal of Medicine* 340 (14): 1131–6.

Strange, S. 1995, 'The defective state', *Daedalus* 24: 56.

    1996, *The retreat of the state: the diffusion of power in the world economy*, Cambridge Studies in International Relations, no. 49, Cambridge University Press.

Styblo, K. and Bumgarner, R. 1991, 'Tuberculosis can be controlled with existing technologies: evidence', in *Tuberculosis Surveillance Research Unit Progress Report 1991*, The Hague: Tuberculosis Surveillance Unit, pp. 60–72.

Subramaniam, A. 1995, 'Putting some numbers on the TRIPS pharmaceutical debate', *International Journal of Technology Management* 10 (1/3): 151–68.

Summerfield, D. 1991, 'The psychosocial effects of conflict in the Third World', *Development in Practice* 1: 159–73.

Sur, S. 1997, 'The state between fragmentation and globalisation', *European Journal of International Law* 8 (3): 421–34.

Swan, M. and Zwi, A. 1997, *Private practitioners and public health: close the gap or increase the distance*, PHP Publication no. 24, Department of Public Health and Policy, London School of Hygiene and Tropical Medicine.

Swiss, S. and Giller, J. E. 1993, 'Rape as a crime of war: a medical perspective', *Journal of the American Medical Association* 270 (5): 612–5.

Taitz, L. 2000, 'Health ministers vow to provide cheap AIDS drugs', *Sunday Times*, 18 June.

Tapiola, K. 1999a, 'Address of Mr Kari Tapiola, Deputy Director-General, International Labour Office', ILO Symposium on Labour Issues in the Context of Economic Integration and Free Trade, Port of Spain, 20–22 January 1999 <http://www.ilo.org/public/english...speeches/1999/tapiola/1trinida.htm>.

1999b, 'Introduction to Workers' Rights and Human Rights in the Framework of the ILO: the Declaration on Fundamental Principles and Rights at Work and its Follow-up', Workshop on Workers' Rights and Human Rights, 12 February 1999, Bangkok, Thailand <http://www.ilo.org/public/english...speeches/1999/tapiola/2bangkok.htm>.

Tarabusi, C. C. and Vickery, G. 1998, 'Globalisation in the pharmaceutical industry: Part I', *International Journal of Health Services* 28 (1): 67–105.

TDR/WHO 1999, 'Innovative private sector venture under way', *TDR News* 58: 3.

Theobald, S. 1999, 'New international division of labour, new occupational health hazards: community responses to the electronic industry in Thailand', Paper presented at the International Roundtable on 'Responses to globalization: rethinking equity in health', organised by the Society for International Development and WHO, Geneva, 12–14 July, 1999.

t'Hoen, E. 1999, 'Access to essential drugs and globalisation', *Development* 42 (4): 87–91.

Thylefors, B., Négrel, A-D., Pararajasegaram, R. and Dadzie, K. 1995, 'Global data on blindness', *Bulletin of the World Health Organization* 73 (1): 115–21.

Tollman, S. M. and Hsiao, W. C. 1998, 'Pursuing equity without getting beat', *Social Science and Medicine* 47 (12): 1901–3.

Toole, M., Waldman, R. and Zwi, A. 2000, 'Complex humanitarian emergencies', in Merson, M. H., Black, R. E. and Mills, A. J. (eds.) *International public health: diseases, programs, systems and policies*, Gaithersburg: Apsen Publishers, pp. 439–513.

Tooze, R. 1997, 'International political economy in an age of globalization', in Baylis, J. and Smith, S. (eds.) *The globalization of world politics: an introduction to international relations*, Oxford University Press.

Trebilcock, M. and House, R. 1999, *The regulation of international trade*, London: Routledge.

Tsui, A., Wasserheit, J.N. and Haaga, J. (eds.) 1997, *Reproductive health in developing countries: expanding dimensions, building solutions*, Washington DC: National Academy Press.

TUAC 1999, 'Building the social dimension of the global economy – the agenda following the Seattle WTO Ministerial Council – the OECD's role', TUAC Discussion Note for consultations with the OECD Liaison Committee, 10 December 1999, Paris: Trade Union Advisory Committee <http://www.tuac.org/statemen/communiq/liaison99e.htm>.

Turmen, T. 1999, 'Making globalisation work for better health', *Development* 42 (4): 8–11.

Twigg, J. 1999, 'Obligatory medical insurance in Russia: the participants' perspective', *Social Science and Medicine* 49: 371–82.

Ugalde, A. and Jackson, J. 1995, 'The World Bank and international health policy: a critical review', *Journal of International Development* 7 (3): 525–42.

Ugalde, A., Selva-Sutter, E., Castillo, C., Paz, C. and Cañas, S. 2000, 'The health costs of war: can they be measured? Lessons from El Salvador', *British Medical Journal* 321: 169–72.

UNAIDS 1998, Press release, UNAIDS statement commending Glaxo Wellcome for reducing cost of AZT for pregnant women with HIV in the developing world, <http://www.unaids.org/whatsnew/press/eng/pressarc98/glaxo.html>.

1999, International Partnership against HIV/AIDs in Africa, meeting of the UNAIDS cosponsoring agencies and secretariat, resolution to create and support the partnership <http://www.unaids.org/dispdocument/cpp/fn561.html>.

UNDP 1997, *Governance for sustainable human development: A UNDP policy document*, New York: Management Development and Governance Division.

1998, 'The global sustainable development facility', Internal document, New York: UNDP, July 1998.

1999, *Human development report 1999: globalization with a human face*, New York: Oxford University Press for the United Nations Development Programme.

UNFPA 1999, 'Final report of the Hague Forum: taking the ICPD agenda forward', New York.

UNFPA/Australian National University 1998, *Southeast Asian populations in crisis: challenges to the implementation of the ICPD programme of action*, New York: United Nations Population Fund.

UNHCR 1995, *Sexual violence against refugees: guidelines on prevention and response*, Geneva.

UNICEF 1990, 'Revitalizing primary health care/maternal and child health: the Bamako Initiative, progress report', Executive Board Doc. E/ICEF/1990/L.3, 20 February, New York.

United Nations 1994a, *Population and development, volume 1: programme of action adopted at the International Conference on Population and Development, Cairo, 5–13 September 1994*, New York: Department for Economic and Social Information and Policy Analysis, United Nations.

1994b, *World population prospects: the 1993 revision*, New York: United Nations.

1995, *Fourth World Conference on Women: platform of action, Beijing September 4–15, 1995*, New York: Department for Economic and Social Information and Policy Analysis, United Nations.

1998, 'Joint Statement on Common Interests by UN Secretary-General and International Chamber of Commerce', press release SG/2043, 9 February, New York: United Nations.

1999a, 'Report of the working group of intergovernmental experts on the human rights of migrants, submitted in accordance with Commission on Human Rights Resolution 1998/16', Commission on Human Rights, Economic and Social Council, 9 March [http://www.unhchr.ch/Huridocda].

1999b, 'The global compact' <http://www.unglobalcompact.org>.

2000, Security Council, adopting 'historic' resolution 1308 on HIV/AIDS, calls for pre-deployment testing, counselling for peace keeping personnel, Security Council press release 6890, 17 July, New York.

United States Trade Representative 1999, 'The protection of intellectual property and health policy', press release, December 1, Washington DC: Office of the USTR.

UNRISD 1995, 'States of disarray; the social effects of globalization', an UNRISD report for the World Summit for Social Development, Geneva: United Nations Research Institute for Social Development.

Unwin, N., Alberti, G., Aspray, T. *et al.* 1998, 'Economic globalisation and its effect on health. Some diseases could be eradicated for the cost of a couple of fighter planes', *British Medical Journal* 316 (7142): 1401–2.

Uplekar, M. W. and Rangan, S. 1993, 'Private doctors and tuberculosis control in India', *Tubercle and Lung Disease* 74: 332–7.

1995, *Tackling TB: the search for solutions*, Mumbai, India: Foundation for Research in Community Health.

Uplekar, M., Juvekar, S., Morankar, S., Ranga, S. and Nunn, P. 1998, 'After health sector reform, whither lung health?', *International Journal of Tuberculosis and Lung Disease* 2 (4): 324–9.

Vaillancourt, D., Brown, S. and others 1993, *Population, health and nutrition: annual operational review for fiscal year 1992*, Washington DC: World Bank.

van der Gaag, J. and Precker, A. 1997, 'Health care for aging populations: issues and options', in Prescott, N. (ed.) *Choices in financing health care and old age security*, World Bank Discussion Paper 392, Washington DC: World Bank.

van der Heijden, T. and Jitta, J. 1993, *Economic survival strategies of health workers in Uganda: Study Report*, Kampala: Child Health and Development Centre, p. 19.

Van de Ven, W. 1996, 'Market-oriented health care reforms: trends and future options', *Social Science and Medicine* 43 (5): 655–66.

Varley, A. and Blasco, M. 2000, 'Reaping what you sow? Older women, housing and family dynamics in urban Mexico' in United Nations International Research and Training Institute for the Advancement of Women (INSTRAW) (ed.) *Women's life cycle and ageing*, Santo Domingo: INSTRAW.

Vateesatokit, P., Hughes, B. and Ritthphakdee, B. 2000, 'Thailand: winning battles, but the war's far from over': *Tobacco Control* 9: 122–7.

Velasquez, G. and Boulet, P. 1999, 'Essential drugs in the new international economic environment', *Bulletin of the World Health Organization* 77 (3): 288–92.

Venkataswamy, P. and Brilliant, G. 1981, 'Social and economic barriers to cataract surgery in rural south India: a preliminary report', *Visual Impairment and Blindness* December: 405–8.

Voelker, R. 1996, 'Shoe leather therapy is gaining on TB', *Journal of the American Medical Association* 275 (10): 743–4.

Vos, E. T., Timaeus, I. M., Huttly, S. R. A., Murray, C. J. L. and Michaud, C. M. (forthcoming), 'Mauritius health sector reform national burden of disease study', in *Global Burden of Diseases*.

Waddell, S. 1999, 'The evolving strategic benefits for business in collaborations with nonprofits in civil society: a strategic resources, capabilities and competencies perspective', Unpublished.

Waddington, C. J. and Enyimayew, K. A. 1989, 'A price to pay: the impact of user charges in Ashanti-Akim district of Ghana', *International Journal of Health Planning and Management* 4: 17–47.

Walker, A. and Maltby, T. 1997, *Ageing Europe*, Buckingham: Open University Press.

Walker, D. and Fox-Rushby, J. (2000), 'Economic evaluation of communicable disease interventions in developing countries: a critical review of the published literature', *Health Economics* 9 (8): 681–98.

Wallack, L. and Montgomery, K. 1992, 'Advertising for all by the year 2000: public health implications for less developed countries', *Journal of Public Health Policy* 13 (2): 204–23.

Wallack, L. and Sforza, M. 1999, *Whose trade organization? Corporate globalization and the erosion of democracy; an assessment of the World Trade Organization.* Washington, DC: Public Citizen.

Wallerstein, I. 1991, *Geopolitics and geoculture*, Cambridge University Press.

Walsh, J. and Warren, K. 1980, 'Selective primary health care: an interim strategy for disease control in developing countries', *Social Science and Medicine* 14C (2): 145–63.

Walt, G. 1994, *Health policy: an introduction to process and power*, London: Zed Books.

1999. 'The politics of tuberculosis: the role of process and power', in Porter, J. D. H. and Grange, J. G. (eds.) *Tuberculosis – an interdisciplinary perspective*, London: Imperial College Press, pp. 67–98.

Walt, G. and Gilson, L. 1994, 'Reforming the health sector in developing countries: the central role of policy analysis', *Health Policy and Planning* 9 (45): 353–70.

Walt, G., Pavignani, E., Gilson, L. and Buse, K. 1999, 'Managing external resources in the health sector: are there lessons for SWAPS?' *Health Policy and Planning* 14 (3): 273–84.

Walzer, M. 1995, 'The concept of civil society', in Walzer, M. (ed.) *Toward a global civil society*, London: Blackwell, pp. 7–28.

Wamai, G. 1992, *Community financing in Uganda: Kasangati Health Centre Cost Recovery Programme*, Kampala: UNICEF.

Wapner, P. 2000, 'The normative promise of nonstate actors: a theoretical account of global civil society', in Wapner, P. and Ruiz, L. E. J. (eds.)

Principled world politics: the challenge of normative international relations, Langham, MD: Rowman and Littlefield.

Warner, K. E. and Hutton, R. C. 1980, 'Cost–benefit and cost-effectiveness analysis in health care: growth and composition of the literature', *Medical Care* 18 (11): 1069–84.

Warnes, A., King, R., Williams, A. and Patterson, G. 1999, 'The well-being of British expatriate retirees in southern Europe', *Ageing and Society* 19 (6): 717–40.

Watts, C., Keogh, E., Ndlovu, M. and Kwaramba, R. 1998, 'Withholding sex and forced sex: dimensions of violence against Zimbabwean women', *Reproductive Health Matters* 6 (12): 57–65.

Weber, H. W. 1899, 'On prevention of tuberculosis', *Tuberculosis* 14–19, 50–5, 101–11.

Weick, K. E. 1999, 'Sensemaking as an organizational dimension of global change', in Cooperider, D. L. and Dutton, J. E. (eds.), *Organizational dimensions of global change, no limits to co-operation*, London: Sage, 39–56.

Weinberg, J. 1993, *The development of independent hospital boards: report of a study visit to The Gambia and Ghana carried out on behalf of the Overseas Development Administration*, London: UK Overseas Development Administration.

Weiss, T. G. 1997, 'A research note about military–civilian humanitarianism: more questions than answers', *Disasters* 21 (2): 95–117.

Wesseling, C., McConnell, R., Partanen, T. and Hogstedt, C. 1997, 'Agricultural pesticide use in developing countries: health effects and research needs', *International Journal of Health Services* 27 (2): 273–308.

White House 1999, *A national security strategy for a new century*, Washington DC: The White House.

2000, 'Access to HIV/AIDS pharmaceuticals and medical technologies', Executive Order 13155, <http://www.pub.whitehouse.gov/uri...ma.eop.gov.us/2000/5/10/12.text.2>.

WHO 1964, *Tuberculosis: eighth report of the WHO Expert Advisory Committee*, no. 290, Geneva.

1974, WHO Technical Report Series, no. 552, Geneva.

1978, *Primary health care*, Geneva: World Health Organisation.

1982, WHO Technical Report Series, no. 671, Geneva.

1987, 'Financing health development: options, experiences and experiments', unpublished report, Geneva.

1988, *TB control as an integral part of primary health care*, Geneva.

1991a, *The public/private mix in national health systems and the roles of ministries of health: report of an interregional meeting. 22–26 July, Morelos State, Mexico*, Geneva.

1991b, 'Environmental health in urban development. Report of a WHO expert committee', WHO Technical Report Series, no. 807, May, Geneva.

1992, 'Our planet, our health; report of the WHO Commission on Health and Environment', Geneva.

1994, *A global emergency*, WHO/TB/94.177, Geneva.

1995, 'Global strategy on occupational health for all: the way to health at work'. Recommendation of the second meeting of the WHO Collaborating Centres in Occupational Health, Beijing, China, 11–14 October, 1994, WHO/OCH/95.1.

1996a, 'Public policy towards the private health sector, a WHO position', Geneva (draft).

1996b, *Tuberculosis in the era of HIV: a partnership*, WHO/TB/96.204, Geneva.

1996c, *A deadly partnership: tuberculosis in the era of HIV*, Geneva: WHO Global Tuberculosis Programme/UNAIDS.

1998a, *Food safety and globalisation of trade in food: a challenge to the public health sector*, Geneva.

1998b, *Globalisation and access to drugs: perspectives on the WHO/TRIPS Agreement*, Geneva: WHO Action Programme on Essential Drugs.

1998c, *Tuberculosis global surveillance*, Geneva.

1998d, 'Asia is 'Epicentre' of world's tuberculosis emergency', press release, Geneva, 23 November.

1998e, *TB advocacy – a practical guide*, WHO/TB/98.239, Geneva.

1998f *The world health report, Life in the 21st century: a vision for all*, Geneva.

1999a, *Guidelines for drug donations*, Geneva.

1999b, 'WHO guidelines on interaction with commercial enterprises', preliminary version, July 1999, Geneva.

1999c, *The world health report 1999: making a difference*, Geneva.

1999d, *Global tuberculosis control, WHO report 1999*, WHO/TB/99.259, Geneva.

1999e, 'Occupational health' <Http://www.who.int/aboutwho/en/promoting/occupat.htm>.

1999f, 'Occupational health. Ethically correct, economically sound', WHO fact sheet no. 84, June 1999, Geneva.

1999g, 'WHO/DFID peace through health programme, a case study prepared by the WHO field team in Bosnia and Herzegovina, September 1998', Copenhagen.

2000a, *The world health report 2000. Health systems: improving performance*, Geneva.

2000b, 'Towards a strategic agenda for the WHO Secretariat', Executive Board Doc. EB105/2, 24 January 2000, Geneva.

2000c, *Country profile*, Geneva: World Health Organisation/The Stop TB Initiative.

WHO/FRH 1997, *Violence against women*, mimeo document WHO/FRH/WHD/97.8, Geneva: WHO.

WHO/UNICEF 1978, *Alma-Ata: primary health care*, Geneva and New York.

Wibulpolprasert, S. 1999, 'Globalisation and access to essential drugs: case study from Thailand', Paper presented at Amsterdam meeting on Globalisation and Access to Essential Drugs, November 1999.

Widdus, R., Chacko, S., Holm, K. and Currat, L. (forthcoming), *Towards better defining public private partnerships for health*, Global Forum for Health Research, Geneva: GFHR.

WiLDAF 1995, 'Women in law and development in Africa', Annual Report, Harare.

Williams, A. 1992, 'Cost-effectiveness analysis: is it ethical?', *Journal of Medical Ethics* 18: 7–11.

Williamson, E. O. 1987, cited in Bennett, S. 1997.

Wilson, D., Cawthorne, P., Ford, N. and Aongsonwang, S. 1999, 'Global trade and access to medicines: AIDS treatment in Thailand', *The Lancet* 354: 9193–5.

Wood, K., Maforah, F. and Jewkes, R. 1998, ' "He forced me to love him": putting violence on adolescent sexual health agendas', *Social Science and Medicine* 47 (2): 233–42.

Woodward, D. 1999, *Tackling the crisis in global finance*, CIIR Comment Series, London: Catholic Institute for International Relations.

Working Group on priority-setting 2000, 'Priority-setting for health research: lessons from developing countries', *Health Policy and Planning* 15 (2): 130–6.

World Bank 1987, *Financing health services in developing countries: an agenda for reform*, A World Bank Policy Study, Washington DC.

   1993, *World development report 1993: investing in health*, Washington DC.

   1994a, *Governance: the World Bank's experience*, Washington DC.

   1994b, *Averting the old age crisis: policies to protect the old and promote growth*, Oxford University Press for the World Bank.

   1995, *World development report 1995: workers in an integrating world*, New York: Oxford University Press.

   1997a, *Health, nutrition & population sector strategy*, Washington DC.

   1997b, *World development report 1997: the state in a changing world*, Washington DC.

   1998a, *World Bank development indicators 1998*, Oxford University Press.

   1998b, *World development report 1998*, Oxford University Press.

   2000, *Assessing globalization*, Briefing Paper, April, Washington DC.

Wouters, A. M. 1991, 'Essential national health research in developing countries: health care financing and the quality of care', *International Journal of Health Planning and Management* 6: 253–71.

   1995, 'Improving quality through cost recovery in Niger', *Health Policy and Planning* 10 (3): 257–70.

Wouters, A. M., Adeyi, O. and Morrow, R. 1993, Quality of health care and its role in cost recovery with a focus on empirical findings about willingness to pay for quality improvements (Phase 1), Major Applied Research Paper no. 8, Health Financing and Sustainability (HFS) Project, Bethesda: Abt Associates Inc.

WTO 1996, *United States – standards for reformulated and conventional gasoline: Appellate Body report and panel report*, WT/DS2/9, Geneva.

   1998a, *EC – measures concerning meat and meat products (hormones): report of the Appellate Body*, WT/DS26/AB/R, Geneva.

   1998b, 'Health and social services', background note by the secretariat (de-restricted document), S/C/W/50, 18 September 1998 (98–3558), Council for Trade in Services, WTO, Geneva.

   1999a, *Trading into the future*, Geneva.

   1999b, WTO official website (WTO: a training package): <http://www.wto.org/ wto/eol/e/wto03/wto3_21.htm> visited on 20 December 1999.

   2000, 'Canada – patent protection of pharmaceutical products – complaint by the European communities and their member states – report of the panel', WTO WT/DS114/R, Geneva.

Yach, D. and Bettcher, D. 1998a, 'The globalization of public health, I: threats and opportunities', *American Journal of Public Health* 88 (5): 735–8.

1998b, 'The globalization of public health, II: the convergence of self-interest and altruism', *American Journal of Public Health* 88 (5): 738–41.

Yamey, G. 1999, 'Agencies urge end to global trade restrictions on essential medicines', *British Medical Journal* 319: 455.

Yepes, F. and Sanchez, L. H., in press, 'Reforming pluralist systems: the case of Colombia', in Mills, A. (ed.) *Reforming health sectors*, London: Kegan Paul.

Yesudian, C. A. K. 1994, 'Behaviour of the private health sector in the health market of Bombay', *Health Policy and Planning* 9 (1): 72–80.

Yip, W. C. and Hsiao, W. C. 1999, *Organizational reform in the public hospital sector in Hong Kong*, Boston, MA: Harvard University Press.

Yoder, R. A. 1989, 'Are people willing and able to pay for health services?', *Social Science and Medicine* 29: 35–42.

Zwi, A. and Mills, A. 1995, 'Health policy in less developed countries: past trends and future directions', *Journal of International Development* 7 (3): 299–328.

Zwarenstein, M., Schoeman, J. H., Vundule, C., Lombard, C. J. and Tatley, M. 1998, 'Randomised controlled trial of self-supervised and directly observed treatment of tuberculosis', *The Lancet* 352: 1340–3.

Index

References to notes are indicated by 'n'; those to boxes, figures and tables by '*b*', '*f*' and '*t*'.

Printed in the United Kingdom
by Lightning Source UK Ltd.
120440UK00001B/307

9 780521 009430